TAKING SIDES

Clashing Views on Controversial

Social Issues

ELEVENTH EDITION

TAKING SIDES

Clashing Views on Controversial

Social Issues

ELEVENTH EDITION

Selected, Edited, and with Introductions by

Kurt Finsterbusch
University of Maryland

McGraw-Hill/Dushkin
A Division of The McGraw-Hill Companies

*To my wife, Meredith Ramsay, who richly shares with me a
life of the mind and much, much more.*

Photo Acknowledgment
Cover image: © 2001 by PhotoDisc, Inc.

Cover Art Acknowledgment
Charles Vitelli

Library of Congress Cataloging-in-Publication Data
Main entry under title:
Taking sides: clashing views on controversial social issues/selected, edited, and with introductions
by Kurt Finsterbusch.—11th ed.
Includes bibliographical references and index.
1. Social behavior. 2. Social problems. I. Finsterbusch, Kurt, *comp.*
302
0-07-241400-6
95-83865

Printed on Recycled Paper

Preface

The English word *fanatic* is derived from the Latin *fanum*, meaning temple. It refers to the kind of madmen often seen in the precincts of temples in ancient times, the kind presumed to be possessed by deities or demons. The term first came into English usage during the seventeenth century, when it was used to describe religious zealots. Soon after, its meaning was broadened to include a political and social context. We have come to associate the term *fanatic* with a person who acts as if his or her views were inspired, a person utterly incapable of appreciating opposing points of view. The nineteenth-century English novelist George Eliot put it precisely: "I call a man fanatical when... he... becomes unjust and unsympathetic to men who are out of his own track." A fanatic may hear but is unable to listen. Confronted with those who disagree, a fanatic immediately vilifies opponents.

Most of us would avoid the company of fanatics, but who among us is not tempted to caricature opponents instead of listening to them? Who does not put certain topics off limits for discussion? Who does not grasp at euphemisms to avoid facing inconvenient facts? Who has not, in George Eliot's language, sometimes been "unjust and unsympathetic" to those on a different track? Who is not, at least in certain very sensitive areas, a *little* fanatical? The counterweight to fanaticism is open discussion. The difficult issues that trouble us as a society have at least two sides, and we lose as a society if we hear only one side. At the individual level, the answer to fanaticism is listening. And that is the underlying purpose of this book: to encourage its readers to listen to opposing points of view.

This book contains 38 selections presented in a pro and con format. A total of 19 different controversial social issues are debated. The sociologists, political scientists, economists, and social critics whose views are debated here make their cases vigorously. In order to effectively read each selection, analyze the points raised, and debate the basic assumptions and values of each position, or, in other words, in order to think critically about what you are reading, you will first have to give each side a sympathetic hearing. John Stuart Mill, the nineteenth-century British philosopher, noted that the majority is not doing the minority a favor by listening to its views; it is doing *itself* a favor. By listening to contrasting points of view, we strengthen our own. In some cases we change our viewpoints completely. But in most cases, we either incorporate some elements of the opposing view—thus making our own richer—or else learn how to answer the objections to our viewpoints. Either way, we gain from the experience.

Organization of the book   Each issue has an issue *introduction*, which sets the stage for the debate as it is argued in the YES and NO selections. Each issue concludes with a *postscript* that makes some final observations and points the way to other questions related to the issue. In reading the issue and forming your own opinions you should not feel confined to adopt one or the other of the positions presented. There are positions in between the given views or totally outside them, and the *suggestions for further reading* that appear in each issue postscript should help you find resources to continue your study of the subject. At the back of the book is a listing of all the *contributors to this volume*, which will give you information on the social scientists whose views are debated here. Also, on the *On the Internet* page that accompanies each part opener, you will find Internet site addresses (URLs) that are relevant to the issues in that part.

Changes to this edition   This new edition has been significantly updated. There are five completely new issues: *Do the New Sex Roles Burden Women More Than Men?* (Issue 3); *Should Same-Sex Marriages Be Legally Recognized?* (Issue 5); *Is the Underclass the Major Threat to American Ideals?* (Issue 8); *Has Welfare Reform Benefited the Poor?* (Issue 12); and *Is Capital Punishment Justified?* (Issue 17). Also, the question for Issue 19 concerning the quality of life in the United States has been changed to form a new issue. The Yes-side selection for this issue has been replaced. In addition, for the issues on moral decline (Issue 1), communication between men and women (Issue 4), economic inequality (Issue 7), affirmative action (Issue 9), school vouchers (Issue 13), and population growth (Issue 18), one or both of the selections were replaced to bring a fresh perspective to the debates. In all, there are 18 new selections. The issues that were dropped from the previous edition were done so on the recommendation of professors who let me know what worked and what could be improved. Wherever appropriate, new introductions and postscripts have been provided.

A word to the instructor   An *Instructor's Manual With Test Questions* (multiple-choice and essay) is available through the publisher for the instructor using *Taking Sides* in the classroom. A general guidebook, *Using Taking Sides in the Classroom*, which discusses methods and techniques for integrating the pro-con approach into any classroom setting, is also available. An online version of *Using Taking Sides in the Classroom* and a correspondence service for *Taking Sides* adopters can be found at http://www.dushkin.com/usingts/.

Taking Sides: Clashing Views on Controversial Social Issues is only one title in the Taking Sides series. If you are interested in seeing the table of contents for any of the other titles, please visit the Taking Sides Web site at http://www.dushkin.com/takingsides/.

Acknowledgments   We received many helpful comments and suggestions from our friends and readers across the United States and Canada. Their suggestions have markedly enhanced the quality of this edition of *Taking*

Sides and are reflected in the new issues and the updated selections. Our thanks go to those who responded with specific suggestions for this edition:

Bonnie Ach
Chapman University

Fasih Ahmed
North Carolina Agricultural and Technical State University

Donald Anspach
University of Southern Maine

Susanne Blieberg Seperson
Dowling College

Olga Bright
Chaffey College

Jami Brown
Riverside Community College

Deborah Burris-Kitch
University of La Verne

Ting-Shih Chia
Morningside College

James Crispino
University of Connecticut

Peter Heckman
Nebraska Wesleyan University

Frederick Hendrickson
Bellarmine College

Antonio F. Holland
Lincoln University

Shirin Hollis
Southern Connecticut State University

Karen M. Jennison
University of Northern Colorado

Kristine Kleptach Jamieson
Ashland University

Cynthia Marconi-Hick
Richard Stockton College of New Jersey

Terry Mills
University of Florida

Kristin Park
Westminster College

Joann Sloan
Gordon College

June E. Warner
Hagerstown Junior College

I also wish to acknowledge the encouragement and support given to this project over the years by Mimi Egan, former publisher for the Taking Sides series. I am grateful as well to Theodore Knight, list manager for the Taking Sides series, and Juliana Gribbins, developmental editor.

I want to thank my wife, Meredith Ramsay, for her example and support.

I also want to thank George McKenna for many years as a close colleague and through many editions of this book.

Kurt Finsterbusch
University of Maryland

Contents In Brief

Contents

Editor and author Jeff Grabmeier presents evidence showing that women experience more stress than men and then analyzes why. Author Susan Faludi argues that men have been socialized into a sex role that cannot be successfully fulfilled due to current conditions.

Author Philip Yancey argues that men and women have strikingly different communication styles because they grow up in different cultures. A man is usually concerned about enhancing or maintaining status as he communicates, while a woman will usually communicate in ways that gain or maintain closeness. Professor of psychology Mary Crawford argues that the thesis that men and women have radically different communication styles is greatly exaggerated in the media and is based on simplistic stereotypes.

Editor and author Andrew Sullivan argues that the secular liberal state must grant the right of same-sex partners to marry. To not do so would be blatant discrimination. Professor of management and public policy James Q. Wilson presents arguments against legally recognizing same-sex marriages.

Sociologist David Popenoe contends that families play important roles in society but how the traditional family functions in these roles has declined dramatically in the last several decades, with very adverse effects on children. Family historian Stephanie Coontz argues that current discussion of family decline includes a false idealization of the traditional family of the past and misleading interpretations of current data on families. She finds that the trends are both positive and negative.

Political sociologist G. William Domhoff argues that the "owners and top-level managers in large income-producing properties are far and away the dominant power figures in the United States" and that they have inordinate influence in the federal government. Jeffrey M. Berry, a professor of political science, contends that public interest pressure groups that have entered the political arena since the end of the 1960s have effectively challenged the political power of big business.

Issue 11.   Should Government Intervene in a Capitalist Economy?   188

Author Ernest Erber argues that capitalism creates serious social problems that require government intervention to correct. Economists Milton and Rose Friedman maintain that the market operates effectively and protects citizens better when permitted to work without the interference of government regulations.

Issue 12.   Has Welfare Reform Benefited the Poor?   208

Ron Haskins, staff director for the House Human Resources Subcommittee, states that both the poor and the taxpayers are better off due to the recent welfare reform. Haskins uses examples of former welfare recipients to support his assertion. Author Karen Houppert describes cases of welfare recipients who were denied the assistance to which they were entitled. Houppert also examines the bureaucratic problems that resulted in harmful consequences for the poor, which she asserts are a direct result of welfare reform.

Issue 13.   Are Vouchers the Solution to the Ills of Public Education?   226

Gary Rosen, an associate editor of *Commentary*, examines the criticisms of public education and argues that vouchers and choice are well suited to correct its deficiencies without damaging education or society. Albert Shanker, president of the American Federation of Teachers until his death in 1998, argues that there is no evidence that privatizing the public schools works or that the public wants vouchers. He maintains that the public wants discipline and academic standards, which can be provided by public schools modeled after those of countries with better primary and secondary education than the United States.

Marcia Angell, executive editor of *The New England Journal of Medicine*, presents medical and ethical reasons justifying doctor-assisted suicide, including that it honors the autonomy of the patient and is merciful in cases when pain cannot be adequately relieved. Paul R. McHugh, director of the Department of Psychiatry and Behavioral Sciences at the Johns Hopkins University School of Medicine, argues that sick people who wish to kill themselves suffer from verifiable mental illness and that, since they can be treated for their pain and depressed state, physicians cannot be allowed to kill them.

PART 5   CRIME AND SOCIAL CONTROL   259

John J. DiIulio, Jr., a professor of politics and public affairs, analyzes the enormous harm done—especially to the urban poor and, by extension, to all of society—by street criminals and their activities. Professor of philosophy Jeffrey Reiman argues that the dangers posed by negligent corporations and white-collar criminals are a greater menace to society than are the activities of typical street criminals.

Ethan A. Nadelmann, director of the Lindesmith Center, a drug policy research institute, argues that history shows that drug prohibition is costly and futile. Examining the drug policies in other countries, he finds that decriminalization plus sane and humane drug policies and treatment programs can greatly reduce the harms from drugs. James A. Inciardi, director of the Center for Drug and Alcohol Studies at the University of Delaware, and his associate Christine A. Saum argue that legalizing drugs would not eliminate drug-related criminal activity and would greatly increase drug use. Therefore, the government should continue the war against drugs.

Editor and author Robert W. Lee argues that capital punishment is needed to deter people from committing murder and other heinous crimes, but more importantly, it is the punishment that is the most appropriate for these crimes. Legal scholar Eric M. Freedman counters that the death penalty does not deter crime and has unacceptable negative consequences, including the potential of killing innocent people, reducing public safety, and imposing considerable costs on society.

PART 6   THE FUTURE: POPULATION/ENVIRONMENT/ SOCIETY   315

Bioscientists David Pimentel and Marcia Pimentel describe the decline and also the limits of the resources used to produce food. They warn that further population growth is likely to increase worldwide malnourishment. Professor of economics D. Gale Johnson argues that world food security will increase in the next quarter century because incomes are rising. Johnson states that food production increases will exceed increases in demand.

Author Gregg Easterbrook contends that despite some worrisome trends, "American life is getting better." He maintains that incomes, education levels, and lifespans are increasing, while many negative indicators are declining. Sociology professor Beth A. Rubin asserts that Americans have not only lost income on average over the past 25 years, but they have also increasingly experienced insecurity and anxiety in their jobs and instability in their family relationships.

Introduction

Debating Social Issues

Kurt Finsterbusch

What Is Sociology?

"I have become a problem to myself," St. Augustine said. Put into a social and secular framework, St. Augustine's concern marks the starting point of sociology. We have become a problem to ourselves, and it is sociology that seeks to understand the problem and, perhaps, to find some solutions. The subject matter of sociology, then, is ourselves—people interacting with one another in groups and organizations.

Although the subject matter of sociology is very familiar, it is often useful to look at it in an unfamiliar light, one that involves a variety of theories and perceptual frameworks. In fact, to properly understand social phenomena, it *should* be looked at from several different points of view. In practice, however, this may lead to more friction than light, especially when each view proponent says, "I am right and you are wrong," rather than, "My view adds considerably to what your view has shown."

Sociology, as a science of society, was developed in the nineteenth century. Auguste Comte (1798–1857), the French mathematician and philosopher who is considered to be the father of sociology, had a vision of a well-run society based on social science knowledge. Sociologists (Comte coined the term) would discover the laws of social life and then determine how society should be structured and run. Society would not become perfect, because some problems are intractable, but he believed that a society guided by scientists and other experts was the best possible society.

Unfortunately, Comte's vision was extremely naive. For most matters of state there is no one best way of structuring or doing things that sociologists can discover and recommend. Instead, sociologists debate more social issues than they resolve.

The purpose of sociology is to throw light on social issues and their relationship to the complex, confusing, and dynamic social world around us. It seeks to describe how society is organized and how individuals fit into it. But neither the organization of society nor the fit of individuals is perfect. Social disorganization is a fact of life—at least in modern, complex societies such as the one we live in. Here, perfect harmony continues to elude us, and "social problems" are endemic. The very institutions, laws, and policies that produce benefits also produce what sociologists call "unintended effects"—unintended and undesirable. The changes that please one sector of the society may displease another, or the changes that seem so indisputably healthy at first turn out to have a dark underside to them. The examples are endless. Modern urban life gives people privacy and freedom from snooping neighbors that the small town never afforded; yet that very privacy seems to breed an uneasy sense of anonymity and loneliness. Take another example: Hierarchy is necessary for organizations to function efficiently, but hierarchy leads to the creation of a ruling elite. Flatten out the hierarchy and you may achieve social equality—but at the price of confusion, incompetence, and low productivity.

This is not to say that all efforts to effect social change are ultimately futile and that the only sound view is the tragic one that concludes "nothing works." We can be realistic without falling into despair. In many respects, the human condition has improved over the centuries and has improved as a result of conscious social policies. But improvements are purchased at a price—not only a monetary price but one involving human discomfort and discontent. The job of policymakers is to balance the anticipated benefits against the probable costs.

It can never hurt policymakers to know more about the society in which they work or the social issues they confront. That, broadly speaking, is the purpose of sociology. It is what this book is about. This volume examines issues that are central to the study of sociology.

Culture and Values

A common value system is the major mechanism for integrating a society, but modern societies contain so many different groups with differing ideas and values that integration must be built as much on tolerance of differences as on common values. Furthermore, technology and social conditions change, so values must adjust to new situations, often weakening old values. Some people (often called conservatives) will defend the old values. Others (often called liberals) will make concessions to allow for change. For example, the protection of human life is a sacred value to most people, but some would compromise that value when the life involved is a 90-year-old comatose man on life-support machines who had signed a document indicating that he did not want to be kept alive under those conditions. The conservative would counter that once we make the value of human life relative, we become dangerously open to greater evils—that perhaps society will come to think it acceptable to terminate all sick, elderly people undergoing expensive treatments. This is only one example of how values are hotly debated today. Two debates on values are presented in Part 1. In Issue 1, David Whitman challenges the common perception that morals have declined in America, while Gertrude Himmelfarb provides empirical support for the declining morality thesis. In Issue 2, Peter Brimelow argues that the current levels of immigration are too high and that the immigrant cultures are too different from American culture to be assimilated. Thus, immigration is threatening America's cultural unity. John Isbister, in opposition, argues that the cultural impacts of immigration are positive and that any of its economic harms are negligible.

Sex Roles, Gender, and the Family

An area that has experienced tremendous value change in the last several decades is sex roles and the family. Women in large numbers have rejected major aspects of their traditional gender roles and family roles while remaining strongly committed to much of the mother role and to many feminine characteristics. Men have changed much less but their situation has changed considerably. Issue 3 considers whether current sex roles are more stressful for women or for men. Jeff Grabmeier contends that women suffer more stress than men because current practices still favor men and that women are not able to cope as well as men with current sex role expectations. Susan Faludi argues the opposite. Men's sex roles are incongruent with the current conditions and men do not know how to deal with the situation. Issue 4 focuses on the causes of communication problems between men and women. It has recently been advanced that such problems are largely the result of radically different conversation styles between the genders. Philip Yancey champions this view, contending that men's concerns about maintaining status and women's concerns about maintaining connections and closeness affects their interpretations of what they hear and say to each other. Mary Crawford asserts that this view has become popularized and exaggerated by the media and that the basis of the thesis is demeaning to women. Issue 5 debates whether same-sex marriages should be legal. Andrew Sullivan argues that "marriage is . . . the highest public recognition of a private commitment. . . . Denying it to homosexuals is the most public affront possible to their public equality." The opposing selection is a critical review and rebuttal of Sullivan's assertions by James Q. Wilson. Issue 6, which has been much debated by feminists and their critics, asks, Is the decline of the traditional family a national crisis? David Popenoe is deeply concerned about the decline of the traditional family, while Stephanie Coontz thinks that such concern amounts to little more than nostalgia for a bygone era.

Stratification and Inequality

Issue 7 centers around a sociological debate about whether or not increasing economic inequality is a serious problem. Sheldon Danziger and Deborah Reed assert that it is, while Christopher C. DeMuth argues that consumption patterns indicate that inequality has actually decreased in recent decades. Many commentators on American life decry the pathologies of the underclass as the shame of America. Charles Murray is a leading proponent of this view and his article is republished in this volume. Barry Schwartz critiques Murray's view and argues that the current advanced stage of capitalism is largely responsible for eroding American ideals and producing the underclass.

Today one of the most controversial issues regarding inequalities is affirmative action. Is equality promoted or undermined by such policies? Walter E. Williams and Wilbert Jenkins take opposing sides on this question in Issue 9.

Political Economy and Institutions

Sociologists study not only the poor, the workers, and the victims of discrimination but also those at the top of society—those who occupy what the late sociologist C. Wright Mills used to call "the command posts." The question is whether the "pluralist" model or the "power elite" model is the one that best fits the facts in America. Does a single power elite rule the United States, or do many groups contend for power and influence so that the political process is accessible to all? In Issue 10, G. William Domhoff argues that the business elite have a dominating influence in government decisions and that no other group has nearly as much power. Jeffrey M. Berry counters that liberal citizen groups have successfully opened the policy-making process and made it more participatory. Currently, grassroots groups of all kinds have some power and influence. The question is, how much?

The United States is a capitalist welfare state, and the role of the state in capitalism (more precisely, the market) and in welfare is examined in the next two issues. Issue 11 considers whether or not the government should step in and attempt to correct for the failures of the market through regulations, policies, and programs. Ernest Erber argues that an active government is needed to protect consumers, workers, and the environment; to bring about greater equality; and to guide economic and social change. Milton and Rose Friedman argue that even well-intended state interventions in the market usually only make matters worse and that governments cannot serve the public good as effectively as competitive markets can. One way in which the government intervenes in the economy is by providing welfare to people who cannot provide for their own needs in the labor market. Issue 12 debates the wisdom of welfare reform policies. In it, Ron Haskins argues that the Work Opportunity Reconciliation Act, signed in 1996, is a great success. It has reduced welfare rolls by 40 percent in less than 3 years without significant harm to welfare recipients. Karen Houppert counters that welfare reform has allowed state and local governments that administer the welfare programs to slash or withhold mandated benefits with painful and unjust results.

Education is one of the biggest jobs of government as well as the key to individual prosperity and the success of the economy. For decades the American system of education has been severely criticized. Recently the criticism has brought education into an ideological debate over the proper role of the government, private enterprise, and markets in public education. In Issue 13, Gary Rosen views public education as a colossal failure. He states that public education can be fixed by voucher programs as demonstrated by the success of the few voucher programs that already exist. Albert Shanker, in reply, looks to schools in countries in which students are performing exemplarily, noting that these nations have not turned to privatization. He concludes that improvements in public education can be accomplished without resorting to vouchers, which he maintains that the public does not want anyway.

The final issue in this section—doctor-assisted suicide—is truly one of life and death. The actions of Dr. Jack Kevorkian, who has assisted in over 100 patient suicides, have brought this issue into the public light. In Issue 14,

Marcia Angell presents medical and ethical reasons why she believes that doctor-assisted suicide is merciful and right. Paul R. McHugh maintains that suicidal patients suffer from depression and that they can and should be treated therapeutically, not murdered.

Crime and Social Control

Crime is interesting to sociologists because crimes are those activities that society makes illegal and will use force to stop. Why are some acts made illegal and others (even those that may be more harmful) not made illegal? Surveys indicate that concern about crime is extremely high in America. Is the fear of crime, however, rightly placed? Americans fear mainly street crime, but Jeffrey Reiman argues in Issue 15 that corporate crime—also known as "white-collar crime"—causes far more death, harm, and financial loss to Americans than street crime. In contrast, John J. DiIulio, Jr., points out the great harm done by street criminals, even to the point of social disintegration in some poor neighborhoods. Much of the harm that DiIulio describes is related to the illegal drug trade, which brings about such bad consequences that some people are seriously talking about legalizing drugs in order to kill the illegal drug business. Ethan A. Nadelmann argues this view in Issue 16, while James A. Inciardi and Christine A. Saum argue that legalization would greatly expand the use of dangerous drugs and increase the personal tragedies and social costs resulting therefrom. Finally, Issue 17 asks whether capital punishment is justified. Robert W. Lee insists that some crimes are so heinous that only execution is an appropriate form of punishment. Furthermore, the death penalty is needed to deter murder. Eric M. Freedman asserts that the death penalty does not reduce crime, is extraordinarily expensive, and diverts scarce funds from more helpful purposes. Capital punishment also leads to the execution of many innocent people.

The Future: Population/Environment/Society

Many social commentators speculate on "the fate of the earth." The environmentalists have their own vision of apocalypse. They see the possibility that the human race could overshoot the carrying capacity of the globe. The resulting collapse could lead to the extinction of much of the human race and the end of free societies. Population growth and increasing per capita levels of consumption, say some experts, are leading us to this catastrophe. Others believe that these fears are groundless. In Issue 18, David Pimentel and Marcia Pimental debate D. Gale Johnson over whether or not the world is threatened by population growth.

The last issue in this book tries to assess the state of the nation in terms of its economic, environmental, social, psychological, moral, and political health. Beth A. Rubin presents trends showing that Americans are losing out economically, socially, and psychologically. Gregg Easterbrook presents many different trends that in his opinion show that "American life is getting better." His review of the facts includes statistics on accidents, murders, crime, drugs, alcohol, sex, the economy, standards of living, the environment, health, and human rights.

The Social Construction of Reality

An important idea in sociology is that people construct social reality in the course of interaction by attaching social meanings to the reality they are experiencing and then responding to those meanings. Two people can walk down a city street and derive very different meanings from what they see around them. Both, for example, may see homeless people—but they may see them in different contexts. One fits them into a picture of once-vibrant cities dragged into decay and ruin because of permissive policies that have encouraged pathological types to harass citizens; the other observer fits them into a picture of an America that can no longer hide the wretchedness of its poor. Both feel that they are seeing something deplorable, but their views of what makes it deplorable are radically opposed. Their differing views of what they have seen will lead to very different prescriptions for what should be done about the problem.

The social construction of reality is an important idea for this book because each author is socially constructing reality and working hard to persuade you to see his or her point of view; that is, to see the definition of the situation and the set of meanings he or she has assigned to the situation. In doing this, each author presents a carefully selected set of facts, arguments, and values. The arguments contain assumptions or theories, some of which are spelled out and some of which are unspoken. The critical reader has to judge the evidence for the facts, the logic and soundness of the arguments, the importance of the values, and whether or not omitted facts, theories, and values invalidate the thesis. This book facilitates this critical thinking process by placing authors in opposition. This puts the reader in the position of critically evaluating two constructions of reality for each issue instead of one.

Conclusion

Writing in the 1950s, a period that was in some ways like our own, the sociologist C. Wright Mills said that Americans know a lot about their "troubles" but they cannot make the connections between seemingly personal concerns and the concerns of others in the world. If they could only learn to make those connections, they could turn their concerns into *issues*. An issue transcends the realm of the personal. According to Mills, "An issue is a public matter: some value cherished by publics is felt to be threatened. Often there is a debate about what the value really is and what it is that really threatens it."

It is not primarily personal troubles but social issues that I have tried to present in this book. The variety of topics in it can be taken as an invitation to discover what Mills called "the sociological imagination." This imagination, said Mills, "is the capacity to shift from one perspective to another—from the political to the psychological; from examination of a single family to comparative assessment of the national budgets of the world. . . . It is the capacity to range from the most impersonal and remote transformations to the most intimate features of the human self—and to see the relations between the two." This book, with a range of issues well suited to the sociological imagination, is intended to enlarge that capacity.

On the Internet ...

Internet Philosophical Resources on Moral Relativism

This Web site for *Ethics Updates* offers discussion questions, a bibliographical guide, and a list of internet resources concerning moral relativism.

> http://ethics.acusd.edu/relativism.html

The International Center for Migration, Ethnicity, and Citizenship

The center is engaged in scholarly research and public policy analysis bearing on international migration, refugees, and the incorporation of newcomers in host countries.

> http://www.newschool.edu/icmec/

National Immigrant Forum

This pro-immigrant organization examines the effects of immigration on U.S. society. Click on the links for discussion of underground economies, immigrant economies, race and ethnic relations, and other topics.

> http://www.immigrationforum.org

The National Network for Immigrant and Refugee Rights (NNIRR)

The NNIRR serves as a forum to share information and analysis, to educate communities and the general public, and to develop and coordinate plans of action on important immigrant and refugee issues.

> http://www.nnirr.org

PART 1

Culture and Values

*S*ociologists recognize that a fairly strong consensus on the basic values of a society contributes greatly to the smooth functioning of that society. The functioning of modern, complex urban societies, however, often depends on the tolerance of cultural differences and equal rights and protections for all cultural groups. In fact, such societies can be enriched by the contributions of different cultures. But at some point the cultural differences may result in a pulling apart that exceeds the pulling together. One cultural problem is the perceived moral decline which may involve a conflict between old and new values. Another problem is whether current immigrants to the United States bring appropriate values and skills.

- Is America in Moral Decline?

- Is Third World Immigration a Threat to America's Way of Life?

ISSUE 1

Is America in Moral Decline?

YES: Gertrude Himmelfarb, from *The De-Moralization of Society: From Victorian Virtues to Modern Values* (Alfred A. Knopf, 1995)

NO: David Whitman, from *The Optimism Gap: The I'm OK— They're Not Syndrome and the Myth of American Decline* (Walker & Company, 1998)

ISSUE SUMMARY

YES: Gertrude Himmelfarb, a professor emeritus of history, details some of the increasing moral problems in America and interprets them as being part of a larger pattern, which she calls "the de-moralization of society."

NO: Writer David Whitman empirically tests the moral decline thesis and finds that, according to the indicators that he employs, it is a myth.

Morality is the glue that holds society together. It enables people to deal with each other in relative tranquility and generally to their mutual benefit. Morality influences us both from the outside and from the inside. The morality of others affects us from outside as social pressure. Our conscience is morality affecting us from inside, even though others, especially parents, influence the formation of our conscience. Because parents, churches, schools, and peers teach us their beliefs and values (their morals) and the rules of society, most of us grow up wanting to do what is right. We also want to do things that are pleasurable. In a well-functioning society the right and the pleasurable are not too far apart, and most people lead morally respectable lives. On the other hand, no one lives up to moral standards perfectly. In fact, deviance from some moral standards is common, and when it becomes very common the standard changes. Some people interpret this as moral decline, while others interpret it as simply a change in moral standards or even as progress.

The degree of commitment to various moral precepts varies from person to person. Some people even act as moral guardians and take responsibility for encouraging others to live up to the moral standards. One of their major tactics is to cry out against the decline of morals. There are a number of such voices speaking out in public today. In fact, many politicians seem to try to outdo each other in speaking out against crime, teenage pregnancy, divorce, violence in the media, latchkey children, irresponsible parenting, etc.

Cries of moral decline have been ringing out for centuries. In earlier times the cries were against sin, debauchery, and godlessness. Today the cries are often against various aspects of individualism. Parents are condemned for sacrificing their children for their own needs, including their careers. Divorced people are condemned for discarding spouses instead of working hard to save their marriages. Children of elderly parents are condemned for putting their parents into nursing homes to avoid the inconvenience of caring for them. The general public is condemned for investing so little time in others and their communities while pursuing their own interests. These criticisms against individualism may have some validity. On the other hand, individualism has some more positive aspects, including enterprise and inventiveness, which contribute to economic growth; individual responsibility; advocacy of human rights; reduced clannishness and prejudice toward other groups; and an emphasis on self-development, which includes successful relations with others.

The morality debate is important because moral decline not only increases human suffering but also weakens society and hinders the performance of its institutions. The following selections require some deep reflection on the moral underpinnings of American society as well as other societies, and they invite the reader to strengthen those underpinnings.

Many have decried the high levels of crime, violence, divorce, and opportunism, but few argue the thesis of the moral decline of America as thoroughly and as passionately as Gertrude Himmelfarb, the author of the following selection. But is she reading the facts correctly? According to David Whitman in the second selection, the common viewpoint that a serious moral decline is in progress is a myth. He argues that numerous morality indicators do not show the decline that the decline thesis expects. Therefore, even in the face of the statistics on crime and divorce, Whitman concludes that there has not been a deterioration of moral conduct.

Gertrude Himmelfarb

 **YES**

A De-Moralized Society

The current statistics are not only more troubling than those a century ago; they constitute a trend that bodes even worse for the future than for the present. Where the Victorians had the satisfaction of witnessing a significant improvement in their condition, we are confronting a considerable deterioration in ours....

In the United States, the figures are no less dramatic. Starting at 3 percent in 1920 (the first year for which there are national statistics), the illegitimacy ratio rose gradually to slightly over 5 percent by 1960, after which it grew rapidly: to almost 11 percent in 1970, over 18 percent in 1980, and 30 percent by 1991— a tenfold increase from 1920, and a sixfold increase from 1960....

In teenage illegitimacy the United States has earned the dubious distinction of ranking first among all industrialized nations. The rate tripled between 1960 and 1991: for whites it increased almost fivefold; for blacks the increase was less spectacular, but the final rate was almost four times that of the whites. In 1990, one in ten teenage girls got pregnant, half of them giving birth and the other half having abortions.... In 1970, 5 percent of fifteen-year-old girls in the United States had had sexual intercourse; in 1988, 25 percent had....

There are no national crime statistics for the United States for the nineteenth century and only partial ones (for homicides) for the early twentieth century. Local statistics, however, suggest that as in England the decrease in crime started in the latter part of the nineteenth century (except for a few years following the Civil War) and continued into the early twentieth century. There was even a decline of homicides in the larger cities, where they were most common; in Philadelphia, for example, the rate fell from 3.3 per 100,000 population in midcentury to 2.1 by the end of the century.

National crime statistics became available in 1960, when the rate was under 1,900 per 100,000 population. That figure doubled within the decade and tripled by 1980. A decline in the early 1980s, from almost 6,000 to 5,200, was followed by an increase to 5,800 in 1990; the latest figure, for 1992, is somewhat under 5,700. The rate of violent crime (murder, rape, robbery, and aggravated assault) followed a similar pattern, except that the increase after 1985 was more precipitous and continued until 1992, making for an almost fivefold rise from 1960. In 1987, the Department of Justice estimated that eight of every ten Americans would be a victim of violent crime at least once in their lives. The incidence of nonviolent crime is obviously greater; in 1992 alone, one in four households experienced such a crime.

Homicide statistics go back to the beginning of the century, when the national rate was 1.2 per 100,000 population. That figure skyrocketed during Prohibition, reaching as high as 9.7 by one account (6.5 by another) in 1933, when Prohibition was repealed. The rate dropped to between 5 and 6 during the 1940s and to under 5 in the fifties and early sixties. In the mid-sixties, it started to climb rapidly, more than doubling between 1965 and 1980. A decline in the early eighties was followed by another rise; in 1991 it was just short of its 1980 peak. . . .

There are brave souls, inveterate optimists, who try to put the best gloss on the statistics. But it is not much consolation to be told that the overall crime rate in the United States has declined slightly from its peak in the early 1980s, if the violent crime rate has risen in the same period—and increased still more among juveniles and girls (an ominous trend, since the teenage population is also growing). Nor that the divorce rate has fallen somewhat in the past decade, if it doubled in the previous two decades; if more people, including parents, are cohabiting without benefit of marriage (the rate in the United States has increased sixfold since 1970); and if more children are born out of wedlock and living with single parents. (In 1970, one out of ten families was headed by a single parent; in 1990, three out of ten were.) Nor that the white illegitimacy ratio is considerably lower than the black illegitimacy ratio, if the white ratio is rapidly approaching the black ratio of a few decades ago, when Daniel Patrick Moynihan wrote his percipient report about the breakdown of the black family. (The black ratio in 1964, when that report was issued, was 24.5 percent; the white ratio now is 22 percent. In 1964, 50 percent of black teenage mothers were single; in 1991, 55 percent of white teenage mothers were single.)

Nor is it reassuring to be told that two-thirds of new welfare recipients are off the rolls within two years, if half of those soon return, and a quarter of all recipients remain on for more than eight years. Nor that divorced mothers leave the welfare rolls after an average of five years, if never-married mothers remain for more than nine years, and unmarried mothers who bore their children as teenagers stay on for ten or more years. (Forty-three percent of the longest-term welfare recipients started their families as unwed teenagers.)

Nor is the cause of racial equality promoted by the news of an emerging "white underclass," smaller and less conspicuous than the black (partly because it is more dispersed) but rapidly increasing. If, as has been conclusively demonstrated, the single-parent family is the most important factor associated with the "pathology of poverty"—welfare dependency, crime, drugs, illiteracy, homelessness—a white illegitimacy rate of 22 percent, and twice that for white women below the poverty line, signifies a new and dangerous trend. This has already reached a "tipping point" in some working-class communities, creating a white underclass with all the characteristics of such a class. (Charles Murray finds a similar underclass developing in England, with twice the illegitimacy rate of the rest of the population; there it is a purely class rather than racial phenomenon.)

Nor can one be sanguine about statistics suggesting that drug use in the United States has fallen among casual users, if it has risen among habitual users; or that heroin addiction is decreasing, if crack-cocaine addiction is increasing (or, as more recent statistics show, both are on the rise); or that drug addiction among juveniles is lagging behind alcoholism. Nor can one take much satisfaction in the knowledge that the infant mortality rate has fallen, if it is disproportionately high in some groups, not because prenatal care is unavailable, but because single parents often do not avail themselves of it or because their drug or alcohol addiction has affected their infants....

✦

In his essay "Defining Deviancy Down," Senator Moynihan has taken the idea of deviancy a step further by describing the downward curve of the *concept* of deviancy. What was once regarded as deviant behavior is no longer so regarded; what was once deemed abnormal has been normalized. As deviancy is defined downward, so the threshold of deviancy rises: behavior once stigmatized as deviant is now tolerated and even sanctioned. Mental patients can rarely be institutionalized or even medicated against their will; free to live on the street, they are now treated, and appear in the statistics, not as mentally incapacitated but as "homeless." Divorce and illegitimacy, once seen as betokening the breakdown of the family, are now viewed benignly as "alternative life styles"; illegitimacy has been officially rebaptized as "nonmarital childbearing"; and divorced and unmarried mothers are lumped together in the category of "single parent families." And violent crime has become so endemic that we have practically become inured to it. The St. Valentine's Day Massacre in Chicago in 1929, when four gangsters killed seven other gangsters, shocked the nation and became legendary, immortalized in encyclopedias and history books; in Los Angeles today as many people are killed every weekend.

It is ironic to recall that only a short while ago criminologists were accounting for the rise of the crime rates in terms of our "sensitization to violence." As a result of the century-long decline of violence, they reasoned, we had become more sensitive to "residual violence"; thus more crimes were being reported and apprehended. This "residual violence" has by now become so overwhelming that, as Moynihan points out, we are being desensitized to it.

Charles Krauthammer has proposed a complementary concept: "Defining Deviancy Up." As deviancy is normalized, so the normal becomes deviant. The kind of family that has been regarded for centuries as natural and moral—the "bourgeois" family, as it is invidiously called—is now seen as pathological, concealing behind the facade of respectability the new "original sin," child abuse. While crime is underreported because we have become desensitized to it, child abuse is grossly overreported, including fantasies imagined (often inspired by therapists and social workers) long after the supposed events. Similarly, rape has been "defined up" as "date rape," to include sexual relations that the participants themselves may not have perceived as rape at the time.

The combined effect of defining deviancy up and defining it down has been to normalize and legitimize what was once regarded as abnormal and illegitimate, and, conversely, to stigmatize and discredit what was once normal and respectable. This process, too, has occurred with startling rapidity. One might expect that attitudes and values would lag behind the reality, that people would continue to pay lip service to the moral principles they were brought up with, even while violating those principles in practice. What is striking about the 1960s "sexual revolution," as it has properly been called, is how revolutionary it was, in sensibility as well as reality. In 1965, 69 percent of American women and 65 percent of men under the age of thirty said that premarital sex was always or almost always wrong; by 1972, those figures had plummeted to 24 percent and 21 percent. For women over the age of thirty, the figures dropped from 91 percent to 62 percent, and for men from 62 percent to 47 percent—this in seven short years....

Language, sensibility, and social policy conspire together to redefine deviancy. But the true effect may better be conveyed by an almost random array of facts. In his book on the underclass, Myron Magnet presents a sampling of statistics:

> By 1970 a baby born and raised in a big city had a greater chance of being murdered than a World War II GI had of dying in battle. Today, a twelve-year-old American boy has an 89% chance of becoming a victim of violent crime in his lifetime.... In mid-1989, one out of every four young black American males was either in jail or on probation—a larger proportion than was in college.

For a long time social critics and policy-makers have found it hard to face up to the realities of our moral condition, in spite of the statistical evidence. They criticize the statistics themselves or try to explain them away....

These realities have been difficult to confront because they violate the dominant ethos, which assumes that moral progress is a necessary by-product of material progress. It seems incomprehensible that in this age of free, compulsory education, illiteracy should be a problem, not among immigrants but among native-born Americans; or illegitimacy, at a time when sex education, birth control, and abortion are widely available; or drug addiction, once associated with primitive cultures and bohemian individuals. We rarely question that assumption about moral progress because we are suspicious of the very idea of morality. Moral principles, still more moral judgments, are thought to be at best an intellectual embarrassment, at worst evidence of an illiberal and repressive disposition. It is this reluctance to speak the language of morality, far more than any specific values, that separates us from the Victorians.

Most of us are uncomfortable with the idea of making moral judgments even in our private lives, let alone with the "intrusion," as we say, of moral judgments into public affairs. We are uncomfortable not only because we have come to feel that we have no right to make such judgments and impose them upon others, but because we have no confidence in the judgments themselves, no assurance that our principles are true and right for us, let alone for others. We are constantly beseeched to be "nonjudgmental," to be wary of crediting our beliefs with any greater validity than anyone else's, to be conscious of how "Eurocentric" and "culture-bound" we are. *"Chacun à son goût,"* we say of morals, as of taste; indeed, morals have become a matter of taste.

Public officials in particular shy away from the word "immoral," lest they be accused of racism, sexism, elitism, or simply a lack of compassion. When members of the president's cabinet were asked whether it is immoral for people to have children out of wedlock, they drew back from that distasteful word. The Secretary of Health and Human Services replied, "I don't like to put this in moral terms, but I do believe that having children out of wedlock is just wrong." The Surgeon General was more forthright: "No. Everyone has different moral standards.... You can't impose your standards on someone else."

It is not only our political and cultural leaders who are prone to this failure of moral nerve. Everyone has been infected by it, to one degree or another....

In Victorian England, moral principles and judgments were as much a part of social discourse as of private discourse, and as much a part of public policy as of personal life. They were not only deeply ingrained in tradition; they were also embedded in two powerful strains of Victorian thought: Utilitarianism on the one hand, Evangelicalism and Methodism on the other. These may not have been philosophically compatible, but in practice they complemented and reinforced each other, the Benthamite calculus of pleasure and pain, rewards and punishments, being the secular equivalent of the virtues and vices that Evangelicalism and Methodism derived from religion.

It was this alliance of a secular ethos and a religious one that determined social policy, so that every measure of poor relief or philanthropy, for example, had to justify itself by showing that it would promote the moral as well as the material well-being of the poor. The principle of "less eligibility," the "workhouse test," the distinction between "pauper" and "poor," the stigma attached to the "able-bodied pauper," indeed, the word "pauper" itself—all of which figured so largely in the New Poor Law—today seem invidious and inhumane. At the time, however, they were the result of a conscious moral decision: an effort to discourage dependency and preserve the respectability of the independent poor, while providing at least minimal sustenance for the indigent.

In recent decades we have so completely rejected any kind of moral calculus that we have deliberately, systematically divorced welfare—no longer called "relief"—from moral sanctions or incentives. This reflects in part the theory that society is responsible for all social problems and should therefore assume the task of solving them; and in part the prevailing spirit of relativism, which makes it difficult to pass any moral judgments or impose any moral conditions upon the recipients of relief. We are now confronting the consequences of this policy of moral neutrality. Having made the most valiant attempt to "objectify" the problem of poverty, to see it as the product of impersonal economic and social forces, we are discovering that the economic and social aspects of that problem are inseparable from the moral and personal ones. And having made the most determined effort to devise social policies that are "value-free," we find that these policies imperil both the moral and the material well-being of their intended beneficiaries.

In de-moralizing social policy—divorcing it from any moral criteria, requirements, even expectations—we have demoralized, in the more familiar sense, both the individuals receiving relief and society as a whole. Our welfare system is counterproductive not only because it aggravates the problem of welfare, creating more incentives to enter and remain within it than to try to avoid or escape from it. It also has the effect of exacerbating other more serious social problems. Chronic dependency is an integral part of the "social pathology" that now constitutes almost a single "social problem." ...

Just as many intellectuals, social critics, and policymakers were reluctant for so long to credit the unpalatable facts about crime, illegitimacy, or dependency, so they find it difficult to appreciate the extent to which these facts themselves are a function of values—the extent to which "social pathology" is a function of "moral pathology" and social policy a function of moral principle.

The moral divide has become a class divide. The "new class," as it has been called, is not in fact all that new; it is by now firmly established in the media, the academy, the professions, and the government. In a curious way, it is the mirror image of the "underclass." One might almost say that the two have a symbiotic relationship to each other. In its denigration of "bourgeois values" and the "Puritan ethic," the new class has legitimated, as it were, the values of the underclass and illegitimated those of the working class, who are still committed to bourgeois values and the Puritan ethic....

By now this "liberated," anti-bourgeois ethic no longer seems so liberating. The moral and social statistics have become so egregious that it is now finally permissible to speak of the need for "family values." Under the headline "Courage to Say the Obvious," the black liberal columnist William Raspberry explained that he meant no disrespect for the many admirable single women who raise decent families, but he was worried about social policies that were likely to produce more single mothers. This column, and others like it, appeared in April 1993, soon after *The Atlantic* featured a long article by Barbara Dafoe Whitehead summarizing the recent work of social scientists about the family. The article created a sensation, partly because of the provocative title, "Dan Quayle Was Right," and partly because of the message encapsulated on the cover: "After decades of public dispute about so-called family diversity, the evidence from social-science research is coming in: The dissolution of two-parent families, though it may benefit the adults involved, is harmful to many children, and dramatically undermines our society...."

One of the most effective weapons in the arsenal of the "counter-counterculture" is history—the memory not only of a time before the counterculture but also of the evolution of the counterculture itself. In 1968, the English playwright and member of Parliament A. P. Herbert had the satisfaction of witnessing the passage of the act he had sponsored abolishing censorship on the stage. Only two years later, he complained that what had started as a "worthy struggle for reasonable liberty for honest writers" had ended as the "right to represent copulation, veraciously, on the public stage." About the same time, a leading American civil-liberties lawyer, Morris Ernst, was moved to protest that he had meant to ensure the publication of Joyce's *Ulysses,* not the public performance of sodomy.

In the last two decades, the movements for cultural and sexual liberation in both countries have progressed far beyond their original intentions. Yet few people are able to resist their momentum or to recall their initial principles. In an unhistorical age such as ours, even the immediate past seems so remote as to be antediluvian; thus anything short of the present state of "liberation" is regarded as illiberal. And in a thoroughly relativistic age such as ours, any assertion of value—any distinction between the publication of *Ulysses* and the public performance of sodomy—is thought to be arbitrary and authoritarian. . . .

The main thing the Victorians can teach us is the importance of values— or, as they would have said, "virtues"—in our public as well as private lives. And not so much the specifically Victorian virtues that we may well value today, as the importance of an ethos that does not denigrate or so thoroughly relativize values as to make them ineffectual and meaningless.

⋅◈⋅

The Victorians were, candidly and proudly, "moralists." In recent decades that has almost become a term of derision. Yet contemplating our own society, we may be more respectful of Victorian moralism. We may even be on the verge of assimilating some of that moralism into our own thinking. It is not only "values" that are being rediscovered, but "virtues" as well. . . .

Industrialism and urbanism—"modernism," as it is now known—so far from contributing to the de-moralization of the poor, seems to have had the opposite effect. At the end of the nineteenth century, England was a more civil, more pacific, more humane society than it had been in the beginning. "Middle-class" manners and morals had penetrated into large sections of the working classes. The traditional family was as firmly established as ever, even as feminist movements proliferated and women began to be liberated from their "separate spheres." Voluntary associations and public agencies mitigated some of the worst effects of industrialism and urbanism. And religion continued to thrive, in spite of the premature reports of its death. (It even managed to beget two of the most important institutions of the twentieth century, the British trade-union movement and the Labour Party, both of which were virtually born in the chapel.)

If Victorian England did not succumb to the moral and cultural anarchy that is said to be the inevitable consequence of economic individualism, it is because of a powerful ethos that kept that individualism in check, as it also kept in check the anarchic impulses in human nature. For the Victorians, the individual, or "self," was the ally rather than the adversary of society. Self-help was seen in the context of the community as well as the family; among the working classes this was reflected in the virtue of "neighbourliness," among the middle classes, of philanthropy. Self-interest stood not in opposition to the general interest but, as Adam Smith had it, as the instrument of the general interest. Self-discipline and self-control were thought of as the source of self-respect and self-betterment; and self-respect as the precondition for the respect and approbation of others. The individual, in short, was assumed to have responsibilities as well as rights, duties as well as privileges.

That Victorian "self" was very different from the "self" that is celebrated today. Unlike "self-help," "self-esteem" does not depend upon the individual's actions or achievements; it is presumed to adhere to the individual regardless of how he behaves or what he accomplishes. Moreover, it adheres to him regardless of the esteem in which he is held by others, unlike the Victorian's self-respect which always entailed the respect of others. The current notions of self-fulfillment, self-expression, and self-realization derive from a self that does not have to prove itself by reference to any values, purposes, or persons outside itself—that simply is, and by reason of that alone deserves to be fulfilled and realized. This is truly a self divorced from others, narcissistic and solipsistic. It is this self that is extolled in the movement against "co-dependency," which aspires to free the self from any dependency upon others and, even more, from any responsibility to others. Where the interrelationship of dependency and responsibility was once regarded as a natural human condition, the source of such virtues as love, friendship, loyalty, and sociability, "co-dependency" is now seen as a pathological condition, a disease requiring a radical cure.

This is the final lesson we may learn from the Victorians: that the ethos of a society, its moral and spiritual character, cannot be reduced to economic, material, political, or other factors, that values—or better yet, virtues—are a determining factor in their own right. So far from being a "reflection," as the Marxist says, of the economic realities, they are themselves, as often as not, the crucial agent in shaping those realities. If in a period of rapid economic and social change, the Victorians managed to achieve a substantial improvement in their "condition" and "disposition," it may be that economic and social change do not necessarily result in personal and public disarray. If they could retain and even strengthen an ethos that had its roots in religion and tradition, it may be that we are not as constrained by the material circumstances of our time as we have thought. A post-industrial economy, we may conclude, does not necessarily entail a postmodernist society or culture.

It is often said that there is in human beings an irrepressible need for spiritual and moral sustenance. Just as England experienced a resurgence of religion when it seemed most unlikely (the rise of Puritanism in the aftermath of the Renaissance, or of Wesleyanism in the age of deism), so there emerged, at the very height of the Enlightenment, the movement for "moral reformation." Today, confronted with an increasingly de-moralized society, we may be ready for a new reformation, which will restore not so much Victorian values as a more abiding sense of moral and civic virtues.

NO

David Whitman

The Optimism Gap

Much of what everyone "knows" about the state of our nation is wrong. A large majority of Americans now believe that the nation is in decline. The causes of this decline are both familiar and disputed. Conservatives blame family breakdown, crime, and spiritual sloth for our national atrophy. Liberals attribute the decline to the forces of modern-day capitalism, racism, and greed; the poor and the working-class stiffs in the factories can no longer get ahead the way they once did, or so the argument goes. Yet while liberals and conservatives disagree about first causes, they nonetheless agree that the nation, like Rome before the fall, has already been compromised. The American Dream is now endangered....

The Myth of Social Regression

> The trouble with this country is that there are too many people going about saying "the trouble with this country is..."

> — Sinclair Lewis

... Is America, in fact, in a state of decline?... To evaluate whether America is declining or advancing, it is necessary to look at whether the nation today is better or worse off in various respects than in the past. Yet the country's political leaders repeatedly duck the compared-to-what question. They are notorious for taking horrifying news stories and transmogrifying them into tales of national atrophy. In 1995, for example, Americans learned of the brutal murder of Deborah Evans and two of her children by three accomplices. One of the accomplices performed a crude C-section on Evans after she died in order to remove a 38-week-old baby whom the alleged murderer claimed for her own. Was the grisly, bizarre murder unusual?

Not according to Newt Gingrich. Here is how the House Speaker analyzed its meaning in a speech to the Republican Governors Association:

> This is not an isolated incident; there's barbarity after barbarity. There's brutality after brutality. And we shake our heads and say "well, what went wrong?" What's going wrong is the welfare system which subsidized people for doing nothing; a criminal system which tolerated drug dealers; an educational system which allows kids to not learn.... And then we end up with the final culmination of a drug-addicted underclass with no sense of humanity, no sense of civilization, and no sense of the rules of life in which human beings respect each other.... The child who was killed was endowed by God. And because we aren't willing to say that any more in a public place, and we're not willing to be tough about this any more, and we don't tell four-, five-, and six-year-olds "there are things you can't do, we will not tolerate drug dealing," we then turn around one day and find that we tolerated the decay of our entire civilization. And it's not just violence. In last year's National Assessment of Educational Progress, 74 percent of the fourth-graders could not read at fourth-grade level.... A civilization that only has 26 percent of its fourth-graders performing at fourth-grade level is a civilization in danger of simply falling apart.

...What is striking about all this is that Gingrich, the former history professor, makes no reference to history. When Gingrich's claims are placed in context, they evaporate. For example, the reading scores for fourth graders that Gingrich decried were all *lower* a quarter century ago when the NAEP tests began for white, black, and Hispanic students. If the current NAEP scores testify to a civilization in danger of falling apart, think of how endangered American society was a quarter century ago. (Gingrich also botched the test results. The test scores showed that about 60 percent of fourth graders were not "proficient" readers, not that 74 percent of them read below grade level. By definition, 50 percent of those tested read above "grade level.")

Similar questions might be posed about Gingrich's claims about the criminal justice system. Does law enforcement really "tolerate" drug dealers? More drug dealers are locked up, serving longer sentences, today than ever before. That does not mean drug dealing has been halted, but it does not suggest a policy of looking the other way. What about the notion that out streets are marked by barbarity after barbarity? Are Americans significantly more likely to murder each other today than a quarter century ago? Not really. The homicide rate was a hair higher in 1995 than in 1970 (8.2 homicides per 100,000 inhabitants in 1995 versus 7.9 homicides per 100,000 inhabitants in 1970). By 1971, and for the remainder of the 1970s in fact, the homicide rate was substantially *higher* than in 1995....

The Good News Surprise

Not all of the news about America is good. Yet most of the country's fundamental economic and social trends have improved over the last quarter century. That fact would surprise millions of Americans who feel as though they are living in Babylon.

Given that the Soviet Union has collapsed, that the threat of nuclear an-
nihilation has almost vanished, and that the nation is now inundated with
immigrants who cling to rafts, wade, swim, and run to reach our borders, it
may seem an odd time to herald the demise of America. Quite apart from the
question of America's standing in the world community, however, many domestic indexes have actually improved. In fact, much of what people presume
about key social trends in America is wrong. Here are just a few examples at
odds with the conventional wisdom:

Crime

Violent crime in the United States appears to be at its lowest level in a quarter century. There are two ways of tracking trends in crime. The first is to
examine the Federal Bureau of Investigation's *Uniform Crime Reports,* which
tabulate crimes reported to law enforcement agencies from around the nation.
The second source of evidence is the Justice Department's annual national victimization surveys, which are huge polls that randomly sample approximately
100,000 people. The victimization surveys cover crimes not reported to police.
(Only about a third of all crimes are reported to law enforcement agencies, and
this fraction can change over time.) As a result, the victimization surveys are
more representative than conventional crime statistics and are favored by many
criminologists.

In 1996, violent crime rates were at their lowest levels since the victimization surveys started in 1973. According to the Justice Department reports,
violent crime rates peaked 17 years ago, in 1981, and the rates of aggravated
assault and rape are now lower than at any time in the previous 23 years.
Meanwhile, property crime, which accounts for the bulk of all crime, had also
plummeted to its lowest level since the federal surveys began. In 1996, the rates
of household theft and burglary were about half of what they had been in 1973.
The drop in property crime is so substantial that New York City now has a lower
theft and burglary rate than London, and Los Angeles has fewer burglaries than
Sydney, Australia.

Victimization surveys have one important gap: They do not track murders,
since homicide victims cannot be interviewed after the fact. However, the FBI's
Uniform Crime Reports do track homicides and the murder totals are considered
accurate, because homicide is a crime that is hard to underreport. In 1996, the
homicide rate of 7.4 murders per 100,000 inhabitants was well below the peak
of 10.2 murders per 100,000 people in 1980. It was, in fact, virtually identical to
the homicide rate in 1969, higher than in the 1950s, but lower than in 1931–34.
Most of this well-publicized drop in violent crime has been concentrated in the
nation's largest cities. In New York and Boston, fewer people were murdered
in 1996 than at any time since the 1960s. In Los Angeles, fewer people were
murdered in 1997 than in any year since 1977—even though the city now has
700,000 more residents. . . .

Drugs

Annual government surveys show that illicit drug use among the general population is at levels far below those of a decade or more ago. Overall drug use

peaked in 1979, when the nation had 25 million users, almost twice the current number. Since 1992, illicit drug use has essentially stabilized but at lower levels. Cocaine use hit its high in 1985, when 3 percent of adults, or 5.7 million Americans, reported they had used cocaine the previous month. By 1996, just 0.8 percent of Americans reported use of cocaine in the past month, and the number of current cocaine users had dropped by almost three-fourths since 1985, to 1.75 million. Among high school seniors, marijuana and LSD use has edged upward since 1992. But student use of marijuana remains well below the levels of the late 1970s and early 1980s, as does the use of most hard drugs. In 1981, 21.7 percent of high school seniors reported using an illicit drug other than marijuana during the month previous to when they were surveyed; in 1997, half as many (10.7 percent) did so. High school seniors were also three times more likely to use cocaine in 1985 than they are today....

Scholastic Achievement

Despite much-heralded reports of a nation at educational risk, high school students today do as well as or slightly better than their predecessors of the mid-1970s on both aptitude and achievement tests. As Derek Bok writes in his book *The State of the Nation,* "Contrary to all the alarmist talk, there are even some recent signs of modest improvement" in academic achievement.

The case that student aptitude has fallen rests largely on the fact that Scholastic Aptitude Test (SAT) scores declined between the early 1960s and 1970s and have never fully recovered. However, there are two reasons why those declines don't mean that today's students are performing worse than their parents.

First, only about half of all high school seniors take the SAT each year, and the sample is far from representative. In six states in 1993, more than 70 percent of high school seniors took the SAT, but in ten other states less than 10 percent of seniors did so. Unlike the SAT, the Preliminary Scholastic Aptitude Test (PSAT) is given to representative samples of high school juniors. Both the math and verbal PSAT scores have stayed the same from 1959 to the present....

Race

In the last quarter century, the black middle class has mushroomed. In 1996, black median family income, adjusted for inflation, was at an all-time high, and black poverty and infant mortality rates had edged downward to an all-time low. In 1970, about 1 out of every 17 blacks in the 25- to 34-year-old age group had earned a four-year college degree. By 1994, 1 in 8 had done so.

Orlando Patterson, a left-leaning Harvard sociologist, summarizes the import of these shifts in his 1997 book *The Ordeal of Integration.* "African Americans," he writes, "from a condition of mass illiteracy fifty years ago, are now among the most educated groups of people in the world, with median years of schooling and college completion rates higher than those of most European nations. Although some readers may think this observation is a shocking overstatement, it is not." ...

As Patterson acknowledges, a minority of blacks in urban ghettos have fared disastrously in the last 25 years. But the big picture is inescapable: Most blacks have prospered, and overt white racism has dramatically declined since the 1960s. Overwhelming majorities of whites today support the principle of equal treatment for the races in schools, jobs, housing, and other public spheres. Interracial friendships and marriages have blossomed as well. In 1970, just 2.6 percent of all new marriages involving an African-American mate were inter-racial marriages; today, more than 12 percent are interracial unions. Whites' greater openness to interracial marriages is one of the more dramatic attitudi-nal shifts in the last 25 years. In 1972, only a quarter of whites approved of marriages between blacks and whites. (In 1958, just 4 percent did so.) By 1997, however, over 60 percent of whites approved of interracial marriages. . . .

The Myth of Moral Decline . . .

The Family Values Conundrum

Since 1970, divorce and out-of-wedlock childbearing have skyrocketed in the United States. Many single-parent families manage to flourish, but on average, children raised by single parents are more likely than children raised by both their biological parents to be poor, drop out of school, become pregnant while in their teens, go to juvenile correction facilities, and be unemployed as adults.

. . . [M]any Americans, laypeople and scholars alike, exaggerate the conse-quences of family breakdown. The crude one-to-one correlation that exists in public discussion—more kids born out of wedlock automatically equals higher crime rates, weaker moral standards, worse schools, sicker children, and so on —has not been borne out in recent years. Crime rates have dropped, scholastic achievement has stabilized or edged upward, and infant mortality has declined, even as the out-of-wedlock birth ratio has risen. Nor is it clear that the ethical standards of Americans have declined.

Here again, when members of the public voice their distress about fam-ily breakdown, they are almost always referring to *other* people's families, not their own.

. . . Americans aren't just pleased with their own family life; they are de-lighted. In a 1997 Mother's Day survey, the Pew Research Center found that 93 percent of mothers with kids under 18 felt their children were a source of happiness all or most of the time; 90 percent said their marriage made them happy all or most of the time; and just 2 percent of moms reported being dis-satisfied with the job they were doing rearing their children. In poll after poll, less than 10 percent of Americans say they are worse parents than were their own parents, and compared to the moms and dads of twenty years ago, today's parents are actually much more likely to rate traditional values, such as hard work, religion, patriotism, and having children as being "very important." In their own lives, three out of four adults don't find it difficult to meet their com-mitments to their families, kids, and employers—even though 90 percent also believe that a "major problem with society" is that people don't live up to their commitments. . . .

The essential paradox is that while Americans believe today's moral break-down was spawned by the permissiveness of the 1960s, they embrace, on a case-by-case basis, most of the liberties that were part of the 1960s revolution. When Americans are asked, as they were in a 1996 *Wall Street Journal* poll, what kind of impact various social movements have had on today's values, they almost invariably think they are beneficial. Roughly 80 percent of those surveyed by the *Journal* said that the civil rights movement, the environmental movement, and the women's movement all had a positive impact on people's values.

The previous year, the Gallup Organization also quizzed members of the public about whether they thought various changes had been good or bad for society. Hefty majorities of Americans thought the greater openness today toward divorced people was good for society, as was the greater openness about sex and the human body, changes in the role of women, greater cultural and ethnic diversity, the increased willingness to question government authority, and the greater attention paid to equality for racial and ethnic minorities. In only one instance (society's increased acceptance of homosexuality) did most people think social change had harmed society....

By All That's Holy

The problem of "family breakdown" can be thought of as a surrogate Rorschach test. Voters hear of its poignant consequences among divorced friends, or see news stories about latch-key kids and crack babies, and before long, every problem starts looking as though it can ultimately be traced back to family breakdown. One might, for example, infer that organized religion is slipping if out-of-wedlock childbearing and single-parenting are mushrooming. In fact, three in four Americans believe the nation is in spiritual decline. Yet the sway of organized religion is much greater in the United States today than in most Western nations, and the religiosity of Americans is at near record levels.

As Seymour Martin Lipset, a neoconservative intellectual, sums up in his 1996 book *American Exceptionalism,* "The historical evidence indicates that religious affiliation and belief in America are much higher in the twentieth century than in the nineteenth, and have not decreased in the post–World War II era.... The standard evidence marshalled to argue that America is experiencing a value crisis is unconvincing." Such counterconventional claims are hard for members of the public to accept, again, because of the optimism gap. Two-thirds of the electorate think that religion is losing its influence on American life. Yet 62 percent say that religion's influence is increasing in their own lives, according to a 1994 *U.S. News & World Report* poll.

Today, a solid majority of Americans belong to churches and synagogues, much as they have since the 1930s, when scientific polling began. In 1997, 68 percent of Americans reported belonging to a church or synagogue, not much below the 73 percent who said they belonged in both 1965 and 1952. Some members of the clergy have asserted that these high levels of church membership conceal a dip in religious commitment and belief. It's true that weekly attendance at religious services was "only" 41 percent in 1997. This was down a bit from its peak in 1958, when 49 percent of Americans said they had attended services the previous week. But attendance in 1997 was very similar to attendance in 1950, when 39 percent of Americans said they had attended a service the previous week. In 1997, the Gallup poll replicated one of its surveys on Americans' religious practices from 1947. The fifty-year update found that the same percentage of Americans pray today (90 percent), believe in God (96 percent), and attend church once a week. About the only difference between the two eras was that Americans were actually more likely to give grace or give thanks aloud in 1997 than in 1947 (63 percent compared to 43 percent).

George Gallup, Jr., summarizes the evidence by observing that "the religious beliefs and practices of Americans today look very much like those of the 1930s and 1940s. The percent of the populace who are active church members today closely matches the figures recorded in the 1930s." Nor is it the case, as Roger Finke and Rodney Stark point out in their influential book *The Churching of America, 1776–1990*, that acceptance of traditional religious doctrine is down. Most Americans still say that religion is central to their own lives: Roughly 60 percent of adults think that religion "can answer all or most of today's problems," and one in three view at least one religious TV show each week. After reviewing church membership records and other historical evidence, Finke and Stark conclude that "to the degree that denominations rejected traditional doctrines and ceased to make serious demands on their followers, they ceased to prosper. The churching of America was accomplished by aggressive churches committed to vivid otherworldliness."

The Ethics "Crisis"

Conceivably, the nation could still be in moral decline even when its citizens claim to be deeply religious. A skeptic might suggest that Americans are simply bigger hypocrites than ever. In 1993, Everett Carll Ladd, the president of the Roper Center for Public Opinion Research, attempted to assess that proposition by examining whether the unethical behavior of Americans had risen in recent decades. In an article titled "The Myth of Moral Decline," Ladd reports his findings: There is no compelling evidence that Americans' moral conduct or ethical standards are slipping, but ever since the introduction of polling in the mid-1930s, most Americans have felt moral standards were in decline. In 1963, for instance, only a third of all adults said they were satisfied "with the honesty and standards of behavior of people in the country today."

Ladd acknowledges there is abundant evidence that large numbers of modern-day Americans err and sin. Yet in tracking trends over time, there is little proof that the moral state of the country's citizenry has deteriorated. Philanthropic giving as a percentage of personal income declined slightly between 1969 and 1972 but has essentially remained steady ever since. However, because Americans' personal incomes have risen substantially since the 1950s, individual citizens are now donating more money to charities than their parents did, even after accounting for inflation. Volunteering seems to have become *more* common. When the Gallup poll first queried people in 1977 about their participation in charitable and social service activities that aid the poor, the sick, and the elderly, a quarter of the populace said they participated. By 1994, that number had doubled to almost half of all adults....

William Bennett may have best summed up the zeitgeist of the day when he observed that "these are times in which conservatives are going to have to face the fact that there is some good news on the landscape. We're going to have to learn to live with it." In some measure, Bennett's curmudgeonly response to good news reflects the fact that conservatives are loath to credit Bill Clinton for progress. But his begrudging acceptance of the good news is also part of an age-old tradition. From era to era, the electorate's mood has swung from boosterish optimism—as during the first two decades after World War II—to the stubborn skepticism popular today. Over a century ago, Charles Dickens deftly captured this skeptical attitude toward politics and public life in his travel journal, *American Notes*. "It is an essential part of every national character to pique itself mightily upon its faults," he observed, "and to deduce tokens of its virtue or its wisdom from their very exaggeration." In America's case, Dickens argued, the "one great blemish in the popular mind ... and the prolific parent of an innumerable brood of evils, is Universal Distrust. Yet the American citizen plumes himself upon this spirit, even when he is sufficiently dispassionate to perceive the ruin it works; and will often adduce it ... as an instance of the great sagacity and acuteness of the people."

POSTSCRIPT

Is America in Moral Decline?

Handwringing over weakening morals has long been a favorite pastime. Yet are Americans less moral today than they were a century ago? Consider that slavery has been abolished, civil rights for minorities have been won and generally accepted, tolerant attitudes have greatly increased, and genocide toward American Indians ceased a long time ago. How could Americans have made so much progress if they have been getting much worse for hundreds of years? Such reflections cast suspicion over the moral decline thesis. On the other hand, this thesis is supported by many trends, such as the recently stalled increases in crime and divorce. The issue is important because morality is a distinctive trait of the human species and essential to cooperative interactions. If morality declines, coercive restraint must increase to hold harmful behaviors in check, but self-restraint is much less costly than police restraint.

The issue of the trends in morality requires an examination of the blessings and curses of individualism and capitalism. One tenet of individualism is that we should be tolerant of each other's lifestyle choices. Though this may be kindly in the short run, according to Himmelfarb, it demoralizes social policy and weakens society in the long run. Capitalism would be another demoralizing factor because it encourages self-interest and the passion for personal gain. Higher education may be another culprit because it relativizes values. In general, the forces behind the demoralization of society as described by Himmelfarb are not likely to be reversed in the medium-term future.

Most of the relevant literature is on aspects of the moral decline. Few works challenge the decline thesis. Examples include Nicholas Lemann's "It's Not as Bad as You Think It Is," *The Washington Monthly* (March 1997) and Gregg Easterbrook's "America the O.K.," *The New Republic* (January 4 & 11, 1999). For an exposition of the moral decline thesis, see Charles Derber's *The Wilding of America: How Greed and Violence Are Eroding Our Nation's Character* (St. Martin's Press, 1996); Robert Bork's *Slouching Towards Gomorrah* (Regan Books, 1996); and Richard Sennett's *The Corrosion of Character* (W. W. Norton, 1998). Richard Stivers attributes the moral decline to a culture of cynicism in *The Culture of Cynicism: American Morality in Decline* (Basil Blackwell, 1994).

ISSUE 2

Is Third World Immigration a Threat to America's Way of Life?

YES: Peter Brimelow, from *Alien Nation: Common Sense About America's Immigration Disaster* (Random House, 1995)

NO: John Isbister, from *The Immigration Debate: Remaking America* (Kumarian Press, 1996)

ISSUE SUMMARY

YES: Peter Brimelow, a writer and senior editor of *Forbes* and *National Review*, asserts that the large influx of immigrants from non-European countries threatens to undermine the cultural foundations of American unity.

NO: John Isbister, a provost at the University of California, Santa Cruz, cites research showing that immigration does not have the many negative impacts that people like Brimelow fear. He argues that immigration has a negligible effect on earnings and public finances and that its cultural impacts "will make it more obvious that the United States is a plural and not a unicultural society."

In his 1996 State of the Union speech, President Bill Clinton promised a 50 percent increase in border patrols to try to dramatically reduce illegal immigration. Polls show that this stand is a popular one. There is also much support for cutting back on legal immigration.

Today the number of legal immigrants to America is close to 1 million per year, and illegal ("undocumented") immigrants probably number well over that figure. In terms of numbers, immigration is now comparable to the level it reached during the early years of the twentieth century, when millions of immigrants arrived from southern and eastern Europe. A majority of the new immigrants, however, do not come from Europe but from what has been called the "Third World"—the underdeveloped nations. The largest percentages come from Mexico, the Philippines, Korea, and the islands of the Caribbean, while European immigration has shrunk to about 10 percent. Much of the reason for this shift has to do with changes made in U.S. immigration laws during the 1960s. Decades earlier, in the 1920s, America had narrowed its gate to people from certain regions of the world by imposing quotas designed to preserve the balance of races in America. But in 1965 a series of amendments to the Immigration Act put all the world's people on an equal footing in terms of immigration. The result, wrote journalist Theodore H. White, was "a stampede, almost an invasion" of Third World immigrants. Indeed, the 1965 amendments made it even easier for Third World immigrants to enter the country because the new law gave preference to those with a family member already living in the United States. Since most of the European immigrants who settled in the early part of the century had died off, and since few Europeans had immigrated in more recent years, a greater percentage of family-reuniting immigration came from the Third World.

Immigrants move to the United States for various reasons: to flee tyranny and terrorism, to escape war, or to join relatives who have already settled. Above all, they immigrate because in their eyes America is an island of affluence in a global sea of poverty; here they will earn many times what they could only hope to earn in their native countries. One hotly debated question is, What will these new immigrants do to the United States—or for it?

Part of the debate has to do with bread-and-butter issues: Will new immigrants take jobs away from American workers? Or will they fill jobs that American workers do not want anyway, which will help stimulate the economy? Behind these economic issues is a more profound cultural question: Will these new immigrants add healthy new strains to America's cultural inheritance, broadening and revitalizing it? Or will they cause the country to break up into separate cultural units, destroying America's unity? Of all the questions relating to immigration, this one seems to be the most sensitive.

In 1992 conservative columnist Patrick Buchanan set off a firestorm of controversy when he raised this question: "If we had to take a million immigrants next year, say Zulus or Englishmen, and put them in Virginia, which group would be easier to assimilate and cause less problems for the people of Virginia?" Although Buchanan later explained that his intention was not to denigrate Zulus or any other racial group but to simply talk about assimilation into Anglo-American culture, his remarks were widely characterized as racist and xenophobic (related to a fear of foreigners). Whether or not that characterization is justified, Buchanan's question goes to the heart of the cultural debate over immigration, which is the tension between unity and diversity.

In the selections that follow, Peter Brimelow contends that immigrants are harming America both economically and culturally. He argues that the sheer number of immigrants from other cultures threatens to overwhelm traditional safeguards against cultural disintegration. This foreign influx is changing America from a nation into a collection of separate nationalities. John Isbister challenges the economic harm thesis and argues that the cultural impacts of immigration "are positive, constructive changes, that most Americans will benefit from living in a more multicultural society and that the tension between the different ethnic groups can be alleviated."

Peter Brimelow  **YES**

Alien Nation: Common Sense About America's Immigration Disaster

The Immigration Inundation

In 1991, the year of Alexander's birth, the Immigration and Naturalization Service reported a total of over 1.8 million legal immigrants. That was easily a record. It exceeded by almost a third the previous peak of almost 1.3 million, reached eighty-four years earlier at the height of the First Great Wave of Immigration, which peaked just after the turn of the century.

The United States has been engulfed by what seems likely to be the greatest wave of immigration it has ever faced. The INS estimates that 12 to 13 million legal and illegal immigrants will enter the United States during the decade of the 1990s. The Washington, D.C.–based Federation for American Immigration Reform (FAIR), among the most prominent of the groups critical of immigration policy, thinks the total will range between 10 and 15 million. An independent expert, Daniel James, author of *Illegal Immigration—An Unfolding Crisis*, has argued that it could be as high as 18 million.

And the chaotic working of current U.S. immigration law has created a peculiar, but little-understood, reality. *The extraordinary truth is that, in almost all cases, Americans will have little more say over the arrival of these new claimants on their national community—and voters on their national future—than over the arrival of Alexander.*

This is because it's not just illegal immigration that is out of control. So is legal immigration. *U.S. law in effect treats immigration as a sort of imitation civil right, extended to an indefinite group of foreigners who have been selected arbitrarily and with no regard to American interests.*

Whether these foreigners deign to come and make their claim on America —and on the American taxpayer—is pretty much up to them.

America's One-Way Immigration Debate

Everyone knows that there are two sides to every question, except the typical American editor ordering up a story about immigration, for whom there is only one side: immigration good, concern about immigration bad.

This results in the anecdotal happy-talk good-news coverage of immigration that we all know and love:

> XYZ was just Harvard's valedictorian—XYZ arrived in the U.S. speaking no English three months ago—XYZ PROVES THE AMERICAN DREAM IS STILL ALIVE!—despite those nasty nativists who want to keep all the XYZs out.

Now, the achievement of immigrants to the United States (more accurately, of some immigrants to the United States) is indeed one of the most inspiring, and instructive, tales in human history. Nevertheless, there are still two sides to the question. Thus we might, equally reasonably, expect to see balancing anecdotal coverage like this:

> In January 1993, a Pakistani applicant for political asylum (and, simultaneously, for amnesty as an illegal immigrant) opens fire on employees entering CIA headquarters, killing two and wounding three! In February 1993, a gang of Middle Easterners (most illegally overstaying after entering on nonimmigrant visas—one banned as a terrorist but admitted on a tourist visa in error) blow up New York's World Trade Center, killing six and injuring more than 1,000!! In December 1993, a Jamaican immigrant (admitted as a student but stayed, illegal status automatically regularized after marriage to a U.S. citizen) opens fire on commuters on New York's Long Island Rail Road, killing six and wounding 19!!! WHAT'S GOING ON??!!?

The case of Colin Ferguson, arrested in the Long Island Rail Road shootings, is particularly instructive. . . .

Ferguson's own writings showed him to be motivated by hatred of whites. And this racial antagonism is a much deeper problem. In any rational mind, it must raise the question: *Is is really wise to allow the immigration of people who find it so difficult and painful to assimilate into the American majority?*

Because the fact cannot be denied: if Ferguson and the others had not immigrated, those fourteen Americans would not have been killed.

Although we might reasonably expect to see such balancing media coverage of immigration, don't hold your breath. There are powerful taboos preventing it. . . . The result, however, is that the American immigration debate has been a one-way street. Criticism of immigration, and news that might support it, just tends not to get through.

This is no mere journalism-school game of balancing anecdotes. It involves the broadest social trends. For example, the United States is in the midst of a serious crime epidemic. Yet almost no Americans are aware that *aliens make up one quarter of the prisoners in federal penitentiaries*—almost three times their proportion in the population at large.

Indeed, many problems that currently preoccupy Americans have an unspoken *immigration dimension. . . .*

The education crisis. Americans are used to hearing that their schools don't seem to be providing the quality of education that foreigners get. Fewer of them know that the U.S. education system is also very expensive by international standards. Virtually none of them know anything about the impact of immigration on that education system.

Yet the impact of immigration is clearly serious. For example, in 1990 almost one child in every twenty enrolled in American public schools either could not speak English or spoke it so poorly as to need language-assistance programs. This number is increasing with striking speed: only six years earlier, it had been one child in thirty-one. Current law is generally interpreted as requiring schools to educate such children in their native language. To do so, according to one California estimate, requires spending some 65 percent more per child than on an English-speaking child....

[T]he immigration resulting from current public policy

1. is dramatically larger, less skilled and more divergent from the American majority than anything that was anticipated or desired
2. is probably not beneficial economically—and is certainly not necessary
3. is attended by a wide and increasing range of negative consequences, from the physical environment to the political
4. is bringing about an ethnic and racial transformation in America without precedent in the history of the world—an astonishing social experiment launched with no particular reason to expect success...

What About My Grandfather?

Many Americans have difficulty thinking about immigration restriction because of a lurking fear: *This would have kept my grandfather out....*

But it must also be stressed: *that was then; this is now.* There are important differences between the last Great Wave of Immigration and today's.

1. Then, there was an "Open Door" (essentially—and with the major exception of the restriction on Asians). Now, the 1965 reform has reopened the border in a perversely unequal way. Essentially, it has allowed immigrants from some countries to crowd out immigrants from others....
2. Then, immigrants came overwhelmingly from Europe, no matter how different they seemed at the time; now, immigrants are overwhelmingly visible minorities from the Third World. Not withstanding which—
3. Then, there was an aggressive public and private "Americanization" campaign...; now, there's "multiculturalism"—i.e., immigrants are officially not expected to assimilate.
4. Then, there was no welfare state and immigrants who failed often went home; now, there is a welfare state—and fewer immigrants leave.
5. Then, *immigration was stopped.* There was a pause for digestion—the Second Great Lull—that lasted some forty years. Now, there's no end in sight.

... [A]n implicit accusation of racism is the common reaction of a vocal minority of Americans to news of their country's shifting ethnic balance....

I say a vocal minority because I think the vast majority of Americans regard as just a matter of common sense that the composition of a country's population cannot, in fact, be changed without risking dramatic consequences....

[T]here are some extraordinary aspects of the impending ethnic revolution that, by any standard, deserve discussion in a democracy:

- *It is unprecedented in history.* No sovereign state has ever undergone such a radical and rapid transformation.
- *It is wholly and entirely the result of government policy.* Immigration is causing both the shifting American ethnic balance and also the projected massive increase in overall population. Left to themselves, pre-1965 Americans would be stabilizing both their ethnic proportions and their overall numbers.

... [T]here's a plain fact to be considered: the evidence that multiracial societies work is—what shall we say?—*not very encouraging.*

There have, of course, been multiracial societies (strictly speaking, usually multiethnic) in the past. Famous examples are the Roman Empire, or the Arab Caliphate, which briefly ruled from Spain to Samarkand in the name of Muhammad. But these were old-fashioned despotisms, not modern democracies. And, even so, ethnic divisions still kept surfacing. The ancestors of the modern Iranians repeatedly rebelled against Arab rule, although they tended to justify their revolts in terms of a convenient Islamic heresy.

Heterogeneous empires that lasted, such as the Eastern Roman Empire of Byzantium, which survived until 1453, were generally based on a core ethnic group—distinctly like our old friend, the "racial hegemony of white Americans." In the case of Byzantium, for instance, this core group was Greek.

In modern times, there has been a lot of seductive murmuring about internationalism, united nations, new world orders, and so on. But, meanwhile, the role of ethnicity and race has proved to be elemental—absolute—fundamental. Look at the record, working back from the present:

- *Eritrea,* a former Italian colony ruled by Ethiopia since 1952, revolt begins in 1960s, finally splits off 1993.
- *Czechoslovakia,* founded 1918, splits into Czech and Slovak ethnic components, 1993.
- *Soviet Union,* founded 1922, splits into multiple underlying ethnic components, 1991. (Some of the underlying components are themselves promptly threatened with further ethnic fragmentation —Georgia, Moldova.)
- *Yugoslavia,* founded 1918, splits into multiple underlying ethnic components, 1991. (An earlier breakup averted by imposition of royal dictatorship, 1929.)
- *Lebanon,* founded 1920, progressive destabilization caused by its Muslim component's faster growth results in civil war, effective partition under Syrian domination, after 1975.

- *Cyprus,* independent 1960, repeated violence between Greeks and Turks results in military intervention by Turkey, effective partition with substantial ethnic cleansing, 1974.
- *Pakistan,* independent 1947, ethnically distinct eastern component rebels, splits off after Indian military intervention, 1971.
- *Malaysia,* independent 1963, political conflict between ethnic Malays and Chinese, Chinese-dominated Singapore expelled, 1965.

And these are just the cases where ethnic and racial differences have actually succeeded in breaking a country up. Many other cases are not yet resolved, because of often-bloody repression.

Here's a partial list: *India*—protracted separatist revolts by Sikhs, Kashmiris, northeastern hill tribes. *Sri Lanka*—protracted separatist revolt by Tamils. *Turkey, Iraq, Iran*—separatist revolts by Kurds. *Sudan, Chad*—endemic warfare between Arab north, black south. *Nigeria*—secession of Ibo-majority "Biafra" crushed in 1967–70 civil war. *Liberia*—English-speaking descendants of freed American slaves overthrown by tribal forces 1981, civil war renders more than half the population refugees. *Ulster*—protracted campaign by members of province's Catholic Irish minority to force the Ulster Protestant ("Scotch-Irish") majority to accept its transfer to the Irish Republic. Some of these conflicts have been very violent—over 1 million deaths each in Nigeria and Sudan.

And there's a whole further category of disputes that are being conducted, mostly, through political means. For example: *Belgium*—Flemish and Walloon; *Canada*—French and English; even *Brazil*—a movement in the predominantly white southern states Rio Grande do Sul, Santa Catarina and Paraná to separate from the mixed-race north.

What a record! You would think it would inspire at least some caution about the prospects for multiethnic, multiracial, multicultural harmony within the same political framework.

But you would be wrong. The recent record seems to have made very little impression on the American political elite....

How Much Economic Growth Are We Talking About Anyway?

Oddly, American economists have made very little effort to measure the overall economic benefits of immigration. But the answer seems to be clear: *immigration doesn't contribute that much to economic growth....*

In 1992, the economic surplus generated by immigrants and accruing to native-born Americans was very small: about one to three tenths of 1 percent of total U.S. economic output, or between $6 billion and $18 billion.

That's 0.2 or 0.3 percent! In an economy whose long-run average annual growth is about 2 percent anyway!! Within the normal margin of error for economic projections—*so it may be, for practical purposes, infinitesimal!!!...*

Another point:

If immigration is indeed causing a net loss to taxpayers of $16 billion—as
George Borjas estimates—**that means its economic effects are neutral. It's**
a wash!!!

America is being transformed for—*nothing?*
Yep. That's what it looks like.
However, note that this Borjas back-of-the-envelope calculation has a sub-
tle but ugly implication:

The overall economic surplus generated by immigrants and accruing to
native-born Americans might be very small—but immigration might still
be causing a significant redistribution of income within the native-born
American community.

This happens because the small amount by which immigrants drive down
the wages for all American workers, nationwide, adds up to a sizeable sum—
which goes to American owners of capital. Borjas estimates it could be 2 percent
of GNP, or as much as $120 billion. . . .

However, this is the ugly implication: the American elite's support for
immigration may not be idealistic at all, but self-interested—as a way to prey on
their fellow Americans. . . .

Is the United States Still Capable
of Absorbing Immigrants?

Let's be clear about this: the American experience with immigration has been
triumphant success. It has so far transcended anything seen in Europe as to
make the application of European lessons an exercise to be performed with
care.

But there are very clear reasons why the American nation has been able
to absorb and assimilate immigrants. In considering further immigration, its
enthusiasts must ask themselves honestly: *do these reasons still apply?*

One reason America could assimilate immigrants, as we have seen, is that
there were regular pauses for digestion. Another reason is that the American
political elite *wanted the immigrants to assimilate.* And it did not hesitate to
ensure that they did.

Over two hundred years of U.S. history, a number of tried-and-true, but
undeniably tough, assimilation techniques had been perfected. But today, they
have been substantially abandoned.

The economic culture of the United States has changed significantly—
from classical liberalism to government-regulated welfare statism. Earlier immigrants were basically free to succeed or fail. And many failed: as we have
seen, as many as 40 percent of the 1880–1920 immigrants went back home. But
now, public policy interposes itself, with the usual debatable results. . . .

And it's not just the American economic culture that has changed. So has
the political culture. Almost a century ago, the last Great Wave of immigrants

were met with the unflinching demand that they "Americanize." Now they are told that they should retain and reinforce their diversity....

Is the United States still capable of absorbing immigrants? Is it still trying? Consider these policies:

1. *Massive, heterogeneous immigration.*
2. *"Bilingualism"*—i.e., foreign languageism—and
3. *"Multiculturalism"*—i.e., non-Americanism—in the education system.
4. *"Affirmative Action"*—i.e., government-mandated discrimination against white Americans.
5. *Systematic attack on the value of citizenship,* by making it easier for aliens to vote, receive government subsidies, etc.

Sounds much more like deconstructionism—the deconstruction of the American nation as it existed in 1965.

NO

John Isbister

The Immigration Debate

The Debate

Immigration has become one of the most contentious topics of debate in the United States. It is not surprising.

In 1965, Congress reformed the country's immigration law, removing the system of quotas based on national origins that had been in place since the 1920s. The architects of the 1965 act wanted to expunge what they saw as racial discrimination in the country's immigration legislation. They did not expect, however, that the new law would lead to much of a shift in either the number or the national origins of the country's immigrants. Yet, since 1965, an enormous change has occurred in both. The amount of immigration has reached levels seen only once before, at the turn of the present century. The United States now accepts more immigrants than all other countries combined. The principal sources of immigration have changed completely, from Europe with its white populations to the third world countries of Latin America and Asia. The pressure for immigration from foreign countries has grown faster than the legal gates have been opening, so the number of undocumented immigrants has increased too.

As immigration has grown, opposition to it has grown as well. The country is flooded with proposals to reduce the flow of immigrants, to change the priority categories, to tighten controls at the border and to penalize immigrants, both legal and illegal. The Commission on Immigration Reform, headed by former Representative Barbara Jordan of Texas, recommended in 1995 that immigration be cut by one-third, and President Clinton endorsed the recommendation. The opposition is similar to the resistance that built up against the great influx of immigrants at the beginning of the century. Public opinion against that wave became so strong that Congress passed a series of acts in the 1920s severely restricting the number of new entrants. Today's critics of immigration would like to see the same sort of policy response.

Public opinion polls show strong resistance to immigration, even among some ethnic groups that include a large proportion of recent immigrants. A Roper poll showed that 55 percent of the population is in favor of a temporary freeze on immigration. A poll that divided its respondents by ethnicity

From John Isbister, *The Immigration Debate: Remaking America* (Kumarian Press, 1996). Copyright © 1996 by John Isbister. Reprinted by permission of Kumarian Press, West Hartford, CT. Notes omitted.

showed that 70 to 80 percent of not only Anglos but also Mexican Americans, Puerto Ricans and Cuban Americans agreed with the statement, "There are too many immigrants coming to the U.S." A *Newsweek* poll found that 60 percent of Americans think that immigration is a "bad thing" for the country, and 62 percent think that immigrants take the jobs of American workers. In 1994, Californians voted by a 59–41 margin for Proposition 187, to cut undocumented immigrants and their children off from all public expenditures except emergency medical care. A Field poll showed that almost half of Californians favored a constitutional amendment to deny citizenship to the American-born children of undocumented immigrants. Any number of other polls show the same thing: the majority of Americans are at least skeptical about the value of immigration and, for the most part, are hostile to it.

Little about the debate is new; most of the arguments, both pro and con, have surfaced many times in the past. In the thirteen colonies of the eighteenth century, for example, the predominant opinion was that immigration was essential to prosperity and that any attempt to restrict it was illegitimate. Among the grievances listed in the Declaration of Independence was that the king had:

> endeavoured to prevent the population of these States; for that purpose obstructing the Laws for Naturalization of Foreigners; refusing to pass others to encourage their migration hither.

It had to be a certain *type* of immigrant, however; non-English newcomers were suspect. In the *Federalist Papers,* John Jay wrote,

> Providence has been pleased to give this one connected country to one united people—a people descended from the same ancestors, speaking the same language, professing the same religion, attached to the same principles of government, very similar in their manners and customs.

Benjamin Franklin, writing in 1775, was more explicitly racist:

> Why should the *Palatine Boors* be suffered to swarm into our settlements, and by herding together establish their language and manners to the exclusion of ours? Why should *Pennsylvania,* founded by the *English,* become a colony of *Aliens,* who will shortly be so numerous as to Germanize us instead of our Anglifying them, and will never adopt our language or customs, any more than they can acquire our complexion....

The Economic Debate

Much of the debate has focused on the economic consequences of immigration, both short and long term. Some proponents of immigration argue that the newcomers contribute to the vitality of the American economy, helping to improve the standard of living of everyone, whether immigrant or native. Others do not go so far but argue that immigrants at least cause no economic harm to Americans. Those on the other side of the economic debate claim that immigrants impose significant material burdens on Americans and that they reduce the country's prospects for long-term prosperity....

What the Empirical Studies Show

What do the cross-sectional studies tell us? Briefly, they show that immigration has little if any economic impact on the wages and employment opportunities of residents, even residents who are unskilled, low paid or racial minorities.

As an example, Robert LaLonde and Robert Topel used the 1970 and 1980 censuses to study the effects of immigration in 119 standard metropolitan statistical areas. They found that immigration had only a slight effect on earnings. According to their calculations, a 100 percent increase in immigration to a city would cause only a 3 percent decline in the earnings of the immigrants themselves and a 1 percent decline in the earnings of African American and Latino residents....

The rest of the cross-sectional empirical work leads to similar conclusions. The great majority of the studies find that immigration has little or no effect on the wages and employment of natives, even on the wages and employment of disadvantaged subgroups.

Can the Empirical Studies Be Reconciled With the Models?

We are left with a puzzle. Why is it that the theoretical models predict that immigration will harm the employment and wages of resident Americans, particularly disadvantaged Americans, yet most of the empirical research cannot identify such an effect? Normally in such a case, one would treat the models as hypotheses to be tested and conclude that the empirical tests have disproved the hypotheses. In this case, however, the models were not really tested directly, because time series studies were not possible.

It is easy to think of reasons why the cross-sectional empirical studies might be misleading. Perhaps immigration into a city tends to reduce the wages of low-skilled workers, as the models predict, but within a short time the flow of both labor and capital within the United States responds so as to negate the initial effect of immigration in those cities....

After dozens of sophisticated studies, ... we are still uncertain about the short-run economic impact of immigration. Immigration may have negative economic effects that our statistical methods are incapable of detecting. The case is not proved, however. One can certainly come up with an argument to support the validity of the empirical studies. For example, if immigration attracts new capital into the country, it may have no overall effect on wages.

It is frustrating to learn that economists, with all their high-powered methodological tools, cannot give a clear answer to a simple, important question: how does immigration affect the earnings of American residents, in particular the most disadvantaged Americans? Nevertheless, that is the state of the professional literature.

Are Immigrants a Fiscal Burden?

... None of the research to date has been adequately designed to provide a fully persuasive answer to the question of whether immigration creates a fiscal burden on residents. The studies are in an accounting rather than an economic mode. They attempt to count the expenditures that are made on immigrants and the taxes paid by immigrants. Even this is exceptionally difficult to do, and every one of the studies can be criticized for being incomplete in one way or another. Few of them even attempt to measure the indirect market effects of immigration on the public finances. For example, if immigration leads to an increase in aggregate demand and the consequent creation of new jobs, some of which are held by previously unemployed natives, the taxes paid by these new employees and the reduction in unemployment insurance payments should be counted as a fiscal benefit of immigration. . . .

It is hard to identify all the ways in which immigrants affect the revenues and expenditures of the different governments, let alone measure the effects. Taken together, however, most of the studies seem to indicate that immigrants have not been a net burden to U.S. governments—that government expenditures on the immigrants have not exceeded tax revenues paid by the immigrants. Immigrants may even have been a net asset. . . .

. . . At the level of state governments, the situation may vary according to the state.

It appears . . . that in the country as a whole, immigrants probably impose no burden on resident taxpayers and may even contribute more than they use. At the state level, however, and even more so at the local level in communities where immigration has been heavy, there are a number of cases of immigrants imposing a fiscal burden. However, because every study to date has been seriously incomplete, we have only hints about the true fiscal impact of immigration, not proof. . . .

Making a Multicultural Society Work

The consequences of immigration into the United States are not limited to the economy. Just as important, perhaps more important, are the social and cultural impacts of immigration, particularly those resulting from changes in the ethnic composition of the population. . . . If immigration continues at its current rate, the time will come, a couple of generations hence, when Anglos will be a minority of the population and Latinos, not African Americans, will be the next largest group.

Many Americans oppose these changes, believing that their country is turning into something they do not like and did not agree to. Journalist Peter Brimelow writes, "The onus is on those who favor the major change in the ethnic balance entailed by current immigration levels to explain exactly what they have against the American nation as it had evolved by 1965 (90 per cent white, primarily from Italy, Germany, Ireland and Britain). While they're at it, they can explain just what makes them think that multi-racial societies work."

[The remainder of this selection] provides a response to Brimelow's challenge, arguing that the changes in the U.S. population caused by immigration are positive, constructive changes, that most Americans will benefit from living in a more multicultural society and that the tension between the different ethnic groups can be alleviated.

The Mosaic of American Life

American culture is based on a multitude of different nationalities and ethnicities. "It never happened that a group of people called Americans came together to form a political society called America," writes political philosopher Michael Walzer. "The people are Americans only by virtue of having come together." American culture does not derive from a single folk tradition; it is not based on a particular religion or a single race. It embodies many folkways, many religions, many races.

The principal metaphor for how the various traditions came together in America used to be the melting pot. The groups were thought to have mixed together so thoroughly that they created a new culture, one that was common to most Americans and that erased the immigrant past. The ideology of the melting pot is still alive, but at the end of the twentieth century it is weak. It is now apparent that the nineteenth-century immigrant groups did not assimilate as thoroughly as was once thought, that the melting pot never worked with African and Native Americans and that the latest waves of immigrants show few signs of disappearing into an undifferentiated brew. Replacing the melting pot is the pluralist, multicultural image of the mosaic, in which immigrants and their descendants are understood as retaining important parts of their ethnic identities, and together constituting a varied, diverse nation. . . .

The metaphor of the melting pot misses . . . the essence of American culture. To be sure, the experience of being in America has changed people. African Americans are not Africans; neither, however, are they just Americans. They are African Americans, and their experience of the United States is strongly influenced by that fact. This is also true for the Jews, the Puerto Ricans, the Mexicans, the Chinese and many other groups that have come in large numbers to the United States. In their seminal 1963 study *Beyond the Melting Pot,* Nathan Glazer and Daniel Patrick Moynihan rejected the idea of a uniform American culture, at least in the neighborhoods of New York. Scholarly work since that time has expanded their ideas. In his 1993 book *A Different Mirror,* for example, Ronald Takaki interprets the full sweep of American history as being dominated by the interactions of immigrant and ethnic groups.

To the extent that the melting pot is a valid idea at all, its contents are white. The melting pot brought together English, Irish, Swedes, Italians, Hungarians, Russians and other European groups and made a country out of them. In the first part of the twentieth century, this seemed a remarkable achievement, because the history of immigration had been fraught with suspicion, disdain and discrimination. The English once thought of the Irish immigrants as scruffy and papist; at a later date, the English and Irish together thought that the Italians and Greeks were barbarian. Yet by the first half of the twentieth century, the distinctions between the European groups were blurring. They retained ethnic organizations, with the Jews being perhaps the strongest in maintaining their communities. They cooperated together in business and in politics, however; they sometimes moved into the same suburbs, and their children intermarried. The ethnic identities did not disappear, but they were on the road to becoming footnotes to an American identity.

If that sort of description rings true for some Irish and Poles, however, it does not for African and Native Americans. One can take the melting pot seriously as the central process of American civilization only if one thinks that non-white groups were not really part of that civilization. Many people have exactly that opinion. For example, Brimelow's popular book on immigration, *Alien Nation,* overflows with observations that the United States is properly a white nation and should stay that way. "The American nation has always had a specific ethnic core. And that core has been white," he writes. Later, he writes, "And—if only for my son Alexander's sake—I'd like it to stay that way." In spite of Brimelow's protestations that his views are not racist, the words speak for themselves.

Like it or not, non-whites have always been a fundamental component of American culture, since the first day a settler encountered a Native on the shore of the Atlantic, and since the first docking of a slave ship. Today, there are many more non-white groups. The majority of Latinos and Asians in the United States are the descendants of fairly recent immigrants, or immigrants themselves, so it is early to judge how those groups will assimilate into mainstream culture, or if mainstream culture will be there when they do. So far, however, they are not melting with other Americans nearly as completely as the different European groups did. They face racial discrimination that is different from and deeper than anything the Europeans faced. Their ethnic organizations and ethnic identities seem to be stronger.

If immigration continues at its current pace, therefore, and if third world countries of origin still predominate, so that non-Anglo ethnic groups continue to grow as proportions of the population, each passing decade will make it more obvious that the United States is a plural and not a unicultural society. . . .

Immigration as a Threat to the Dominant Culture

The majority of white Americans think of themselves as Americans, not any particular kind of Americans. They often think of themselves as people without any particular culture, just "people." The truth, however, is that they have merged not into a common American culture but into the dominant American culture, so dominant that they can be blinded into thinking of it as the only culture. Thus Bette Hammond . . . complains that today's immigrants want to be in America but they do not want to be American. She means, presumably, that they do not want to be part of the predominantly white, Anglo, middle-class culture that the melting pot has produced. The non-white groups tend to see it differently. They cannot be part of that dominant culture, they believe, because they are excluded from it and oppressed by it.

Anglos who fear the new immigration understand this on some level. They know, and fear, that the forces of the melting pot are not strong enough to assimilate the latest wave of newcomers completely . . . Today's immigrants look different, they speak differently, they have different values, different family structures, different commitments, different heritages. Mainstream-culture Americans often fear that this new multiculturalism is altering the life to which they are accustomed. . . .

Immigration Seen Through Multicultural Lenses

Those who see the country as pluralist, myself included, do not share the fears of the uniculturalists. The essence of American life is that it is composed of different groups, different cultures, races, religions, attitudes, folkways and ideologies, differences that give the country its distinctiveness. Current immigration is sure to change the mixture, but change is not new; the cultural mixture of America has been changing continuously.

Brimelow's question was: what was wrong with the American nation as it was in 1965, 90 percent white? The answer is that there were serious problems, as the civil rights movement and the explosions in the central cities revealed. America has always been multicultural, but it has been a peculiar kind of multiculturalism: not equally powerful cultures enriching one another on a reciprocal basis, but a dominant culture set against subservient cultures fighting to secure places for themselves. Today's immigration creates the possibility that the United States may become a country without a dominant race and without a dominant culture. If Anglos become a minority by the second half of the twenty-first century, and if the different ethnic groups achieve political representation, they will have the power to protect their interests and their cultures. As the sizes of the different racial and ethnic groups become more comparable, the likelihood of one group dominating the others will become correspondingly less.

The alternative to an egalitarian, reciprocal, multicultural society is not the single culture imagined by the uniculturalists. The implication of Brimelow's description ("90 per cent white, primarily from Italy, Germany, Ireland and Britain") is that the United States really could be a country with a single culture, much like some imagine France or Japan to be. It never has been, however, and it cannot be. The most important theme in American cultural history, since the seventeenth century, has been racial conflict. The conflicts have been marked by slavery, unequal power, widely disparate economic statuses, personal prejudice and institutional discrimination. Although the terms of the confrontation have shifted, whites and non-whites are still unequal in status. The alternatives before the country, therefore, are not a single culture versus many cultures, but multiculturalism marked by dominance, subordination and conflict versus multiculturalism marked by equality of status and reciprocity.

How can the first kind of country be transformed into the second? There is no single answer. I am enough of an optimist, however, to think that I have been living in the United States during a generation of change—through the civil rights movement, through political action, through education, through the assertion of legal rights, through cooperation by people of good will and through immigration. The shift in immigration legislation from a racist to a nondiscriminatory basis in 1965 has allowed and will continue to allow the relative numbers of the different ethnic groups to change in such a way that they confront one another on a more equal basis.

Numbers matter. In order for the different groups to relate to one another on an equal basis, without the members of one group feeling that they have to suppress their values and their interests, all the groups need to be not equal in size but well represented. As Anglos move toward minority status, and as Latinos and Asian Americans grow proportionately and African Americans retain their current relative representation, the interactions among the different groups may become more direct, clearer, more reciprocal, more equal. The United States will not become multicultural because it always has been, but its multiculturalism will become healthier, its citizens less constrained by structures of discrimination....

What will be distinctive about the United States is that the mix of cultures will be so rich. Even today, the representation of different groups in the United States is broader than in any other country; as immigration proceeds, the combination of ethnic groups will approach that of the world as a whole. Anglos will probably continue to be overrepresented and Asians underrepresented, in comparison to their proportions in the world's population, but the former will be less than half and the latter will constitute a substantial number.

One of the reasons that it is important for America to become a country in which different cultural groups encounter one another on the basis of equality and respect is that America could become a model to the world. The world needs models of cultural respect.

POSTSCRIPT

Is Third World Immigration a Threat to America's Way of Life?

Former representative Silvio Conte (R-Massachusetts) said at a citizenship ceremony, "You can go to France, but you will never be a Frenchman. You can go to Germany but you will never be a German. Today you are all Americans, and that is why this is the greatest country on the face of the earth." At one time America's open doors to immigrants was one of the prides of America. For some people, like Isbister, it still is. He thinks that an integrated, multicultural society is a culturally rich society and that immigration is making America stronger. Many people disagree because they fear the consequences of today's immigration. Brimelow worries that, although the new immigrants may want to assimilate, they have reached such a critical mass that the United States has lost the ability to absorb everyone into its own, slowly dissipating culture. The result is that immigrants are encouraged to maintain and promote the cultures that they arrive with, which further dilutes the original culture of America. Isbister counters that Brimelow's fears are that the white America that he identifies with will lose some of its dominance. That is, the America that Brimelow wants to protect is a racist, white America. Isbister argues that America has always been multicultural and that it will gain from being multicultural.

For a fascinating study of the roots of American traditional culture, see David Hackett Fischer, *Albion's Seed: Four British Folkways in America* (Oxford University Press, 1989). Stanley Lieberson and Mary C. Waters, in *From Many Strands* (Russell Sage Foundation, 1988), argue that ethnic groups with European origins are assimilating, marrying outside their groups, and losing their ethnic identities. Richard D. Alba's study "Assimilation's Quiet Tide," *The Public Interest* (Spring 1995) confirms these findings.

Several major works debate whether or not immigrants, on average, economically benefit America and can assimilate. Sources that argue that immigrants largely benefit America include Julian L. Simon, *The Economic Consequences of Immigration,* 2d ed. (University of Michigan Press, 1999) and *Immigration: The Demographic and Economic Facts* (Cato Institute, 1995).

Sources that argue that immigrants have more negative than positive impacts include George Borjas, *Heaven's Door: Immigration Policy and the American Economy* (Princeton University Press, 1999) and Roy Beck, *The Case Against Immigration* (W. W. Norton, 1996).

On the Internet . . .

American Men's Studies Association

The American Men's Studies Association is a not-for-profit professional organization of scholars, therapists, and others interested in the exploration of masculinity in modern society.

`http://members.aol.com/amsapage/`

American Studies Web

This eclectic site provides links to a wealth of resources on the Internet related to gender studies.

`http://www.georgetown.edu/crossroads/asw/`

Feminism and Women's Resources

This site for feminism and women's resources includes information on and links to women's organizations, women's resources, and other organizations and links of interest.

`http://zeno.ibd.nrc.ca/~mansfield/feminism/`

Feminist Internet Gateway

The Feminist Internet Gateway provides affirmative action links, resources from the feminist majority foundation, information for empowering women in business, sexual harassment information, and much more.

`http://www.feminist.org/gateway/sd_exec2.html`

GLAAD: Gay and Lesbian Alliance Against Defamation

GLAAD, formed in New York in 1985, seeks to improve the public's attitudes toward homosexuality and to put an end to discrimination against lesbians and gay men.

`http://www.glaad.org`

SocioSite

This site provides insights into a number of issues that affect family relationships. It covers wide-ranging issues regarding women and men, family and children, and much more.

`http://www.pscw.uva.nl/sociosite/TOPICS/Women.html`

PART 2

Sex Roles, Gender, and the Family

*T*he modern feminist movement has advanced the causes of women to the point where there are now more women in the workforce in the United States than ever before. Professions and trades that were traditionally regarded as the provinces of men have opened up to women, and women now have easier access to the education and training necessary to excel in these new areas. But what is happening to sex roles, and what are the effects of changing sex roles? How have stress caused by current sex roles, male-female communication difficulties, the demand for the right to same-sex marriages, and the deterioration of the traditional family structure affected men and women? The issues in this part address these sorts of questions.

- Do the New Sex Roles Burden Women More Than Men?

- Are Communication Problems Between Men and Women Largely Due to Radically Different Conversation Styles?

- Should Same-Sex Marriages Be Legally Recognized?

- Is the Decline of the Traditional Family a National Crisis?

ISSUE 3

Do the New Sex Roles Burden
Women More Than Men?

YES: Jeff Grabmeier, from "The Burden Women Bear: Why They Suffer More Distress Than Men," *USA Today Magazine* (July 1995)

NO: Susan Faludi, from *Stiffed: The Betrayal of the American Man* (William Morrow and Company, 1999)

ISSUE SUMMARY

YES: Editor and author Jeff Grabmeier presents evidence showing that women experience more stress than men and then analyzes why.

NO: Author Susan Faludi argues that men have been socialized into a sex role that cannot be successfully fulfilled due to current conditions.

The publication of Betty Friedan's *The Feminine Mystique* (W. W. Norton, 1963) is generally thought of as launching the modern women's movement, and since that time significant changes have occurred in American society. Occupations and professions, schools, clubs, associations, and governmental positions that were by tradition or law previously reserved for men only are now open to women. Women are found in increasing numbers among lawyers, judges, physicians, and elected officials. In 1981 President Ronald Reagan appointed the first woman, Sandra Day O'Connor, to the Supreme Court. In 1983 the first American woman astronaut, Sally Ride, was included in the crew of a space shuttle, and women have been on more recent space shuttle missions, as well. The service academies have accepted women since 1976, and women in the military participated in the U.S. invasion of Panama in December 1989 and in the Persian Gulf War in 1990. Elizabeth Watson became the first woman to head a big-city police department when the mayor of Houston appointed her as chief of police in January 1990.

These sorts of changes—quantifiable and highly publicized—may signal a change in women's roles. Women now engage in occupations that were previously exclusive to men, and can pursue the necessary training and education required to do so. Paula Span, in "It's a Girl's World," *The Washington Post Magazine* (June 22, 1997), quotes her daughter as saying, "Most of my girlfriends and I feel like we could do anything.... Being female isn't a restriction." Now most women of working age are either in school or the labor force, even those with children. As a result, the problem for women today has less to do with occupational exclusion than with the stress of inclusion.

But what about men today? To the extent that sex bias remains they are the advantaged sex. However, do they really have it made? Some would argue that they do not. Men may experience less stress as Jeff Grabmeier, author of the first selection, asserts, but they die younger. In fact, between the ages of 15 and 24, when sex roles take full hold, the death rate for men is over three times the death rate for women. Furthermore, if death by heart disease is likely to be related to stress, it should be noted that men die of heart disease at almost twice the age-adjusted death rate as women. One reason may be that men who work full time on average spend substantially more time working and commuting than women who work full time.

Neither stress data nor death-rate data can tell us the extent that sex roles affect the differential rates. Biological differences also play a role and the extent of this role is not clear. At this point, therefore, the discussion should focus on what burdens sex roles create for women and men. Current sex roles for women give them primary responsibility for household and child care so they end up with a second work shift if they choose to have a career as well as a family. According to Grabmeier, women are not too happy about this. He states that, based on his interviews with women, "well over half the women expressed anger, hostility, and resentment toward their husbands or partners for failing to share child care and household responsibilities." The aggravation is due in large part to differential sex role changes. Women's roles have changed due to the women's movement, the increasing financial need for two paychecks, and the opportunities of an expanding white-collar economy. However, the sex roles for men have not changed very much. Men's sex role problem can be seen as two-sided. One side of the problem is that men are still socialized to conform to masculine sex roles but are not given real opportunities to fulfill these roles in today's society. This is why Susan Faludi, in her selection, states that men are made to feel like failures. The other side of the problem is that men experience expectations from women to be more feminine and to increasingly perform what many men think of as women's tasks. On the one side they are failures in their own eyes and on the other side they are failures in women's eyes.

In the following selection, Grabmeier argues that women suffer a greater burden than men and uses data on stress to support his conclusions. He discusses the biological reasons for this, but emphasizes that roles for women have changed dramatically without a commensurate change in the traditional dominant roles for men. Women often blame themselves for their problems, which worsens them, according to Grabmeier. Faludi counters that men, particularly working class men, are frustrated by a world for which their socialization has not prepared them. In combination with mortality and disease statistics, Faludi's analysis supports the conclusion that men are more burdened by modern sex roles than women.

The Burden Women Bear: Why They Suffer More Distress Than Men

Who suffers more in life, men or women? This was a great issue to bring up around the office coffee machine or at cocktail parties because it not only made for lively conversation, it also was one of those questions that couldn't be settled simply by calling the reference desk at the local library.

Recently, though, evidence is growing that women, in fact, do suffer more than men. Blame it on biology, the stress of combining parenthood and career, living in a male-centered society, or all of the above. A study at Ohio State University by sociologists John Mirowsky and Catherine Ross shows that females experience symptoms of psychological distress—including sadness, anger, anxiety, malaise, and physical aches and pains—about 30% more often than males. Their work complements earlier research that found women about twice as likely as men to experience major clinical depression.

"Women genuinely suffered more distress than men by all the measures in our study," Mirowsky indicates. He and Ross interviewed 1,282 women and 749 men aged 18 to 90 and asked them on how many of the last seven days they had experienced various emotions. In each case, women reported more days with symptoms of distress than men. Don't assume women feel more of everything than men, however. The female participants experienced happiness 3.3% less often than the males.

In the past, assertions about women's surplus of suffering have been dismissed because they were thought to be more emotional than men. In other words, females simply complained more than males, who hid their pain behind a stoic facade. Mirowsky and Ross examined that possibility and found that women did indeed express their emotions more than men. About 68% of the males in the study agreed or strongly agreed that they kept their emotions to themselves, compared to 50% of the females who responded similarly. Even after the researchers took these differences into account, women still showed more signs of distress than men. "Women do express their emotions more, but that doesn't mean they aren't truly more depressed," Mirowsky maintains.

There is no simple explanation for why women suffer more distress than men. Most experts believe a combination of factors, including biological differences, puts females at greater risk for some psychological troubles. Scientists have discovered that imbalances of certain neurotransmitters in the brain—particularly norepinepherine and serotonin—are related to depression. Low levels of serotonin may lead to depression, anxiety, anger, eating disorders, and impulsive behavior, points out Henry Nasrallah, chairperson of psychiatry. "We don't know why, but women may have less stable brain systems for regulating these neurotransmitters. Female hormones are believed to play a role in the regulation of neurotransmitters that affect mood and that may explain why females are more likely to experience clinical depression. Fluctuations in hormone levels, for example, have been associated with the well-known premenstrual syndrome, which afflicts some women."

Just how much of a role biology plays in women's distress remains unclear. "There is usually an interplay between biological, psychological, and social factors," says Nasrallah. "Clearly there are biological factors that contribute a great deal to behavior and mood in men and women."

Blaming biology for distress can be a two-edged sword. It can help to mobilize medical resources and make physicians take such problems seriously, but also may take the focus off social factors that contribute to the situation.

This two-edged sword is painfully apparent for those with a uniquely female form of distress—postpartum depression. Women suffering from this syndrome have formed national interest groups seeking, in part, to get more medical attention for their problems, notes Verta Taylor, a professor of sociology who has studied their cause. However, these women walk a fine line between looking for medical solutions and pushing for their partners to provide more help in caring for children.

For a book she is writing, Taylor interviewed more than 100 women who said they suffered emotional problems—ranging from "baby blues" to clinical depression—after the birth or adoption of a baby. This illness, which afflicts more than three-quarters of new mothers, may last weeks or, as one woman told Taylor, it "didn't end until [my son] left home for college."

Taylor indicates that the question of whether postpartum depression has biological roots is a hotly debated topic. She found that women physicians who suffered from it were more likely than male doctors to believe that the disorder is the result of a deficiency in the hormone progesterone. Accordingly, women physicians were more likely to advocate progesterone therapy to treat the biochemical basis of the illness.

Nasrallah says most medical professionals believe that postpartum depression is an illness with biochemical causes that must be treated with antidepressants. However, the less serious postpartum blues usually can be treated with rest, family support, and reassurance.

Even women who believe their postpartum depression has a biochemical aspect don't blame their condition simply on hormonal imbalances, Taylor points out. They echo the grievances of many working mothers—with and without postpartum depression—who complain of not getting enough support from husbands and partners. "A majority of the women I interviewed saw their excessive worry and irritability as the inevitable result of trying to combine and balance the demands of a 'second shift' of child care, housework, and a marriage with a paid job. Well over half the women expressed anger, hostility, and resentment toward their husbands or partners for failing to share child care and household responsibilities."

The problem, according to history professor Susan Hartmann, is that women now have more opportunities outside the home, but still do most of the household chores. "The old norms haven't changed that much. Women are still expected to take care of the home and children. But a majority of women also have taken on the responsibility of work. They've added new roles and responsibilities without significant changes in their old ones."

Although men sometimes may help out, there usually isn't a true sharing of household and child care responsibilities in American society. When men care for their children, for instance, it often is seen as "babysitting." When women do it, that simply is part of being a mother.

There is ample evidence that women still shoulder most of the responsibility of caring for kids, housework, and day-to-day chores. Margaret Mietus Sanik, an associate professor of family resource management, conducts studies of time use in families. She has found that, in couples with a new child, mothers spend about 4.6 hours per day in infant care, compared to about 1.3 for fathers. New mothers also lose more of their leisure time—about 3.8 hours a day—than their husbands, who give up approximately one hour. The result is that women often feel overworked and underappreciated.

A recent U.S. government survey of 250,000 working women found that stress was the most mentioned problem by respondents. The number-one issue females would like to talk about with Pres. Clinton is their inability to balance work and family, the survey found.

With the often overwhelming demands of juggling a career and family, it is no wonder that employed women suffer more depression than men. That doesn't mean that full-time homemakers have it better; in fact, research suggests they actually have higher levels of psychological distress than employed women. While working women can derive satisfaction from multiple roles at home and in the workplace, stay-at-home moms have only their homemaker role, Mirowsky indicates. They may feel isolated and out of step with the rest of society because parenting apparently is not highly valued in American culture.

Moreover, whether they want to work or not, housewives are economically dependent on their husbands, which is a powerful cause of distress. "In our culture, economic independence gives you status in the eyes of the community and a sense of security and self-worth," Mirowsky explains. "Housewives don't have that economic security. What we have found is that women are psychologically better off if they are employed."

In her studies of postpartum depression, Taylor has found that society's expectations of mothers also can put a suffocating burden on women. It is expected that a new mother will be happy, overjoyed even, and more than willing to put her baby's needs above her own. "But motherhood is often difficult, and women can find that their feelings are out of sync with societal expectations. They may feel as though their negative feelings are proof that they're not being a good mother, which compounds their feelings of distress, depression, anger, anxiety, and guilt."

If the stress of work and caring for children contributes to women's higher levels of distress, what about single, childless females? According to Mirowsky, they show less evidence of distress than other women, but more than men. That is because females face more than just role overload, she maintains. Women in the U.S. are paid about 75% of what men receive, are more likely to live in poverty, face a greater threat of physical and sexual abuse, and live in a culture that often promotes near-unattainable ideals for physical perfection. "Women just face a lot of problems and obstacles that men don't have to deal with. I'm surprised women don't feel more distress."

Psychological Strategies

Adding to the situation is the fact that women tend to use psychological strategies that amplify and prolong their distress. Psychologists have found that, when females are faced with problems, they are more likely than males to think continually about troubling issues. They also are more apt to blame themselves. The result is that women can be caught in a cycle of worry and depression instead of working to find a way out. Men, on the other hand, tend to take action in dealing with problems. They are more likely to place the blame elsewhere and find activities such as sports or hobbies to distract them.

All of this ruminating about their troubles leads women to more than just depression. One of the key findings about women's distress is the amount of anger they feel, Mirowsky and Ross discovered. The stereotype has been that women get depressed and men get angry, but their study revealed that the female subjects actually experienced anger about 29% more often than the males. "Anger is depression's companion—not its substitute," Mirowsky notes.

The anger gap actually was larger than the difference in depression. The researchers found that women were more angry and anxious than men who were equally depressed. Females in the study also were more likely to express their anger through yelling at others. "We thought this was particularly interesting because yelling is crossing the line between an emotion and an action," Mirowsky says. "Our interpretation is that women are yelling at their children more often than their husbands do."

While women are at home getting angry and depressed, maybe men are handling their distress another way—by drinking alcohol and taking drugs. Research has shown that males are more likely than females to abuse alcohol and drugs, but Mirowsky doesn't think that explains the distress gap. "In one sense, if alcohol and drugs really did help eliminate distress, then our findings would make sense—it would explain why men feel less distressed than women. In actuality, there's no evidence that alcohol or drugs help people, or men in particular, feel better." One study, for instance, found that alcoholism and drug abuse increase the odds of a major depressive episode more than fourfold. "Alcohol and drug use probably produces more distress than it prevents," Mirowsky claims.

No matter how you look at the evidence, he suggests, it seems clear that women really do suffer more psychological distress. Is there anything that can be done about it? There is not much females can change concerning their biology, although serious depression often can be treated with anti-depressant drugs. Many of the problems require fundamental changes in how government, business, and society treat women. Taylor says they want their concerns taken seriously. Because females traditionally have been seen as emotional, their problems haven't been given much weight. "Whatever causes higher rates of distress in women, it's not treated. If women feel it and suffer from it, then it should be seen as real."

One thing they are doing is organizing to make their voices heard. Some groups, such as the National Organization for Women, are well-known for their efforts to improve the lot of females. Taylor notes that women with postpartum depression have organized two national groups to present their issues to the public and the medical community. Their efforts, while specifically for the benefit of those with postpartum depression, really involve issues of concern to many females, she states. "The leaders of these groups argue all the time in their speeches that we need men to get more involved in parenting. Women are under this tremendous strain because they are almost solely responsible for parenting. Men have to assume a larger role, and that's a societal problem that requires changing how we structure gender roles."

Working women face special problems that need to be addressed by business and government, experts say. A recent survey by the U.S. government of 250,000 working women has put the spotlight on some of the issues women face, such as lack of adequate child care and unequal pay with men. "I think that more and more businesses are trying to recognize the needs of women in the workforce, yet the progress has been slow," Hartmann points out. "The situation for working women may get incrementally better, but I don't see any major improvements soon."

Social change is always slow and uneven, Mirowsky feels, but it is necessary if the distress gap is to be eased. "People may debate whether there's a difference in the quality of life for men and women in the United States. The evidence, however, suggests the quality of life is poorer for many women, and it's something that needs to be addressed."

NO

Susan Faludi

Stiffed: The Betrayal of the American Man

The American Century Versus the Century of the Common Man

... [A]s the nation wobbled toward the millennium, its pulse-takers seemed to agree that a domestic apocalypse was under way: American manhood was under siege....

If so many concurred in the existence of a male crisis, consensus collapsed as soon as anyone asked the question: Why? Not that there was a shortage of responses. Everyone proposed a favorite whipping boy—or, more often, whipping girl—and blame-seekers on all sides went after their selected culprits with righteous and bitter relish.

As a feminist and a journalist, I began investigating this crisis where you might expect a feminist journalist to begin: at the weekly meetings of a domestic-violence group.... What did I expect to divine about the broader male condition by monitoring a weekly counseling session for batterers?... I can see now that I was operating from an assumption both underexamined and dubious: that the male crisis in America was caused by something men were *doing* unrelated to something being done to them, and that its cure was surely to be found in figuring out how to get men to *stop* whatever it was. I had my own favorite whipping boy, suspecting that the crisis of masculinity was caused by masculinity on the rampage. If male violence was the quintessential expression of masculinity run amok, out of control and trying to control everything in its path, then a domestic-violence therapy group must be at the very heart of this particular darkness.

... The two counselors who ran the group, which was called Alternatives to Violence, worked hard to make "control" a central issue. Each new member would be asked to describe to the group what he had done to a woman, a request that was generally met with sullen reluctance, vague references to "the incident," and invariably the disclaimer "I was out of control." The counselors would then expend much energy showing him how he had, in fact, been in control the entire time. He had chosen his fists, not a knife; he had hit her in the stomach, not the face; he had stopped before landing a permanently injurious blow, and so forth. One session was devoted to reviewing "The Power and

Control Wheel," a mimeographed chart that enumerated the myriad ways men could victimize their mates. No doubt the moment of physical contact for these men had grown out of a desire for supreme control fueled by a need to dominate. I cannot conceive of a circumstance that would exonerate such violence. By making the abusive spouse take responsibility for his actions, the counselors were pursuing a worthy goal. But the logic behind the violence still remained elusive.

A serviceman who had turned to nightclub bouncer jobs and pastry catering after his military base shut down seemed to confirm the counselors' position one evening shortly before his "graduation" from the group. "I denied it before," he said of the night he pummeled his girlfriend, who had also worked on the base. As he spoke he studied his massive, callused hands, lying uselessly on his lap. "I thought I'd blacked out. But looking back at that night when I beat her with an open hand, I didn't black out. I was feeling good. I was in power, I was strong, I was in control. I felt like a *man.*" But what struck me most strongly was what he said next: that moment of control had been the only one in his recent life. "That feeling of power," he said, "didn't last long. Only until they put the cuffs on. Then I was feeling again like I was no man at all."

He was typical in this regard. The men I got to know in the group had without exception lost their compass in the world. They had lost or were losing jobs, homes, cars, families. They had been labeled outlaws but felt like castoffs. Their strongest desire was to be dutiful and to belong, to adhere with precision to the roles society had set out for them as men. In this respect, they were prototypical modern wife beaters, who, demographic research suggests, are commonly ill equipped to fulfill the requirements of expected stereotypical sex roles, men who are socially isolated, afflicted with a sense of ineffectuality, and have nothing but the gender rule book to fall back on. . . .

There was something almost absurd about these men struggling, week after week, to recognize themselves as dominators when they were so clearly dominated, done in by the world. "That 'wheel' is misnamed," a laid-off engineer ruefully told the counselors. "It should be called the Powerlessness and Out-of-Control Wheel." The men had probably felt in control when they beat their wives, but their everyday experience was of feeling controlled—a feeling they had no way of expressing because to reveal it was less than masculine, would make each of them, in fact, "no man at all." For such men, the desire to be in charge was what they felt they must do to survive in a nation that *expected* them to dominate. . . .

More than a quarter century ago, women began to suspect in their own lives "a problem with no name." Even the most fortunate woman in postwar, suburban America, maneuvering her gleaming Hoovermatic across an expansive rec room, sensed that she'd been had. Eventually, this suspicion would be expressed in books—most notably Betty Friedan's *The Feminine Mystique*—that traced this uneasiness back to its source: the cultural forces of the mass media, advertising, pop psychology, and all the other "helpful" advice industries. Women began to free themselves from the box in which they were trapped by feeling their way along its contours, figuring out how it had been constructed around them, how it was shaped and how it shaped them, how their reflections on its mirrored walls distorted who they were or might be. Women were able to take action, paradoxically, by understanding how they were acted upon. "Women have been largely man-made," Eva Figes wrote in 1970 in *Patriarchal Attitudes.* What had been made by others women themselves could unmake. Once their problems could be traced to external forces generated by a male society and culture, they could see them more clearly and so challenge them.

Men feel the contours of a box, too, but they are told that box is of their own manufacture, designed to their specifications. Who are they to complain? The box is there to showcase the man, not to confine him. After all, didn't he build it—and can't he destroy it if he pleases, if he is a *man*? For men to say they feel boxed in is regarded not as laudable political protest but as childish and indecent whining. How dare the kings complain about their castles?

Women's basic grievances are seen as essentially reasonable; even the most blustery antifeminist these days is quick to say that, of course, he favors equal pay and equal opportunity. What women are challenging is something that everyone can see. Men's grievances, by contrast, seem hyperbolic, almost hysterical; so many men seem to be doing battle with phantoms and witches that exist only in their own overheated imaginations. Women see men as guarding the fort, so they don't see how the culture of the fort shapes men. Men don't see how they are influenced by the culture either; in fact, they prefer not to. If they did, they would have to let go of the illusion of control....

The very paradigm of modern masculinity—that it is all about being the master of your universe—prevents men from thinking their way out of their dilemma, from taking active political steps to resolve their crisis. If they are the makers of history, not the subjects of historical forces, then how can they rise up?

... Yet clearly masculinity is shaped by society. Anyone wondering how mutable it is need only look at how differently it is expressed under the Taliban in Kabul or on the streets of Paris. Witness men walking with their arms wrapped around each other in Istanbul or observe the Mexican immigrant to Los Angeles whose manhood is so linked to supporting a family that any job, even a busboy's, holds a masculine pride. As anthropologist David D. Gilmore demonstrated in *Manhood in the Making,* his comprehensive cross-cultural survey of masculine ideals, manliness has been expressed as laboring-class loyalty in Spain, as diligence and discipline in Japan, as dependence on life outside the home in the company of men in Cyprus, as gift-giving among Sikhs, as the restraint of temper and the expression of "creative energy" among the Gisu of Uganda, and as entirely without significance to the Tahitians. "Manliness is a symbolic script," Gilmore concluded, "a cultural construct, endlessly variable and not always necessary."

It should be self-evident that ideas of manhood vary and are contingent on the times and the culture. Despite that, contemporary discussion about what bedevils men fixes almost exclusively on the psychological and the biological....

Cause Without a Rebel

A question that has plagued feminists like myself is the nature of male resistance to female change. Why are so many men so disturbed by the prospect of women's independence? Why do so many men seem to begrudge it, resent it, fear it, fight it with an unholy passion? The question launched my inquiry. But in the end, much to my surprise, it was not the question that most compelled me. It is not the question, finally, that drives this [selection]. Because the more I explored the predicament of postwar men, the more familiar it seemed to me. The more I consider what men have lost—a useful role in public life, a way of earning a decent and reliable living, appreciation in the home, respectful treatment in the culture—the more it seems that men of the late twentieth century are falling into a status oddly similar to that of women at mid-century. The fifties housewife, stripped of her connections to a wider world and invited to fill the void with shopping and the ornamental display of her ultrafeminity, could be said to have morphed into the nineties man, stripped of his connections to a wider world and invited to fill the void with consumption and a gym-bred display of his ultra-masculinity. The empty compensations of a "feminine mystique" are transforming into the empty compensations of a masculine mystique; with a gentlemen's cigar club no more satisfying than a ladies' bake-off, the Nike Air Jordan no more meaningful than the Dior New Look.

And so my question changed. Instead of wondering why men resist women's struggle for a freer and healthier life, I began to wonder why men refrain from engaging in their own struggle. Why, despite a crescendo of random tantrums, have they offered no methodical, reasoned response to their predicament? Given the untenable and insulting nature of the demands placed on men to prove themselves in our culture, why don't men revolt?

Like many women, I was drawn to feminism out of a desire to challenge the silence of my sex. It has come to seem to me that, under all the rantings of men seeking to drown out the female voice, theirs is as resounding a silence. Why haven't men responded to the series of betrayals in their own lives—to the failures of their fathers to make good on their promises—with something co-equal to feminism? When the frontier that their fathers offered them proved to be a wasteland, when the enemy their fathers sent them to crush turned out often to be women and children trembling in thatched huts, when the institutions their fathers claimed would buoy them downsized them, when the women their fathers said wanted their support got their own jobs, when the whole deal turned out to be a crock and it was clear that they had been thoroughly stiffed, why did the sons do nothing?

The feminine mystique's collapse a generation earlier was not just a crisis but a historic opportunity for women. Women responded to their "problem with no name" by naming it and founding a political movement, by beginning the process of freeing themselves. Why haven't men done the same? This seems to me to be the real question that lurks behind the "masculinity crisis" facing American society: not that men are fighting against women's liberation, but that they have refused to mobilize for their own—or their society's—liberation.

Not that traditional male roles are endangered, but that men themselves are in danger of not acting.

Many in the women's movement and in the mass media complain that men just "don't want to give up the reins of power." But that would seem to have little applicability to the situations of most men, who individually feel not the reins of power in their hands but its bit in their mouths. What's more likely is that they are clinging to a phantom status. A number of men I interviewed, as they argued for the importance of having a male head of the household, tellingly demoted that to an honorary post: it's important, they would say, that every home have a "figurehead." But even the natural reluctance to give up a position of putative superiority, no matter how compromised, is not enough to explain a deeper male silence.

To understand why men are so reluctant to break with the codes of manhood sanctioned in their childhood, perhaps we need to understand how strong the social constraints on them are. It's not just women who are bombarded by cultural messages about appropriate gender behavior. In the past half century, Madison Avenue, Hollywood, and the mass media have operated relentlessly on men, too. The level of mockery, suspicion, and animosity directed at men who step out of line is profound, and men respond profoundly—with acquiescence. But that is not a wholly satisfying explanation either, for haven't women, the object of such commercial and political manipulation, kicked over these traces successfully?

If men do not respond, then maybe it is because their society has proposed no route for them to venture down. Surely the culture has not offered an alternative vision of manhood. No one has: not the so-called men's movement, which clings to its dusted-off copies of *Grimms' Fairy Tales* and its caveman clichés; not conservative or liberal political leaders who call for a remilitarized model of manhood with work camps and schools run by former generals; not the Promise Keepers or Nation of Islam ministers, whose programs of male contrition and resurrection are fantasies of past fantasies; not a gay culture, which, as it gets increasingly absorbed into the larger commercial culture, becomes increasingly muted in its challenge of masculine roles; not even the women's movement, which clamors for men to change but has yet to conceptualize that change. But then, did feminists wait upon men to craft their revolution for them? Didn't the women's movement make its own way, without any assistance —no, with much resistance—from the dominant culture? So why can't men act? The ultimate answer has deep ramifications not only for men but for feminists. Eventually I came to believe that, far from being antagonists, they were each poised at this hour to be vital in the other's advance. But that answer came at the end. First I had to begin....

My travels led me to a final question: Why don't contemporary men rise up in protest against their betrayal? If they have experienced so many of the same injuries as women, the same humiliations, why don't they challenge the culture as women did? Why can't men seem to act?

The stock answers that have been offered to explain men's reluctance to break out of stereotypical male models don't suffice. Men aren't simply refusing to "give up the reins of power," as some feminists have argued. The reins have already slipped from most of their hands, anyway.... While the pressures on men to imagine themselves in power and in control of their emotions are impediment to male revolt, a more fundamental obstacle overshadows them. If men have feared to tread where women have rushed in, then maybe that's because women have had it easier in one very simple regard: women could frame their struggle as a battle against men....

Because the women who engaged in the feminist campaigns of the seventies were fighting the face of "male domination," they were able to take advantage of a ready-made model for revolt. To wage their battle, they could unfurl a well-worn map and follow a reliable strategy. Ironically, it was a male strategy—feminists grabbed hold of the blueprint for the American male paradigm and made good use of it. They had at the ready all the elements required to make that paradigm work. They had a clearly defined oppressive enemy: the "patriarchy." They had a real frontier to conquer and clear for other women: all those patriarchal institutions, both the old ones that still rebuffed women, like the U.S. Congress or U.S. Steel, and the new ones that tried to remold women, like Madison Avenue or the glamour and media-pimp kingdoms of Bert Parks and Hugh Hefner. Feminists also had their own army of "brothers": sisterhood. Each GI Jane who participated in this struggle felt she was useful. Whether she was distributing leaflets or working in a women's-health clinic, whether she was lobbying legislators to pass a child-care bill or tossing her bottles of Clairol in a "freedom trash can," she was part of a greater glory, the advancement of her entire sex. Many women whose lives were touched by feminism felt in some way that they had reclaimed an essential usefulness; together, they had charged the barricades that kept each of them from a fruitful, thriving life. Women had discovered a good fight, and a flight path to adult womanhood. Traveling along with trajectory of feminism, each "small step" for a woman would add up finally to a giant leap for womankind, not to mention humankind.

The male paradigm of confrontation, in which an enemy could be identified, contested, and defeated, was endlessly transferable. It proved useful as well to activists in the civil-rights movement and the antiwar movement, the gay-rights movement and the environmental movement. It was, in fact, the fundamental organizing principle of virtually every concerted countercultural campaign of the last half century. Yet it could launch no "men's movement." Herein lies the bedeviling paradox, and the source of male inaction: the model women have used to revolt is the exact one men not only can't use but are trapped in. The solution for women has proved the problem for men.

The male paradigm is peculiarly unsuited to mounting a challenge to men's predicament. Men have no clearly defined enemy who is oppressing them. How can men be oppressed when the culture has already identified them as the oppressors, and when they see themselves that way? As one man wrote plaintively to Promise Keepers, "I'm like a kite with a broken string, but I'm also holding the tail." In an attempt to employ the old paradigm, men have invented antagonists to make their problems visible, but with the passage of time, these culprits—scheming feminists, affirmative-action proponents, job-grabbing illegal aliens, the wife of a president—have come to seem increasingly unconvincing as explanations for their situation. Defeating such paper tigers offers no sense of victory. Nor do men have a clear frontier on which to challenge their intangible enemies. What new realms should they be gaining—the media, entertainment, and image-making institutions of corporate America? But these are institutions, they are told, that are already run by men; how can men invade their own territory? . . .

Social responsibility is not the special province of masculinity; it's the lifelong work of all citizens in a community where people are knit together by meaningful and mutual concerns. But if husbanding a society is not the exclusive calling of "husbands," all the better for men's future. Because as men struggle to free themselves from their crisis, their task is not, in the end, to figure out how to be masculine—rather, their masculinity lies in figuring out how to be human. The men who worked at the Long Beach Naval Shipyard didn't come there and learn their crafts as riggers, welders, and boilermakers to *be* masculine; they were seeking something worthwhile to *do*. Their sense of their own manhood flowed out of their utility in a society, not the other way around. Conceiving of masculinity as something to *be* turns manliness into a detachable entity, at which point it instantly becomes ornamental, and about as innately "masculine" as fake eyelashes are inherently "feminine." Michael Bernhardt was one man who came to understand this in his difficult years after he returned from Vietnam. "All these years I was trying to be all these stereotypes" of manhood, he said, "and what was the use? . . . I'm beginning to think now of not even defining it anymore. I'm beginning to think now just in terms of people." From this discovery follow others, like the knowledge that he no longer has to live by the "scorecard" his nation handed him. He can begin to conceive of other ways of being "human," and hence, of being a man.

And so with the mystery of men's nonrebellion comes the glimmer of an opening, an opportunity for men to forge a rebellion commensurate with women's and, in the course of it, to create a new paradigm for human progress that will open doors for both sexes. That was, and continues to be, feminism's dream, to create a freer, more humane world. Feminists have pursued it, particularly in the last two centuries, with great determination and passion. In the end, though, it will remain a dream without the strength and courage of men who are today faced with a historic opportunity: to learn to wage a battle against no enemy, to own a frontier of human liberty, to act in the service of a brotherhood that includes us all.

POSTSCRIPT

Do the New Sex Roles Burden Women More Than Men?

Sex roles are currently in transition. At the moment both men and women face challenges in fulfilling their sex roles. Much of this has to do with the pace of life. Both men and women are overwhelmed because they are short on time and loaded with choices and demands. But notice that most people do not want to go back to earlier days. A few men may long for frontier challenges and many women want to stay home while their children are young, but most want sex roles to continue to evolve in the direction they are going. The major influence on the changes in sex roles has been feminism and the women's movement.

Over the past 30 years, there has been a deluge of books, articles, and periodicals devoted to expounding feminist positions. Important recent statements by feminist leaders are Barbara A. Crow ed., *Radical Feminism: A Documentary Reader* (New York University Press, 2000); Gloria Steinem's book, *Outrageous Acts and Everyday Rebellions,* 2d ed. (Henry Holt, 1995) and article "Revving Up for the Next 25 Years," *Ms.* magazine (September/October 1997); and Patricia Ireland, *What Women Want* (Penguin, 1996). For a history of the women's movement see Kathleen C. Berkeley, *The Women's Liberation Movement in America* (Greenwood Press, 1999). For the impact of the women's movement on American society and culture see Cassandra L. Langer, *A Feminist Critique: How Feminism Has Changed American Society, Culture, and How We Live from the 1940's to the Present* (IconEditions, 1996) and Ruth Rosen, *The World Split Open: How the Modern Women's Movement Changed America* (Viking, 2000). For some recent discussions of the demands of work and family on women see Arlie Russell Hochschild, *The Second Shift* (Avon Books, 1997); Daphne Spain and Suzanne M. Bianchi, *Balancing Act: Motherhood, Marriage, and Employment Among American Women* (Russell Sage Foundation, 1996); and Nancy Kaltreider ed., *Dilemmas of a Double Life: Women Balancing Careers and Relationships* (Jason Aronson, 1997). For some analyses of the sex role problems of men see Michael S. Kimmel, *Manhood in America: A Cultural History* (Free Press, 1996); Stephen Wicks, *Warriors and Wildmen: Men, Masculinity, and Gender* (Bergin & Carvey, 1996); Joseph A. Kuypers, ed., *Men and Power* (Prometheus Books, 1999); John MacInnes, *The End of Masculinity: The Confusion of Sexual Genesis and Sexual Difference in Modern Society* (Open University Press, 1998); and Warren Farrell, *The Myth of Male Power* (Simon & Schuster, 1993). Perhaps the final resolution of this issue is described in Pepper Schwartz' *Peer Marriage: How Love Between Equals Really Works* (Free Press, 1994).

ISSUE 4

Are Communication Problems Between Men and Women Largely Due to Radically Different Conversation Styles?

YES: Philip Yancey, from "Do Men and Women Speak the Same Language?" *Marriage Partnership* (Fall 1993)

NO: Mary Crawford, from *Talking Difference: On Gender and Language* (Sage Publications, 1995)

ISSUE SUMMARY

YES: Author Philip Yancey argues that men and women have strikingly different communication styles because they grow up in different cultures. A man is usually concerned about enhancing or maintaining status as he communicates, while a woman will usually communicate in ways that gain or maintain closeness.

NO: Professor of psychology Mary Crawford argues that the thesis that men and women have radically different communication styles is greatly exaggerated in the media and is based on simplistic stereotypes.

In 1992 John Gray published his best-selling book *Men Are from Mars, Women Are from Venus* (HarperCollins), which promises greatly improved relationships between men and women if they understand that men and women are different and if they accept rather than resent their differences. Here are some selections from the book:

> One of the biggest differences between men and women is how they cope with stress. Men become increasingly focused and withdrawn while women become increasingly overwhelmed and emotionally involved. At these times, a man's needs for feeling good are different from a woman's. He feels better by solving problems while she feels better by talking about problems. Not understanding and accepting these differences creates unnecessary friction in our relationships (p. 29).

When a Martian gets upset he never talks about what is bothering him. He would never burden another Martian with his problem unless his friend's assistance was necessary to solve the problem. Instead he becomes very quiet and goes to his private cave to think about his problem, mulling it over to find a solution. When he has found a solution, he feels much better and comes out of his cave (p. 30).

When a Venusian becomes upset or is stressed by her day, to find relief, she seeks out someone she trusts and then talks in great detail about the problems of her day. When Venusians share feelings of being overwhelmed, they suddenly feel better. This is the Venusian way.

On Venus sharing your problems with another actually is considered a sign of love and trust and not a burden. Venusians are not ashamed of having problems. Their egos are dependent not on looking "competent" but rather on being in loving relationships....

A Venusian feels good about herself when she has loving friends with whom to share her feelings and problems. A Martian feels good when he can solve his problems on his own in his cave (p. 31).

Some claim to be greatly helped by Gray's message. Others find it demeaning to characterize women as irrational, passive, and overly dependent on others. Critics also feel that it counsels women to accept boorish and uncaring behavior in men, while telling men that they only have to listen to women more to make them happy. Gray's message gets a strong reaction because it addresses a very important issue: how can men and women better understand each other?

This issue fascinates sociologists because it plunges them into questions about the construction of reality, perceptions of reality, differential socialization, and power in male-female relationships. Gray himself is constructing reality as he sees it in his book, and according to his reality many difficulties between men and women are not anyone's fault but are just misunderstandings. His reality leaves power out, but a sociologist will always take it into account. In fact, sociologists would note that men and women differ not only in their socialization but also in their relative power in their relationships. The person with greater income, education, and job status will feel freer to determine when, where, how, and about what the pair talks.

The differences in male-female communication styles that Philip Yancey identifies in the following selection are similar to Gray's. He says that men are more concerned about hierarchy and that women are more concerned about relationships, but it is a matter of degree. He, like Gray, works for better understanding between men and women. In the second selection, Mary Crawford reacts strongly to the proponents of gender differences in communication because she feels that their construction of gendered reality is superficial and puts women down.

Philip Yancey

 **YES**

Do Men and Women Speak the Same Language?

For five years my wife, Janet, and I met in a small group with three other couples. Sometimes we studied the Bible, sometimes we read books together, sometimes we spontaneously discussed topics like money and sex. Almost always we ended up talking about our marriages. Finally we decided the time had come to investigate an explosive topic we had always avoided: the differences between men and women. We used the book *You Just Don't Understand* [William Morrow & Company, 1990], by Deborah Tannen, as the springboard for our discussions. That study of the different communication styles of men and women had risen to the top of The New York Times bestseller list. Books on gender differences tend to portray one party as the "right" party. Women are sensitive, compassionate, peace-loving, responsible, nurturing; men are boorish slobs whose idea of "bonding" is to slouch in front of a TV with their buddies watching other men chase little round balls. Or, men are rational, organizational geniuses who run the world because they are "hardwired" with leadership skills that women can never hope to master. But in her book, Tannen strives to avoid such bias, focusing instead on what it takes for men and women to understand each other.

She sees males as more competitive, aggressive, hierarchical and emotionally withdrawn. Females, she concludes, are quieter, more relational and mutually supportive. Naturally, any generalities about gender differences do not apply to all men or all women. Yet we found one point of commonality that helped us all: Male/female relationships represent a classic case of cross-cultural communication. The key to effective relationships is to understand the vast "cultural" gap between male and female.

Anyone who has traveled overseas knows that barriers exist between cultures, language being the most obvious. The barriers between men and women can be just as real, and just as frustrating. Typically, says Tannen, men and women don't recognize these differences; they tend to repeat the same patterns of miscommunication, only more forcefully. As a result, marriages often resemble the stereotypical tourist encounter: One party speaks loudly and slowly in a language the other does not comprehend.

The Male/Female Culture Gap

"Shared meaning" is a good, concise definition of culture. By virtue of growing up in the United States, I share the meaning of things like Bart Simpson, baseball and the Fourth of July with 250 million other people, and no one else in the world. Our couples group found that some problems come about because one spouse enters marriage with a different set of "shared meanings" than the other. Consider routine dinner conversation. For some of us, interrupting another's conversation seems an act of impoliteness or hostility; for others, it expresses friendly engagement. Angie, one of the women in our group, said, "When Greg first came to my Italian family's get-togethers he would hardly speak. We usually had a fight on the way home. We later figured out he felt shut down whenever someone interrupted him in the middle of a story or a comment. Well, in my family interrupting is a sign of involvement. It means we're listening to you, egging you on.

"Greg comes from a German family where everyone politely takes turns responding to the previous comment. I go crazy—their conversation seems so boring and stilted. It helped us both to realize there is no 'right' or 'wrong' style of conversation—we were simply acting out of different cultural styles."

Everyone grows up with "rules" or assumptions about how life is supposed to operate. Marriage forces into close contact two people with different sets of shared meanings and then requires them to negotiate a common ground. Bill and Holly told of a disagreement that nearly ruined their Christmas vacation. Bill said, "We visited Holly's family, which is huge and intimidating. That Christmas, one of the sisters bought a VCR and television to present to the parents, without consulting the rest of the family. 'You guys can chip in anything you want,' she told her siblings and in-laws. 'I'll sign the card and present the gift as being from all of us.'

"To me this looked like a set-up job," Bill continued. "I felt pressure to come up with our fair share, which was a lot more than we would have spent on our own. I felt manipulated and angry, and Holly couldn't understand my feelings. She said her sister was absolutely sincere. 'Our family doesn't keep score,' she said. 'Ellen spontaneously felt like buying a present, and she'll be content whether everyone chips in one-eighth or if no one contributes anything. It's not 'tit-for-tat' like your family.'

"Holly was probably right. My family does keep score. You send a letter, you expect one in return. You give a gift, you expect one of equal value. I'm finally coming to grasp that Holly's family doesn't operate like mine."

Another couple, Gayle and Don, identified on-timeness as their major cross-cultural disagreement. Gayle grew up in a family that didn't notice if they were 10 or 15 minutes late, but Don wears a digital watch and follows it punctually. Several times a week they clash over this common cross-cultural difference. In Germany the trains run on time; in Mexico they get there—eventually.

Cross-cultural differences may seem trivial but, as many couples learn, on small rocks great ships wreck. It helps to know in advance where the rocks are.

Cross-Gender Communication

Communication can either span—or widen—the gender gap. Research shows that boys and girls grow up learning different styles of communicating. Boys tend to play in large groups that are hierarchically structured, with a leader who tells the others what to do and how to do it. Boys reinforce status by giving orders and enforcing them; their games have winners and losers and are run by elaborate rules. In contrast, girls play in small groups or in pairs, with "best friends." They strive for intimacy, not status.

These gender patterns continue into adulthood. A man relates to the world as an individual within a hierarchy; he measures himself against others and judges success or failure by his movement up or down the ladder. A woman approaches the world as a network of many social connections. For women, writes Deborah Tannen, "conversations are negotiations for closeness in which people try to seek and give confirmation and support, and to reach consensus."

Tannen's studies of the corporate world show it to be a male-dominated culture where men tend to make pronouncements, to surround themselves with symbols of status, to position themselves against one another, and to improve their standing by opposition. Women, though, tend to seek approval from others and thereby gain their sense of worth. Women are more inclined to be givers of praise than givers of information.

Our couples group agreed that Tannen's observations about the corporate world ring true. "I feel trapped," said Gayle, a management consultant. "At work I find myself changing in order to meet male expectations. I can't be tentative or solicit other people's reactions. I have to appear strong and confident whether I genuinely feel that way or not. I feel I'm losing my femininity."

Because women rely so strongly on feedback from others, they may hesitate to express themselves in a forthright, direct manner. As one psychologist says, "A man might ask a woman, 'Will you please go the store?' where a woman might say, 'I really need a few things from the store, but I'm so tired.'" A man might judge such behavior sneaky or underhanded, but such indirectness is actually the norm in many cultures.

For example, a direct approach such as, "I want to buy that cabbage for 50 cents" will get you nowhere in a Middle Eastern or African market. Both parties expect an elaborate social dance of bluff and innuendo. "If indirectness is understood by both parties, then there is nothing covert about it," Tannen concludes. The challenge in marriage is for both parties to recognize a communication style and learn to work within it.

Battle of the Sexes

We discovered that each couple in our group had what we called a Blamer and a Blamee; two of the Blamers were husbands, two were wives. The Blamer was usually a perfectionist, very detail-and task-oriented, who expected unrealistically high standards of the spouse. "No matter what I do," said one Blamee, "I can never measure up to my husband's standard of cooking or housekeeping or reading or sex, or anything. It's like I'm constantly being graded on my performance. And it doesn't motivate me to improve. I figure I'm not going to satisfy him anyway, so why try?"

All of us would like to make a few changes in the person we live with, but attempts to coax those changes often lead to conflict. And in conflict, gender differences rise quickly to the surface. Men, who grow up in a hierarchical environment, are accustomed to conflict. Women, concerned more with relationship and connection, prefer the role of peacemaker.

In my own marriage, for example, Janet and I view conflict through different eyes. As a writer, I thrive on criticism. I exchange manuscripts with other writers, and I've learned the best editors are the least diplomatic ones. I have two friends who pepper my manuscripts with words like "Ugh!" and "Awk!", and I would hesitate to publish any book without first running it through their gauntlet. In addition, I've gotten used to receiving heated letters from readers. Complimentary letters sound alike; angry letters fascinate me.

Janet, though, tends to feel criticism as a personal attack. I have learned much by watching her manage other people. Sensitive to criticism herself, she has become masterful at communicating criticism to others. When I managed employees in an office setting I would tend to blunder in with a straightforward approach: "There are five things you're doing right and five things you're doing wrong." After numerous failures, I began to see that the goal in criticism is to help the other person see the problem and desire to change. I have learned the necessity of communicating cross-culturally in my conflicts. When dealing with gluttons for punishment like me, I can be as direct as I want. For more sensitive persons, I need to exercise the skills I've gleaned from diplomats like my wife.

As our small group discussed various styles, we arrived at the following "guidelines" for conflict:

First, identify your fighting style. We tend to learn fighting styles from the family we grow up in. In Angie's Italian family, the fighting style was obvious: yell, argue and, if necessary, punch your brother in the nose. She approached marriage much the same way, only without the punches. Meanwhile, her husband would clam up and walk away from an argument. Angie thought Greg was deliberately ignoring her, and their conflicts never got resolved until they sought counseling. There, they realized that Greg was walking away because he knew he had no chance against Angie's well-honed fighting skills. Once both of them realized the dynamics behind their dead-end conflicts, they were able to make appropriate adjustments and change the "rules of engagement."

Second, agree on rules of engagement. Every couple needs to negotiate what constitutes "fighting fair." The couples in our group agreed to avoid these things: fighting in public, straying from the topic at hand, bringing up old history, threatening divorce and using sex as a way to paper over conflict. It's also helpful to consider additional rules, such as "Don't pretend to go along with a decision and then bring it up later as a matter of blame;" and "Don't resort to 'guerrilla warfare'—getting revenge by taking cheap shots after an argument is over."

Third, identify the real issue behind the conflict. A hidden message often underlies conflict. For example, women are sometimes accused of "nagging." On the surface, their message is the specific complaint at hand: not spending enough time with the kids, not helping with housework, coming home late from work. Actually, Deborah Tannen writes, there is another message at work:

"That women have been labeled 'nags' may result from the interplay of men's and women's styles, whereby many women are inclined to do what is asked of them and many men are inclined to resist even the slightest hint that anyone, especially a woman, is telling them what to do. A woman will be inclined to repeat a request that doesn't get a response because she is convinced that her husband would do what she asks if he only understood that she really wants him to do it. But a man who wants to avoid feeling that he is following orders may instinctively wait before doing what she asked in order to imagine that he is doing it of his own free will. Nagging is the result, because each time she repeats the request, he again puts off fulfilling it."

Spouses need to ask themselves questions like, "Is taking out the garbage really the issue, or is it a husband's crusty resistance to anything that infringes on his independence?"

Man Talk, and Woman Talk

In conversation, men and women appear to be doing the same thing—they open their mouths and produce noise. However, they actually use conversation for quite different purposes. Women use conversation primarily to form and solidify connections with other people. Men, on the other hand, tend to use words to navigate their way within the hierarchy. They do so by communicating their knowledge and skill, imparting information to others.

Women excel at what Tannen calls "private speaking" or "rapport-talk." Men feel most comfortable in "public speaking" or "report talk." Even though women may have more confidence in verbal ability (aptitude tests prove their superior skill), they are less likely to use that ability in a public context. Men feel comfortable giving reports to groups or interrupting a speaker with an objection—these are skills learned in the male hierarchy. Many women might perceive the same behavior as putting themselves on display. For example, at a party the men tell stories, share their expertise and tell jokes while the women usually converse in smaller groups about more personal subjects. They are busy connecting while the men are positioning themselves.

Our couples' group discussion became heated when we brought up another female trait that commonly goes by the name "bitching" (Tanner substituted the much more respectable term "ritual lament"). "Yeah, let's talk about this!" Greg said. "I remember one ski trip when I met some of my buddies in Colorado. We spent three days together before our wives joined us. We guys were having a great time, but when the women showed up everything changed. Nothing was right: The weather was too cold and the snow too crusty, the condo was drafty, the grocery store understocked, the hot tub dirty. Every night we heard them complain about sore muscles and raw places where the ski boots rubbed.

"The guys would listen to the griping, then just look at each other and say, 'The women are here!' It was incredible. We were living and skiing in exactly the same conditions. But before the women arrived, we had peace. Afterward, we heard nothing but gripes."

Tannen's explanation is that women tend to bond in pain. Through griping, they reaffirm connections with each other. For men, the immediate response to a complaint is to fix the problem. Otherwise, why complain? Women don't necessarily want the problem solved—who can "fix" the weather, for example? They merely want to feel understood and sympathized with.

Coming Together

Over several months our couples group gained an appreciation for the profound differences between male and female, but also a respect for how difficult it can be to pin down those differences.

Mary Crawford  **NO**

Talking Difference: On Gender and Language

Talking Across the Gender Gap

People believe in sex differences. As one best-selling book puts it, when it comes to communication, *Men are from Mars, Women are from Venus* (Gray, 1992). Social scientists have helped to create and confirm that belief by conducting innumerable studies of every conceivable linguistic and stylistic variation between the sexes and by developing theories that stress differences rather than similarities and overlap (West and Zimmerman, 1985). In *Language and Woman's Place* (1975) the linguist Robin Lakoff proposed that women use a speech style that is ineffectual because it is overly polite, hesitant, and deferent. The assertiveness training movement of the 1970s and 1980s—a therapeutic fad led by psychologists whose clients were largely women—engaged perhaps hundreds of thousands of people in attempts to change their way of communicating. A rationale for the movement was that some people (especially women) suffer from poor communication skills and irrational beliefs that prevent them from expressing themselves clearly and directly. More recently, linguists and communication experts have created another conceptual bandwagon by applying theories of cross-cultural communication to women and men. According to this view, 'men from Mars' and 'women from Venus' are fated to misunderstand each other unless they recognize their deeply socialized differences.

The view of gender and language encoded in these writings and therapies is that fundamental differences between women and men shape the way they talk. The differences are conceived as located within individuals and prior to the talk—as differences in personality traits, skills, beliefs, attitudes, or goals. For the millions of people who have become acquainted with issues of gender and language through reading best-selling books telling women how to be more assertive or how to understand the 'opposite' sex, or through watching television talk shows featuring communication experts who claim that talk between women and men is cross-cultural communication, a powerful narrative frame is provided and validated: that gender is difference, and difference is static, bipolar, and categorical. Absorbing such messages, it would be very difficult *not* to believe that women and men are indeed opposite sexes when it comes to talk....

Two Sexes, Two Cultures

Cross-Cultural Talk...

Talking Across the Gender Divide

... When we think of distinct female and male subcultures we tend to think of societies in which women and men spend virtually their entire lives spatially and interactionally segregated; for example, those which practice purdah. In Western societies, however, girls and boys are brought up together. They share the use of common space in their homes; eat, work, and play with their siblings of both sexes; generally attend co-educational schools in which they are aggregated in many classes and activities. Both sexes are supervised, cared for, and taught largely by women in infancy and early childhood, with male teachers and other authority figures becoming more visible as children grow older. Moreover, they see these social patterns mirrored and even exaggerated in the mass media. How can the talk of Western women and men be seen as talk across cultures?

The two-cultures model was first applied to the speech of North American women and men by Daniel Maltz and Ruth Borker, who proposed that difficulties in cross-sex and cross-ethnic communication are 'two examples of the same larger phenomenon: cultural difference and miscommunication' (1982: 196). Maltz and Borker acknowledge the argument that American women and men interact with each other far too much to be characterized as living in different subcultures. However, they maintain that the social rules for friendly conversation are learned between the ages of approximately 5 and 15, precisely the time when children's play groups are maximally segregated by sex. Not only do children voluntarily choose to play in same-sex groups, they consciously exaggerate differences as they differentiate themselves from the other sex. Because of the very different social contexts in which they learn the meanings and goals of conversational interaction, boys and girls learn to use language in different ways.

Citing research on children's play, Maltz and Borker (1982) argue that girls learn to do three things with words:

1. to create and maintain relationships of closeness and equality;
2. to criticize others in acceptable (indirect) ways;
3. to interpret accurately and sensitively the speech of other girls.

In contrast, boys learn to do three very different things with words:

1. to assert one's position of dominance;
2. to attract and maintain an audience;
3. to assert oneself when another person has the floor.

The Two-Cultures Approach as Bandwagon

... The new twist in the two-cultures model of communication is to conceive relationship difficulties not as women's deficiencies but as an inevitable result of deeply ingrained male–female differences. The self-help books that encode a two-cultures model make the paradoxical claim that difference between the sexes is deeply socialized and/or fundamental to masculine and feminine natures, and at the same time subject to change and manipulation if the reader only follows prescribed ways of talking. Instead of catchy slogans and metaphors that stigmatize women (*Women who Love too Much,* Doris Doormat v. Agatha Aggressive) the equally catchy new metaphors glorify difference.

... Deborah Tannen's *You just don't Understand: Women and Men in Conversation* (1990)... has become a phenomenal success in the US. Acclaimed in the popular press as the 'Rosetta Stone that at last deciphers the miscommunication between the sexes' and as 'a Berlitz guidebook to the language and customs of the opposite gender [sic]'... Tannen claims that childhood play has shaped world views so that, when adult women and men are in relationships 'women speak and hear a language of connection and intimacy, while men speak and hear a language of status and independence' (1990:42). The contrasting conversational goals of intimacy and independence lead to contrasting conversational styles. Women tell each other of their troubles, freely ask for information and help, and show appreciation of others' helping efforts. Men prefer to solve problems rather than talk about them, are reluctant to ask for help or advice, and are more comfortable in the roles of expert, lecturer, and teacher than learner or listener. Men are more talkative in public, women in private. These different styles are labelled 'report talk' (men's) and 'rapport talk' (women's).

Given the stylistic dichotomy between the sexes, miscommunication is almost inevitable; however, no one is to blame. Rather, another banner proclaims, 'The Key is Understanding:' 'Although each style is valid on its own terms, misunderstandings arise because the styles are different. Taking a cross-cultural approach to male–female conversations makes it possible to explain why dissatisfactions are justified without accusing anyone of being wrong or crazy' (1990:47).

You just don't Understand makes its case for the two-cultures model skillfully and well using techniques that have become standard in popular writing about behavior: characterizations of 'most' women and men, entertaining anecdotes, and the presentation of research findings as fact.... Instead of advocating conversational formulae or regimented training programs for one sex, it recommends simply that people try to understand and accept sex differences and to be as flexible in style as possible....

The Two-Cultures Approach: An Evaluation

Beyond Deficiencies and Blame

Proponents of the two-cultures model maintain that it is an advance over approaches that blame particular groups for miscommunication....

Unlike earlier approaches, the two-cultures model does not characterize women's talk as deficient in comparison to a male norm. In contrast to the notion of an ineffectual 'female register' or the prescriptive masculine ideals of the assertiveness training movement, the two-cultures model problematizes the behavior of men as well as women. To John Gray, neither Mars nor Venus is a superior home. To Deborah Tannen, 'report talk' and 'rapport talk' are equally limiting for their users in cross-sex communication. The speech style attributed to men is no longer 'standard' speech or 'the language,' but merely one way of negotiating the social landscape.

A model of talk that transcends woman-blaming is less likely to lead to woman-as-problem research programs or to widespread attempts to change women through therapy and skills training. Moreover, ways of talking thought to characterize women can be positively revalued within this framework. In a chapter on gossip, Tannen notes that the negative connotation of the word reflects men's interpretation of women's ways of talking. But gossip can be thought of as 'talking about' rather than 'talking against.' It can serve crucial functions of establishing intimacy and rapport. . . .

Doing Gender, Doing Power

The two-cultures approach fails to theorize how power relations at the structural level are recreated and maintained at the interactional level. The *consequences* of 'miscommunication' are not the same for powerful and powerless groups. As Deborah Cameron (1985: 150) points out, 'The right to represent and stereotype is not mutual.' Stereotypes of less powerful groups (immigrants, people of color) as inadequate speakers serve to ensure that no one need take seriously what these people say. People of color may have their own set of negative stereotypes of white people, but 'these are the ideas of people without power. They do not serve as a base for administrative procedures and decisions, nor do they get expressed routinely in mass media.' Recent research on the relationship between power and stereotyping suggests that people in power stereotype others partly as a cognitive 'shortcut' that minimizes the need to attend to them as individuals. People without power, of course, must attend carefully to their 'superiors' in order to avoid negative judgment or actual harm and cannot afford to use schematic shortcuts (Fiske, 1993).

'Negotiating status' is an evaluatively neutral term for interpersonal behaviors that consolidate power and maintain dominance. Ignoring the enactment of power and how it connects to structural power in gender relations does a disservice to sociolinguistics, distorting its knowledge base and undermining other more legitimate research approaches (Freed, 1992). Moreover, it badly misrepresents communication phenomena. Nancy Henley and Cheris Kramarae (1991) provide a detailed analysis of six 'cultural differences' in female–male speech styles taken from Maltz and Borker (1982), showing that they may be more plausibly interpreted as manifestations and exercises of power. For example, men's tendency to interpret questions as requests for information, and problem-sharing as an opportunity to give expert advice, can be viewed as prerogatives of power. In choosing these speech strategies, men take to themselves the voice of authority.

This failure to recognize structural power and connect it with international power has provoked the strongest criticisms of the two-cultures approach. In a review of *You just don't Understand,* Senta Troemel-Ploetz (1991) pointed out that if the majority of relationships between women and men in our society were not fundamentally asymmetrical to the advantage of men,

> we would not need a women's liberation movement, women's commis-
> sions, houses for battered women, legislation for equal opportunity, an-
> tidiscrimination laws, family therapy, couple therapy, divorce . . . If you leave
> out power, you do not understand any talk, be it the discussion after your
> speech, the conversation at your own dinner-table, in a doctor's office, in the
> back yards of West Philadelphia, in an Italian village, on a street in Turkey,
> in a court room or in a day-care center, in a women's group or at a UN
> conference. It is like saying Black English and Oxford English are just two
> different varieties of English, each valid on its own; it just so happens that
> the speakers of one variety find themselves in high-paying positions with
> a lot of prestige and power of decision-making, and the others are found
> more in low-paying jobs, or on the streets and in prisons. They don't always
> understand each other, but they both have the best intentions; if they could
> only learn a bit from each other and understand their differences as a matter
> of style, all would be well. (Troemel-Ploetz, 1991: 497–8)

No one involved in debating the two-cultures approach denies that men have more social and political power than women. Maltz and Borker (1982: 199) acknowledge that power differentials 'may make some contribution' to communication patterns. However, they do not theorize the workings of power in interaction or advocate structural changes to reduce inequity.

The Bandwagon Revisited

There is no inherent limitation to the two-cultures approach that would pre-vent its development as a theory of difference *and* dominance, a theory that could encompass the construction of gendered subjectivities, the reproduction of inequality in interaction, and the role of interaction in sustaining gendered social structures. It is therefore the more disappointing that in the popularized versions that have influenced perhaps millions of people, it is flattened into an account of sex dichotomies. And this is why the model has been so harshly evaluated by feminist scholars. Perhaps unfortunately, the more egregious ver-sions have been largely ignored and the more scholarly one attacked. Deborah Tannen's critics have charged that, despite the absence of overt women-blaming and the positive evaluation of 'feminine' modes of talk, the interpretations she offers often disguise or gloss over inequity, and privilege men's interpretations (Freed, 1992; Troemel-Ploetz, 1991). They have accused her of being an apol-ogist for men, excusing their insensitivity, rudeness, and dominance as mere stylistic quirks, and encouraging women to make the adjustments when needs conflict (Freed, 1992). Indeed, the interpretations Tannen offers for the many anecdotes that enliven her book often read as though the past two decades of women's studies scholarship had never occurred, and there were no feminist analyses available with which to contextualize gendered behavior (Troemel-Ploetz, 1991).

You just don't Understand is apolitical—a choice which is in itself a political act, and a significant one at that, given that the book has sold well over a million copies. Like the popular psychology of the assertiveness training movement, it does not threaten the status quo (Troemel-Ploetz, 1991). Like its pop-psychology companions on the bookstore shelves, it offers something to both the powerful and those over whom they have power: to men, a compelling rationale of blame-free difference and to women a comforting promise of mutual accommodation.

Let us consider [two] examples, from [two] types of conversational setting, to illustrate how the accounts of interaction in *You just don't Understand* might be reinterpreted in light of research on women and gender. The first is an anecdote about Josh and Linda. When an old friend calls Josh at work with plans for a visit nearby on business, Josh invites him to spend the weekend and makes plans to go out with him Friday night. These plans are made without consulting with Linda, who protests that Josh should have checked with her, especially since she will be returning from a business trip herself that day. Tannen's explanation of the misunderstanding is in terms of an autonomy/intimacy dichotomy. Linda likes to have her life entwined with Josh's, to consult and be consulted about plans. Josh feels that checking with her implies a loss of independence. 'Linda was hurt because she sensed a failure of closeness in their relationship... he was hurt because he felt she was trying to control him and limit his freedom' (1990: 27).

No resolution of the conflict is provided in the anecdote; the implication is that Josh's plans prevail. Interpreting this story in terms of women's needs for intimacy and men's for autonomy glosses the fact that Josh has committed mutual resources (living space, food, the time and work required to entertain a houseguest) on behalf of himself and his partner without acknowledgement that the partner should have a voice in that decision. His behavior seems to reflect the belief that the time and energy of others (women) are to be accommodated to men. As a test of the fairness of his behavior, imagine that Josh were living with a male housemate. To invite a mutual weekend guest without consulting the housemate would be considered overtly rude. The housemate (but not the woman in a heterosexual couple) would be warranted in refusing to cooperate, because he is seen as entitled to make his own plans and control his own resources. A sense of entitlement to act entirely on one's own and make decisions unilaterally is 'part of the social empowerment that men enjoy. It has precious little to do with communicative style or language' (Freed, 1992: 4)....

In a section titled 'First Me, Then Me,' Tannen describes her own experience of discourse in a professional setting. Seated at a faculty dinner next to a woman, she enjoyed a mutually informative and pleasant discussion in which each talked about her research and explored connections and overlaps. Turning to a male guest, she initiated a conversation in a similar way. However, the conversation proceeded very differently:

> During the next half hour, I learned a lot about his job, his research, and his background. Shortly before the dinner ended there was a lull, and he asked me what I did. When I said I was a linguist, he became excited and told me about a research project he had conducted that was related to neurolinguistics. He was still telling me about his research when we all got up to leave the table. (1990: 126)

Lecturing, says Tannen, is part of a male style. And women let them get away with it. Because women's style includes listening attentively and not interrupting, they do not jump in, challenge, or attempt to deflect the lecturer. Men assume that if their partner had anything important to say, she would say it. The two styles interact to produce silent women, who nod and smile although they are bored, and talkative men, who lecture at length though they themselves may be bored and frustrated by the lack of dialogue. Thus, apparent conversational dominance is not something men deliberately do to women. Neither is it something women culpably permit. The imbalance is created by 'habitual styles.'

The stylistic interpretation discounts the possibility that the male academic in this example did not want to hear about his female dinner companion's research because he did not care about it. That women and what they do are valued less than men and what they do is one of the fundamental insights of feminism. The history of women in the professions provides ample evidence of exclusion, discrimination, and marginalization. Methods vary: plagiarizing women's work (Spender, 1989), denigrating them as unfeminine while stealing their ideas (Sayre, 1975), denying them employment (Crawford, 1981; Scarborough and Furumoto, 1987) and recognition (Nochlin, 1971). When women compete successfully in male domains, they are undermined by sexual harassment (Gutek, 1985) and by being represented as sex objects (a long-running 1980s ad campaign featured female physicians and attorneys making medical rounds and appearing in court in their underwear) (Lott, 1985). In short, there is not yet much reason to believe that women in the professions are routinely taken as seriously as their male peers. And the academy is no exception. What Tannen explains as mere stylistic differences have the effect of keeping women and their work invisible, and have had documented consequences on women's hiring, promotion, and tenure (Caplan, 1993)....

A Rhetoric of Reassurance

The rhetoric of difference makes everyone—and no one—responsible for interpersonal problems. Men are not to blame for communication difficulties; neither is a social system in which gender governs access to resources. Instead, difference is reified: 'The culprit, then is not an individual man or even men's styles alone, but the difference between women and men's styles' (Tannen, 1990: 95).

One of the most striking effects achieved in these books is to reassure women that their lot in heterosexual relationships is normal. Again and again, it is stressed that no one is to blame, that miscommunication is inevitable, that unsatisfactory results may stem from the best of intentions. As these explanations dominate the public realm of discourse about gender, they provide 'one more pseudo-explanation' and 'one more ingenious strategy for not tackling the root causes of women's subordinate status' (Cameron, in press).

Its very ubiquity has made inequality of status and power in heterosexual relationships seem unremarkable, and one of the most important contributions of feminist research has been to make it visible (Wilkinson and Kitzinger,

1993). In the discourse of miscommunication the language feminists have developed to theorize status and power is neutralized. Concepts such as sexism, sex discrimination, patriarchy, and gender inequity are barely mentioned, and conversational strategies that have the effect of silencing women are euphemized as stylistic 'asymmetries.' For example, Tannen explains that when men do most of the talking in a group, it is not because they intend to prevent women from speaking or believe that women have nothing important to say. Rather, they see the women as *equals,* and expect them to compete in the same style they themselves use. Thus, an inequity that feminists have conceptualized in terms of power differentials is acknowledged, but explained as an accidental imbalance created by style and having little to do with a gendered social order.

Power dynamics in heterosexual relationships are obscured by the kinds of intentions imputed to speakers. Both books presume an innocence of communicative intent. In the separate and simplistic worlds of Martians and Venusians, women just want to be cherished and men just want to be needed and admired. In the separate worlds of 'report talk' and 'rapport talk', the goal may be sex-specific but the desire is the same: to be understood and responded to in kind. In *You just don't Understand,* each anecdote is followed by an analysis of the intentions of *both* speakers, a practice that Tannen (1992) feels reflects her fairness to both sexes. But this symmetry is false, because the one kind of intention that is never imputed to any speaker is the intent to dominate. Yet people are aware of such intentions in their talk, and, when asked, can readily describe the verbal tactics they use to 'get their own way' in heterosexual interactions (Falbo, 1982; Falbo and Peplau, 1980; Kelley et al., 1978). Tannen acknowledges the role of power in conversational dynamics (cf. p. 283, 'We enact and create our gender, and our inequality, with every move we make'). But the rhetorical force of the anecdotes is about difference. When an anecdote seems obviously explainable in terms of dominance strategies, the possibility of such an account is often acknowledged but discounted. The characteristics that the two-cultures model posit for females' speech are ones appropriate to friendly conversation, while the characteristics posited for men's speech are not neutral, but indicate uncooperative, dominating and disruptive interaction (Henley and Kramarae, 1991). Whose needs are being served when intent to dominate is ruled out *a priori* in accounting for cross-sex conversation?

Many of the most compelling anecdotes describe situations in which a woman is hurt, frustrated or angered by a man's apparently selfish or dominating behavior, only to find that her feelings were unwarranted because the man's intentions were good. This is psychologically naive. There is no reason to believe that *post hoc* stated intentions are a complete and sufficient description of conversational motives. . . .

The emphasis on interpreting a partner's intentions is problematic in other ways as well. As Nancy Henley and Cheris Kramarae (1991: 42) point out, '[F]emales are required to develop special sensitivity to interpret males' silence, lack of emotional expressiveness, or brutality, and to help men express themselves, while men often seem to be trained deliberately to misinterpret much of women's meaning.' Young girls are told that hitting, teasing, and insults are to be read as signs of boys' 'liking.' Adolescent girls are taught to take responsibility for boys' inexpressiveness by drawing them out in conversation, steering talk to topics that will make them feel comfortable, and being a good listener. . . .

Analyzing conversation in terms of intentions has a very important implication: it deflects attention from *effects*, including the ways that everyday action and talk serve to recreate and maintain current gender arrangements.

POSTSCRIPT

Are Communication Problems Between Men and Women Largely Due to Radically Different Conversation Styles?

One of Crawford's concerns is the demeaning picture of women that the literature on gender differences in communication styles often suggests. Men are problem solvers and stand on their own two feet, while women are people pleasers and dependent. Men, however, could also feel put down. According to the theory, men are predominantly interested in defending and advancing their status, even to the point of stepping on toes and jeopardizing closeness. This makes men out to be rather immoral. Self-promotion and the need to dominate others is not sanctioned by most religions or appreciated much by most people. Women come closer to religious and popular ideals than men do. To their credit, they bond, love, and share more through communication than men do, and women do so without necessarily sacrificing their competence in the process.

Many issues regarding gender differences in communication styles remain murky. Everyone, including Crawford, acknowledges that there are talking differences between genders, but how big are these differences? This relates to the large question of how different men and women are on other significant dimensions. What causes these differences? To what extent are they biological and hormonal, and to what extent are they due to differential socialization and different positions in society? How changeable are these differences? Should they be changed?

The past two decades have produced considerable research on gender differences in communication styles, which is reflected in several readers and academic works. Deborah Tannen is prominent in this literature, see Tannen's *You Just Don't Understand: Women and Men in Conversation* (Ballantine Books, 1991); *Gender and Discourse* (Oxford University Press, 1994); and her edited book *Gender and Conversational Interaction* (Oxford University Press, 1993). See also Deborah Cameron, ed., *The Feminist Critique of Language: A Reader*, 2d ed. (Routledge, 1998); Jennifer Coates, ed., *Language and Gender: A Reader* (Blackwell, 1998); Ruth Wodak, ed., *Gender and Discourse* (Sage Publications, 1997); Mary Bucholtz, A. C. Liang, and Laurel A. Sutton, eds., *Reinventing Identities: The Gendered Self in Discourse* (Oxford University Press, 1999); Mary Ritchie Key, *Male/Female Language* (Scarecrow Press, 1996); and Victoria L. Bergwall, Janet M. Bing, and Alice F. Freed, eds., *Rethinking Language and Gender Research: Theory and Practice* (Longman, 1996).

ISSUE 5

Should Same-Sex Marriages Be Legally Recognized?

YES: Andrew Sullivan, from *Virtually Normal: An Argument About Homosexuality* (Alfred A. Knopf, 1995)

NO: James Q. Wilson, from "Against Homosexual Marriage," *Commentary* (March 1996)

ISSUE SUMMARY

YES: Editor and author Andrew Sullivan argues that the secular liberal state must grant the right of same-sex partners to marry. To not do so would be blatant discrimination.

NO: Professor of management and public policy James Q. Wilson presents arguments against legally recognizing same-sex marriages.

In 1979 in Sioux Falls, South Dakota, Randy Rohl and Grady Quinn became the first acknowledged homosexual couple in America to receive permission from their high school principal to attend the senior prom together. The National Gay Task Force hailed the event as a milestone in the progress of human rights. It is unclear what the voters of Sioux Falls thought about it, since it was not put up to a vote. However, if their views were similar to those of voters in Dade County, Florida; Houston, Texas; Wichita, Kansas; and various localities in the state of Oregon, they probably were not pleased. In referenda held in these and other areas, voters have reversed decisions by legislators and local boards that banned discrimination by sexual preference.

Yet the attitude of Americans toward the rights of homosexuals is not easy to pin down. Voters have also defeated resolutions such as the one in California in 1978 that would have banned the hiring of homosexual schoolteachers, or the one on the Oregon ballot in 1992 identifying homosexuality as "abnormal, wrong, unnatural and perverse." In some states, notably Colorado, voters have approved initiatives widely perceived as antihomosexual. But, almost invariably, these resolutions have been carefully worded so as to appear to oppose "special" rights for homosexuals. In general, polls show that a large majority of Americans believe that homosexuals should have equal rights with heterosexuals with regard to job opportunities. On the other hand, many view homosexuality as morally wrong.

Currently, same-sex marriages are not legally recognized by Congress. In the Defense of Marriage Act of 1996, Congress defined marriage as heterosexual. A state does not have to recognize another state's nonheterosexual marriage. The legal situation is constantly changing because several states are experimenting with new laws. A few states permit same-sex marriage but most do not.

The issue of same-sex marriage fascinates sociologists because it represents a basic change in a major social institution and is being played out on several fields: legal, cultural/moral, and behavioral. The legal debate will be decided by courts and legislatures; the cultural/moral debate is open to all of us; and the behavioral debate will be conducted by the activists on both sides. In the readings that follow, Andrew Sullivan presents some of the arguments in favor of same-sex marriages and James Q. Wilson responds to Sullivan's assertions with his counterarguments.

Andrew Sullivan  **YES**

Virtually Normal

In everyone there sleeps
A Sense of life lived according to love.
To some it means the difference they could make
By loving others, but across most it sweeps
As all they might have been had they been loved.
That nothing cures.

— Philip Larkin

If there were no alternative to today's conflicted politics of homosexuality, we might be condemned to see the proponents of the four major positions fight noisily while society stumbles from one awkward compromise to another. But there is an alternative: a politics that can reconcile the best arguments of liberals and conservatives, and find a way to marry the two. In accord with liberalism, this politics respects the law, its limits, and its austerity. It places a high premium on liberty, and on a strict limit to the regulation of people's minds and actions. And in sympathy with conservatism, this politics acknowledges that in order to create a world of equality, broader arguments may often be needed to persuade people of the need for change, apart from those of rights and government neutrality. It sees that beneath politics, human beings exist whose private lives may indeed be shaped by a shift in public mores.

This politics begins with the view that for a small minority of people, from a young age, homosexuality is an essentially involuntary condition that can neither be denied nor permanently repressed. It is a function of both nature and nurture, but the forces of nurture are formed so early and are so complex that they amount to an involuntary condition. It is *as if* it were a function of nature. Moreover, so long as homosexual adults as citizens insist on the involuntary nature of their condition, it becomes politically impossible simply to deny or ignore the fact of homosexuality.

This politics adheres to an understanding that there is a limit to what politics can achieve in such a fraught area as homosexuality, and trains its focus not on the behavior of citizens in civil society but on the actions of the public and allegedly neutral state. While it eschews the use of law to legislate culture, it strongly believes that law can affect culture indirectly by its insistence on the equality of all citizens. Its goal in the area of homosexuality is simply to ensure that the liberal state live up to its promises for all its citizens. It would seek full public equality for those who, through no fault of their own, happen to be homosexual; and it would not deny homosexuals, as the other four politics do, their existence, integrity, dignity, or distinctness. It would attempt neither to patronize nor to exclude.

This politics affirms a simple and limited principle: that all *public* (as opposed to private) discrimination against homosexuals be ended and that every right and responsibility that heterosexuals enjoy as public citizens be extended to those who grow up and find themselves emotionally different. *And that is all.* No cures or re-educations, no wrenching private litigation, no political imposition of tolerance; merely a political attempt to enshrine formal public equality, whatever happens in the culture and society at large. For these reasons, it is the only politics that actually tackles the *political* problem of homosexuality; the only one that fully respects liberalism's public-private distinction; and, ironically, as we shall see, the only one that cuts the Gordian knot of the shame and despair and isolation that many homosexuals feel. For these reasons, perhaps, it has the least chance of being adopted by homosexuals and heterosexuals alike.

What would it mean in practice? Quite simply, an end to all proactive discrimination by the state against homosexuals. That means an end to sodomy laws that apply only to homosexuals; a recourse to the courts if there is not equal protection of heterosexuals and homosexuals in law enforcement; an equal legal age of consent to sexual activity for heterosexuals and homosexuals, where such regulations apply; inclusion of the facts about homosexuality in the curriculum of every government-funded school, in terms no more and no less clear than those applied to heterosexuality (although almost certainly with far less emphasis, because of homosexuality's relative rareness when compared with heterosexuality); recourse to the courts if any government body or agency can be proven to be engaged in discrimination against homosexual employees; equal opportunity and inclusion in the military; and legal homosexual marriage and divorce....

Its most powerful and important elements are equal access to the military and marriage. The military ban is by far the most egregious example of proactive public discrimination in the Western democracies. By conceding the excellent service that many gay and lesbian soldiers have given to their country, the U.S. military in recent years has elegantly clarified the specificity of the government's unfairness. By focusing on the mere public admission of homosexuality in its 1993 "don't ask, don't tell" compromise, the military isolated the core issue at the heart of the equality of homosexual persons. It argued that homosexuals could serve in the military; that others could know they were homosexuals; that *they* could know they were homosexuals; but that if they ever so much as mentioned this fact, they were to be discharged. The prohibition was not against homosexual acts as such—occasional lapses by heterosexuals were not to be grounds for expulsion. The prohibition was not even against homosexuality. The prohibition was against homosexuals' being honest about their sexuality, because that honesty allegedly lowered the morale of others.

Once the debate has been constructed this way, it will eventually, surely, be won by those advocating the admission of open homosexuals in the military. When this is the sole argument advanced by the military—it became the crux of the debate on Capitol Hill—it has the intellectual solidity of a pack of cards. One group is arbitrarily silenced to protect not the rights but the sensibilities of the others. To be sure, it won the political battle; but it clearly lost the moral and intellectual war, as subsequent court tests demonstrated. It required one of the most respected institutions in American society to impose upon its members a rule of fundamental dishonesty in order for them to perform their duties. It formally introduced hypocrisy as a rule of combat. . . .

If this politics is feasible, both liberal and conservative dead ends become new beginnings. The liberal can campaign for formal public equality—for the abolition of sodomy laws, equal protection in public employment and institutions, the end of the ban on openly gay men and lesbians in the military—and rightly claim that he is merely seeing that all citizens in their public capacity are treated equally. But he can also argue fervently for freedom of expression—for those on both sides of the cultural war—and for freedom of economic contract. And he can concentrate his efforts on the work of transforming civil society, the place where every liberal longs to be.

And the conservative, while opposing "special rights," is able to formulate a vision of what values the society wants to inculcate. He can point to the virtues of a loyal and dedicated soldier, homosexual or heterosexual, and celebrate his patriotism; he can involve another minority group in the collective social good. He can talk about relations between heterosexuals and homosexuals not under the rubric of a minority group seeking preferences from a majority group, but as equal citizens, each prepared and willing to contribute to the common good, so long as they are treated equally by the state.

But the centerpiece of this new politics goes further than this. The critical measure for this politics of public equality–private freedom is something deeper and more emotional, perhaps, than the military.

It is equal access to civil marriage.

As with the military, this is a question of formal public discrimination, since only the state can grant and recognize marriage. If the military ban deals with the heart of what it means to be a citizen, marriage does even more so, since, in peace and war, it affects everyone. Marriage is not simply a private contract; it is a social and public recognition of a private commitment. As such, it is the highest public recognition of personal integrity. Denying it to homosexuals is the most public affront possible to their public equality.

This point may be the hardest for many heterosexuals to accept. Even those tolerant of homosexuals may find this institution so wedded to the notion of heterosexual commitment that to extend it would be to undo its very essence. And there may be religious reasons for resisting this that, within certain traditions, are unanswerable. But I am not here discussing what churches do in their private affairs. I am discussing what the allegedly neutral liberal state should do in public matters. For liberals, the case for homosexual marriage is overwhelming. As a classic public institution, it should be available to any two citizens.

Some might argue that marriage is by definition between a man and a woman; and it is difficult to argue with a definition. But if marriage is articulated beyond this circular fiat, then the argument for its exclusivity to one man and one woman disappears. The center of the public contract is an emotional, financial, and psychological bond between two people; in this respect, heterosexuals and homosexuals are identical. The heterosexuality of marriage is intrinsic only if it is understood to be intrinsically procreative; but that definition has long been abandoned in Western society. No civil marriage license is granted on the condition that the couple bear children; and the marriage is no less legal and no less defensible if it remains childless. In the contemporary West, marriage has become a way in which the state recognizes an emotional commitment by two people to each other for life. And within that definition, there is no public way, if one believes in equal rights under the law, in which it should legally be denied homosexuals....

But perhaps surprisingly... one of the strongest arguments for gay marriage is a conservative one. It's perhaps best illustrated by a comparison with the alternative often offered by liberals and liberationists to legal gay marriage, the concept of "domestic partnership." Several cities in the United States have domestic partnership laws, which allow relationships that do not fit into the category of heterosexual marriage to be registered with the city and qualify for benefits that had previously been reserved for heterosexual married couples. In these cities, a variety of interpersonal arrangements qualify for health insurance, bereavement leave, insurance, annuity and pension rights, housing rights (such as rent-control apartments), adoption and inheritance rights. Eventually, the aim is to include federal income tax and veterans' benefits as well. Homosexuals are not the only beneficiaries; heterosexual "live-togethers" also qualify.

The conservative's worries start with the ease of the relationship. To be sure, potential domestic partners have to prove financial interdependence, shared living arrangements, and a commitment to mutual caring. But they don't need to have a sexual relationship or even closely mirror old-style marriage. In principle, an elderly woman and her live-in nurse could qualify, or a pair of frat buddies. Left as it is, the concept of domestic partnership could open a Pandora's box of litigation and subjective judicial decision making about who qualifies. You either are or you're not married; it's not a complex question. Whether you are in a domestic partnership is not so clear.

More important for conservatives, the concept of domestic partnership chips away at the prestige of traditional relationships and undermines the priority we give them. Society, after all, has good reasons to extend legal advantages to heterosexuals who choose the formal sanction of marriage over simply living together. They make a deeper commitment to one another and to society; in exchange, society extends certain benefits to them. Marriage provides an anchor, if an arbitrary and often weak one, in the maelstrom of sex and relationships to which we are all prone. It provides a mechanism for emotional stability and economic security. We rig the law in its favor not because we disparage all forms of relationship other than the nuclear family, but because we recognize that not to promote marriage would be to ask too much of human virtue....

Any heterosexual man who takes a few moments to consider what his life would be like if he were never allowed a formal institution to cement his relationships will see the truth of what I am saying. Imagine life without a recognized family; imagine dating without even the possibility of marriage. Any heterosexual woman who can imagine being told at a young age that her attraction to men was wrong, that her loves and crushes were illicit, that her destiny was single-hood and shame, will also appreciate the point. Gay marriage is not a radical step; it is a profoundly humanizing, traditionalizing step. It is the first step in any resolution of the homosexual question—more important than any other institution, since it is the most central institution to the nature of the problem, which is to say, the emotional and sexual bond between one human being and another. If nothing else were done at all, and gay marriage were legalized, ninety percent of the political work necessary to achieve gay and lesbian equality would have been achieved. It is ultimately the only reform that truly matters.

... It has become a truism that in the field of emotional development, homosexuals have much to learn from the heterosexual culture. The values of commitment, of monogamy, of marriage, of stability are all posited as models for homosexual existence. And, indeed, of course, they are. Without an architectonic institution like that of marriage, it is difficult to create the conditions for nurturing such virtues, but that doesn't belie their importance.

It is also true, however, that homosexual relationships, even in their current, somewhat eclectic form, may contain features that could nourish the broader society as well. Precisely because there is no institutional model, gay relationships are often sustained more powerfully by genuine commitment. The mutual nurturing and sexual expressiveness of many lesbian relationships, the solidity and space of many adult gay male relationships, are qualities sometimes lacking in more rote, heterosexual couplings. Same-sex unions often incorporate the virtues of friendship more effectively than traditional marriages; and at times, among gay male relationships, the openness of the contract makes it more likely to survive than many heterosexual bonds. Some of this is unavailable to the male-female union: there is more likely to be greater understanding of the need for extramarital outlets between two men than between a man and a woman; and again, the lack of children gives gay couples greater freedom. Their failures entail fewer consequences for others. But something of the gay relationship's necessary honesty, its flexibility, and its equality could undoubtedly help strengthen and inform many heterosexual bonds....

As I've just argued, I believe strongly that marriage should be made available to everyone, in a politics of strict public neutrality. But within this model, there is plenty of scope for cultural difference. There is something baleful about the attempt of some gay conservatives to educate homosexuals and lesbians into an uncritical acceptance of a stifling model of heterosexual normality. The truth is, homosexuals are not entirely normal; and to flatten their varied and complicated lives into a single, moralistic model is to miss what is essential and exhilarating about their otherness.

NO

James Q. Wilson

Against Homosexual Marriage

Our courts, which have mishandled abortion, may be on the verge of mishandling homosexuality. As a consequence of two pending decisions, we may be about to accept homosexual marriage.

In 1993 the supreme court of Hawaii ruled that, under the equal-protection clause of that state's constitution, any law based on distinctions of sex was suspect, and thus subject to strict judicial scrutiny. Accordingly, it reversed the denial of a marriage permit to a same-sex couple, unless the state could first demonstrate a "compelling state interest" that would justify limiting marriages to men and women.... [I]n the meantime, the executive branch of Hawaii appointed a commission to examine the question of same-sex marriages; its report, by a vote of five to two, supports them. The legislature, for its part, holds a different view of the matter, having responded to the court's decision by passing a law unambiguously reaffirming the limitation of marriage to male-female couples.

... [S]ince the United States Constitution has a clause requiring that "full faith and credit shall be given to the public acts, records, and judicial proceedings of every other state," a homosexual couple in a state like Texas, where the population is overwhelmingly opposed to such unions, may soon be able to fly to Hawaii, get married, and then return to live in Texas as lawfully wedded....

Contemporaneous with these events, an important book has appeared under the title *Virtually Normal*. In it, Andrew Sullivan, the editor of the *New Republic,* makes a strong case for a new policy toward homosexuals. He argues that "all *public* (as opposed to private) discrimination against homosexuals be ended.... *And that is all.*" The two key areas where this change is necessary are the military and marriage law. Lifting bans in those areas, while also disallowing antisodomy laws and providing information about homosexuality in publicly supported schools, would put an end to the harm that gays have endured. Beyond these changes, Sullivan writes, American society would need no "cures [of homophobia] or reeducations, no wrenching private litigation, no political imposition of tolerance."

It is hard to imagine how Sullivan's proposals would, in fact, end efforts to change private behavior toward homosexuals, or why the next, inevitable, step would not involve attempts to accomplish just that purpose by using cures and reeducations, private litigation, and the political imposition of tolerance. But apart from this, Sullivan—an English Catholic, a homosexual, and someone who has on occasion referred to himself as a conservative—has given us the most sensible and coherent view of a program to put homosexuals and heterosexuals on the same public footing. . . .

                                              ✥

Sullivan recounts three main arguments concerning homosexual marriage, two against and one for. He labels them prohibitionist, conservative, and liberal. (A fourth camp, the "liberationist," which advocates abolishing all distinctions between heterosexuals and homosexuals, is also described—and scorched for its "strange confluence of political abdication and psychological violence.") I think it easier to grasp the origins of the three main arguments by referring to the principles on which they are based.

The prohibitionist argument is in fact a biblical one; the heart of it was stated by Dennis Prager in an essay in the *Public Interest* ("Homosexuality, the Bible, and Us," Summer 1993). When the first books of the Bible were written, and for a long time thereafter, heterosexual love is what seemed at risk. In many cultures—not only in Egypt or among the Canaanite tribes surrounding ancient Israel but later in Greece, Rome, and the Arab world, to say nothing of large parts of China, Japan, and elsewhere—homosexual practices were common and widely tolerated or even exalted. The Torah reversed this, making the family the central unit of life, the obligation to marry one of the first responsibilities of man, and the linkage of sex to procreation the highest standard by which to judge sexual relations. Leviticus puts the matter sharply and apparently beyond quibble:

> Thou shalt not live with mankind as with womankind; it is an abomination. . . . If a man also lie with mankind, as he lieth with a woman, both of them have committed an abomination; they shall surely be put to death; their blood shall be upon them.

Sullivan acknowledges the power of Leviticus but deals with it by placing it in a relative context. What is the nature of this "abomination"? Is it like killing your mother or stealing a neighbor's bread, or is it more like refusing to eat shellfish or having sex during menstruation? Sullivan suggests that all of these injunctions were written on the same moral level and hence can be accepted or ignored *as a whole*. He does not fully sustain this view, and in fact a refutation of it can be found in Prager's essay. In Prager's opinion and mine, people at the time of Moses, and for centuries before him, understood that there was a fundamental difference between whom you killed and what you ate, and in all likelihood people then and for centuries earlier linked whom you could marry closer to the principles that defined life than they did to the rules that defined diets.

The New Testament contains an equally vigorous attack on homosexuality by St. Paul. Sullivan partially deflects it by noting Paul's conviction that the earth was about to end and the Second Coming was near; under these conditions, all forms of sex were suspect. But Sullivan cannot deny that Paul singled out homosexuality as deserving of special criticism. He seems to pass over this obstacle without effective retort.

Instead, he takes up a different theme, namely, that on grounds of consistency many heterosexual practices—adultery, sodomy, premarital sex, and divorce, among others—should be outlawed equally with homosexual acts of the same character. The difficulty with this is that it mistakes the distinction alive in most people's minds between marriage as an institution and marriage as a practice. As an institution, it deserves unqualified support; as a practice, we recognize that married people are as imperfect as anyone else. Sullivan's understanding of the prohibitionist argument suffers from his unwillingness to acknowledge this distinction.

⋅◈⋅

The second argument against homosexual marriage—Sullivan's conservative category—is based on natural law as originally set forth by Aristotle and Thomas Aquinas and more recently restated by Hadley Arkes, John Finnis, Robert George, Harry V. Jaffa, and others. How it is phrased varies a bit, but in general its advocates support a position like the following: man cannot live without the care and support of other people; natural law is the distillation of what thoughtful people have learned about the conditions of that care. The first thing they have learned is the supreme importance of marriage, for without it the newborn infant is unlikely to survive or, if he survives, to prosper. The necessary conditions of a decent family life are the acknowledgement by its members that a man will not sleep with his daughter or a woman with her son and that neither will openly choose sex outside marriage.

Now, some of these conditions are violated, but there is a penalty in each case that is supported by the moral convictions of almost all who witness the violation. On simple utilitarian grounds it may be hard to object to incest or adultery; if both parties to such an act welcome it and if it is secret, what differences does it make? But very few people, and then only ones among the overeducated, seem to care much about mounting a utilitarian assault on the family. To this assault, natural-law theorists respond much as would the average citizen—never mind "utility," what counts is what is right. In particular, homosexual uses of the reproductive organs violate the condition that sex serve solely as the basis of heterosexual marriage.

To Sullivan, what is defective about the natural-law thesis is that it assumes different purposes in heterosexual and homosexual love: moral consummation in the first case and pure utility or pleasure alone in the second. But in fact, Sullivan suggests, homosexual love can be as consummatory as heterosexual. He notes that as the Roman Catholic Church has deepened its understanding of the involuntary—that is, in some sense genetic—basis of homosexuality, it has attempted to keep homosexuals in the church as objects of affection and nurture, while banning homosexual acts as perverse.

But this, though better than nothing, will not work, Sullivan writes. To show why, he adduces an analogy to a sterile person. Such a person is permitted to serve in the military or enter an unproductive marriage; why not homosexuals? If homosexuals marry without procreation, they are no different (he suggests) from a sterile man or woman who marries without hope of procreation. Yet people, I think, want the form observed even when the practice varies; a sterile marriage, whether from choice or necessity, remains a marriage of a man and a woman. To this Sullivan offers essentially an aesthetic response. Just as albinos remind us of the brilliance of color and genius teaches us about moderation, homosexuals are a "natural foil" to the heterosexual union, "a variation that does not eclipse the theme." Moreover, the threat posed by the foil to the theme is slight as compared to the threats posed by adultery, divorce, and prostitution. To be consistent, Sullivan once again reminds us, society would have to ban adulterers from the military as it now bans confessed homosexuals.

But again this misses the point. It would make more sense to ask why an alternative to marriage should be invented and praised when we are having enough trouble maintaining the institution at all. Suppose that gay or lesbian marriage were authorized; rather than producing a "natural foil" that would "not eclipse the theme," I suspect such a move would call even more seriously into question the role of marriage at a time when the threats to it, ranging from single-parent families to common divorces, have hit record highs. Kenneth Minogue recently wrote of Sullivans's book that support for homosexual marriage would strike most people as "mere parody," one that could further weaken an already strained institution.

To me, the chief limitation of Sullivan's view is that it presupposes that marriage would have the same, domesticating effect on homosexual members as it has on heterosexuals, while leaving the latter largely unaffected. Those are very large assumptions that no modern society has ever tested.

Nor does it seem plausible to me that a modern society resists homosexual marriages entirely out of irrational prejudice. Marriage is a union, sacred to most, that unites a man and woman together for life. It is a sacrament of the Catholic Church and central to every other faith. Is it out of misinformation that every modern society has embraced this view and rejected the alternative? Societies differ greatly in their attitude toward the income people may have, the relations among their various races, and the distribution of political power. But they differ scarcely at all over the distinctions between heterosexual and homosexual couples. The former are overwhelmingly preferred over the latter. The reason, I believe, is that these distinctions involve the nature of marriage and thus the very meaning—even more, the very possibility—of society....

⋙◉⋘

Let us assume for the moment that a chance to live openly and legally with another homosexual is desirable. To believe that, we must set aside biblical injunctions, a difficult matter in a profoundly religious nation. But suppose we manage the diversion, perhaps on the grounds that if most Americans skip church, they can as readily avoid other errors of (possibly) equal magnitude.

Then we must ask on what terms the union shall be arranged. There are two alternatives—marriage or domestic partnership.

Sullivan acknowledges the choice, but disparages the domestic-partnership laws that have evolved in some foreign countries and in some American localities. His reasons, essentially conservative ones, are that domestic partnerships are too easily formed and too easily broken. Only real marriages matter. But—aside from the fact that marriage is in serious decline, and that only slightly more than half of all marriages performed in the United States this year will be between never-before-married heterosexuals—what is distinctive about marriage is that it is an institution created to sustain child-rearing. Whatever losses it has suffered in *this* respect, its function remains what it has always been.

The role of raising children is entrusted in principle to married heterosexual couples because after much experimentation—several thousand years, more or less—we have found nothing else that works as well. Neither a gay nor a lesbian couple can of its own resources produce a child; another party must be involved. What do we call this third party? A friend? A sperm or egg bank? An anonymous donor? There is no settled language for even describing, much less approving of, such persons.

Suppose we allowed homosexual couples to raise children who were created out of a prior heterosexual union or adopted from someone else's heterosexual contact. What would we think of this? There is very little research on the matter. Charlotte Patterson's famous essay, "Children of Gay and Lesbian Parents" (*Journal of Child and Development,* 1992), begins by conceding that the existing studies focus on children born into a heterosexual union that ended in divorce or that was transformed when the mother or father "came out" as a homosexual. Hardly any research has been done on children acquired at the outset by a homosexual couple. We therefore have no way of knowing how they would behave. And even if we had such studies, they might tell us rather little unless they were conducted over a very long period of time.

But it is one thing to be born into an apparently heterosexual family and then many years later to learn that one of your parents is homosexual. It is quite another to be acquired as an infant from an adoption agency or a parent-for-hire and learn from the first years of life that you are, because of your family's position, radically different from almost all other children you will meet. No one can now say how grievous this would be. We know that young children tease one another unmercifully; adding this dimension does not seem to be a step in the right direction.

Of course, homosexual "families," with or without children, might be rather few in number. Just how few, it is hard to say. Perhaps Sullivan himself would marry, but, given the great tendency of homosexual males to be promiscuous, many more like him would not, or if they did, would not marry with as much seriousness.

That is problematic in itself. At one point, Sullivan suggests that most homosexuals would enter a marriage "with as much (if not more) commitment as heterosexuals." Toward the end of this book, however, he seems to withdraw from so optimistic a view. He admits that the label "virtually" in the title of his book is deliberately ambiguous, because homosexuals as a group are *not* "normal." At another point, he writes that the "openness of the contract" between two homosexual males means that such a union will in fact be more durable than a heterosexual marriage because the contract contains an *"understanding of the need for extramarital outlets"* (emphasis added). But no such "understanding" exists in heterosexual marriage; to suggest that it might in homosexual ones is tantamount to saying that we are now referring to two different kinds of arrangements. To justify this difference, perhaps, Sullivan adds that the very "lack of children" will give "gay couples greater freedom." Freedom for what? Freedom, I think, to do more of those things that heterosexual couples do less of because they might hurt the children.

✑

The courts in Hawaii and in the nation's capital must struggle with all these issues under the added encumbrance of a contemporary outlook that makes law the search for rights, and responsibility the recognition of rights. Indeed, thinking of laws about marriage as documents that confer or withhold rights is itself an error of fundamental importance—one that the highest court in Hawaii has already committed. "Marriage," it wrote, "is a state-conferred legal-partnership status, the existence of which gives rise to a multiplicity of rights and benefits...." A state-conferred legal partnership? To lawyers, perhaps; to mankind, I think not....

Our challenge is to find a way of formulating a policy with respect to homosexual unions that is not the result of a reflexive act of judicial rights-conferring, but is instead a considered expression of the moral convictions of a people.

POSTSCRIPT

Should Same-Sex Marriages Be Legally Recognized?

The issue of the rights of homosexuals creates a social dilemma. Most people would agree that all members of society should have equal rights. However, the majority may disapprove of the lifestyles of a minority group and pass laws against some of their behaviors. The question is: When do these laws violate civil rights? Are laws against same-sex marriage such a violation?

There is a considerable literature on homosexuality. Recent works on the history of the gay rights movement include Dudley Clendinen and Adam Nagourney, *Out for Good: The Struggle to Build a Gay Rights Movement in America* (Simon & Schuster, 1999); Ronald J. Hunt, *Historical Dictionary of the Gay Liberation Movement* (Scarecrow Press, 1999); and John Loughery, *The Other Side of Silence: Men's Lives and Gay Identities: A Twentieth-Century History* (Henry Holt, 1998). For broad academic works on homosexuality see Kath Weston, *Long Slow Burn: Sexuality and Social Science* (Routledge, 1998); Alan Sinfield, *Gay and After* (Serpent's Tail, 1998); and Michael Ruse, *Homosexuality: A Philosophical Inquiry* (Blackwell, 1998). Recent works that focus on homosexual rights include David A. J. Richards, *Identity and the Case for Gay Rights* (University of Chicago Press, 1999); Morris B. Kaplan, *Sexual Justice* (Routledge, 1997); James Button, et al., *Private Lives, Public Conflicts: Battles Over Gay Rights in American Communities* (CQ Press, 1997); and Carl F. Stychin, *A Nation by Rights: National Cultures, Sexual Identity Politics, and the Discourse of Rights* (Temple University Press, 1998). On the antigay rights movement see Stephanie L. Whitt and Suzanne McCorkle, eds., *Anti-Gay Rights: Assessing Voter Initiatives* (Praeger, 1997). For an examination of prejudice against homosexuals see Gregory M. Herek, ed., *Stigma and Sexual Orientation: Understanding Prejudice Against Lesbians, Gay Men, and Bisexuals* (Sage, 1998). For a reader on same-sex marriage see Andrew Sullivan, *Same-Sex Marriage, Pro and Con: A Reader* (Random House, 1997). The best work on human sexual practices is Edward O. Laumann, John H. Gagnon, Robert T. Michael, and Stuart Michaels, *The Social Organization of Sexuality: Sexual Practices in the United States* (University of Chicago Press, 1994).

ISSUE 6

Is the Decline of the Traditional Family a National Crisis?

YES: David Popenoe, from "The American Family Crisis," *National Forum: The Phi Kappa Phi Journal* (Summer 1995)

NO: Stephanie Coontz, from *The Way We Really Are: Coming to Terms With America's Changing Families* (Basic Books, 1997)

ISSUE SUMMARY

YES: Sociologist David Popenoe contends that families play important roles in society but how the traditional family functions in these roles has declined dramatically in the last several decades, with very adverse effects on children.

NO: Family historian Stephanie Coontz argues that current discussion of family decline includes a false idealization of the traditional family of the past and misleading interpretations of current data on families. She finds that the trends are both positive and negative.

The state of the American family deeply concerns many Americans. About 40 percent of marriages end in divorce, and only 27 percent of children born in 1990 are expected to be living with both parents by the time they reach age 17. Most Americans, therefore, are affected personally or are close to people who are affected by structural changes in the family. Few people can avoid being exposed to the issue: violence in the family and celebrity divorces are standard fare for news programs, and magazine articles decrying the breakdown of the family appear frequently. Politicians today try to address the problems of the family. Academics have affirmed that the family crisis has numerous significant negative effects on children, spouses, and the rest of society.

Sociologists pay attention to the role that the family plays in the functioning of society. For a society to survive, its population must reproduce (or take in many immigrants), and its young must be trained to perform adult roles and to have the values and attitudes that will motivate them to contribute to society. Procreation and socialization are two vital roles that families traditionally have performed. In addition, the family provides economic and emotional support for its members, which is vital to their effective functioning in society.

Today the performance of the family is disappointing in all of these areas. Procreation outside of marriage has become common, and it has been found to lead to less than ideal conditions for raising children. The scorecard on American family socialization is hard to assess, but there is concern about such issues as parents' declining time with and influence on their children and latchkey children whose parents work and who must therefore spend part of the day unsupervised. The economic performance of two-parent families is improving because more mothers are entering the labor force, but this gain is often related to a decline in emotional support. Single-parent families tend to perform less well on both counts. Overall, the high divorce rate and the frequency of child and spousal abuse indicate that the modern family fails to provide adequate social and emotional support.

Although most experts agree that the American family is in crisis, there is little agreement about what, if anything, should be done about it. After all, most of these problems result from the choices that people make to try to increase their happiness. People end unhappy marriages. Married women work for fulfillment or financial gain. Unwed mothers decide to keep their children. The number of couples who choose to remain childless is growing rapidly. These trends cannot be changed unless people start choosing differently. As yet there is no sign of this happening. Does this mean that the weakening of the family is desirable? Few would advocate such an idea, but perhaps some weakening must be accepted as the consequence of embracing other cherished values.

In the selections that follow, David Popenoe argues that the family is the key institution in society. Since it plays many important roles, its functional decline, which is largely due to cultural trends, has many adverse social impacts, including greatly harming children. He concludes by suggesting what needs to be done to strengthen families and family life. Stephanie Coontz provides a much different assessment of the present state of the family as compared with earlier times. She maintains that the family crisis thesis ignores the many strengths of American families today, overemphasizes certain negative trends, and misinterprets several of them. She tries to set the record straight and to counter much of the misinformation that the media produces.

David Popenoe

 **YES**

The American Family Crisis

Throughout our nation's history, we have depended heavily on the family to provide both social order and economic success. Families have provided for the survival and development of children, for the emotional and physical health of adults, for the special care of the sick, injured, handicapped, and elderly, and for the reinforcement of society's values. Today, America's families face growing problems in each of these areas, and by many measures are functioning less well than ever before—less well, in fact, than in other advanced, industrialized nations.

The most serious negative effects of the functional decline of families have been on children. Evidence suggests that today's generation of children is the first in our nation's history to be less well-off psychologically and socially than their parents were at the same age. Alarming increases have occurred in such pathologies as juvenile delinquency, violence, suicide, substance abuse, eating disorders, nonmarital births, psychological stress, anxiety, and unipolar depression.

Such increases are especially troubling because many conditions for child well-being have improved. Fewer children are in each family today; therefore, more adults are theoretically available to care for them. Children are in some respects healthier and materially better off; they have completed more years in school, as have their parents. Greater national concern for children's rights, for child abuse, and for psychologically sound childrearing practices is also evident.

Family Origins and History

As the first social institution in human history, the family probably arose because of the need for adults to devote a great amount of time to childrearing. Coming into the world totally dependent, human infants must, for a larger portion of their lives than for any other species, be cared for and taught by adults. To a unique degree, humans nurture, protect, and educate their offspring. It is hard to conceive of a successful society, therefore, that does not have families that are able to raise children to become adults who have the capacity to love and to work, who are committed to such positive social values as honesty, respect, and responsibility, and who pass these values on to the next generation.

Infants and children need, at minimum, one adult to care for them. Yet, given the complexities of the task, childrearing in all societies until recent years has been shared by many adults. The institutional bond of marriage between biological parents, with the essential function of tying the father to the mother and child, is found in virtually every society. Marriage is the most universal social institution known; in no society has nonmarital childbirth, or the single parent, been the cultural norm. In all societies the biological father is identified where possible, and in almost all societies he plays an important role in his children's upbringing, even though his primary task is often that of protector and breadwinner.

In the preindustrial era, however, adult family members did not necessarily consider childrearing to be their primary task. As a unit of rural economic production, the family's main focus typically was economic survival. According to some scholars, rather than the family being for the sake of the children, the children, as needed workers, were for the sake of the family. One of the most important family transitions in history was the rise in industrial societies of what we now refer to as the "traditional nuclear family": husband away at work during the day and wife taking care of the home and children full time. This transition took place in the United States beginning in the early 1800s. The primary focus of this historically new family form was indeed the care and nurturing of children, and parents dedicated themselves to this effort.

Over the past thirty years, the United States (along with other modern societies) has witnessed another major family transformation—the beginning of the end of the traditional nuclear family. Three important changes have occurred:

- The divorce rate increased sharply (to a level currently exceeding 50 percent), and parents increasingly decided to forgo marriage, with the consequence that a sizable number of children are being raised in single-parent households, apart from other relatives.
- Married women in large numbers left the role of full-time mother and housewife to go into the labor market, and the activities of their former role have not been fully replaced.
- The focus of many families shifted away from childrearing to the psychological well-being and self-development of their adult members. One indication of this latter focus is that, even when they have young children to raise, parents increasingly break up if their psychological and self-fulfillment needs are unmet in the marriage relationship.

We can never return to the era of the traditional nuclear family, even if we wanted to, and many women and men emphatically do not. The conditions of life that generated that family form have changed. Yet the one thing that has not changed through all the years and all the family transformations is the need for children to be raised by mothers and fathers. Indeed, in modern, complex societies in which children need an enormous amount of education and psychological security to succeed, active and nurturing relationships with adults may be more critical for children than ever.

Unfortunately, the amount of time children spend with adults, especially their parents, has been dropping dramatically. Absent fathers, working mothers, distant grandparents, anonymous schools, and transient communities have become hallmarks of our era. Associated with this trend in many families, and in society as a whole, is a weakening of the fundamental assumption that children are to be loved and valued at the highest level of priority.

The Individualism Trend

To understand fully what has happened to the family, we must look at the broader cultural changes that have taken place, especially changes in the values and norms that condition everyday choices. Over recent centuries in industrialized and industrializing societies, a gradual shift has occurred from a "collectivist" culture (I am using this term with a cultural and not a political meaning) toward an individualistic culture. In the former, group goals take precedence over individual ones. "Doing one's duty," for example, is more important than "self-fulfillment," and "social bonds" are more important than "personal choice." In individualistic cultures, the welfare of the group is secondary to the importance of such personal goals as self-expression, independence, and competitiveness.

Not surprisingly, individualistic societies rank higher than collectivist societies in political democracy and individual development. But the shift from collectivism to individualism involves social costs as well as personal gains—especially when it proceeds too far. Along with political democracy and individual development, individualistic societies tend to have high rates of individual deviance, juvenile delinquency, crime, loneliness, depression, suicide, and social alienation. In short, these societies have more free and independent citizens but less social order and probably a lower level of psychological well-being.

"Communitarian" Individualism

The United States has long been known as the world's most individualistic society. Certainly, we place a high value on this aspect of our society, and it is a major reason why so many people from other countries want to come here. Yet for most of our history, this individualism has been balanced, or tempered, by a strong belief in the sanctity of accepted social organizations and institutions, such as the family, religion, voluntary associations, local communities, and even the nation as a whole. While individualistic in spirit, people's identities were rooted in these social units, and their lives were directed toward the social goals that they represented. Thus, the United States has been marked for much of its history, not by a pure form of individualism, but by what could be termed a "communitarian" or balanced individualism.

"Expressive" Individualism

As the individualism trend has advanced, however, a more radical or "expressive" individualism has emerged, one that is largely devoted to "self-indulgence" or "self-fulfillment" at the expense of the group. Today, we see a large number of people who are narcissistic or self-oriented, and who show concern for social institutions only when these directly affect their own well-being. Unfortunately, these people have a tendency to distance themselves from the social and community groupings that have long been the basis for personal security and social order. Since the 1950s, the number of people being married, visiting informally with others, and belonging to voluntary associations has decreased, and the number of people living alone has increased.

In turn, the traditional community groupings have been weakened. More people are viewing our once accepted social institutions with considerable skepticism. As measured by public opinion polls, confidence in such public institutions as medicine, higher education, the law, the press, and organized religion has declined dramatically. As measured by people voting with their feet, trust in the institution of marriage also had declined dramatically. And, as we see almost every night on the news, our sense of cultural solidarity seems to be diminishing.

The highly disturbing actions of inner-city residents that we have witnessed in the urban riots of recent years could be considered less a departure from everyday American cultural reality than a gross intensification of it. Few social and cultural trends found in the inner city are not also present in the rest of the nation. Indeed, with respect to the family, the characteristics of the African American family pronounced by President Lyndon Johnson in 1965 to be in a state of "breakdown" are very similar to the family characteristics of America as a whole in 1994!

In summary, for the good of both the individual and society, the individualism trend in the United States has advanced too far. The family holds the key. People need strong families to provide them with the identity, belonging, discipline, and values that are essential for full individual development. The social institutions of the surrounding community depend on strong families to teach those "civic" values—honesty, trust, self-sacrifice, personal responsibility, respect for others—that enable them to thrive. But let us not forget that strong families depend heavily on cultural and social supports. Family life in an unsupportive community is always precarious and the social stresses can be overwhelming.

Not to Forget the Gains

While I have presented a fairly grim picture in describing these cultural changes, it is important to add that not every aspect of our society has deteriorated. In several key areas, this nation has seen significant social progress. For instance, we are a much more inclusive society today—segregation and racism have diminished, and we now accept more African Americans, Hispanics, and other minority groups into the mainstream. The legal, sexual, and financial emancipation of women has become a reality as never before in history. With advances in medicine, we have greater longevity and, on the whole, better physical health. And our average material standard of living, especially in the possession of consumer durables, has increased significantly.

The Nuclear Family and Marriage

Given our nation's past ability to accept positive social change, we can have some confidence in our capacity to solve the problem of family decline. In seeking solutions, we should first consider what family structure is best able to raise children who are autonomous and socially responsible, and also able to meet adult needs for intimacy and personal attachment. Considering the available evidence, as well as. the lessons of recent human experience, unquestionably the family structure that works best is the nuclear family. I am not referring to the traditional nuclear family, but rather to the nuclear family that consists of a male and a female who marry and live together and share responsibility for their children and for each other.

Let us look, for a moment, at other family forms. No advanced, Western society exists where the three-generation extended family is very important and where it is not also on the wane. Some scholars suggest that a new extended family has emerged with the trend toward "step" and "blended" families. "Isn't it nice," they say, "that we now have so many new relatives!" The final verdict is not yet in on stepfamilies, but preliminary evidence from the few empirical studies that have been done sends quite the opposite message, and it is a chilling one. For example, a recent British study of 17,000 children born in 1958 concluded that "the chances of stepchildren suffering social deprivation before reaching twenty-one are even greater than those left living after divorce with a lone parent." Similar findings are turning up in the United States.

How are the single-parent families doing? Accumulating evidence on the personal and social consequences of this family type paints an equally grim picture. A 1988 survey by the National Center for Health Statistics found, for example, that children from single-parent families are two to three times more likely to have emotional and behavioral problems than children from intact families, and reduced family income is by no means the only factor involved. In their new book *Growing Up With a Single Parent,* Sara McLanahan and Gary Sandefur, after examining six nationally representative data sets containing over 25,000 children from a variety of racial and social class backgrounds, conclude that "children who grow up with only one of their biological parents are disadvantaged across a broad array of outcomes... they are twice as likely to drop out of high school, 2.5 times as likely to become teen mothers, and 1.4 times as likely to be idle—out of school and out of work—as children who grow up with both parents." The loss of economic resources, they report, accounts for only about 50 percent of the disadvantages associated with single parenthood.

Toward Solutions

Of course, many people have no other choice than to live in step- and single-parent families. These families can be successful, and their members deserve our continuing support. Nevertheless, the benefits that strong nuclear families bring to a high-achieving, individualistic, and democratic society are absolutely clear. For example, a committed marriage, which is the basis of the strong nuclear family, brings enormous benefits to adults. It is ironic in this age of self-fulfillment, when people are being pulled away from marriage, that a happy marriage seems to provide the best source of self-fulfillment. By virtually every measure, married individuals are better off than single individuals.

Another reason for supporting strong nuclear families is that society gains enormously when a high percentage of men are married. While unmarried women take relatively good care of themselves, unmarried men often have difficulty in this regard. In general, every society must be wary of the unattached male, for he is universally the cause of numerous social ills. Healthy societies are heavily dependent on men being attached to a strong moral order, which is centered in families, both to discipline sexual behavior and to reduce competitive aggression. Men need the moral and emotional instruction of women more than vice versa. Family life, especially having children, is for men a civilizing force of no mean proportions.

We should be seriously concerned, therefore, that men currently spend more time living apart from families than at probably any other time in American history. About a quarter of all men aged twenty-five to thirty-four live in nonfamily households, either alone or with an unrelated individual. In 1960, average Americans spent 62 percent of their adult lives with spouse and children, which was the highest in our history; by 1980, they spent 43 percent, the lowest in our history. This trend alone may help to account for the high and rising crime rates over the past three decades. During this period, the number of reported violent crimes per capita, largely committed by unattached males, increased by 355 percent.

Today, a growing portion of American men are highly involved in child care, providing more help with the children than their own fathers did. Yet, because they did not stay with or marry the mothers of their children, or because of divorce, a large number of men have abandoned their children entirely.

Between 1960 and 1990 the percentage of children living apart from their biological fathers more than doubled, from 17 percent to 36 percent. In general, childrearing women have become increasingly isolated from men. This is one of the main reasons why nothing would benefit the nation more than a national drive to promote strong marriages.

The New Familism: A Hopeful Trend

One bright spot in this picture is what some of us have called "the new familism," a growing realization in America that, "yes, the family really is in trouble and needs help." Public opinion polls indicate that nearly two-thirds of Americans believe "family values have gotten weaker in the United States." Both major political parties and our President now seem to be in agreement.

Two primary groups are involved in this cultural mini-shift: the maturing baby boomers, now at the family stage of their life cycle, and the "baby-boom echo" children of the divorce revolution. The middle-aged baby boomers, spurred by growing evidence that children have been hurt by recent family changes, have been instrumental in shifting the media in a profamily direction. And many of the echo children of the 1970s, with their troubled childhoods, are coming into adulthood with a resolve not to repeat their parents' mistakes. They tend to put a high premium on marital permanence, perhaps because they have been unable to take the family for granted as many of their parents—the children of the familistic 1950s—did. But one concern is this: will they have the psychological stability to sustain an intimate relationship, or will their insecure childhoods make it impossible for them to fulfill their commitment to a lasting marriage?

Unfortunately, studies of the long-term effects of divorce on children and adolescents provide no optimism in this regard.

A couple of other factors seem to be working in a profamily direction. One is AIDS, which has now noticeably slowed the sexual revolution. As one entertainment figure recently said (with obvious dismay), "dating in Hollywood just isn't what it used to be." Neither, I must add, is dating what it used to be on the college campus, but the changes so far have not been very remarkable. Another factor is that cultural change is often reflected in cycles, and some cycles of change are patterned in generational terms. We know that not all cultural values can be maximized simultaneously. What one generation comes to value because they have less of it, their parents' generation rejected. This factor leads us to believe that the nation as a whole may be primed in the 1990s to run away from the values of radical individualism and more fully embrace the ideals of family and other social bonds.

Conclusion

In thinking about how to solve America's family crisis, we should keep the following considerations uppermost in mind:

- As a society, we cannot return to the era of the traditional nuclear family. But, we must do everything possible to strengthen the husband-wife nuclear family that stays together and takes responsibility for its children. Every child both wants—and needs—a mother and a father.
- Fundamental to strengthening the nuclear family is a renewed emphasis on the importance of marriage, which is the social institution designed primarily to hold men to the mother-child unit. It is extremely important for our children, and for our society, that men are attached to childrearing families.

- With even the strongest of marriages, parents have great difficulty raising children in an unsupportive and hostile environment. We must seek to renew the sinews of community life that can support families, maintain social order, and promote the common good. We should give as much attention to recreating a "family culture" as we are now giving to strengthening a "work culture."

- As an overall approach to promoting family life, nothing is more important than trying to diminish and even turn back the trend toward radical individualism. Social bonds, rather than personal choice, and community needs, rather than individual autonomy, must be accorded a higher priority in our culture—and in our lives.

The Way We Really Are

Introduction

Five years ago I wrote a book called *The Way We Never Were: American Families and the Nostalgia Trap*. As a family historian bothered by widespread misconceptions in the popular press about "traditional" families, I hoped to get people to look more realistically at the strengths, weaknesses, and surprising variability of family life in the past.

My book went to press just as Dan Quayle issued his famous condemnation of Murphy Brown, the fictional television character who decided to bear her child out of wedlock. The ensuing polemics over whether Murphy Brown was setting a bad example for our nation's youth were followed by an all-out war over family values as the 1992 election approached. Since much of the discussion focused on the contrast between today's families and "the way things used to be," I began to get calls from congressional committees, reporters, and television producers asking me for a historical perspective on these issues. Soon I found myself in the thick of a national debate over what was happening to the American family. . . .

In my last book, I demonstrated the tremendous variety of family types that have worked—and not worked—in American history. When families succeeded, it was often for reasons quite different than stereotypes about the past suggest—because they were flexible in their living arrangements, for example, or could call on people and institutions beyond the family for assistance or support. And when families failed, the results were often devastating. There never was a golden age of family life, a time when all families were capable of meeting the needs of their members and protecting them from poverty, violence, or sexual exploitation.

The "traditional" sexual double standard, for example, may have led more middle-class girls to delay sex at the end of the nineteenth century than today, but it also created higher proportions of young female prostitutes. Respect for elders may have received more lip service in the past, but elders were until very recently the segment of the population most likely to be destitute.

Yet knowing there was no golden age in history does not satisfy most people. Okay, they say, so the past wasn't great, and people have been lamenting the

From Stephanie Coontz, *The Way We Really Are: Coming to Terms With America's Changing Families* (Basic Books, 1997). Copyright © 1997 by Basic Books, a division of HarperCollins Publishers, Inc. Reprinted by permission of Basic Books, a member of Perseus Books, L.L.C. Notes omitted.

"breakdown of the family" or the "crisis of modern youth" since colonial days. It may be entertaining to know that John Watson, the most famous child psychiatrist of the early twentieth century, predicted in 1928 that marriage would be dead by 1977, and that in 1977, noted sociologist Amitai Etzioni announced that "by mid-1990 not one American family will be left." But even a stopped clock is right twice a day. What if these fears are finally coming true? Am I claiming that the more things change, the more they remain the same? Do I think people are crazy to feel anxious about recent trends in family life?

"Perhaps it's good to have our illusions about the past shattered," people often say, "but once we reject the lies and the myths, what do we put in their place?" Are the only lessons from history negative? Isn't there anything positive families can learn from history and sociology? . . .

Boosting Our Social Intelligence: Putting Family and Personal Trends in Context

Understanding the history of families and the structural constraints under which they operate can prevent our emotional and social IQs from being stunted by what sometimes seems like a national campaign to "dumb us down." Politicians have become experts in squeezing the complexity out of issues to produce compressed, thirteen-second sound bites. Think-tank publicists bombard us with the out-of-context snippets of information sometimes called "factoids." . . .

Care must be taken in interpreting headlines about the explosion of unwed motherhood. Unwed motherhood has increased dramatically since 1970, but it's easy to overstate *how* dramatically, because much illegitimacy was covered up in the past and reporting methods have recently become much more sophisticated. In the past, notes Sam Roberts, many unwed mothers would tell census workers that they were separated, "resulting in the anomaly of many more 'separated' women than men." At least 80 percent of the increase in unwed motherhood reported between 1981 and 1983, explains Steve Rawlings of the Census Bureau, came from "refinements in survey procedures that were introduced early in the 1980s. This represents 10 to 15 percent of the total increase between 1970 and 1993 (or 20 to 25 percent of the increase since 1980)." And though newspapers routinely use unwed motherhood and single parenthood interchangeably, many unwed mothers are part of cohabitating couples. Five states, including California, further distort the statistics by assuming a woman is unmarried if she has a different last name than the father listed on the birth certificate!

It's also important to distinguish between the ratio of unmarried to married births and the rate of births to unmarried women. Between 1960 and 1990, the nonmarital birth ratio increased by more than 500 percent, from 5.3 percent of all births to 28 percent. But birth rates to unmarried women only increased by a factor of 1.73, not quite twofold. What explains the larger figure is that births to unmarried women rose while births to married women fell, increasing the *relative* proportion of unmarried births much more than their *absolute* numbers. In some cases, a fall in marital fertility may be so large that unwed births become a larger proportion of all births even when rates of unwed childbearing are flat or falling. The probability that an unmarried African-American woman would have a child actually fell from 9.8 to 9.0 percent between 1960 and 1990, for example; but because married-couple childbearing decreased among African Americans even more sharply, the proportion of black children born to unwed mothers rose.

I'm not saying that the media intend to mislead. But in many cases, lack of historical perspective makes intelligent, dedicated reporters vulnerable to manipulation by people who wish to magnify one particular set of the factoids that continuously streak across our information horizon....

The result is that many pronouncements about the family, often by the same commentators, have a peculiarly manic-depressive quality. On the one hand, there are the doomsday predictions. New consensus spokesman David Popenoe warns that the decay of family life is "unique and unprecedented" and that the final collapse of "the last vestige of the traditional family unit" is imminent. "Marriage is dying," says Robert Rector of the Heritage Foundation; the next ten years will "decide whether or not marriage and family survive in this nation." Our failure to halt the decay of marriage, says the Council on Families in America, is "nothing less than an act of cultural suicide."

On the other hand, these catastrophic assertions are periodically interspersed with cheerful assurances that things may be turning around. Popenoe sees hopeful signs of a "new familism" in "the nation as a whole." Charles Murray of the American Enterprise Institute thinks we may be moving toward "the restoration of a culture in which family, parenthood, ... morality, and the virtues are all perceived and valued in ways that our grandparents would find familiar."

Such wild fluctuations in assessments result from a lack of historical context. By contrast, once people understand the complicated *mix* of long-term changes in family trends, social institutions, and cultural mores, they are less likely to think that any one-size-fits-all quick fix can turn everything around, for better or for worse. They're more likely to be realistic about what can and can't be changed, what we need to adjust to and what we may be able to resist.

For example, take the question of whether marriage is a dying institution. In 1867 there were 9.6 marriages per 1,000 people. A hundred years later, in 1967, there were 9.7. The rate reached a low of 7.9 in 1932 and an all-time high of 16.4 in 1946, a peak quickly followed by a brief but huge surge in divorce. Marriage rates fell again from the early 1950s to 1958, rose slowly until the end of the 1960s, and then began to decline again. But the proportion of women who remain single all their lives is *lower* today than at the turn of the century, and fewer women now feel they have to forgo marriage entirely in order to do anything else in their lives. Periodic predictions to the contrary, it is unlikely that we will someday record the demise of the last married couple in America.

Nevertheless, marriage is certainly a *transformed* institution, and it plays a smaller role than ever before in organizing social and personal life. One reason is that marriage comes much later, for most people, than in the past. Men's average age at first marriage today is not unprecedented, though it has now regained the previous record high of 1890. But the average age of marriage for contemporary women is two years higher than its historical peak in 1890 and almost four years higher than in the 1950s. This figure approaches the highest age ever recorded for Western Europe, a region where marriage has always taken place later than almost anywhere else in the world. And although fewer women stay single all their lives than in 1900, a higher proportion of women than ever before experience a period of independent living and employment before marriage. Women's expectations of both marriage and work are unlikely to ever be the same as in the past.

The second reason for marriage's more limited role in people's lives is that it is no longer expected to last "until death do us part." Divorce rates in America rose steadily until World War II, fell briefly during the 1950s, and took off again during the late 1960s. The divorce rate crested near the end of the 1970s, leveled off in the 1980s, and very slightly receded from 1988 to 1993. This last trend was heralded by many commentators as a "real turnaround," a sign that Americans "are turning conservative, pro-family." But while demographers now say that only 40 percent, rather than 50 percent, of marriages will end in divorce, these remain among the highest divorce rates ever recorded. Furthermore, the cumulative effects of past divorces continue to mount. In 1960 there were 35 divorced men and women for every 1,000 married ones. By 1990 there were 140 divorced individuals for every 1,000 married ones.

People often misunderstand what statisticians mean when they estimate that one in every two or three marriages will end in divorce. The calculations refer to the chances of a marriage ending in divorce within 40 years. While rising divorce rates have increased the number of marriages at risk for dissolution, the gradual extension of life spans ensures that a marriage today has the potential to last three times longer than one of 200 years ago. Thus while the number of people who divorce is certainly unprecedented, so is the number of couples who celebrate their fortieth wedding anniversaries. In fact, the chances of doing so have never been better.

On the other hand, the average marriage that ends in divorce lasts only 6.3 years. We may be seeing more marriages that last longer and are more fulfilling than at any time in our history. But we are also seeing more marriages that are *less* committed and of shorter duration than in the past. Sociologist Valerie Oppenheimer suggests we are experiencing growing polarization between increasing numbers of very "high-quality," long-lasting marriages *and* increasing numbers of short-lived, medium- to "low-quality" ones where the partners are not committed enough to stay and work things through. Understanding this polarization helps explain some of the ambivalence Americans have about modern families. Very few people in a modern high-quality marriage would trade it for an older model where limited communication and a high degree of sexual dissatisfaction were taken for granted. And few adults in a very low-quality marriage, or their children, want to be trapped there for life. But the commitments and consequences of "medium-quality" marriages are more ambiguous, especially for kids, and this worries many Americans.

Often their worry takes the form of a debate over whether we should return to the family forms and values of the 1950s. That decade is still close enough that many people derive their political position on the issue from personal experience. At forums I've conducted across the country, some people raised in 1950s families tell of tormented childhoods in alcoholic, abusive, or conflict-ridden families. They cannot understand, they say vehemently, why anyone would regret the passing of the 1950s for a single moment. My research validates their experience. These individuals were not alone.

But other people remember 1950s families that shielded them from adult problems and disputes. Many had unmistakably happy parents. Others had secure childhoods but learned later that one or both of their parents were miserable. Some of these individuals are now sorry that their parents stayed together, but many more say they are glad not to have known about their parents' problems and grateful for whatever kept their families together. They are also thankful that the media did not expose them to many adult realities that today's children see or read about every day. My research validates their experience too.

The only way to get past the polarized personal testimonies for and against 1950s families is to put their strengths and weaknesses into historical perspective. This permits a more balanced assessment of what we have gained and lost since then. It also helps us distinguish historical precedents we may be able to draw on from new issues requiring new responses. . . .

Why Working Mothers Are Here to Stay

The 1950s was clearly out of balance in one direction, with almost half the adult population restricted in their access to economic and political roles beyond the family. But the last few decades have been out of balance in the opposite direction. Many of us now feel that our expanding roles beyond the family have restricted our access to family life.

At first glance, it appears that the new imbalance results from women, especially mothers, entering the workforce. Certainly, that trend has produced a dramatic change in relation to the decade that most people use as their measure of "traditional" family life. In 1950, only a quarter of all wives were in the paid labor force, and just 16 percent of all children had mothers who worked outside the home. By 1991, more than 58 percent of all married women, and nearly two-thirds of all married women with children, were in the labor force. Of the total number of children in the country, 59 percent, including a majority of preschoolers, had mothers who worked outside the home.

But to analyze today's family imbalance as a conflict between work and mothering is to misread family history and to misdirect future family policy. Historically, productive work by mothers as well as fathers (and by young people) has not only been compatible with family life but has also strengthened family relationships. What's really out of balance is the relationship between market activities and nonmarket ones (including community as well as family ties). Our jobs don't make room for family obligations. The purchase of goods and services often substitutes for family or neighborhood activities. Phone calls, beepers, faxes and e-mail constantly intrude into family time. To correct this imbalance, we need to reorganize work to make it more compatible with family life. We need to reorganize family life to make sure that all members share in the work needed to sustain it. We need to redirect technology so that it serves rather than dominates our social and interpersonal relationships.

Instead, however, the family consensus brokers encourage us to cobble together personal marital arrangements that combine what they consider to be the best family features from both the 1950s and the 1990s. They reason that if we could convince women to take time off from work while their children are young, bolster male wages enough that more families could afford to make this choice, increase the incentives for marriage, and combat the excesses of individualism that lead to divorce or unwed motherhood, then surely we could solve the conflicts that parents now experience in balancing work and family. While recommending that men should help out more at home and expressing abstract support for equal pay and promotion opportunities for women on the job, the family values think tanks nevertheless propose that parents revive "relatively traditional marital gender roles" for the period "when children are young," cutting back on mothers' paid work.

In the absence of wider social change in work policies and family support systems, this is the individual solution that many men and women try to work out. And it may be a reasonable stopgap measure for parents who can afford it. But when such personal accommodations are put forward as an overarching political program for family life, they cease to sound quite so reasonable. . . .

Women, the argument goes, are happy to care for children, but men's biological drives point them in a different direction. Men have to be coaxed and guided into responsible fatherhood, and societies have historically achieved this by granting husbands special status as moral educators, family authority figures, and breadwinners. When society stops viewing breadwinning "as a father's special task," we lose our most powerful way "to motivate fathers to provide for their children."

The family values crusaders believe that all men and women, at least during their parenting years, should organize their families with the man as primary provider and protector and the wife as primary nurturer. Before and after child rearing, a woman is welcome to work; but unless she has no other option, she should engage in "sequencing"—alternating work and child raising rather than trying to combine them. Popenoe proposes the wife take "at least a year" off work, then work part-time until her children are in their early to mid-teens. Even when both husband and wife are employed, the woman should remain primarily responsible for nurturing, with the man as "junior partner" at home. Husbands should help out more than in the past, but anything that smacks of "androgyny" is to be avoided like the plague. Society, he argues, must "disavow the popular notion of radical feminists that 'daddies can make good mommies.' "

Hostility to women's economic independence is a consistent subtext in "new consensus" writing. "Policies that encourage mothers to work instead of marry" are a large part of America's social problem, says Wade Horn of the National Fatherhood Initiative. Without providing any evidence, Dan Quayle claims studies show "that children whose parents work are *less likely* to have Mommy's undivided attention than children whose mothers stay home." Isn't it odd how quickly a discussion of working *parents* becomes an indictment of *Mommy*? According to this agenda, a male breadwinner–female homemaker division of labor is not an individual family choice but the correct model for every family. Women are told that there are compensations for giving up their aspirations to economic equality: "Even though the man is the head of the family, the woman is the neck, and she turns the head any way she wants." But if women are not willing to "give back" family leadership, groups such as the Promise Keepers advise men to "take it back.... Be sensitive. Treat the lady gently and lovingly. But lead!"

While we can debate the *merits* of these proposals for America's families, I am more interested in examining their *practicality*. How likely is it that a majority of mothers will once more withdraw from paid employment during the early years of child rearing? What can historical and sociological analysis teach us about how realistic it is to propose that we revive the breadwinner identity as the basis for men's commitment to marriage and child raising?

The Late Birth and Short Life of the Male Breadwinner Family

One of the most common misconceptions about modern marriage is the notion that coprovider families are a new invention in human history. In fact, today's dual-earner family represents a return to older norms, after a very short interlude that people mistakenly identify as "traditional."

Throughout most of humanity's history women as well as men were family breadwinners. Contrary to cartoons of cavemen dragging home food to a wife waiting at the campfire, in the distant past of early gathering and hunting societies women contributed as much or more to family subsistence as men. Mothers left the hearth to forage for food, hunt small animals, trade with other groups, or tend crops.

On this continent, neither Native American, African-American, nor white women were originally seen as economic dependents. Among European colonists, men dominated women, but their authority was based on legal, political, and religious coercion, not on men's greater economic importance. The most common words for wives in seventeenth- and eighteenth-century colonial America were "yoke-mates" or "meet-helps," labels that indicated women's economic partnership with men. Until the early nineteenth century, men and women worked together on farms or in small household businesses, alongside other family members. Responsibility for family life and responsibility for breadwinning were not two different, specialized jobs.

But in the early 1800s, as capitalist production for the market replaced home-based production for local exchange and a wage-labor system supplanted widespread self-employment and farming, more and more work was conducted in centralized workplaces removed from the farm or home. A new division of labor then grew up within many families. Men (and older children) began to specialize in work outside the home, withdrawing from their traditional child-raising responsibilities. Household work and child care were delegated to wives, who gave up their older roles in production and barter. While slaves and free blacks continued to have high labor force participation by women, wives in most other ethnic and racial groups were increasingly likely to quit paid work outside the home after marriage.

But it's important to remember that this new division of work between husbands and wives came out of a *temporary* stage in the history of wage labor and industrialization. It corresponded to a transitional period when households could no longer get by primarily on things they made, grew, or bartered, but could not yet rely on purchased consumer goods. For example, families no longer produced their own homespun cotton, but ready-made clothing was not yet available at prices most families could afford. Women still had to sew clothes from cloth that men purchased with their pay. Most families still had to grow part of their food and bake their own bread. Food preparation and laundering required hours of work each day. Water often had to be hauled and heated.

Somebody had to go out to earn money in order to buy the things the family needed; but somebody else had to stay home and turn the things they bought into things they could actually use. Given the preexisting legal, political, and religious tradition of patriarchal dominance, husbands (and youths of both sexes) were assigned to work outside the home. Wives assumed exclusive responsibility for domestic matters that they had formerly shared with husbands or delegated to older children and apprentices. Many women supplemented their household labor with income-generating work that could be done at or around home—taking in boarders, doing extra sewing or laundering, keeping a few animals, or selling garden products. But this often arduous work was increasingly seen as secondary to wives' primary role of keeping house, raising the children, and getting dinner on the table.

The resulting identification of masculinity with economic activities and femininity with nurturing care, now often seen as the "natural" way of organizing the nuclear family, was in fact a historical product of this nineteenth-century transition from an agricultural household economy to an industrial wage economy. So even as an ideal, the male breadwinner family was a comparatively late arrival onto the historical scene. As a reality—a family form in which most people actually lived—it came about even later....

The Revival of Women's Role as Family Coprovider

... For approximately 50 years, from the 1920s through the 1960s, the growth in married women's work outside the home was smaller than the decline in child labor, so that the male breadwinner family became increasingly dominant. But even at its high point in the 1950s, less than 60 percent of American children spent their youth in an Ozzie and Harriet-type family where dad went to work and mom stayed home. And by the 1970s the fifty-year reign of this family form was definitely over....

After 1973, real wages for young men began falling, creating a larger proportion of families where the mother worked just to keep the family afloat. Housing inflation meant that families with young children were especially likely to need the wife to work, in order to afford the new home that their growing family motivated them to buy. By 1989, almost 80 percent of all home buyers came from two-income households. Another incentive was the rising cost of higher education, which increased nearly three times faster than house-hold income between 1980 and 1994.

Today most families can no longer think of the earnings that wives and mothers bring home as a bonus that can be put aside when family needs call. Nor, increasingly, do the jobs women hold allow them the luxury of choosing to cut back or quit when family priorities change, any more than their husbands' jobs would. By 1993, married women working full-time contributed 41 percent of their families' incomes. Indeed, in 23 percent of two-earner couples, the wives earned *more* than their husbands.

The sequencing of mothering and paid employment that characterized many women's activities over the past 100 years is becoming a thing of the past. Through most of this century, even though labor participation rates for women rose steadily, they dropped significantly when women were in their twenties and thirties. By 1990, however, labor-force participation rates no longer dipped for women in their child-raising years. Today, fewer and fewer women leave their jobs while their children are very young.

Proponents of the modified male breadwinner family believe that if we could drastically reduce the number of single-mother households, raise wages for men, and convince families to get by on a little less, we might be able to get wives to quit work during their child-raising years. Polls consistently show that many women would like to cut back on work hours, though not quit entirely (and it's interesting that an almost equal number of men would also like to cut back their hours). But a return to the norm of male breadwinner families is simply not feasible for most Americans.

Why Wives and Mothers Will Continue to Work Outside the Home

It's not just a dollars-and-cents issue. Most women would not give up the sat-isfactions of their jobs even if they could afford to quit. They consistently tell interviewers they like the social respect, self-esteem, and friendship networks they gain from the job, despite the stress they may face finding acceptable child care and negotiating household chores with their husbands. In a 1995 survey by Louis Harris & Associates, for example, less than a third of working women said they would prefer to stay home even if money were no object.

Another reason women do not want to quit work is that they are not will-ing to surrender the increased leverage it gives them in the family. The simple truth is that women who do not earn income have much less decision-making power in marital relations than women who do. And no amount of goodwill on the part of husbands seems to lessen this imbalance. In one in-depth study of American families, researchers found that the primary determinant of power in all couples was who brings in the money. The only exception was among lesbians. Lesbian couples might be persuaded to have one partner stay home with the kids and the other earn the money, but I doubt that the Institute for American Values would consider this a positive step in the direction of "marital role complementarity."

Aside from women's own motivations to remain at work, the issue of whether a family can afford to have the wife stay home is quite debatable. One of the most longstanding American traditions, much older than the ideal of the male breadwinner, is the search for socioeconomic mobility. That's why many families came to America in the first place. It's what people were seeking when they crossed the plains in covered wagons, why farmers switched from diversified family crops to specialized market production, what parents have expected education to provide for their children.

From the mid-nineteenth to the mid-twentieth century, there were three main routes to family economic advancement. One was child labor, allowing parents to accumulate enough to buy a house and possibly send a later generation to school. Another was the move from farm to city, to take advantage of higher wage rates in urban areas. The third was investment in increased training and education for male members of the family.

But child labor was abolished in the early twentieth century, and even before 1950 most men had already obtained nonfarm jobs. By the mid-1960s there were diminishing returns to the gains families could expect from further education or training for men. As these older strategies ceased to guarantee continued mobility, women's employment became so central to family economic advancement that it could less and less often be postponed or interrupted for full-time child raising.

In other words, even for families where the uninterrupted work of wives isn't essential for minimum family subsistence, it is now the main route to even a modest amount of upward mobility. Those who tell women who "don't need to work" that they should go back to full-time child rearing are contradicting many of the other ideals most Americans hold dear. We're talking about abandoning the American dream here. The only way to get a significant number of families to make this choice would be to foster a thoroughly untraditional—some might even say un-American—acceptance of a stationary standard of living, a no-growth family economy. Some families may harbor such subversive ideals; yet the chances are slim that this will become a mass movement any time soon.

POSTSCRIPT

Is the Decline of the Traditional Family a National Crisis?

Popenoe admits that there are many positive aspects to the recent changes that have affected families, but he sees the negative consequences, especially for children, as necessitating actions to counter them. He recommends a return to family values and speaks out against the individualistic ethos. Coontz contends that the traditional family form that people like Popenoe are nostalgic for was atypical in American history and cannot be re-created. Furthermore, a closer look at the data indicates that the institution of the family is not in crisis. While admitting that many marriages fail, Coontz asserts that many families are strong.

Support for Coontz's point of view can be found in E. L. Kain, *The Myth of Family Decline* (D. C. Heath, 1990); J. F. Gubrium and J. A. Holstein, *What Is a Family?* (Mayfield, 1990); and Rosalind C. Barnett and Caryl Rivers, *She Works/He Works: How Two-Income Families Are Happier, Healthier, and Better Off* (HarperCollins, 1997). Recent works describing the weakening of the family and marriage include Richard T. Gill, *Posterity Lost: Progress, Ideology, and the Decline of the American Family* (Rowman & Littlefield, 1997); Dana Mack, *The Assault on Parenthood: How Our Culture Undermines the Family* (Simon & Schuster, 1997); Maggie Gallagher, *The Abolition of Marriage: How We Destroy Lasting Love* (Regnery, 1996); and Barbara Dafoe Whitehead, *The Divorce Culture: How Divorce Became an Entitlement and How It Is Blighting the Lives of Our Children* (Alfred A. Knopf, 1997). David Popenoe and Jean Bethke Elshtain's book *Promises to Keep: Decline and Renewal of Marriage in America* (Rowman & Littlefield, 1996) discusses the decline but also signs of renewal of marriage. Works that analyze changes in marriage and the family include Andrew Cherlin's *Marriage, Divorce, Remarriage,* rev. ed. (Harvard University Press, 1992); Betty Farrell's *Family: The Making of an Idea, an Institution, and a Controversy in American Culture* (Westview Press, 1999); Karla B. Hackstaff's *Marriage in a Culture of Divorce* (Temple University Press, 1999); Jessica Weiss's *To Have and to Hold: Marriage, the Baby Boom, and Social Change* (University of Chicago Press, 2000); Barbara J. Risman's *Gender Vertigo: American Families in Transition* (Yale University Press, 1998); and Ronald D. Taylor and Margaret C. Wang, eds., *Resilience Across Contexts: Family, Work, Culture, and Community* (Lawrence Erlbaum, 2000). For two major works on aspects of familial changes, see David Blankenhorn, *Fatherless America: Confronting Our Most Urgent Social Problem* (Basic Books, 1995) and Sara McLanahan and Gary Sandefur, *Growing up With a Single Parent: What Hurts and What Helps* (Harvard University Press, 1994).

On the Internet ...

Statistical Resources on the Web: Sociology

This Web site provides links to data on poverty in the United States. Included is a link that contains both current and historical poverty data.

`http://www.lib.umich.edu/libhome/Documents.center/stats.html`

Institute for Research on Poverty (IRP)

The Institute for Research on Poverty researches the causes and consequences of social inequality and poverty in the United States. This Web site includes frequently asked questions about poverty and links to other internet resources on the subject.

`http://www.ssc.wisc.edu/irp/`

Yahoo! Full Coverage: Affirmative Action

This links you to the Yahoo! search engine for the topic of affirmative action.

`http://fullcoverage.yahoo.com/fc/US/Affirmative_Action`

PART 3

Stratification and Inequality

*W*hy is there so much poverty in a society as rich as ours? Why has there been such a noticeable increase in inequality over the past quarter century? Although the ideal of equal opportunity for all is strong in the United States, many charge that the American political and economic system is unfair. Does extensive poverty demonstrate that policymakers have failed to live up to United States egalitarian principles? Are American institutions deeply flawed in that they provide fabulous opportunities for the educated and rich and meager opportunities for the uneducated and poor? Is the American stratification system at fault or are the poor themselves at fault? And what about the racial gap? The civil rights movement and the Civil Rights Act have made America more fair than it was, so why does a sizeable racial gap remain? Various affirmative action programs have been implemented to remedy unequal opportunities, but some argue that this is discrimination in reverse. In fact, California passed a referendum banning affirmative action. Where should America go from here? Social scientists debate these questions in this part.

- Is Increasing Economic Inequality a Serious Problem?

- Is the Underclass the Major Threat to American Ideals?

- Has Affirmative Action Outlived Its Usefulness?

ISSUE 7

Is Increasing Economic Inequality a Serious Problem?

YES: Sheldon Danziger and Deborah Reed, from "Winners and Losers: The Era of Inequality Continues," *Brookings Review* (Fall 1999)

NO: Christopher C. DeMuth, from "The New Wealth of Nations," *Commentary* (October 1997)

ISSUE SUMMARY

YES: Policy researchers Sheldon Danziger and Deborah Reed demonstrate the dramatic increase in income inequality that has occurred over the past quarter century. They also suggest policies for improving the conditions of the poor.

NO: Christopher C. DeMuth, president of the American Enterprise Institute for Public Policy Research, argues that the "recent increase in income inequality... is a very small tick in the massive and unprecedented leveling of material circumstances that has been proceeding now for almost three centuries and in this century has accelerated dramatically."

The cover of the January 29, 1996, issue of *Time* magazine bears a picture of 1996 Republican presidential candidate Steve Forbes and large letters reading: "DOES A FLAT TAX MAKE SENSE?" During his campaign Forbes expressed his willingness to spend $25 million of his own wealth in pursuit of the presidency, with the major focus of his presidential campaign being a flat tax, which would reduce taxes substantially for the rich. It seems reasonable to say that if the rich pay less in taxes, others would have to pay more. Is it acceptable for the tax burden to be shifted away from the rich in America? Forbes believed that the flat tax would benefit the poor as well as the rich. He theorized that the economy would surge ahead because investors would shift their money from relatively nonproductive, but tax-exempt, investments to productive investments. This is an example of the trickle-down theory, which states that helping the rich stimulates the economy, which helps the poor. In fact, the trickle-down theory is the major rationalization for the view that great economic inequality benefits all of society.

Inequality is not a simple subject. For example, America is commonly viewed as having more social equality than the more hierarchical societies of Europe and Japan, but America has more income inequality than almost all other industrial societies. This apparent contradiction is explained when one recognizes that American equality is not in income but in the opportunity to obtain higher incomes. The issue of economic inequality is further complicated by other categories of equality/inequality, which include political power, social status, and legal rights.

Americans believe that everyone should have an equal opportunity to compete for jobs and awards. This belief is backed up by free public school education, which provides poor children with a ladder to success, and by laws that forbid discrimination. Americans, however, do not agree on many specific issues regarding opportunities or rights. For example, should society compensate for handicaps such as disadvantaged family backgrounds or the legacy of past discrimination? This issue has divided the country. Americans do not agree on programs such as income-based scholarships, quotas, affirmative action, or the Head Start compensatory education program for poor preschoolers.

America's commitment to political equality is strong in principle, though less strong in practice. Everyone over 18 years old gets one vote, and all votes are counted equally. However, the political system tilts in the direction of special interest groups; those who do not belong to such groups are seldom heard. Furthermore, as in the case of Forbes, money plays an increasingly important role in political campaigns.

The final dimension of equality/inequality is status. Inequality of status involves differences in prestige, and it cannot be eliminated by legislation. Ideally, the people who contribute the most to society are the most highly esteemed. To what extent does this principle hold true in the United States?

The Declaration of Independence proclaims that "all men are created equal," and the Founding Fathers who wrote the Declaration of Independence went on to base the laws of the land on the principle of equality. The equality they were referring to was equality of opportunity and legal and political rights for white, property-owning males. They did not mean equality of income or status, though they recognized that too much inequality of income would jeopardize democratic institutions. In the two centuries following the signing of the Declaration, nonwhites and women struggled for and won considerable equality of opportunity and rights. Meanwhile, income gaps in the United States have been widening.

In the readings that follow, Sheldon Danziger and Deborah Reed argue that the growing inequality in America is due to economic changes that have been particularly hard on the poor and that government policies are needed to improve working conditions and opportunities. Christopher C. DeMuth admits that incomes have become more unequally distributed, but he argues that consumption, a better indicator of living conditions, has become much more equally distributed.

Sheldon Danziger and Deborah Reed  **YES**

Winners and Losers

Income inequality in the United States has grown substantially in the past quarter-century. Even the long ongoing economic recovery of the 1990s has done little to stem the tide. In the near future, market forces are unlikely to alleviate the hardship for low-income families who have borne the brunt of economic changes. Several public policy reforms, however, could raise the living standards of low-income families and workers.

A Quarter-Century of Growing Inequality

According to Census Bureau statistics, U.S. family income inequality (by numerous summary measures) has climbed almost continuously from a postwar low in the late 1960s. It has been higher during the 1990s than in any decade since the end of World War II. Most industrialized nations have also experienced growing income inequality, but in the United States, where the existing income disparity was greater, the rise has been more rapid. The difference, primarily, is that other countries have been more effective in countering the increased inequality generated by market forces through labor market and tax and transfer policies.

One way to measure inequality is by the relative income gap between the upper and lower "middle class." Figure 1 shows a near-steady rise in the ratio of family income at the 75th percentile to that at the 25th percentile—the "75–25" ratio—from 1973 to 1997. In 1973, an upper-middle-income family had 2.4 times the income of a lower-middle-income family. The ratio increased to a peak of 3.1 in 1993, falling only slightly—to 3.0—by 1997.

During the 1970s, inequality rose because the income of families in the upper middle of the distribution grew faster than the income of those in the lower middle. Between 1973 and 1979, income at the 75th percentile grew 9 percent, from $64,000 to $70,000, while income at the 25th percentile grew 4.5 percent, from $26,300 to $27,500. But during the 1980s and 1990s, incomes for families at the upper middle rose while incomes for those at the lower middle fell. By 1997, family income at the 75th percentile had grown to $80,500 while income at the 25th percentile had fallen to $26,900 (incomes in 1998 dollars, adjusted to represent a family of four).

From Sheldon Danziger and Deborah Reed, "Winners and Losers: The Era of Inequality Continues," *Brookings Review* (Fall 1999). Copyright © 1999 by *Brookings Review*. Reprinted by permission.

Figure 1

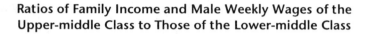

Ratios of Family Income and Male Weekly Wages of the
Upper-middle Class to Those of the Lower-middle Class

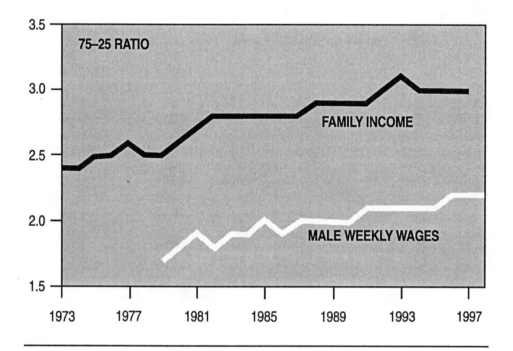

At the extremes of the distribution, family income fell at the bottom and grew at the top over the past quarter-century. Between 1973 and 1997 the income of families at the 10th percentile fell 7 percent, while income at the 90th percentile grew 38 percent (see figure 2). In fact, inequality increased throughout the distribution, as the size of each bar in figure 2 increases from the lowest- through the median to the highest-income families.

Changes in inequality can also be evaluated by comparing the share of people who are poor—those living in families below the poverty line—with the share who are "rich"—those living in families with incomes more than seven times the poverty line (about $105,000 for a family of four in 1997 using an alternative price index). Between 1973 and 1997, the share of people who were poor increased 1.2 percentage point to 11.8 percent while the share of those who were rich increased 8.1 percentage points to 14.3 percent—yet one more indication that economic growth has raised incomes at the top of the distribution while allowing absolute incomes at the bottom to stagnate or fall.

Figure 2

Percentage Change in Real Family Income and Male Weekly Wages

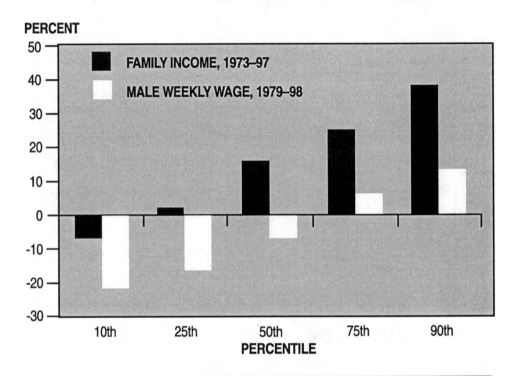

Despite the Economic Boom, the Gap Remains

Although the robust economic recovery of the 1990s has produced the lowest unemployment and inflation rates in 30 years and has lifted living standards across the income distribution, families below the median have not yet fully recovered from the income stagnation and recessions of the early 1980s and early 1990s. Family income in the lower middle of the distribution remains a few percentage points below its 1989 and 1979 peaks, whereas that in the upper middle has increased a few percentage points since 1989 and 15 percent since 1979. As figure 1 shows, family income inequality fell slightly as the economy recovered from the recession of the early 1990s. But as of 1997, the 75–25 ratio was still higher than it was in 1973, 1979, and 1989, the last three business cycle peaks.

Changes in the distribution of male earnings—the largest single component of family income—account for much of the increased family income inequality. Thanks to the current economic expansion, the wages of men at the bottom of the distribution grew between 1996 and 1998, but weekly wages for full-time male workers at the 10th and 25th percentiles, $300 and $432 respectively, remain more than 6 percent below their 1989 business cycle peak and more than 15 percent below the 1979 peak. The 75–25 ratio for men's weekly wages was just below 2.2 in 1998, slightly under its 1997 peak, but well above the 1979 and 1989 peaks (1.7 and 2.0, respectively; see figure 1).

Male earnings inequality rose during 1979–97 because real earnings fell for workers at the median and below and grew for those at the top of the distribution. Figure 2 shows a decline in men's earnings of 22 percent at the 10th percentile, 16 percent at the 25the percentile, and 7 percent at the median. Over the same period, men's earnings grew 6 percent at the 75th percentile and 13 percent at the 90th percentile.

Why Is Inequality Increasing?

Most economists agree that the main source of growing earnings inequality is the rising value of worker skill. In 1979, for example, the median full-time weekly wage for men with college degrees was 29 percent higher than that for men with high school diplomas only. By 1998, college graduates had a 68 percent edge. During 1979–98, real wages increased 8 percent for male college graduates but fell 18 percent for high school graduates. For women, the weekly wage gap between college and high school graduates increased from 43 percent in 1979 to 79 percent in 1998. The work experience differential increased as well, with earnings of workers with substantial labor market experience growing relative to those of new labor market entrants.

There is some disagreement over the relative importance of various causes of the rising value of skill. Labor-saving technological changes have simultaneously increased the demand for skilled workers who can run sophisticated equipment and reduced the demand for less-skilled workers, many of whom have been displaced by automation. Global competition has increased worldwide demand for the goods and services produced by skilled workers in high-tech industries and financial services. Lower-skilled workers increasingly compete with low-wage production workers in developing countries. Immigration has increased the size of the low-wage workforce and competition for low-skilled jobs. Institutional changes, such as the decline in the real value of the minimum wage and shrinking unionization rates, also moved the economy in the direction of higher earnings inequality.

Developments other than rising earnings inequality also widened the family income gap. In particular, changes in family structure, especially the growing share of female-headed households, increased the number of low-income families. A growing tendency for high-earning men to be married to high-earning women further separates the incomes of dual-earning couples from those of female-headed households.

Implications for the Future

Because growing income inequality arises primarily from long-term structural changes in the labor market that are unlikely to be reversed, U.S. income inequality is likely to remain high in the coming decade.

Even an extension of the current economic boom cannot be expected to close the family income gap any time soon. As figure 1 shows, the greatest single year of improvement in narrowing the family income gap was 1993–94. But the income gap in 1997 was still so large that *nine more years* of the unparalleled progress of 1993–94 would be required to return family income inequality to 1979 levels, almost twelve more such years to return it to 1973 levels.

Because the economic returns to skills have increased so much, the labor market now provides incentives for workers and young people to upgrade their skills through education and training. Indeed, the share of high school graduates entering college has already grown in the past few years. But though the resulting growth in the supply of skilled workers may eventually reduce labor market inequality, the adjustment will take years—years during which the wages of less-skilled workers are likely to remain low.

Nor will all workers respond equally to the incentives to improve their skills. Generally speaking younger Americans are much more likely to undertake substantial investments in education or training programs than are prime-age workers who have been hurt by changes in the labor markets over the past quarter-century and who have relatively few years of work left before retirement. In addition, because of pervasive inequalities in school quality and access, children from the poorest families and from racial and ethnic minorities who are concentrated in the inner cities are likely to respond less than average to the incentives.

Policy Directions

We are concerned about increased inequality over the past quarter-century because of its effects on both the absolute and relative well-being of low-income families and workers. Even without a decline in income for those at the bottom, we care about rising inequality because, as Adam Smith [author of *Wealth of Nations* in 1776] noted, the minimum acceptable standard of living tends to be higher the richer the society. Moreover, according to recent Nobel laureate Amartya Sen, the absolute well-being of the poor in terms of their ability to "participate in the standard activities of the community" depends on their relative well-being in terms of resources.

Increases in inequality over the past quarter-century are likely to have made equality of opportunity harder to attain. The children of the poor are increasingly subject to lower-quality education, lower-quality health care, and more dangerous communities. Concerns about equal opportunity are particularly relevant for children from female-headed households and for those who are racial and ethnic minorities because they are far more likely to grow up in poor families.

Many of the economic forces that have contributed to rising income inequality have also brought positive changes in our economy. Technological changes and increased globalization raise the average standard of living by bringing new goods to consumers and producers and by reducing their prices. The rising value of skill provides incentives for people to upgrade their own skills, which can be financially and personally rewarding. Even if it were possible to slow technological changes or adopt protective barriers to trade, we see no reason to attempt to lower inequality by doing so.

The United States has pursued policies to promote free trade and technological advancement in the interest of growth and efficiency; in doing so it has produced winners and losers. Government policies should therefore help reduce the resulting inequalities by aiding the low-income families and less-skilled workers who have borne the brunt of labor market changes.

Reasoned policy in this area must take into account two realities. First, the recent welfare reform experience has shown that the public favors policies that promote work. Welfare reform has dramatically reduced cash assistance for people who are capable of working, but it has offered expanded wage and child care subsidies. Second, education and well-designed training programs can improve the earnings of workers and promote economic opportunity in the long run. These policies, however, are unlikely to substantially improve the well-being of low-income workers in the coming decade. For the short term, policymakers should expand work-oriented antipoverty policies that raise the incomes of the least-skilled workers.

For people who are able to find jobs, the key elements of support are wage supplements and refundable child care tax credits. The Earned Income Credit, substantially expanded in 1993, has done much to offset the decline in real wages for workers at the bottom of the earnings distribution who work year-round and who have children. Almost all low-income families with children are now eligible for substantial credits from the EITC. For example, a single mother with two children who works year-round, full-time at the minimum wage receives about $3,600 in refundable tax credits. But only a small share of low-wage workers who do not have children receive the EITC, and their maximum credit is only a few hundred dollars. Raising substantially the EITC for childless workers would increase their living standards without taking them through the welfare system and would also make the federal income tax more progressive. Several states have already adopted their own EITCs for families with children, something other states should consider, especially those that continue to impose incomes taxes on the working poor.

In addition, even though the employment rate and earnings of single mothers have increased in the past five years, many single mothers, especially former welfare recipients, with young children are hard pressed to work full-time, year-round because a large portion of their earnings must go to child care. Increasing public subsidies for child care would be particularly beneficial for this group. The Dependent Care Credit (DCC) provides tax relief for families with children, but it is a nonrefundable credit and so benefits only families with positive income tax liabilities. Making the DCC refundable would raise the disposable income of single mothers and other low-income working families who spend substantial sums on child care but do not owe federal income tax. It too would make the federal income tax more progressive.

Finding a job has become more difficult for less-skilled workers over the past quarter-century. In mid-1999, even with the lowest unemployment rate in 30 years, many less-skilled workers are unable to find work. For those who want to work but are unable to find regular employment, transitional public service "jobs of last resort" at wages just below the minimum can provide the basis for a work-oriented safety net. Such "jobs of last resort" are more important than ever now that we have "ended welfare as we know it." During the next recession, many former welfare recipients will find themselves out of work and without recourse to cash assistance because of time limits, sanctions, and other aspects of welfare reform.

Looking Ahead

The good news is that the current economic recovery seems to have slowed the quarter-century trend toward rising income and earnings inequality. The bad news is that inequality is unlikely to return to the level of the late 1970s any time soon, much less to the lower levels of the late 1960s and early 1970s. As this era of inequality continues to unfold, work-oriented policy reforms could, at relatively modest cost, greatly benefit those workers and families most disadvantaged by the structural economic changes that have boosted the fortunes of the rich.

NO

Christopher C. DeMuth

The New Wealth of Nations

The Nations of North America, Western Europe, Australia, and Japan are wealthier today than they have ever been, wealthier than any others on the planet, wealthier by far than any societies in human history. Yet their governments appear to be impoverished—saddled with large accumulated debts and facing annual deficits that will grow explosively over the coming decades. As a result, government spending programs, especially the big social-insurance programs like Social Security and Medicare in the United States, are facing drastic cuts in order to avert looming insolvency (and, in France and some other European nations, in order to meet the Maastricht treaty's criteria of fiscal rectitude). American politics has been dominated for several years now by contentious negotiations over deficit reduction between the Clinton administration and the Republican Congress. This past June, first at the European Community summit in Amsterdam and then at the Group of Eight meeting in Denver, most of the talk was of hardship and constraint and the need for governmental austerity ("Economic Unease Looms Over Talks at Denver Summit," read the *New York Times* headline).

These bloodless problems of governmental accounting are said, moreover, to reflect real social ills: growing economic inequality in the United States; high unemployment in Europe; an aging, burdensome, and medically needy population everywhere; and the globalization of commerce, which is destroying jobs and national autonomy and forcing bitter measures to keep up with the bruising demands of international competitiveness.

How can it be that societies so surpassingly wealthy have governments whose core domestic-welfare programs are on the verge of bankruptcy? The answer is as paradoxical as the question. We have become not only the richest but also the freest and most egalitarian societies that have ever existed, and it is our very wealth, freedom, and equality that are causing the welfare state to unravel.

꩜

That we have become very rich is clear enough in the aggregate. That we have become very equal in the enjoyment of our riches is an idea strongly resisted by many. Certainly there has been a profusion of reports in the media and political speeches about increasing income inequality: the rich, it is said, are getting richer, the poor are getting poorer, and the middle and working classes are under the relentless pressure of disappearing jobs in manufacturing and middle management.

Although these claims have been greatly exaggerated, and some have been disproved by events, it is true that, by some measures, there has been a recent increase in income inequality in the United States. But it is a very small tick in the massive and unprecedented leveling of material circumstances that has been proceeding now for almost three centuries and in this century has accelerated dramatically. In fact, the much-noticed increase in measured-income inequality is in part a result of the increase in real social equality. Here are a few pieces of this important but neglected story.

• First, progress in agriculture, construction, manufacturing, and other key sectors of economic production has made the material necessities of life—food, shelter, and clothing—available to essentially everyone. To be sure, many people, including the seriously handicapped and the mentally incompetent, remain dependent on the public purse for their necessities. And many people continue to live in terrible squalor. But the problem of poverty, defined as material scarcity, has been solved. If poverty today remains a serious problem, it is a problem of individual behavior, social organization, and public policy. This was not so 50 years ago, or ever before.

• Second, progress in public health, in nutrition, and in the biological sciences and medical arts has produced dramatic improvements in longevity, health, and physical well-being. Many of these improvements—resulting, for example, from better public sanitation and water supplies, the conquest of dread diseases, and the abundance of nutritious food—have affected entire populations, producing an equalization of real personal welfare more powerful than any government redistribution of income.

The Nobel prize-winning economist Robert Fogel has focused on our improved mastery of the biological environment—leading over the past 300 years to a doubling of the average human life span and to large gains in physical stature, strength, and energy—as the key to what he calls "the egalitarian revolution of the 20th century." He considers this so profound an advance as to constitute a distinct new level of human evolution. Gains in stature, health, and longevity are continuing today and even accelerating. Their outward effects may be observed, in evolutionary fast-forward, in the booming nations of Asia (where, for example, the physical difference between older and younger South Koreans is strikingly evident on the streets of Seoul).

• Third, the critical *source* of social wealth has shifted over the last few hundred years from land (at the end of the 18th century) to physical capital (at the end of the 19th) to, today, human capital—education and cognitive ability. This development is not an unmixed gain from the standpoint of economic equality. The ability to acquire and deploy human capital is a function of intelligence, and intelligence is not only unequally distributed but also, to a significant degree, heritable. As Charles Murray and the late Richard J. Herrnstein argue in *The Bell Curve,* an economy that rewards sheer brainpower replaces one old source of inequality, socioeconomic advantage, with a new one, cognitive advantage.

⌗

But an economy that rewards human capital also tears down far more artificial barriers than it erects. For most people who inhabit the vast middle range of the bell curve, intelligence is much more equally distributed than land or physical capital ever was. Most people, that is, possess ample intelligence to pursue all but a handful of specialized callings. If in the past many were held back by lack of education and closed social institutions, the opportunities to use one's human capital have blossomed with the advent of universal education and the erosion of social barriers.

Furthermore, the material benefits of the knowledge-based economy are by no means limited to those whom Murray and Herrnstein call the cognitive elite. Many of the newest industries, from fast food to finance to communications, have succeeded in part by opening up employment opportunities for those of modest ability and training—occupations much less arduous and physically much less risky than those they have replaced. And these new industries have created enormous, widely shared economic benefits in consumption; I will return to this subject below.

• Fourth, recent decades have seen a dramatic reduction in one of the greatest historical sources of inequality: the social and economic inequality of the sexes. Today, younger cohorts of working men and women with comparable education and job tenure earn essentially the same incomes. The popular view would have it that the entry of women into the workforce has been driven by falling male earnings and the need "to make ends meet" in middle-class families. But the popular view is largely mistaken. Among married women (as the economist Chinhui Juhn has demonstrated), it is wives of men with high incomes who have been responsible for most of the recent growth in employment.

• Fifth, in the wealthy Western democracies, material needs and desires have been so thoroughly fulfilled for so many people that, for the first time in history, we are seeing large-scale voluntary reductions in the amount of time spent at paid employment. This development manifests itself in different forms: longer periods of education and training for the young; earlier retirement despite longer life spans; and, in between, many more hours devoted to leisure, recreation, entertainment, family, community and religious activities, charitable and other nonremunerative pursuits, and so forth. The dramatic growth of the sports, entertainment, and travel industries captures only a small slice of what has happened. In Fogel's estimation, the time devoted to nonwork activities by the average male head of household has grown from 10.5 hours per week in 1880 to 40 hours today, while time per week at work has fallen from 61.6 hours to 33.6 hours. Among women, the reduction in work (including not only outside employment but also household work, food preparation, childbearing and attendant health problems, and child rearing) and the growth in nonwork have been still greater.

There is a tendency to overlook these momentous developments because of the often frenetic pace of modern life. But our busy-ness actually demonstrates the point: time, and not material things, has become the scarce and valued commodity in modern society.

⌘

One implication of these trends is that in very wealthy societies, income has become a less useful gauge of economic welfare and hence of economic equality. When income becomes to some degree discretionary, and when many peoples' incomes change from year to year for reasons unrelated to their life circumstances, *consumption* becomes a better measure of material welfare. And by this measure, welfare appears much more evenly distributed: people of higher income spend progressively smaller shares on consumption, while in the bottom ranges, annual consumption often exceeds income. (In fact, government statistics suggest that in the bottom 20 percent of the income scale, average annual consumption is about twice annual income—probably a reflection of a substantial underreporting of earnings in this group.) According to the economist Daniel Slesnick, the distribution of consumption, unlike the distribution of reported income, has become measurably *more* equal in recent decades.

If we include leisure-time pursuits as a form of consumption, the distribution of material welfare appears flatter still. Many such activities, being informal by definition, are difficult to track, but Dora Costa of MIT has recently studied one measurable aspect—expenditures on recreation—and found that these have become strikingly more equal as people of lower income have increased the amount of time and money they devote to entertainment, reading, sports, and related enjoyments.

Television, videocassettes, CD's, and home computers have brought musical, theatrical, and other entertainments (both high and low) to everyone, and have enormously narrowed the differences in cultural opportunities between wealthy urban centers and everywhere else. Formerly upper-crust sports like golf, tennis, skiing, and boating have become mass pursuits (boosted by increased public spending on parks and other recreational facilities as well as on environmental quality), and health clubs and full-line book stores have become as plentiful as gas stations. As some of the best things in life become free or nearly so, the price of pursuing them becomes, to that extent, the "opportunity cost" of time itself.

The substitution of leisure activities for income-producing work even appears to have become significant enough to be contributing to the recently much-lamented increase in inequality in measured income. In a new AEI study, Robert Haveman finds that most of the increase in earnings inequality among U.S. males since the mid-1970's can be attributed not to changing labor-market opportunities but to voluntary choice—to the free pursuit of nonwork activities at the expense of income-producing work.

Most of us can see this trend in our own families and communities. A major factor in income inequality in a wealthy knowledge economy is age—many people whose earnings put them at the top of the income curve in their late fifties were well down the curve in their twenties, when they were just getting out of school and beginning their working careers. Fogel again: today the average household in the top 10 percent might consist of a professor or accountant married to a nurse or secretary, both in their peak years of earning. As for the stratospheric top 1 percent, it includes not only very rich people like Bill Cosby but also people like Cosby's fictional Huxtable family: an obstetrician married to a corporate lawyer. All these individuals would have appeared well down the income distribution as young singles, and that is where their young counterparts appear today.

That more young people are spending more time in college or graduate school, taking time off for travel and "finding themselves," and pursuing interesting but low- or non-paying jobs or apprenticeships before knuckling down to lifelong careers is a significant factor in "income inequality" measured in the aggregate. But this form of economic inequality is in fact the social equality of the modern age. It is progress, not regress, to be cherished and celebrated, not feared and fretted over.

POSTSCRIPT

Is Increasing Economic Inequality a Serious Problem?

This debate can be posed in terms of contradictory statements by the two authors: "We are concerned about increased inequality over the past quarter-century because of its effects on both the absolute and relative well-being of low-income families and workers" (Danziger and Reed); "We have become very equal in the enjoyment of our riches" (DeMuth). Both authors support their statements with indicators that measure trends, but they select different indicators. The reader has to decide which set of indicators better describes his or her idea of inequality.

Inequality, stratification, and social mobility are central concerns of sociology, and they are addressed by a large literature. Two important discussions of income inequality are *The Inequality Paradox: Growth of Income Disparity* edited by James A. Auerbach and Richard S. Belous (National Policy Association, 1998); Barry Bluestone and Bennett Harrison, *Growing Prosperity: The Battle for Growth With Equity in the Twenty-First Century* (Houghton Mifflin, 2000); D. G. Champernowne and F. A. Cowell, *Economic Inequality and Income Distribution* (Cambridge University Press, 1998); Richard B. Freeman, *When Earnings Diverge: Causes, Consequences, and Cures for the New Inequality in the U.S.* (National Policy Association, 1997); Andrew Hacker, *Money: Who Has How Much and Why* (Scribner's Reference, 1997); Frank Levy, *The New Dollars and Dreams: American Income and Economic Change* (Russell Sage Foundation, 1998); and Paul Ryscavage, *Income Inequality in America: An Analysis of Trends* (M. E. Sharpe, 1999). For a major structural analysis of inequality, see Peter M. Blau's *Structural Contexts of Opportunities* (University of Chicago Press, 1994). Richard J. Herrnstein and Charles Murray's *The Bell Curve: Intelligence and Class Structure in American Life* (Free Press, 1994) is a controversial work in which the authors conclude that the major cause of income inequality is differences in intelligence. This book is vigorously attacked by Claude S. Fischer et al. in *Inequality by Design: Cracking the Bell Curve Myth* (Princeton University Press, 1996). For a fuller explanation of Danziger's views, see Sheldon Danziger and Peter Gottschalk, *America Unequal* (Harvard University Press, 1995). For a poignant ethnographic study of the poor and their disadvantages, see Elliot Liebow, *Tell Them Who I Am: The Lives of Homeless Women* (Free Press, 1993).

ISSUE 8

Is the Underclass the Major Threat to American Ideals?

YES: Charles Murray, from "And Now for the Bad News," *Society* (November/December 1999)

NO: Barry Schwartz, from "Capitalism, the Market, the 'Underclass,' and the Future," *Society* (November/December 1999)

ISSUE SUMMARY

YES: Author Charles Murray describes destructive behavior among the underclass. Murray asserts that this type of behavior will result in serious trouble for society even though, according to statistics, the number of crimes committed has decreased.

NO: Psychology professor Barry Schwartz states that the underclass is not the major threat to American ideals. He counters that "the theory and practice of free-market economics have done more to undermine traditional moral values than any other social force."

T he Declaration of Independence proclaims the right of every human being to "life, liberty, and the pursuit of happiness." It never defines happiness, but Americans tend to agree that happiness includes doing well financially, getting ahead in life, and maintaining a comfortable standard of living.

The fact is that millions of Americans do not do well and do not live comfortably. They are mired in poverty and seem unable to get out. On the face of it, this fact poses no contradiction to America's commitment to the pursuit of happiness. To pursue is not necessarily to catch.

The real difficulty in reconciling the American ideal with American reality is not the problem of income differentials but the *persistence* of poverty from generation to generation. There are two basic explanations for this problem. One largely blames the poor and the other largely blames the circumstances of the poor and, thus, society.

The explanation that blames the poor is most strongly identified with the culture-of-poverty thesis, according to which a large segment of the poor does not really try to get out of poverty. In its more extreme form this view portrays the poor as lazy, stupid, or base. Poverty is not to be blamed on defects of American society but on personal defects. After all, many successful Americans have worked their way up from humble beginnings, and many immigrant groups have made progress in one generation. Therefore, some believe that the United States provides ample opportunities for those who work hard.

According to this view, available opportunities are ignored by the portion of the poor that embraces what is known as the *culture of poverty*. In other words, the poor have a culture all their own that is at variance with middle-class culture and that hinders their success. Although it may keep people locked into what seems to be an intolerable life, some would assert that this culture nevertheless has its own compensations and pleasures. It does not demand that people postpone pleasure, save money, or work hard.

However, the culture of poverty does not play a major role in today's version of the poor-are-to-blame theory. According to recent versions of this theory, having children out of wedlock, teenage pregnancy, divorce, absent fathers, crime, welfare dependency, and child abuse are what contribute to poverty. The culture of poverty contributes to these practices by being permissive or even condoning. This culture, however, is not antithetical to but is rather shared in part by much of the middle class. The difference is that in the middle class its consequences are usually not as extreme.

According to the second explanation of poverty, the poor have few opportunities and many obstacles to overcome to climb out of poverty. Most of the poor will become self-supporting if they are given the chance. Their most important need is for decent jobs that have the potential for advancement. Many poor people cannot find jobs, and when they do, the jobs are degrading or lack further opportunity.

These two perspectives are expressed in the two selections that follow. Charles Murray blames a segment of the poor that he calls the underclass for their poverty and for much of the harm done to society. Barry Schwartz blames the functioning of capitalism and the stock market for creating obstacles to the poor for getting ahead. Values such as sympathy, fairness, and self control, which sustain a productive and humane society, are undermined, according to Schwartz.

Charles Murray

 **YES**

And Now for the Bad News

Good news is everywhere. Crime rates are falling; welfare rolls are plunging; unemployment is at rock bottom; teenage births are down. Name an indicator, economic or social, and chances are it has taken a turn in the right direction. This happy story is worth celebrating. It is also a story that begs to be disentangled. For what is happening to the nation as a whole is not happening to the sub-population that we have come to call the underclass.

To make the case, I return to three indicators I first selected in the late 1980s to track the course of the underclass: criminality, dropout from the labor force among young men, and illegitimate births among young women. Then and now, these three seemed to me key outcroppings of what we mean by the underclass: people living outside the mainstream, often preying on the mainstream, in a world where the building blocks of a life—work, family and community—exist in fragmented and corrupt forms. Crime offers the most obvious example of a story that needs disentangling. After seven straight years of decline, the crime rate is at its lowest in a quarter-century. Almost everyone feels safer, especially in big cities. But suppose we ask not how many crimes are committed, but how many Americans demonstrate chronic criminality. That number is larger than ever. We don't notice, because so many of the chronically criminal are in jail.

Off the Street

For the past 20 years the United States has engaged in a massive effort to take criminals off the street. As of 1997, more than 1.8 million people were in prisons, jails and juvenile facilities. It has not been an efficient process—many who should be behind bars aren't and vice versa—but the great majority of prisoners are there because they have been a menace to their fellow citizens. To see how our appraisal of the crime problem depends on the imprisonment binge, suppose that in 1997 we imprisoned at the same rate relative to crime that we did in 1980, the year that the crime rate hit its all-time high. At the 1980 rate, 567,000 people would have been incarcerated in 1997, roughly 1.3 million fewer than the actual number. Now suppose that tomorrow we freed 1.3 million prisoners. Recent scholarly estimates of the average number of crimes prevented per year of incarceration range from 12 to 21. Even if these numbers are too high, it is clear that if we set free 1.3 million people now in prison, we would no longer be bragging about a falling crime rate. The only uncertainty is how sky-high the crime rate would be. It is a major accomplishment that crime has gone down. It has been achieved not by socializing the underclass, but by putting large numbers of its members behind bars.

Unemployment is another success story for the nation as a whole. Unemployment rates have dropped for just about any group of people who have been in the labor market, including blacks, and young black males in particular. Suppose we turn instead to a less-publicized statistic, but one of the most significant in trying to track the course of the underclass, the percentage of young males not in the labor force. When large numbers of young men neither work nor look for work, most are living off the underground economy or are dependent on handouts, perhaps moving into the labor force periodically, getting a job, and then quitting or getting fired a few weeks later, consigning themselves to a life at the margins of the economy.

Sudden and unexpected increases in the labor force dropout rates of young black males in the mid-1960s heralded the deterioration of the inner city. The 1990s have seen a new jump in dropout from the labor force that is just as ominous. The increased dropout has occurred selectively, among a subgroup that should have virtually 100% labor-force participation: young men who are no longer in school. The increase in labor force dropout is largest among young black males. Among 16- to 24-year-old black males not in school, the proportion who are not working or looking for work averaged 17% during the 1980s. It first hit 20% in 1992. As of 1997, it stood at 23%. The magnitude of dropout among white males the same age not in school is smaller, 9% in 1997. But the proportional increase since 1990 is substantial, up 25% overall, and concentrated among white teenagers (up 33% since 1990). That these increases in labor-force dropout have occurred despite a sustained period of high demand for workers at all skill levels is astonishing and troubling.

As for illegitimacy, confusion, reigns. Headlines declare that "Illegitimacy is Falling," but the referent is birthrates, illegitimate births per 1,000 unmarried women. The referent for the headlines is also usually blacks, because that's where the dramatic change has occurred: The black illegitimate birth rate for women 15 to 44 fell 18% from 1990 to 1996; the black teenage birth rate fell by even more. But what is happening to the illegitimacy *ratio*—the percentage of babies who are born to unmarried women? The two measures need not track with each other, as the black experience vividly illustrates. Birthrates for unmarried black women and for black teenagers did not begin to drop in 1990. They dropped further and for much longer from 1960 to 1985. But the black illegitimacy ratio rose relentlessly throughout that period. The ratio also rose from 1990 to 1994 as birth rates fell. The good news about the black illegitimacy ratio is that it has since leveled off, even dropping a percentage point—meaning that as of 1997 it stood at a catastrophic 69% instead of a catastrophic 70%.

Most analysts, including me, have focused on the ratio rather than the rate because it is the prevalence of mother-only homes that determines the nature of a neighborhood and the socialization of the next generation. But when we turn from blacks to the national numbers for all races, it doesn't make much difference which measure you think is important. The rate and ratio have both risen substantially over the past few decades. Since 1994 the rate has fallen slightly, while the ratio has been flat at 32%. That is, almost one out of three American babies is now born to an unmarried woman.

The problems associated with illegitimacy have not really leveled off. Because the illegitimacy ratio is so much higher today than 18 years ago, the proportion of American children under 18 who were born to unmarried women will continue to increase. The problems associated with illegitimacy will also continue to increase well into the next century as the babies born in the 1990s grow up. That illegitimacy has stopped rising is a genuinely hopeful sign, but for practical purposes we are at the peak of the problem.

The size of the welfare population was not one of my 1989 indicators for tracking the underclass (it tends to double-count the role of illegitimacy), but recent success on this front has been so dramatic that it should be acknowledged. By "welfare reform" I mean the movement that began in the states in the early 1990s and culminated in the national welfare reform law of 1996. The change has been stunning: In 1993, slightly more than five million families were on welfare. By 1998, that number had dropped to about three million—a 40% drop in five years. The economy gets only a modest part of the credit. During the two preceding booms, welfare soared (in the 1960s) and declined fractionally (in the 1980s).

But once again, disentangling is crucial. For years, liberals defending welfare stressed that half of all women who ever go on welfare exit within a few years (and thus are ordinary women who have hit a rough patch), while conservatives attacking welfare stressed that half the welfare caseload at any point in time consists of women who have been on the rolls for many years (and thus are likely candidates for the underclass). So the crucial question is: How has the 40% reduction in caseload split between the two groups? No one yet knows. Past experience with workfare programs has been that the effect is concentrated on women who fit the profile of the short-term recipient. Answers about the current situation should be forthcoming soon.

The more profound question is what difference it makes if single mothers go to work. Is a community without fathers importantly different just because more mothers are earning a paycheck? One line of argument says yes. Jobs provide regularity, structure and dignity to family life, even if the father is not around. But we know from recent research that the bad effects of single parenting persist for women not on welfare. No counterbalancing body of research demonstrates that it is good for children when a single mother works (rather the opposite). I like to think children who see their mothers working for a living grow up better equipped to make their way in the world than children who watch their mothers live off a welfare check, even if there are no fathers in their lives. But this is a hope, not a finding.

In net, the underclass is as large as or larger than it has ever been. It is probably still growing among males, level or perhaps falling among females. We know for sure that the underclass today is substantially larger than it was at any time in the 1980s when the Reagan administration was being excoriated for ignoring the underclass. Yet the underclass is no longer a political issue. Why? I propose an ignoble explanation. Whatever we might tell ourselves, mainstream Americans used to worry about the underclass primarily insofar as it intruded on our lives. Busing sent children from the wrong side of the tracks into our schools; the homeless infested our public spaces; the pervasive presence of graffiti, street hustlers and clusters of glowering teenagers made us anxious. Most of all, high crime rates twisted urban life into a variety of knots.

It took the better part of three decades, but we dealt with those intrusions. Busing is so far in the past that the word has an archaic ring to it. Revitalized vagrancy laws and shelters took most homeless off the streets. Most of all, we figured out what to do with criminals. Innovations in policing helped, but the key insight was an old one: lock 'em up.

Why is the underclass no longer an issue? Because what bothered us wasn't that the underclass existed, but that it was in our face. Now it is not. So we can forget about it. "For the time being" is the crucial hedge. What about the long term? Can the United States retain its political and social culture in the presence of a permanent underclass? The answer is certainly yes, if an underclass is sufficiently small. As long as it is only a fragment, the disorganization and violence of its culture do not spill over into the mainstream. The answer is certainly no if the underclass is sufficiently large. Trying to decide where the American underclass stands on that continuum raises two questions without clear answers.

First, how much has the culture of the underclass already spilled over into the mainstream? So far, the American underclass has been predominantly urban and black. Urban black culture has been spilling over into mainstream American culture for more than a century now, to America's great advantage. But during the past three decades it has increasingly been infiltrated by an underclass subculture that celebrates a bastardized social code—predatory sex and "getting paid." The violence and misogyny that pervade certain forms of popular music reflect these values. So does the hooker look in fashion, and the flaunting of obscenity and vulgarity in comedy.

Perhaps most disturbing is the widening expression, often approving, of underclass ethics: Take what you want. Respond violently to anyone who antagonizes you. Despise courtesy as weakness. Take pride in cheating (stealing, lying, exploiting) successfully. I do not know how to measure how broadly such principles have spread, but it's hard to deny that they are more openly espoused in television, films and recordings than they used to be. Among the many complicated explanations for this deterioration in culture, cultural spill-over from the underclass is implicated.

Implicated—that's all. There are many culprits behind the coarsening of American life. It should also go without saying that vulgarity, violence and the rest were part of mainstream America before the underclass came along. But these things always used to be universally condemned in public discourse. Now they are not. It is not just that America has been defining deviancy down, slackening old moral codes. Inner-city street life has provided an alternative code and it is attracting converts.

The converts are mainly adolescents, which makes sense. The street ethics of the underclass subculture are not "black." They are the ethics of male adolescents who haven't been taught any better. For that matter, the problem of the underclass itself is, ultimately, a problem of adolescents who haven't been taught any better. There are a lot more white adolescents than black ones, leading to the second question: How fast will the white underclass grow?

National statistics tell us that in the past decade white criminality has not only increased but gotten more violent, that white teenage males are increasingly dropping out of the labor force, and that white illegitimacy has increased rapidly. Anecdotal evidence about changes in white working-class neighborhoods points to increased drug use, worse school performance and a breakdown of neighborhood norms—recalling accounts of black working-class neighborhoods three decades ago. (Systematic documentation of these trends is still lacking.)

Looking ahead, much depends on whether illegitimacy among whites has already reached critical mass—the point at which we can expect accelerated and sustained growth in white crime, labor force dropout and illegitimacy rates. The good news is that the growth in the white illegitimacy ratio has slowed. The bad news is that it stands at 26%-22% for non-Latino whites—which, judging from the black experience in the early 1960s, may be near that point of critical mass. No one knows, of course, whether the subsequent trajectory of events for whites will be the same as it was for blacks, but there is ample cause for worry. European countries with high white illegitimacy ratios offer no comfort. Juvenile crime is increasing rapidly across Europe, along with other indicators of social deterioration in low-income groups.

Jamesian Directions

The most striking aspect of the current situation, and one that makes predictions very dicey, is the degree to which the United States is culturally compartmentalizing itself. America in the 1990s is a place where the local movie theater may play *Sense and Sensibility* next door to *Natural Born Killers*. Brian Lamb (on C-SPAN) is a few channels away from Jerry Springer. Formal balls are in vogue in some circles; mosh pits in others. Name just about any aspect of American life, and a case can be made that the country is going in different directions simultaneously, some of them Jamesian, others Hogarthian.

The Jamesian elements are not confined to a cultured remnant. Broad swaths of American society are becoming more civil and less vulgar, more responsible and less self-indulgent. The good news is truly good, and it extends beyond the statistics. What's more, the bad news may prove manageable. One way to interpret the nation's success in re-establishing public order is that we have learned how to cope with our current underclass. One may then argue that the size of the underclass is stabilizing, meaning that we can keep this up indefinitely. It requires only that we set aside moral considerations and accept that the huge growth of the underclass since 1960 cannot now be reversed.

Welfare reform and the growing school-voucher movement are heartening signs that many are not ready to accept the status quo. But they struggle against a larger movement toward what I have called "custodial democracy," in which the mainstream subsidizes but also walls off the underclass. In effect, custodial democracy takes as its premise that a substantial portion of the population cannot be expected to function as citizens.

At this moment, elated by falling crime rates and shrinking welfare rolls, we haven't had to acknowledge how far we have already traveled on the road to custodial democracy. I assume the next recession will disabuse us. But suppose that our new *modus vivendi* keeps working? We just increase the number of homeless shelters, restore the welfare guarantee, build more prison cells, and life for the rest of us goes on, pleasantly. At some point we will be unable to avoid recognizing that custodial democracy has arrived. This will mark a fundamental change in how we conceive of America. Will anyone mind?

Capitalism, the Market, the "Underclass," and the Future

Ishare Charles Murray's concern that there is bad news lurking in the shadows of what seems to be unalloyed prosperity in millennial America. I share his concerns about urban crime, employment, the fragility of the family, and the coarseness of the culture. But I am also angry. I am angry at the resolute refusal of conservatives like Murray, William Bennett, and James Q. Wilson to face squarely what their colleague Pat Buchanan is willing to face, when he writes:

> Reaganism and its twin sister, Thatcherism, create fortunes among the highly educated, but in the middle and working classes, they generate anxiety, insecurity and disparities.... Tax cuts, the slashing of safety nets and welfare benefits, and global free trade... unleash the powerful engines of capitalism that go on a tear. Factories and businesses open and close with startling speed.... As companies merge, downsize and disappear, the labor force must always be ready to pick up and move on.... The cost is paid in social upheaval and family breakdown.... Deserted factories mean gutted neighborhoods, ghost towns, ravaged communities and regions that go from boom to bust... Conservatism is being confronted with its own contradictions for unbridled capitalism is an awesome destructive force.

Murray's message is that things have not been working nearly as well as we think they have. Crime is down only because we have locked all the hardened criminals away; the tendency to commit crime has not changed. Unemployment is down, but those who remain unemployed are contemptuous of work. Illegitimate births are down, but legitimate births are down even more, as growing numbers of people seem disdainful of marriage. All these signs of moral decay Murray traces to the underclass, and he is especially worried because the middle class seems increasingly to approve of what he calls "underclass ethics." He says that "among the many complicated explanations for this deterioration in culture, cultural spill-over [from the underclass to the rest of us] is implicated."

But Murray also says this: "There are many culprits behind the coarsening of American life. It should also go without saying that vulgarity, violence and the rest were part of mainstream America before the underclass came along.

But these things always used to be universally condemned in public discourse. Now they are not. It is not just that America has been defining deviancy down, slackening old moral codes. Inner-city street life has provided an alternative code and it is attracting converts."

The idea that middle America needs to look at the underclass for examples of coarseness is preposterous. It turns a willful blind eye to what the conservative revolution has brought us. The conservatism that captured America's fancy in the 1980s was actually two distinct conservatisms. It was an *economic* conservatism committed to dismantling the welfare state and turning as many facets of life as possible over to the private sector. And it was a *moral* conservatism committed to strengthening traditional values and the social institutions that foster them. These two conservatisms corresponded to the economic and social agendas that guided the policies of both the Reagan and the Bush administrations. These Presidents and their supporters seemed to share not only the belief that free-market economics and traditional moral values are good, but that they go together.

This has proven to be a serious mistake. The theory and practice of free-market economics have done more to undermine traditional moral values than any other social force. It is not permissive parents, unwed mothers, undisciplined teachers, multicultural curricula, fanatical civil libertarians, feminists, rock musicians, or drug pushers who are the primary sources of the corrosion that moral conservatives are trying to repair. Instead, it is the operation of the market system itself, along with an ideology that justifies the pursuit of economic self-interest as the "American way." And so, I acknowledge that Murray's concerns about the "problem of the underclass" are not being solved by our current prosperity. But I insist that they will never be solved unless we face up squarely to what causes them. And what causes them, I believe, is in large part what is responsible for our current prosperity.

I am not going to argue here that the evils of market capitalism demand that we all gather to storm the barricades and wrest the means of production out of the hands of evil capitalists and turn them over to the state. As everyone says, "the Cold War is over, and we won." State ownership of the means of production is a non-issue. We are all capitalists now. The issues before us really are two. First, what kind of capitalism? Is it the capitalism of Reagan and Thatcher —of unregulated markets and privatization of everything, with government involvement viewed as a cause of waste and inefficiency? Or is it the capitalism of John Maynard Keynes and of Franklin Roosevelt, with significant state regulation of the market and state guarantees of life's necessities? I'm going to argue for the latter—old-fashioned capitalism. The boom we are in the midst of has created perhaps the greatest degree of income inequality in the history of the developed world. What the free market teaches us is that what *anyone* can have not *everyone* can have, often with very painful consequences for the have-nots. And second, if we must live with capitalism, what are we prepared to do to correct the moral corrosion that it brings as a side effect? For in addition to asking what free-market capitalism does *for* people, we must ask what it does *to* people. And I will suggest that it turns people into nasty, self-absorbed, self-interested competitors—that it demands this of people, and celebrates it.

The Market and Inequality

One would think that if the problem is the underclass, the solution—or a solution—is to reduce its numbers. What do we know about the great economic
"boom" we are living in the midst of? The income of the average wage-earning
worker in 1997 was 3.1% lower than it was in 1989. Median family income was
$1000 less in 1997 than in 1989. The typical couple worked 250 more hours
in 1997 than in 1989. So to the extent that average people have been able to
hold their own at all, it is because they worked harder. The median wage of
high school graduates fell 6% between 1980 and 1996 while the median wage of
college graduates rose 12%.

And this picture looks worse if you include benefits. Benefits used to be
the "great equalizer," distributed equally among employees despite huge dis-
parities in salary. For example, the $20,000/year employee and the $500,000/
year employee got the same $4000 medical insurance. But despite IRS efforts
to prevent differential benefits based on income (by making such benefits tax-
able), employers have invented all kinds of tricks. They have introduced lengthy
employment "trial periods" with no benefits. They have resorted to hiring temporary workers who get no benefits. The result is that while 80% of workers
received paid vacations and holidays in 1996, less than 10% in the bottom tenth
of the income distribution did. The result is that while 70% of workers have
some sort of employer funded pension, less than 10% of those in the bottom
tenth of the income distribution do. The result is that while 90% of high wage
employees have health insurance, only 26% of low wage employees do. All told,
about 40 million Americans have no health insurance. The picture looks still
worse if you consider *wealth* rather than income. The richest 1% of Americans
have almost 50% of the nation's wealth. The next 9% have about a third. And
the remaining 90% have about a sixth.

America now has the greatest wealth and income inequality in the developed world, and it is getting bigger every day. Efforts to implement even
modest increases in the minimum wage are met with intense resistance. Further, as pointed out in a recent analysis in the *Left Business Observer,* the United
States has the highest poverty rate of any developed nation, and uses government income transfers to reduce poverty less than any developed nation. Our
two main rivals in these categories are Thatcher's England, and postcommunist,
gangster-capitalist Russia.

Is this massive inequality an accident—an imperfection in an otherwise
wonderful system? I don't think so. Modern capitalism depends on inequality. Modern capitalism is consumer capitalism. People have to buy things. In
1997, $120 billion was spent in the United States on advertising, more than was
spent on all forms of education. Consumer debt, excluding home mortgages, exceeded $1 trillion in 1995—more than $10,000 per household. But people also
need to save, to accumulate money for investment, especially now, in these days
of ferocious global competition. How can you save and spend at the same time?
The answer is that some must spend while others save. Income and wealth inequality allow a few to accumulate, and invest, while most of us spend—even
more than we earn. And this is not an accident, but a structural necessity. There

must be some people who despite society-wide exhortation to spend just cannot spend all they make. These people will provide the capital for investment.

Perhaps this kind of inequality is just the price we pay for prosperity. Concentrating wealth in the hands of the few gives them the opportunity to invest. This investment "trickles down" to improve the lives of all, by improving the products we buy and creating employment opportunities. There is no question that the current political leadership in the U.S.—of both parties—thinks that keeping Wall Street happy is essential to the nation's financial well-being. By encouraging people to buy stocks we put money in the hands of investors who then produce innovation and improvement in economic efficiency. Thus, we reduce capital gains taxes. And we eliminate the deficit to make Wall Street happy, even if it means neglecting the social safety net.

But who gains? It is true that what's good for Wall Street is good for America? On investment, more than 90% of all stock market trades involve just shuffling of paper as shares move from my hands to yours, or vice versa. Almost none of the activity on Wall Street puts capital in the hands of folks who invest in plant and equipment. Similarly, most corporate debt is used to finance mergers and acquisitions, or to buy back stock that later goes to chief executives as performance bonuses.

Why is it that when a company announces major layoffs, its stock goes up? The answer is that layoffs signal higher profits, good news for investors. Why is it that when unemployment rates go down, stock prices go down? The answer is that low unemployment signals potential inflation, bad news for investors. Why is it that banks bailed out a highly speculative hedge fund—for rich folks only—that was able to invest borrowed money (20 times its actual assets) while at the same time lobbying to crack down on personal bankruptcy laws, when the overwhelming majority of those facing personal bankruptcy make less than $20,000/year? The evidence is clear and compelling: the stock market operates to benefit the few at the expense of the many.

So if, as Murray contends (correctly, I think), the underclass is a social problem for America that is not going away, why isn't Murray demanding a set of policies that make it smaller rather than larger. Why isn't he demanding a minimum wage that is a *living* wage, so that parents can *afford* to take care of their children. And in addition, why isn't he demanding high-quality day care, so that the children of single mothers, or of two worker households, won't be neglected. How is that a set of economic policies that has made the underclass bigger glides by free of Murray's wrath, as he chooses to condemn instead the nation's growing enthusiasm for underclass values?

The Market and Morality

... [R]ecent thinkers have realized that we can't take the bourgeois values that support capitalism for granted. Indeed, as Karl Polanyi, in *The Great Transformation,* and Fred Hirsch, in *Social Limits to Growth* argue persuasively, not only can we not take these values for granted, but market capitalism—the very thing that so desperately depends on them—actively undermines them. This, I believe, is the lesson that Murray and his cohort refuses to accept. The so-called "underclass" may threaten the comfort and safety of the middle class, but it is the overclass that threatens the stability and the future prospects of society.

One sees this dramatically in James Q. Wilson's... book *The Moral Sense.* In that book, Wilson argues for a biologically based moral sense in human beings—a sense that almost guarantees such moral traits as sympathy, duty, self-control, and fairness....

Having made the sweeping claim that the market contributes more to the erosion of our moral sense than any other modern social force, I want to defend that claim with some more specific arguments. In particular, I want to discuss the market's negative effects on some of the moral sentiments that Wilson emphasizes and on some of the social institutions that nurture those sentiments.

One of the moral sentiments that is central to Wilson's argument is sympathy, the ability to feel and understand the misfortune of others and the desire to do something to ameliorate that misfortune. Wilson notes correctly that other-regarding sentiments and actions, including sympathy and altruism, are extremely common human phenomena, notwithstanding the efforts of many cynical social scientists to explain them away as subtle forms of self-interested behavior. What the literature on sympathy and altruism have made clear is that they depend on a person's ability to take the perspective of another (to "walk a mile in her shoes"). This perspective-taking ability in turn depends on a certain general cognitive sophistication, on familiarity with the other, and on proximity to the other. What does the market do to sympathy? Well, the market thrives on anonymity. One of its great virtues is that buyers are interchangeable with other buyers and sellers with other sellers. All that matters is price and quality and the ability to pay. Increasingly, in the modern market, transactions occur over long distances. Indeed, increasingly, they occur over telephone lines, as "e-commerce" joins the lexicon. Thus, the social institution that dominates modern American society is one that fosters, both in principle and in fact, social relations that are distant and impersonal—social relations that are the antithesis of what sympathy seems to require.

A second moral sentiment that attracts Wilson's attention is fairness. He correctly notes (as any parent will confirm) that concern about fairness appears early in human development and that it runs deep. Even four-year-olds have a powerful, if imperfect conception of what is and is not fair. What does fairness look like in adults?

[Professors] Daniel Kahneman, Jack Knetsch, and Richard Thaler asked this question by posing a variety of hypothetical business transactions to randomly chosen informants and asking the informants to judge whether the transactions were fair. What these hypothetical transactions had in common was that they all involved legal, profit-maximizing actions that were of questionable moral character. What these researchers found is that the overwhelming majority of people have a very strong sense of what is fair. While people believe that business people are entitled to make a profit, they do not think it fair for producers to charge what the market will bear (for example, to price gouge during shortages) or to lower wages during periods of slack employment. In short, most people think that concerns for fairness should be a constraint on profit-seeking. So far, so good; this study clearly supports Wilson's contention that fairness is one of our moral sentiments.

But here's the bad news. Another investigator posed these same hypotheticals to students in a nationally prominent MBA program. The overwhelming majority of these informants thought that anything was fair, as long as it was legal. Maximizing profit was the point; fairness was irrelevant. In another study, these same hypotheticals were posed to a group of CEOs. What the authors of the study concluded was that their executive sample was less inclined than those in the original study to find the actions posed in the survey to be unfair. In addition, often when CEOs did rate actions as unfair, they indicated in unsolicited comments that they did not think the actions were unfair so much as they were unwise, that is, bad business practice....

To summarize, people care about fairness, but if they are participants in the market, or are preparing to be participants in the market, they care much less about fairness than others do. Is it the ideology of relativism that is undermining this moral sentiment or the ideology of the market?

Another of the moral sentiments Wilson discusses is self-control. What does the market do to self-control? As many have pointed out, modern corporate management is hardly a paradigm of self-control. The combination of short-termism and me-first management that have saddled large companies with inefficiency and debt are a cautionary tale on the evils of self-indulgence. Short-termism is in part structural; managers must answer to shareholders, and in the financial markets, you're only as good as your last quarter. Me-first management seems to be pure greed. Some of the excesses of modern executive compensation have recently been documented by Derek Bok, in his book *The Cost of Talent.* Further, *The Economist,* in a survey of pay published in May of 1999, makes it quite clear that the pay scale of American executives is in another universe from that in any other nation, and heavily loaded with stock options that reward the executive for the company's performance in the stock market rather than the actual markets in goods and services in which the company operates....

The final moral sentiment that Wilson identifies and discusses is duty, "a disposition to honor obligations even without hope of reward or fear of punishment." Wilson is quite right about the importance of duty. If we must rely on threat of punishment to enforce obligations, they become unenforceable. Punishment works only as long as most people will do the right thing most of the time even if they can get away with transgressing....

The enemy of duty is free-riding, taking cost-free advantage of the dutiful actions of others. The more people are willing to be free-riders, the higher the cost to those who remain dutiful, and the higher the cost of enforcement to society as a whole. How does the market affect duty and free-riding? Well, one of the studies of fairness I mentioned above included a report of an investigation of free-riding. Economics students are more likely to be free riders than students in other disciplines. And this should come as no surprise. Free-riding is the "rational, self-interested" thing to do. Indeed, if you are the head of a company, free-riding may even be your fiduciary responsibility. So if free-riding is the enemy of duty, then the market is the enemy of duty.

... In my view, this is what market activity does to all the virtues that Wilson, and Murray long for—it submerges them with calculations of personal preference and self-interest.

If Wilson fails to acknowledge the influence of the market on our moral sense, where then does he look? As I said earlier, he thinks a good deal of human morality reflects innate predisposition. But that disposition must be nurtured, and it is nurtured, according to Wilson, in the family, by what might be described as "constrained socialization." The child is not a miniature adult (socialization is required), but nor is she a blank slate (not anything is possible; there are predispositions on the part of both parents and children for socialization to take one of a few "canonical" forms.) One of the primary mechanisms through which socialization occurs is imitation: "There can be little doubt that we learn a lot about how we ought to behave from watching others, especially others to whom we are strongly attached. . . .

So let us accept Wilson's position about socialization and ask what the adults who the young child will be imitating look like. I believe, following the work of [economist] Fred Hirsch, that in the last few decades there has been an enormous upsurge in what might be called the "commercialization of social relations"—that choice has replaced duty and utility maximization replaced fairness in relations among family members. . . .

Wilson seems mindful of all this. He decries the modern emphasis on rights and the neglect of duty. He acknowledges that modern society has posed a real challenge to the family by substituting labor markets for householding. And he deplores the ideology of choice as applied to the family:

> Not even the family has been immune to the ideology of choice. In the 1960s and 1970s (but less so today) books were written advocating "alternative" families and "open" marriages. A couple could choose to have a trial marriage, a regular marriage but without an obligation to sexual fidelity, or a revocable marriage with an easy exit provided by no-fault divorce. A woman could choose to have a child out of wedlock and to raise it alone. Marriage was but one of several "options" by which men and women could manage their intimate needs, an option that ought to be carefully negotiated in order to preserve the rights of each contracting party. The family, in this view, was no longer the cornerstone of human life, it was one of several "relationships" from which individuals could choose so as to maximize their personal goals.

But instead of attributing this ideology of choice to the market, from which I think it clearly arises, Wilson attributes it to the weakening of cultural standards—to relativism. Indeed he even adopts a Becker-like economic analysis of the family himself, apparently unaware that if people actually thought about their families in the way that he and [economist Gary] Becker claim they do, the family would hardly be a source of any of the moral sentiments that are important to him:

> But powerful as they are, the expression of these [familial] instincts has been modified by contemporary circumstances. When children have less economic value, then, at the margin, fewer children will be produced, marriage (and childbearing) will be postponed, and more marriages will end in

divorce. And those children who are produced will be raised, at the margin, in ways that reflect their higher opportunity cost. Some will be neglected and others will be cared for in ways that minimize the parental cost in personal freedom, extra income, or career opportunities.

Let me be clear that I think Wilson is right about changes that have occurred in the family, and that he is also right about the unfortunate social consequences of those changes. His mistake is in failing to see the responsibility for these changes that must be borne by the spread of market thinking into the domain of our intimate social relations. As I have said elsewhere, there is an opportunity cost to thinking about one's social relations in terms of opportunity costs. In Wilson's terms, that opportunity cost will be paid in sympathy, fairness, and duty. Sociologist Arlie Hochschild has written that "each marriage bears the footprints of economic and cultural trends which originate far outside marriage." Wilson has emphasized the cultural and overlooked the economic. And so, alas, has Murray.

What Economies Do to People

In Arthur Miller's play, *All My Sons*, much of the drama centers around the belated discovery by a son that his father knowingly shipped defective airplane parts to fulfill a government contract during World War II. The parts were installed, some of the planes crashed, and pilots and their crews were killed. The man responsible, the father, is a good man, a kind man, a man who cares deeply about his family and would do anything to protect them and provide for them. His son simply can't imagine that a man like his father is capable of such an act—but he is. As he explains, he was under enormous pressure to deliver the goods. The military needed the parts right away, and failure to deliver would have destroyed his business. He had a responsibility to take care of his family. And anyway, there was no certainty that the parts would not hold up when in use. As the truth slowly comes out, the audience has the same incredulity as the son. How could it be? If a man like that could do a thing like that, then anyone is capable of doing anything.

This, of course, is one of the play's major points. Almost anyone *is* capable of almost anything. A monstrous system can make a monster of anyone, or perhaps more accurately, can make almost anyone do monstrous things. We see this as drama like Miller's are played out in real life, with horrifyingly tragic consequences.

- All too close to the story of *All My Sons*, military contractors have been caught knowingly making and selling defective brake systems for U.S. jet fighters, defective machine gun parts that cause the guns to jam when used, and defective fire-fighting equipment for navy ships.
- An automobile manufacturer knowingly made and sold a dangerous car, whose gas tank was alarmingly likely to explode in rear end collisions. This defect could have been corrected at a cost of a few dollars per car.

- A chemical company continued operating a chemical plant in Bhopal, India long after it knew the plant was unsafe. A gas leak killed more than 2000 people, and seriously injured more than 30,000. The $5 billion company responded to this tragedy by sending $1 million in disaster relief and a shipment of medicines sufficient for about 400 people.
- Other drug and chemical manufacturers make and sell to the Third World products known to be sufficiently dangerous that their sale is banned in the U.S.
- The asbestos industry knowingly concealed the hazardous nature of their products for years from workers who were exposed to carcinogens on a daily basis.
- Trucking companies put trucks on the road more than 30% of which would fail safety inspections and are thus hazards to their drivers as well as to other motorists.
- And of course, we all know now about the tobacco industry.

And it isn't just about dramatic death and destruction. The death and destruction can be slow and torturous:

- Firms get closed down, people put out of work, and communities destroyed, not because they aren't profitable, but because they aren't *as* profitable as other parts of the business.
- People are put to work in illegal sweatshops, or the work is sent offshore, where the working conditions are even worse, but not illegal.

Why does all this abuse occur? What makes people seek to exploit every advantage over their customers? What makes bosses abuse their employees? Do the people who do these things take pleasure from hurting their unsuspecting customers? Do they relish the opportunity to take advantage of people? It does not seem so. When bosses are challenged about their unscrupulous practices, they typically argue that "everybody does it." Understand, the argument is not that since everybody does it, it is all right. The argument is that since everybody does it, you have to do it also, in self-defense. In competitive situations, it seems inevitable that dishonest, inhumane practices will drive out the honest and humane ones; to be humane becomes a luxury that few business people can afford.

I find it unimaginable as I talk to the talented, ambitious, enthusiastic students with whom I work that any of them aspires to a future in which he or she will oversee the production of cars, drugs, chemicals, foods, military supplies, or anything else that will imperil the lives of thousands of people. I even find it unimaginable that any of them will accept such a future. They are good, decent people, as far removed from those who seek to turn human weakness and vulnerability into profit as anyone could be. And yet, I know that some of my former students already have, and some of my current students surely will accept such positions. They will also marry, have families, and raise wonderful children who won't believe their parents could ever do such things.

Surely there is an urgent need to figure out what it is that makes good people do such bad things, and stop it.

The leaders of corporations tell themselves that they have only one mission—to do whatever they can to further the interests of the shareholders, the owners of the company that these leaders have been hired to manage. When the leaders of corporations say these things to themselves, they are telling themselves the truth. They work within a system that asks—even requires—them to be single-minded, no matter how much they wish they could be different. As long as the system has this character, we can expect that only the single-minded will rise to the top. Only rarely will people whose intentions are to change corporate practices go far enough to implement those intentions.

Several years ago United States Catholic Bishops drafted a position paper, a pastoral letter, on the economy. In it they said, "every perspective on economic life that is human, moral, and Christian must be shaped by two questions: What does the economy do *for* people? What does the economy do *to* people?" I have been suggesting that our economy does terrible things *to* people, even to those people who succeed. It makes them into people that they should not and do not want to be, and it encourages them to do things that they should not and do not want to do. No matter what an economy does *for* these people, it cannot be justified if it does these things *to* them. And it seems to me that in the face of massive, antisocial practices like these, blaming the underclass for teaching mainstream America the lessons of incivility is perverse.

POSTSCRIPT

Is the Underclass the Major Threat to American Ideals?

In *Reducing Poverty in America* edited by Michael R. Darby (Sage Publications, 1996), James Q. Wilson summarizes the debate on the causes of poverty as the clash between two views: "The first is incentives or objective factors: jobs, incomes, opportunities. The second is culture: single-parent families, out-of-wedlock births, and a decaying work ethic." Sociologists expect the structural versus individual explanations of poverty to be debated for a long time because both can be seen as at least partially true. The cultural explanation derives from the anthropological studies of Oscar Lewis and was proposed as a major cause of urban poverty in America by Edward Banfield in *The Unheavenly City* (Little, Brown, 1970). Today, the most vigorous proponent of the culture-of-poverty thesis today is Lawrence E. Harrison, who wrote *Who Prospers? How Cultural Values Shape Economic and Political Success* (Basic Books, 1992). In *The Dream and the Nightmare: The Sixties' Legacy to the Underclass* (William Morrow, 1993), Myron Magnet blames the culture of the underclass for their poverty, but he also blames the upper classes for contributing greatly to the underclass's culture. Charles Murray, in *Losing Ground* (Basic Books, 1984), provides empirical support for the idea that welfare is a cause of poverty and not its solution, and concludes that welfare should be abolished.

The counter to the cultural explanation of poverty is the structural explanation. Its most current version focuses on the loss of unskilled jobs. This is the thrust of William Julius Wilson's analysis of the macroeconomic forces that impact so heavily on the urban poor in *The Truly Disadvantaged* (University of Chicago Press, 1987) and in *When Work Disappears: The World of the New Urban Poor* (Alfred A. Knopf, 1996). If Jeremy Rifkin's analysis in *The End of Work: The Decline of the Global Labor Force and the Dawn of the Post-Market Era* (Putnam, 1995) is correct, then this situation will get worse, not better, because new technologies will lengthen unemployment lines unless the economy or the working world is radically restructured. For a similar view, see Stanley Aronowitz and William DiFazio, *The Jobless Future: Sci-Tech and the Dogma of Work* (University of Minnesota Press, 1994).

There are countless works that describe the adverse conditions of the poor. The nineteenth-century English novelist Charles Dickens was a crusader for the poor, and many of his novels, still in print and certainly considered classics, graphically depict the wretchedness of poverty. Michael Harrington described poverty in America in his influential nonfiction book *The Other America* (Macmillan, 1963) at a time when a substantial portion of the country was affluent.

ISSUE 9

Has Affirmative Action Outlived
Its Usefulness?

YES: Walter E. Williams, from "Affirmative Action Can't Be Mended," *Cato Journal* (Spring/Summer 1997)

NO: Wilbert Jenkins, from "Why We Must Retain Affirmative Action," *USA Today Magazine* (September 1999)

ISSUE SUMMARY

YES: Professor of economics Walter E. Williams asserts that "the civil rights struggle for blacks is over and won," so affirmative action policies are unjust and adversely affect society.

NO: History professor Wilbert Jenkins dismisses the arguments against affirmative action as founded on the false logic that since the promised land has been reached, continuing affirmative action would be reverse discrimination. Jenkins maintains that an honest look at the facts reveals that affirmative action is still needed.

In America, equality is a principle as basic as liberty. "All men are created equal" is perhaps the most well known phrase in the Declaration of Independence. More than half a century after the signing of the Declaration, the French social philosopher Alexis de Tocqueville examined democracy in America and concluded that its most essential ingredient was the equality of condition. Today we know that the "equality of condition" that Tocqueville perceived did not exist for women, blacks, Native Americans, and other racial minorities, nor for other disadvantaged social classes. Nevertheless, the ideal persisted.

When slavery was abolished after the Civil War, the Constitution's newly ratified Fourteenth Amendment proclaimed, "No State shall ... deny to any person within its jurisdiction the equal protection of the laws." Equality has been a long time coming. For nearly a century after the abolition of slavery, American blacks were denied equal protection by law in some states and by social practice nearly everywhere. One-third of the states either permitted or forced schools to become racially segregated, and segregation was achieved elsewhere through housing policy and social behavior. In 1954 the Supreme Court reversed a 58-year-old standard that had found "separate but equal" schools compatible with equal protection of the law. A unanimous decision in *Brown v. Board of Education* held that separate is *not* equal for the members of the discriminated-against group when the segregation "generates a feeling of inferiority as to their status in the community that may affect their hearts and minds in a way unlikely ever to be undone." The 1954 ruling on public elementary education has been extended to other areas of both governmental and private conduct, including housing and employment.

Even if judicial decisions and congressional statutes could end all segregation and racial discrimination, would this achieve equality—or simply perpetuate the status quo? Consider that the unemployment rate for blacks today is more than twice that of whites. Disproportionately higher numbers of blacks experience poverty, brutality, broken homes, physical and mental illness, and early deaths, while disproportionately lower numbers of them reach positions of affluence and prestige. It seems possible that much of this inequality has resulted from 300 years of slavery and segregation. Is termination of this ill treatment enough to end the injustices? No, say the proponents of affirmative action.

Affirmative action—the effort to improve the educational and employment opportunities for minorities—has had an uneven history in U.S. federal courts. In *Regents of the University of California v. Allan Bakke* (1978), which marked the first time the Supreme Court dealt directly with the merits of affirmative action, a 5–4 majority ruled that a white applicant to a medical school had been wrongly excluded in favor of a less qualified black applicant due to the school's affirmative action policy. Yet the majority also agreed that "race-conscious" policies may be used in admitting candidates—as long as they do not amount to fixed quotas. The ambivalence of *Bakke* has run through the Court's treatment of the issue since 1978. More recent decisions suggest that the Court is beginning to take a dim view of affirmative action. In 1989, for example, the Court ruled that a city council could *not* set aside a fixed percentage of public construction projects for minority contractors.

Affirmative action is hotly debated outside the courts, and white males have recently been vocal on talk shows and in print about being treated unjustly because of affirmative action policies. In the following selections, Walter E. Williams and Wilbert Jenkins debate the merits of affirmative action. In Williams's view, affirmative action has outlived its usefulness, and the government should follow a policy of strict race neutrality. Jenkins, on the other hand, considers affirmative action an essential means for bringing about the equality that both sides ostensibly want.

Walter E. Williams
 **YES**

Affirmative Action Can't Be Mended

For the last several decades, affirmative action has been the basic component of the civil rights agenda. But affirmative action, in the form of racial
preferences, has worn out its political welcome. In Gallup Polls, between 1987
and 1990, people were asked if they agreed with the statement: "We should
make every effort to improve the position of blacks and other minorities even
if it means giving them preferential treatment." More than 70 percent of the
respondents opposed preferential treatment while only 24 percent supported
it. Among blacks, 66 percent opposed preferential treatment and 32 percent
supported it (Lipset 1992: 66–69).

The rejection of racial preferences by the broad public and increasingly
by the Supreme Court has been partially recognized by even supporters of affirmative action. While they have not forsaken their goals, they have begun
to distance themselves from some of the language of affirmative action. Thus,
many business, government, and university affirmative action offices have been
renamed "equity offices." Racial preferences are increasingly referred to as "diversity multiculturalism." What is it about affirmative action that gives rise to
its contentiousness?

For the most part, post–World War II America has supported civil rights
for blacks. Indeed, if we stick to the uncorrupted concept of civil rights, we
can safely say that the civil rights struggle for blacks is over and won. Civil
rights properly refer to rights, held simultaneously among individuals, to be
treated equally in the eyes of the law, make contracts, sue and be sued, give
evidence, associate and travel freely, and vote. There was a time when blacks
did not fully enjoy those rights. With the yeoman-like work of civil rights organizations and decent Americans, both black and white, who fought lengthy
court, legislative, and street battles, civil rights have been successfully secured
for blacks. No small part of that success was due to a morally compelling appeal to America's civil libertarian tradition of private property, rule of law, and
limited government.

Today's corrupted vision of civil rights attacks that civil libertarian tradition. Principles of private property rights, rule of law, freedom of association,
and limited government are greeted with contempt. As such, the agenda of
today's civil rights organizations conceptually differs little from yesteryear's

From Walter E. Williams, "Affirmative Action Can't Be Mended," *Cato Journal,* vol. 17, no. 1 (Spring/
Summer 1997). Copyright © 1997 by The Cato Institute. Reprinted by permission. Notes and some
references omitted.

restrictions that were the targets of the earlier civil rights struggle. Yesteryear civil rights organizations fought *against* the use of race in hiring, access to public schools, and university admissions. Today, civil rights organizations fight *for* the use of race in hiring, access to public schools, and university admissions. Yesteryear, civil rights organizations fought *against* restricted association in the forms of racially segregated schools, libraries, and private organizations. Today, they fight *for* restricted associations. They use state power, not unlike the racists they fought, to enforce racial associations they deem desirable. They protest that blacks should be a certain percentage of a company's workforce or clientele, a certain percentage of a student body, and even a certain percentage of an advertiser's models.

Civil rights organizations, in their successful struggle against state-sanctioned segregation, have lost sight of what it means to be truly committed to liberty, especially the freedom of association. The true test of that commitment does not come when we allow people to be free to associate in ways we deem appropriate. The true test is when we allow people to form those voluntary associations we deem offensive. It is the same principle we apply to our commitment to free speech. What tests our commitment to free speech is our willingness to permit people the freedom to say things we find offensive.

Zero-Sum Games

The tragedy of America's civil rights movement is that it has substituted today's government-backed racial favoritism in the allocation of resources for yesterday's legal and extra-legal racial favoritism. In doing so, civil rights leaders fail to realize that government allocation of resources produces the kind of conflict that does not arise with market allocation of resources. Part of the reason is that any government allocation of resources, including racial preferential treatment, is a zero-sum game.

A zero-sum game is defined as any transaction where one person's gain necessarily results in another person's loss. The simplest example of a zero-sum game is poker. A winner's gain is matched precisely by the losses of one or more persons. In this respect, the only essential difference between affirmative action and poker is that in poker participation is voluntary. Another difference is the loser is readily identifiable, a point to which I will return later.

The University of California, Berkeley's affirmative action program for blacks captures the essence of a zero-sum game. Blacks are admitted with considerably lower average SAT scores (952) than the typical white (1232) and Asian student (1254) (Sowell 1993: 144). Between UCLA and UC Berkeley, more than 2,000 white and Asian straight A students are turned away in order to provide spaces for black and Hispanic students (Lynch 1989: 163). The admissions gains by blacks are exactly matched by admissions losses by white and Asian students. Thus, any preferential treatment program results in a zero-sum game almost by definition.

More generally, government allocation of resources is a zero-sum game primarily because government has no resources of its very own. When government gives some citizens food stamps, crop subsidies, or disaster relief payments, the recipients of the largesse gain. Losers are identified by asking: where does government acquire the resources to confer the largesse? In order for government to give to some citizens, it must through intimidation, threats, and coercion take from other citizens. Those who lose the rights to their earnings, to finance government largesse, are the losers.

Government-mandated racial preferential treatment programs produce a similar result. When government creates a special advantage for one ethnic group, it necessarily comes at the expense of other ethnic groups for whom government simultaneously creates a special disadvantage in the form of reduced alternatives. If a college or employer has X amount of positions, and R of them have been set aside for blacks or some other group, that necessarily means there are $(X - R)$ fewer positions for which other ethnic groups might compete. At a time when there were restrictions against blacks, that operated in favor of whites, those restrictions translated into a reduced opportunity set for blacks. It is a zero-sum game independent of the race or ethnicity of the winners and losers.

Our courts have a blind-sided vision of the zero-sum game. They have upheld discriminatory racial preferences in hiring but have resisted discriminatory racial preferences in job layoffs. An example is the U.S. Supreme Court's ruling in *Wygant v. Jackson Board of Education* (1986), where a teacher union's collective-bargaining agreement protected black teachers from job layoffs in order to maintain racial balance. Subsequently, as a result of that agreement, the Jackson County School Board laid off white teachers having greater seniority while black teachers with less seniority were retained.

A lower court upheld the constitutionality of the collective bargaining agreement by finding that racial preferences in layoffs were a permissible means to remedy societal discrimination (*Wygant* 1982: 1195, 1201). White teachers petitioned the U.S. Supreme Court, claiming their constitutional rights under the Equal Protection clause were violated. The Court found in their favor. Justice Lewis F. Powell delivered the opinion saying, "While hiring goals impose a diffuse burden, only closing one of several opportunities, layoffs impose the entire burden of achieving racial equity on particular individuals, often resulting in serious disruption of their lives. The burden is too intrusive" (*Wygant* 1986: 283)....

There is no conceptual distinction in the outcome of the zero-sum game whether it is played on the layoff or the hiring side of the labor market.... The diffuseness to which Justice Powell refers is not diffuseness at all. It is simply that the victims of hiring preferences are less visible than victims of layoff preferences as in the case of *Wygant*. The petitioners in *Wygant* were identifiable people who could not be covered up as "society." That differs from the cases of hiring and college admissions racial preferences where those who face a reduced opportunity set tend to be unidentifiable to the courts, other people, and even to themselves. Since they are invisible victims, the Supreme Court and others can blithely say racial hiring goals (and admission goals) impose a diffuse burden.

Tentative Victim Identification

In California, voters passed the California Civil Rights Initiative of 1996 (CCRI) that says: "The state shall not discriminate against, or grant preferential treatment to, any individual or group on the basis of race, sex, color, ethnicity, or national origin in the operation of public employment, public education, or public contracting." Therefore, California public universities can no longer have preferential admission policies that include race as a factor in deciding whom to admit. As a result, the UCLA School of Law reported accepting only 21 black applicants for its fall 1997 class—a drop of 80 percent from the previous year, in which 108 black applicants were accepted. At the UC Berkeley Boalt Hall School of Law, only 14 of the 792 students accepted for the fall 1997 class are black, down from 76 the previous year. At the UCLA School of Law, white enrollment increased by 14 percent for the fall 1997 term and Asian enrollment rose by 7 percent. At UC Berkeley, enrollment of white law students increased by 12 percent and Asian law students increased by 18 percent (Weiss 1997)....

In the case of UC Berkeley's preferential admissions for blacks, those whites and Asians who have significantly higher SAT scores and grades than the admitted blacks are victims of reverse discrimination. However, in the eyes of the courts, others, and possibly themselves, they are invisible victims. In other words, no one can tell for sure who among those turned away would have gained entry to UC Berkeley were it not for the preferential treatment given to blacks....

Affirmative Action and Supply

An important focus of affirmative action is statistical underrepresentation of different racial and ethnic groups on college and university campuses. If the percentages of blacks and Mexican-Americans, for example, are not at a level deemed appropriate by a court, administrative agency, or university administrator, racial preference programs are instituted. The inference made from the underrepresentation argument is that, in the absence of racial discrimination, groups would be represented on college campuses in proportion to their numbers in the relevant population. In making that argument, little attention is paid to the supply issue—that is, to the pool of students available that meet the standards or qualifications of the university in question.

In 1985, fewer than 1,032 blacks scored 600 and above on the verbal portion of the SAT and 1,907 scored 600 and above on the quantitative portion of the examination. There are roughly 58 elite colleges and universities with student body average composite SAT scores of 1200 and above (Sowell 1993: 142). If blacks scoring 600 or higher on the quantitative portion of the SAT (assuming their performance on the verbal portion of the examination gave them a composite SAT score of 1200 or higher) were recruited to elite colleges and universities, there would be less than 33 black students available per university. At none of those universities would blacks be represented according to their numbers in the population.

There is no evidence that suggests that university admissions offices practice racial discrimination by turning away blacks with SAT scores of 1200 or higher. In reality, there are not enough blacks to be admitted to leading colleges and universities on the same terms as other students, such that their numbers in the campus population bear any resemblance to their numbers in the general population.

Attempts by affirmative action programs to increase the percent of blacks admitted to top schools, regardless of whether blacks match the academic characteristics of the general student body, often produce disastrous results. In order to meet affirmative action guidelines, leading colleges and universities recruit and admit black students whose academic qualifications are well below the norm for other students. For example, of the 317 black students admitted to UC Berkeley in 1985, all were admitted under affirmative action criteria rather than academic qualifications. Those students had an average SAT score of 952 compared to the national average of 900 among all students. However, their SAT scores were well below UC Berkeley's average of nearly 1200. More than 70 percent of the black students failed to graduate from UC Berkeley (Sowell 1993: 144).

Not far from UC Berkeley is San Jose State University, not one of the top-tier colleges, but nonetheless respectable. More than 70 percent of its black students fail to graduate. The black students who might have been successful at San Jose State University have been recruited to UC Berkeley and elsewhere where they have been made artificial failures. This pattern is one of the consequences of trying to use racial preferences to make a student body reflect the relative importance of different ethnic groups in the general population. There is a mismatch between black student qualifications and those of other students when the wrong students are recruited to the wrong universities.

There is no question that preferential admissions is unjust to both white and Asian students who may be qualified but are turned away to make room for less-qualified students in the "right" ethnic group. However, viewed from a solely black self-interest point of view, the question should be asked whether such affirmative action programs serve the best interests of blacks. Is there such an abundance of black students who score above the national average on the SAT, such as those admitted to UC Berkeley, that blacks as a group can afford to have those students turned into artificial failures in the name of diversity, multiculturalism, or racial justice? The affirmative action debate needs to go beyond simply an issue of whether blacks are benefited at the expense of whites. Whites and Asians who are turned away to accommodate blacks are still better off than the blacks who were admitted. After all, graduating from the university of one's second choice is preferable to flunking out of the university of one's first choice.

To the extent racial preferences in admission produce an academic mismatch of students, the critics of California's Proposition 209 may be unnecessarily alarmed, assuming their concern is with black students actually graduating from college. If black students, who score 952 on the SAT, are not admitted to UC Berkeley, that does not mean that they cannot gain admittance to one of America's 3,000 other colleges. It means that they will gain admittance to some other college where their academic characteristics will be more similar to those of their peers. There will not be as much of an academic mismatch. To the extent this is true, we may see an *increase* in black graduation rates. Moreover, if black students find themselves more similar to their white peers in terms of college grades and graduation honors, they are less likely to feel academically isolated and harbor feelings of low self-esteem.

Affirmative Action and Justice

Aside from any other question, we might ask what case can be made for the morality or justice of turning away more highly credentialed white and Asian students so as to be able to admit more blacks? Clearly, blacks as a group have suffered past injustices, including discrimination in college and university admissions. However, that fact does not spontaneously yield sensible policy proposals for today. The fact is that a special privilege cannot be created for one person without creating a special disadvantage for another. In the case of preferential admissions at UCLA and UC Berkeley, a special privilege for black students translates into a special disadvantage for white and Asian students. Thus, we must ask what have those individual white and Asian students done to deserve punishment? Were they at all responsible for the injustices, either in the past or present, suffered by blacks? If, as so often is the case, the justification for preferential treatment is to redress past grievances, how just is it to have a policy where a black of today is helped by punishing a white of today for what a white of yesterday did to a black of yesterday? Such an idea becomes even more questionable in light of the fact that so many whites and Asians cannot trace the American part of their ancestry back as much as two or three generations.

Affirmative Action and Racial Resentment

In addition to the injustices that are a result of preferential treatment, such treatment has given rise to racial resentment where it otherwise might not exist. While few people support racial resentment and its manifestations, if one sees some of affirmative action's flagrant attacks on fairness and equality before the law, one can readily understand why resentment is on the rise.

In the summer of 1995, the Federal Aviation Administration (FAA) published a "diversity handbook" that said, "The merit promotion process is but one means of filling vacancies, which need not be utilized if it will not promote your diversity goals." In that spirit, one FAA job announcement said, "Applicants who meet the qualification requirements ... cannot be considered for this position.... Only those applicants who do not meet the Office of Personnel Management requirements ... will be eligible to compete" (Roberts and Stratton 1995: 141).

According to a General Accounting Office report that evaluated complaints of discrimination by Asian-Americans, prestigious universities such as UCLA, UC Berkeley, MIT, and the University of Wisconsin have engaged in systematic discrimination in the failure to admit highly qualified Asian students in order to admit relatively unqualified black and Hispanic students (U.S. GAO 1995).

In Memphis, Tennessee, a white police officer ranked 59th out of 209 applicants for 75 available positions as police sergeant, but he did not get promoted. Black officers, with lower overall test scores than he, were moved ahead of him and promoted to sergeant. Over a two-year period, 43 candidates with lower scores were moved ahead of him and made sergeant (Eastland 1996: 1–2).

There is little need to recite the litany of racial preference instances that are clear violations of commonly agreed upon standards of justice and fair play. But the dangers of racial preferences go beyond matters of justice and fair play. They lead to increased group polarization ranging from political backlash to mob violence and civil war as seen in other countries. The difference between the United States and those countries is that racial preferences have not produced the same level of violence (Sowell 1990). However, they have produced polarization and resentment.

Affirmative action proponents cling to the notion that racial discrimination satisfactorily explains black/white socioeconomic differences. While every vestige of racial discrimination has not been eliminated in our society, current social discrimination cannot begin to explain all that affirmative action proponents purport it explains. Rather than focusing our attention on discrimination, a higher payoff can be realized by focusing on real factors such as fraudulent education, family disintegration, and hostile economic climates in black neighborhoods. Even if affirmative action was not a violation of justice and fair play, was not a zero-sum game, was not racially polarizing, it is a poor cover-up for the real work that needs to be done.

References

Eastland, T. (1996) *Ending Affirmative Action: The Case for Colorblind Justice.* New York: Basic Books.

Lipset, S. M. (1992) "Equal Chances Versus Equal Results." In H. Orlans and J. O'Neill (eds.) *Affirmative Action Revisited; Annals of the American Academy of Political and Social Science* 523 (September): 63–74.

Lynch, F. R. (1989) *Invisible Victims: White Males and the Crisis of Affirmative Action.* New York: Greenwood Press.

Roberts, P. C., and Stratton, L. M. (1995) *The Color Line: How Quotas and Privilege Destroy Democracy.* Washington, D.C.: Regnery.

Sowell, T. (1990) *Preferential Policies: An International Perspective.* New York: William Morrow.

Sowell, T. (1993) *Inside American Education: The Decline, The Deception, The Dogmas.* New York: The Free Press.

United States General Accounting Office (1995) *Efforts by the Office for Civil Rights to Resolve Asian-American Complaints.* Washington, D.C.: Government Printing Office. (December).

Weiss, K. R. (1997) "UC Law Schools' New Rules Cost Minorities Spots." *Los Angeles Times,* 15 May.

Wygant v. Jackson Board of Education (1982) 546 F. Supp. 1195.

Wygant v. Jackson Board of Education (1986) 476 U.S. 267.

NO

Wilbert Jenkins

Why We Must Retain Affirmative Action

The historical origins of affirmative action can be found in the 14th and 15th Amendments to the Constitution, the Enforcement Acts of 1870 and 1871, and the Civil Rights Acts of 1866 and 1875, which were passed by Republican-dominated Congresses during the Reconstruction period. This legislation set the precedent for many of the civil rights laws of the 1950s and 1960s—such as the Civil Rights Act of 1957, the Civil Rights Act of 1964, and the Voting Rights Act of 1965—and paved the way for what would become known as affirmative action.

In spite of the fact that laws designed to promote and protect the civil and political rights of African-Americans were enacted by Congress in the 1950s and 1960s, it was obvious that racism and discrimination against blacks in the area of education and, by extension, the workplace were huge obstacles that needed to be overcome if African-Americans were ever going to be able to carve an economic foundation. Thus, in the 1960s, affirmative action became a part of a larger design by Pres. Lyndon Johnson's War on Poverty program. In a historic 1965 speech at Howard University, the nation's top black school, Johnson illustrated the thinking that led to affirmative action: "You do not take a person who for years has been hobbled by chains and liberate him, bring him to the starting line and say you are free to compete with all the others." Civil rights leader Martin Luther King, Jr., also underscored this belief when he stated that "one cannot ask people who don't have boots to pull themselves up by their own bootstraps."

Policymakers fervently believed that more than three centuries of enslavement, oppression, and discrimination had so economically deprived African-Americans that some mechanism had to be put in place that would at least allow them a fighting chance. Blacks were locked out of the highest paid positions and made considerably fewer dollars than their white counterparts in the same jobs. Moreover, the number of African-Americans enrolling in the nation's undergraduate and graduate schools was extremely low. Affirmative action became a vehicle to correct this injustice. The original intent of affirmative action was not to provide jobs and other advantages to blacks solely because of the color of their skin, but to provide economic opportunities for those who are competent and qualified. Due to a history of discrimination, even those with outstanding credentials were often locked out. As the years wore on, it was deemed necessary to add other minorities—such as Native Americans, Hispanics, and Asian-Americans—as well as women to the list of those requiring affirmative action in order to achieve a measure of economic justice.

A number of conservatives—black and white—such as Armstrong Williams, Linda Chavez, Patrick Buchanan, Robert Novak, Ward Connerly, Clarence Thomas, Clint Bolick, Alan Keyes, and others argue that it is time to scrap affirmative action. This is necessary, they maintain, if the country is truly going to become a color-blind society like King envisioned. People would be judged by the content of their character, not by the color of their skin. Many among these conservatives also maintain that affirmative action is destructive to minorities because it is demeaning, saps drive, and leads to the development of a welfare dependency mentality. Minorities often come to believe that something is owed them.

Thus, conservatives argue against race-based admissions requirements to undergraduate and graduate schools, labeling them preferential treatment and an insult to anyone who is the beneficiary of this practice. In their opinion, it is psychologically, emotionally, and personally degrading for individuals to have to go through life realizing they were not admitted to school or given employment because of their credentials, but in order to fill some quota or to satisfy appearances. It is rather ironic, however, that they are so concerned about this apparent harm to black self-esteem, since there is little evidence that those who have been aided by affirmative action policies feel many doubts or misgivings. The vast majority of them believe they are entitled to whatever opportunities they have received—opportunities, in their estimation, which are long overdue because of racism and discrimination. Consequently, America is only providing them with a few economic crumbs which are rightfully theirs.

Although a number of affirmative action critics argue that lowering admissions standards for minorities creates a class of incompetent professionals —if they are somehow fortunate enough to graduate—the facts run counter to their arguments. For instance, a study conducted by Robert C. Davidson and Ernest L. Lewis of affirmative action students admitted to the University of California at Davis Medical School with low grades and test scores concluded that these students became doctors just as qualified as the higher-scoring applicants. The graduation rate of 94% for special-admissions students compared favorably to that of regular-admissions students (98%). Moreover, despite the fact that regular-admissions students were more likely to receive honors or A grades, there was no difference in the rates at which students failed core courses.

Many whites have been the recipients of some form of preferential treatment. For many years, so-called selective colleges have set less-demanding standards for admitting offspring of alumni or the children of the rich and famous. For example, though former Vice Pres. Dan Quayle's grade-point average was minuscule and his score on the LSAT very low, he was admitted to Indiana University's Law School. There is little evidence that Quayle or other recipients of this practice have developed low self-esteem or have felt any remorse for those whose credentials were better, but nonetheless were rejected because less-qualified others took their slots. The following example further underscores this practice. A number of opponents of affirmative action were embarrassed during 1996 in the midst of passage of Proposition 209, which eliminated affirmative action in California, when the *Los Angeles Times* broke a story documenting the fact that many of them and their children had received preferential treatment in acquiring certain jobs and gaining entry to some colleges.

Some opponents of affirmative action go so far as to suggest that it aggravates racial tensions and leads, in essence, to an increase in violence between whites and people of color. This simply does not mesh with historical reality. Discrimination against and violence toward the powerless always has increased during periods of economic downturns, as witnessed by the depressions of 1873 and 1893. There was nothing akin to affirmative action in this country for nearly two centuries of its existence, yet African-American women were physically and sexually assaulted by whites, and people of color were brutalized, murdered, and lynched on an unprecedented scale. Moreover, there were so many race riots in the summer of 1919 that the author of the black national anthem, James Weldon Johnson, referred to it as "the red summer." The 1920s witnessed the reemergence of a reinvigorated Ku Klux Klan. Many state politicians even went public with their memberships, and the governor of Indiana during this period was an avowed member of the Klan. The 1930s and 1940s did not bring much relief, as attested to by several race riots and Pres. Franklin D. Roosevelt's refusal to promote an anti-lynching bill.

Some of the African-American critics of affirmative action have actually been beneficiaries of such a program. It is unlikely that Clarence Thomas would have been able to attend Yale University Law School or become a justice on the U.S. Supreme Court without affirmative action. Yet, Thomas hates it with a passion, once saying he would be violating "God's law" if he ever signed his name to an opinion that approved the use of race—even for benign reasons—in hiring or admissions.

Opponents of affirmative action from various racial and ethnic backgrounds argue that it may lead to reverse discrimination, whereby qualified whites fail to acquire admission to school, secure employment, or are fired because of their race since prospective slots have to be preserved solely for minorities. It is difficult to say with any degree of certainty how many whites may have been bypassed or displaced because preferences have been given to blacks and other minorities. What can be said, though, with a large measure of accuracy is that whites have not lost ground in medicine and college teaching, despite considerable efforts to open up those fields. In addition, contrary to popular myth, there is little need for talented and successful advertising executives, lawyers, physicians, engineers, accountants, college professors, movie executives, chemists, physicists, airline pilots, architects, etc. to fear minority preference. Whites who lose out are more generally blue-collar workers or persons at lower administrative levels, whose skills are not greatly in demand.

Furthermore, some whites who are passed over for promotion under these circumstances may simply not be viewed as the best person available for the job. It is human nature that those not receiving promotions that go to minorities or not gaining admission to colleges and universities prefer to believe that they have been discriminated against. They refuse to consider the possibility that the minorities could be better qualified. Although some highly qualified white students may be rejected by the University of California at Berkeley, Duke, Yale, Harvard, Stanford, or Princeton, the same students often are offered slots at Brown, Dartmouth, Cornell, Columbia, Michigan, the University of Pennsylvania, and the University of North Carolina at Chapel Hill— all first-rate institutions of higher learning.

Although some white women have been the victims of affirmative action, females, for the most part, arguably have been the largest beneficiaries of it. Over the last quarter-century, their numbers have increased dramatically in such fields as law, medicine, accounting, engineering, broadcasting, architecture, higher education, etc. Nonetheless, many white women vehemently have attacked affirmative action. For example, according to an ABC News poll taken in November, 1996, 52% of white women in California voted to support Proposition 209, which sought to eliminate racial and gender preferences in hiring, college admissions, and Federal contracts. What explains this behavior?

White women believe affirmative action is denying their sons admission to some schools and taking jobs away from their sons and husbands. Many worry about the psychological and emotional toll this could have on their loved ones. In fact, a bipartisan Federal panel found in 1995 that white men hold 95% of the nation's top management jobs although they represent just 43% of the workforce. It thus is apparent that much ground still has to be covered in terms of providing adequate economic opportunities for minorities. Yet, when most critics of affirmative action who favor destroying it are asked the question of what they would replace it with, they are silent.

Tangible Benefits

Affirmative action has produced some tangible benefits for the nation as a whole. As a result of it, the number of minorities attending and receiving degrees from colleges and universities rose in the 1970s and 1980s. This led to an increase in the size of the African-American middle class. An attainment of higher levels of education, as well as affirmative action policies in hiring, helped blacks gain access to some professions that earlier had been virtually closed to them. For instance, it traditionally had been nearly impossible for African-Americans and other minorities to receive professorships at predominantly white schools. Some departments at these schools actively began to recruit and hire minority faculty as their campuses became more diverse.

As expected, African-American, Hispanic, Native American, and Asian-American students demanded that not only should more minority faculty be hired, but that the curriculum be expanded to include courses that deal with the cultural and historical experiences of their past. Some school administrators granted their demands, which has borne fruit in a number of ways. First, given the fact that the U.S. is steadily becoming even more multicultural, it is imperative that Americans learn about and develop an appreciation and respect for various cultures. This could enable those who plan to teach students from several different racial, cultural, and ethnic backgrounds in the public school system to approach their jobs with more sensitivity and understanding. Second, it is often crucial for minority faculty to act as role models, particularly on white campuses. Third, white students could profit by being taught by professors of color. Since a white skin provides everyday advantages, having to face people of color in positions of authority may awaken some whites to realities about themselves and their society they previously have failed to recognize. It also might become obvious to them that certain racial stereotypes fly out of the window in light of intellectual exchanges with professors and peers of color.

Since education is crucial to acquiring economic advancement, it is of paramount importance that as many educational opportunities as possible be extended to the nation's minorities, which many studies indicate will total 50% of the population by 2050. Although much more is needed than affirmative action in order for minorities to gain the necessary access to higher levels of education and hiring, it nevertheless is the best mechanism to ensure at least a small measure of success in this regard. However, it currently is under attack in the areas of higher education, hiring, and Federal contracts. Now is the perfect time to find ways of improving affirmative action, rather than developing strategies aimed at destroying it.

Although a large number of minorities were attending and graduating from colleges and universities in the 1970s and 1980s, this trend had subsided by the 1990s. Tougher admission requirements, rising college costs, cutbacks of scholarships and fellowships or their direct elimination, as well as a reduction of grants and loans to students are contributing factors. Budgetary cuts have had a devastating effect on faculty in general, and minority faculty in particular, since they are often the first to be released from jobs. At a time when tenure and promotion are difficult to attain for most academics, it is almost impossible for some minority faculty.

Indeed, the attack on affirmative action is real. In California, without a commitment to affirmative action, the number of black students has dipped sharply. Applications from "underrepresented" minorities in 1997 on the nine campuses of the University of California dropped five percent, while overall applications rose 2.6%. The losses were even more dramatic at Ues Boalt Hall Law School, where admissions of African-Americans dropped 81% and Hispanics 50%. What are the implications of this for the nation? Certainly there will not be as many choices or opportunities for students and employers who have learned the value of a diverse workforce. This onslaught is contributing to the creation of an atmosphere in which many whites feel comfortable making racially derogatory remarks they would not have dared make a few years ago. For example, a University of Texas law professor remarked that "Blacks and Mexican-Americans are not academically competitive with whites in selective institutions. It is the result primarily of cultural effects. They have a culture that seems not to encourage achievement. Failure is not looked upon with disgrace."

Impact

Three questions beg answering in this racially charged environment: What impact will the attack on affirmative action have on the recruitment of minority student-athletes? Will they eventually be subjected to the same rigorous admissions standards as other students? Even if they are not, will they continue to enroll in large numbers at predominantly white state-supported colleges and universities with steadily decreasing numbers of minority students and faculty? Since minority athletes bring millions of dollars to schools, which, in turn, are used to subsidize the education of whites, I seriously doubt that tougher admission standards will be applied to them so rigorously that they eventually will be driven away from these schools. Administrators could not afford to lose millions of dollars.

Let's for a second imagine what would happen to state colleges that tried to recruit minority athletes to their campuses if they were all white in terms of faculty and student body. Those schools would have a difficult time convincing them to come. Furthermore, private schools not subjected to the same admission requirements would be all too happy to offer minority athletes lucrative financial aid packages.

Many industries began downsizing in the late 1980s and the practice has continued in the 1990s, helping to reverse some of the earlier gains made by minorities. With American society steadily becoming even more multicultural, it makes good business sense to have a workforce that is reflective of this development. In order to make this a reality, affirmative action policies need to be kept in place, not abandoned. Why not use the expertise of African-Americans to target African-American audiences for business purposes or Asian-Americans to tap into potential Asian-American consumers? Businessmen who believe minorities will purchase products as readily from all-white companies as those which are perceived as diverse are seriously misguided.

A diverse workforce also can yield huge economic dividends in the international business sector, as became obvious in 1996 to Republicans who hoped to increase their majority in Congress and ride into the White House by attacking affirmative action policies in hiring. Rep. Dan Burton of Indiana, Speaker of the House Newt Gingrich, and presidential candidate Bob Dole, to name a few, applied pressure on businesses to end affirmative action policies in hiring. Executives informed them that this would be bad business and that the losses in revenue potentially would be staggering. In addition, it would be foolish public relations and substantially would reduce the pool of fine applicants. For the time being, the Republicans eased off.

A diverse workforce in a multicultural society makes practical and ethical sense. With all of the problems that need to be solved—such as disease, hunger, poverty, homelessness, lack of health care, racism, anti-Semitism, sexism, teenage pregnancy, crime, drugs, etc.—why should anyone's input be limited because of sex, race, color, class, or ethnic background? All Americans should be working together in this endeavor. It can best be accomplished by creating a truly diverse workforce through a continuation of affirmative action policies.

In spite of the fact that affirmative action has helped some African-Americans and other minorities achieve a middle-class status, not all have witnessed a significant improvement in their economic condition. For the most part, it has only helped the last generation of minorities. In order to make a significant impact, affirmative action policies need to be in place for several generations. Between 1970 and 1992, the median income for white families, computed in constant dollars, rose from $34,773 to $38,909, an increase of 11.9%. Black family income declined during this period, from $21,330 to $21,162. In relative terms, black incomes dropped from $613 to $544 for each $1,000 received by whites. Moreover, in 1992, black men with bachelor's degrees made $764 for each $1,000 received by white men with such degrees, and black males with master's degrees earned $870 for each $1,000 their white counterparts earned. Overall, black men received $721 for every $1,000 earned by white men.

Even more depressing for blacks is the fact that unemployment rates for them have remained at double-digit levels since 1975, averaging 14.9% for the 1980s, while the average was 6.3% for whites. The number of black children living below the poverty line reached 46.3% by 1992, compared to 12.3% of white children. At the same time, the overall poverty rate among Hispanics increased to 28.2%. Even in professions where blacks made breakthroughs by the early 1990s, they remained underrepresented. This was the case in engineering, law, medicine, dentistry, architecture, and higher education. Although blacks represented 10.2% of the workforce in 1992, they constituted just 3.7% of engineers, 2.7% of dentists, 3.1% of architects, and held 4.8% of university faculty positions.

Furthermore, while 27,713 doctoral degrees were awarded in 1992 to U.S. citizens and aliens who indicated their intention is to remain in America, 1,081, or 3.9%, of these doctorates went to blacks. Given the low percentage of African-Americans receiving doctoral degrees, most college departments in all likelihood will find it difficult to recruit black faculty. With the hatchet steadily chopping affirmative action programs, this may become virtually impossible in the near future. The same holds true for other professions.

The most feasible way to ensure that colleges, universities, and various occupations will not become lily-white again is by the continuation of affirmative action. It gives minority groups that traditionally have been locked out of the education system and the workforce the best opportunity to carve out a solid economic foundation in America. I agree with Pres. Clinton, who said, "Don't end it; mend it."

America has had over 200 years to deliver true justice, freedom, and equality to women and people of color. To believe that it now will make good the promise of equality without some kind of legislation to assist it is to engage in fantasy.

In advocating for affirmative action policies, people of color are not looking for government handouts. They merely are asking that some mechanism be kept in place to help provide the same social and economic opportunities most whites have had and continue to have access to.

POSTSCRIPT

Has Affirmative Action Outlived Its Usefulness?

Despite their basic disagreement, both Williams and Jenkins desire a just society. The authors' main disagreement is on whether or not affirmative action is needed today to achieve this goal. Jenkins suggests that to abandon affirmative action before opportunities are much more equal is to perpetuate injustice. Williams contends that progress in racial justice has advanced to the point that some affirmative action programs are now unjust to whites. He observes that Americans support "soft affirmative action" but are opposed to more aggressive affirmative action. Could less aggressive affirmative action be the way to greater national unity on the race issue?

The writings on this subject are diverse and numerous. For an in-depth discussion of the legal standing of affirmative action, see Girardeau A. Spann, *The Law of Affirmative Action: Twenty-Five Years of Supreme Court Decisions on Race and Remedies* (New York University Press, 2000). For a review of affirmative action programs, see M. Ali Raza et al., *The Ups and Downs of Affirmative Action Preferences* (Greenwood, 1999). William G. Bowen and Derek Bok review affirmative action in college admissions in *The Shape of the River: Long-Term Consequences of Considering Race in College and University Admissions* (Princeton University Press, 1998). For a personal reading of black and white attitudes, see Studs Terkel, *Race: How Blacks and Whites Think and Feel About the American Obsession* (New Press, 1992). For a more academic reading of white racial attitudes, see Paul M. Sniderman and Thomas Piazza, *The Scar of Race* (Harvard University Press, 1993). One way to learn about racism is to read Gregory Howard Williams's story about living as a black after years as a white in *Life on the Color Line: The True Story of a White Boy Who Discovered He Was Black* (E. P. Dutton, 1995). Two works that portray the experiences of racism by the black middle class are Ellis Close, *The Rage of a Privileged Class* (HarperCollins, 1993) and Joe R. Feagin and Melvin P. Sikes, *Living With Racism: The Black Middle-Class Experience* (Beacon, 1994). Two personal accounts of this experience are Brent Staples, *Parallel Time: Growing Up in Black and White* (Pantheon, 1994) and Henry Louis Gates, *Colored People* (Free Press, 1994). Steven L. Carter's *Reflections of an Affirmative Action Baby* (Basic Books, 1991) is based on the author's own experiences under affirmative action. Andrew Hacker argues that affirmative action has relatively minor adverse consequences for whites in *Two Nations: Black and White, Separate, Hostile, Unequal* (Charles Scribner's Sons, 1992). Dinesh D'Souza, in *The End of Racism* (Free Press, 1995), argues that white racism has pretty much disappeared in the United States. The opposite is argued by Joe R. Feagin and Hernan Vera in *White Racism: The Basics* (Routledge, 1995) and by Stephen Steinberg in *Turning Back* (Beacon Press, 1995).

On the Internet...

Economic Report of the President

This report includes current and anticipated trends in the United States and annual numerical goals concerning topics such as employment, production, real income, and federal budget outlays. The database notes employment objectives for significant groups of the labor force, annual numeric goals, and a plan for carrying out program objectives.

http://www.library.nwu.edu/gpo/help/econr.html

Welfare Reform Resources

This Web page, from the National Association of State Universities and Land-Grant Colleges' Web site, contains numerous links to sites on welfare reform. Included are links to the Department of Labor's Welfare-to-Work page and the page for the Welfare Information Network, a clearinghouse for information on welfare reform.

http://www.nasulgc.org/NASULGCOLD/Welfare_Links.htm

National Center for Policy Analysis

Through this site you can read discussions that are of major interest in the study of American politics and government from a sociological perspective.

http://www.public-policy.org/~ncpa/pd/pdindex.html

Policy.com

Visit this site of the "policy community" to examine major issues related to social welfare, welfare reform, social work, and many other topics. The site includes substantial resources for researching issues online.

http://www.policy.com

PART 4

Political Economy and Institutions

*A*re political power and economic power merged within a "power elite" that dominates the U.S. political system? The first issue in this part explores that debate. The second issue concerns the proper role of government in the economy. Some believe that the government must correct for the many failures of the market, while others think that the government usually complicates the workings of the free market. The next debate concerns public policy: What is the impact of the end of the Federal AFDC program? The fourth issue examines the role of the government in public education. Finally, the last issue in this part looks at doctor-assisted suicide for terminally ill patients.

- Is Government Dominated by Big Business?

- Should Government Intervene in a Capitalist Economy?

- Has Welfare Reform Benefited the Poor?

- Are Vouchers the Solution to the Ills of Public Education?

- Should Doctor-Assisted Suicide Be Legalized for the Terminally Ill?

ISSUE 10

Is Government Dominated by Big Business?

YES: G. William Domhoff, from *Who Rules America? Power and Politics in the Year 2000,* 3rd ed. (Mayfield Publishing, 1998)

NO: Jeffrey M. Berry, from "Citizen Groups and the Changing Nature of Interest Group Politics in America," *The Annals of the American Academy of Political and Social Science* (July 1993)

ISSUE SUMMARY

YES: Political sociologist G. William Domhoff argues that the "owners and top-level managers in large income-producing properties are far and away the dominant power figures in the United States" and that they have inordinate influence in the federal government.

NO: Jeffrey M. Berry, a professor of political science, contends that public interest pressure groups that have entered the political arena since the end of the 1960s have effectively challenged the political power of big business.

$\mathbf{S}$ince the framing of the U.S. Constitution in 1787, there have been periodic charges that America is unduly influenced by wealthy financial interests. Richard Henry Lee, a signer of the Declaration of Independence, spoke for many Anti-Federalists (those who opposed ratification of the Constitution) when he warned that the proposed charter shifted power away from the people and into the hands of the "aristocrats" and "moneyites."

Before the Civil War, Jacksonian Democrats denounced the eastern merchants and bankers who, they charged, were usurping the power of the people. After the Civil War, a number of radical parties and movements revived this theme of antielitism. The ferment—which was brought about by the rise of industrial monopolies, government corruption, and economic hardship for western farmers—culminated in the founding of the People's Party at the beginning of the 1890s. The Populists, as they were more commonly called, wanted economic and political reforms aimed at transferring power away from the rich and back to "the plain people."

By the early 1900s the People's Party had disintegrated, but many writers and activists have continued to echo the Populists' central thesis: that the U.S. democratic political system is in fact dominated by business elites. Yet the thesis has not gone unchallenged. During the 1950s and the early 1960s, many social scientists subscribed to the *pluralist* view of America.

Pluralists argue that because there are many influential elites in America, each group is limited to some extent by the others. There are some groups, like the business elites, that are more powerful than their opponents, but even the more powerful groups are denied their objectives at times. Labor groups are often opposed to business groups; conservative interests challenge liberal interests, and vice versa; and organized civil libertarians sometimes fight with groups that seek government-imposed bans on pornography or groups that demand tougher criminal laws. No single group, the pluralists argue, can dominate the political system.

Pluralists readily acknowledge that American government is not democratic in the full sense of the word; it is not driven by the majority. But neither, they insist, is it run by a conspiratorial "power elite." In the pluralist view, the closest description of the American form of government would be neither majority rule nor minority rule but *minorities* rule. (Note that in this context, "minorities" does not necessarily refer to race or ethnicity but to any organized group of people with something in common—including race, religion, or economic interests—not constituting a majority of the population.) Each organized minority enjoys some degree of power in the making of public policy. In extreme cases, when a minority feels threatened, its power may take a negative form: the power to derail policy. When the majority—or, more accurately, a coalition of other minorities—attempts to pass a measure that threatens the vital interests of an organized minority, that group may use its power to obstruct their efforts. (Often cited in this connection is the use of the Senate filibuster, which is the practice of using tactics during the legislative process that cause extreme delays or prevent action, thus enabling a group to "talk to death" a bill that threatens its vital interests.) But in the pluralist view negative power is not the only driving force: when minorities work together and reach consensus on certain issues, they can institute new laws and policy initiatives that enjoy broad public support. Pluralism, though capable of producing temporary gridlock, ultimately leads to compromise, consensus, and moderation.

Critics of pluralism argue that pluralism is an idealized depiction of a political system that is in the grip of powerful elite groups. Critics fault pluralist theory for failing to recognize the extent to which big business dominates the policy-making process. In the selections that follow, G. William Domhoff supports this view, identifies the groups that compose the power elite, and details the way they control or support social, political, and knowledge-producing associations and organizations that advance their interests. Jeffrey M. Berry, in opposition, argues that, thanks to new consumer, environmental, and other citizen groups, big business no longer enjoys the cozy relationship it once had with Washington policymakers.

Who Rules America?

Power and Class in the United States

... [T]he owners and top-level managers in large income-producing properties
are far and away the dominant power figures in the United States. Their corporations, banks, and agribusinesses come together as a *corporate community* that
dominates the federal government in Washington. Their real estate, construction, and land development companies form *growth coalitions* that dominate
most local governments. Granted, there is competition within both the corporate community and the local growth coalitions for profits and investment opportunities, and there are sometimes tensions between national corporations
and local growth coalitions, but both are cohesive on policy issues affecting
their general welfare, and in the face of demands by organized workers, liberals,
environmentalists, and neighborhoods.

As a result of their ability to organize and defend their interests, the owners and managers of large income-producing properties have a very great share
of all income and wealth in the United States, greater than in any other industrial democracy. Making up at best 1 percent of the total population, by the
early 1990s they earned 15.7 percent of the nation's yearly income and owned
37.2 percent of all privately held wealth, including 49.6 percent of all corporate stocks and 62.4 percent of all bonds. Due to their wealth and the lifestyle
it makes possible, these owners and managers draw closer as a common social
group. They belong to the same exclusive social clubs, frequent the same summer and winter resorts, and send their children to a relative handful of private
schools. Members of the corporate community thereby become a *corporate rich*
who create a nationwide *social upper class* through their social interaction....
Members of the growth coalitions, on the other hand, are *place entrepreneurs,*
people who sell locations and buildings. They come together as local upper
classes in their respective cities and sometimes mingle with the corporate rich
in educational or resort settings.

The corporate rich and the growth entrepreneurs supplement their small
numbers by developing and directing a wide variety of nonprofit organizations,
the most important of which are a set of tax-free charitable foundations, think

tanks, and policy-discussion groups. These specialized nonprofit groups constitute a *policy-formation network* at the national level. Chambers of commerce and policy groups affiliated with them form similar policy-formation networks at the local level, aided by a few national-level city development organizations that are available for local consulting.

Those corporate owners who have the interest and ability to take part in general governance join with top-level executives in the corporate community and the policy-formation network to form the *power elite,* which is the leadership group for the corporate rich as a whole. The concept of a power elite makes clear that not all members of the upper class are involved in governance; some of them simply enjoy the lifestyle that their great wealth affords them. At the same time, the focus on a leadership group allows for the fact that not all those in the power elite are members of the upper class; many of them are high-level employees in profit and nonprofit organizations controlled by the corporate rich. . . .

The power elite is not united on all issues because it includes both moderate conservatives and ultraconservatives. Although both factions favor minimal reliance on government on all domestic issues, the moderate conservatives sometimes agree to legislation advocated by liberal elements of the society, especially in times of social upheaval like the Great Depression of the 1930s and the Civil Rights Movement of the early 1960s. Except on defense spending, ultraconservatives are characterized by a complete distaste for any kind of government programs under any circumstances—even to the point of opposing government support for corporations on some issues. Moderate conservatives often favor foreign aid, working through the United Nations, and making attempts to win over foreign enemies through patient diplomacy, treaties, and trade agreements. Historically, ultraconservatives have opposed most forms of foreign involvement, although they have become more tolerant of foreign trade agreements over the past thirty or forty years. At the same time, their hostility to the United Nations continues unabated.

Members of the power elite enter into the electoral arena as the leaders within a *corporate-conservative coalition,* where they are aided by a wide variety of patriotic, antitax, and other single-issue organizations. These conservative advocacy organizations are funded in varying degrees by the corporate rich, direct-mail appeals, and middle-class conservatives. This coalition has played a large role in both political parties at the presidential level and usually succeeds in electing a conservative majority to both houses of Congress. Historically, the conservative majority in Congress was made up of most Northern Republicans and most Southern Democrats, but that arrangement has been changing gradually since the 1960s as the conservative Democrats of the South are replaced by even more conservative Southern Republicans. The corporate-conservative coalition also has access to the federal government in Washington through lobbying and the appointment of its members to top positions in the executive branch. . . .

Despite their preponderant power within the federal government and the many useful policies it carries out for them, members of the power elite are constantly critical of government as an alleged enemy of freedom and economic growth. Although their wariness toward government is expressed in terms of a dislike for taxes and government regulations, I believe their underlying concern is that government could change the power relations in the private sphere by aiding average Americans through a number of different avenues: (1) creating government jobs for the unemployed; (2) making health, unemployment, and welfare benefits more generous; (3) helping employees gain greater workplace rights and protections; and (4) helping workers organize unions. All of these initiatives are opposed by members of the power elite because they would increase wages and taxes, but the deepest opposition is toward any government support for unions because unions are a potential organizational base for advocating the whole range of issues opposed by the corporate rich. . . .

Where Does Democracy Fit In?

. . . [T]o claim that the corporate rich have enough power to be considered a dominant class does not imply that lower social classes are totally powerless. *Domination* means the power to set the terms under which other groups and classes must operate, not total control. Highly trained professionals with an interest in environmental and consumer issues have been able to couple their technical information and their understanding of the legislative and judicial processes with well-timed publicity, lobbying, and lawsuits to win governmental restrictions on some corporate practices. Wage and salary employees, when they are organized into unions and have the right to strike, have been able to gain pay increases, shorter hours, better working conditions, and social benefits such as health insurance. Even the most powerless of people—the very poor and those discriminated against—sometimes develop the capacity to influence the power structure through sit-ins, demonstrations, social movements, and other forms of social disruption, and there is evidence that such activities do bring about some redress of grievances, at least for a short time.

More generally, the various challengers to the power elite sometimes work together on policy issues as a *liberal-labor coalition* that is based in unions, local environmental organizations, some minority group communities, university and arts communities, liberal churches, and small newspapers and magazines. Despite a decline in membership over the past twenty years, unions are the largest and best-financed part of the coalition, and the largest organized social force in the country (aside from churches). They also cut across racial and ethnic lines more than any other institutionalized sector of American society. . . .

The policy conflicts between the corporate-conservative and liberal-labor coalitions are best described as *class conflicts* because they primarily concern the distribution of profits and wages, the rate and progressivity of taxation, the usefulness of labor unions, and the degree to which business should be regulated by government. The liberal-labor coalition wants corporations to pay higher wages to employees and higher taxes to government. It wants government to regulate a wide range of business practices, including many that are related to the environment, and help employees to organize unions. The corporate-conservative coalition resists all these policy objectives to a greater or lesser degree, claiming they endanger the freedom of individuals and the efficient workings of the economic marketplace. The conflicts these disagreements generate can manifest themselves in many different ways: workplace protests, industrywide boycotts, massive demonstrations in cities, pressure on Congress, and the outcome of elections.

Neither the corporate-conservative nor the liberal-labor coalition includes a very large percentage of the American population, although each has the regular support of about 25–30 percent of the voters. Both coalitions are made up primarily of financial donors, policy experts, political consultants, and party activists....

Pluralism

The main alternative theory [I] address... claims that power is more widely dispersed among groups and classes than a class-dominance theory allows. This general perspective is usually called *pluralism,* meaning there is no one dominant power group. It is the theory most favored by social scientists. In its strongest version, pluralism holds that power is held by the general public through the pressure that public opinion and voting put on elected officials. According to this version, citizens form voluntary groups and pressure groups that shape public opinion, lobby elected officials, and back sympathetic political candidates in the electoral process....

The second version of pluralism sees power as rooted in a wide range of well-organized "interest groups" that are often based in economic interests (e.g., industrialists, bankers, labor unions), but also in other interests as well (e.g., environmental, consumer, and civil rights groups). These interest groups join together in different coalitions depending on the specific issues. Proponents of this version of pluralism sometimes concede that public opinion and voting have only a minimal or indirect influence, but they see business groups as too fragmented and antagonistic to form a cohesive dominant class. They also claim that some business interest groups occasionally join coalitions with liberal or labor groups on specific issues, and that business-dominated coalitions sometimes lose. Furthermore, some proponents of this version of pluralism believe that the Democratic Party is responsive to the wishes of liberal and labor interest groups.

In contrast, I argue that the business interest groups are part of a tightly knit corporate community that is able to develop classwide cohesion on the issues of greatest concern to it: opposition to unions, high taxes, and government regulation. When a business group loses on a specific issue, it is often because other business groups have been opposed; in other words, there are arguments within the corporate community, and these arguments are usually settled within the governmental arena. I also claim that liberal and labor groups are rarely part of coalitions with business groups and that for most of its history the Democratic Party has been dominated by corporate and agribusiness interests in the Southern states, in partnership with the growth coalitions in large urban areas outside the South. Finally, I show that business interests rarely lose on labor and regulatory issues except in times of extreme social disruption like the 1930s and 1960s, when differences of opinion between Northern and Southern corporate leaders made victories for the liberal-labor coalition possible....

How the Power Elite Dominates Government

This [section] shows how the power elite builds on the ideas developed in the policy-formation process and its success in the electoral arena to dominate the federal government. Lobbyists from corporations, law firms, and trade associations play a key role in shaping government on narrow issues of concern to specific corporations or business sectors, but their importance should not be overestimated because a majority of those elected to Congress are predisposed to agree with them. The corporate community and the policy-formation network supply top-level governmental appointees and new policy directions on major issues.

Once again, as seen in the battles for public opinion and electoral success, the power elite faces opposition from a minority of elected officials and their supporters in labor unions and liberal advocacy groups. These opponents are sometimes successful in blocking ultra-conservative initiatives, but most of the victories for the liberal-labor coalition are the result of support from moderate conservatives....

Appointees to Government

The first way to test a class-dominance view of the federal government is to study the social and occupational backgrounds of the people who are appointed to manage the major departments of the executive branch, such as state, treasury, defense, and justice. If pluralists are correct, these appointees should come from a wide range of interest groups. If the state autonomy theorists are correct, they should be disproportionately former elected officials or longtime government employees. If the class-dominance view is correct, they should come disproportionately from the upper class, the corporate community, and the policy-formation network.

There have been numerous studies over the years of major governmental appointees under both Republican and Democratic administrations, usually focusing on the top appointees in the departments that are represented in the president's cabinet. These studies are unanimous in their conclusion that most top appointees in both Republican and Democratic administrations are corporate executives and corporate lawyers—and hence members of the power elite....

Conclusion

This [section] has demonstrated the power elite's wide-ranging access to government through the interest-group and policy-formation processes, as well as through its ability to influence appointments to major government positions. When coupled with the several different kinds of power discussed in earlier [sections] this access and involvement add up to power elite domination of the federal government.

By *domination,* as stated in the first [section], social scientists mean the ability of a class or group to set the terms under which other classes or groups within a social system must operate. By this definition, domination does not mean control on each and every issue, and it does not rest solely on involvement in government. Influence over government is only the final and most visible aspect of power elite domination, which has its roots in the class structure, the corporate control of the investment function, and the operation of the policy-formation network. If government officials did not have to wait for corporate leaders to decide where and when they will invest, and if government officials were not further limited by the general public's acceptance of policy recommendations from the policy-formation network, then power elite involvement in elections and government would count for a lot less than they do under present conditions.

Domination by the power elite does not negate the reality of continuing conflict over government policies, but few conflicts, it has been shown, involve challenges to the rules that create privileges for the upper class and domination by the power elite. Most of the numerous battles within the interest-group process, for example, are only over specific spoils and favors; they often involve disagreements among competing business interests.

Similarly, conflicts within the policy-making process of government often involve differences between the moderate conservative and ultraconservative segments of the dominant class. At other times they involve issues in which the needs of the corporate community as a whole come into conflict with the needs of specific industries, which is what happens to some extent on tariff policies and also on some environmental legislation. In neither case does the nature of the conflict call into question the domination of government by the power elite.

... Contrary to what pluralists claim, there is not a single case study on any issue of any significance that shows a liberal-labor victory over a united corporate-conservative coalition, which is strong evidence for a class-domination theory on the "Who wins?" power indicator. The classic case studies frequently cited by pluralists have been shown to be gravely deficient as evidence for their views. Most of these studies reveal either conflicts among rival groups within the power elite or situations in which the moderate conservatives have decided for their own reasons to side with the liberal-labor coalition....

More generally, it now can be concluded that all four indicators of power introduced in [the first section] point to the corporate rich and their power elite as the dominant organizational structure in American society. First, the wealth and income distributions are skewed in their favor more than in any other industrialized democracy. They are clearly the most powerful group in American society in terms of "Who benefits?" Second, the appointees to government come overwhelmingly from the corporate community and its associated policy-formation network. Thus, the power elite is clearly the most powerful in terms of "Who sits?"

Third, the power elite wins far more often than it loses on policy issues resolved in the federal government. Thus, it is the most powerful in terms of "Who wins?" Finally, as shown in reputational studies in the 1950s and 1970s, . . . corporate leaders are the most powerful group in terms of "Who shines?" By the usual rules of evidence in a social science investigation using multiple indicators, the owners and managers of large income-producing properties are the dominant class in the United States.

Still, as noted at the end of the first [section], power structures are not immutable. Societies change and power structures evolve or crumble from time to unpredictable time, especially in the face of challenge. When it is added that the liberal-labor coalition persists in the face of its numerous defeats, and that free speech and free elections are not at risk, there remains the possibility that class domination could be replaced by a greater sharing of power in the future.

NO

Jeffrey M. Berry

Citizen Groups and the Changing Nature of Interest Group Politics in America

ABSTRACT: The rise of liberal citizen groups that began in the 1960s has had a strong impact on the evolution of interest group advocacy. The success of these liberal organizations was critical in catalyzing the broader explosion in the numbers of interest groups and in causing the collapse of many subgovernments. New means of resolving policy conflicts had to be established to allow for the participation of broader, more diverse policy communities. Citizen groups have been particularly important in pushing policymakers to create new means of structuring negotiations between large numbers of interest group actors. The greater participation of citizen groups, the increased numbers of all kinds of interest groups, and change in the way policy is made may be making the policymaking process more democratic.

Many protest movements have arisen in the course of American history, each affecting the political system in its own way. The social movements that took hold in the 1960s had their own unique set of roots but seemed to follow a conventional life span. The civil rights and antiwar groups that arose to protest the injustices they saw were classic social movements. Their views were eventually absorbed by one of the political parties, and, after achieving their immediate goals, their vitality was sapped. The antiwar movement disappeared, and black civil rights organizations declined in power. The most enduring and vital citizen groups born in this era of protest were never protest oriented. Consumer groups, environmental groups, and many other kinds of citizen lobbies have enjoyed unprecedented prosperity in the last 25 years. Never before have citizen groups been so prevalent in American politics, and never before have they been so firmly institutionalized into the policymaking process.

The rise of citizen groups has not only empowered many important constituencies, but it has altered the policymaking process as well. This article focuses on how citizen groups have affected interest group politics in general and how these organizations have contributed to the changing nature of public policymaking. A first step is to examine the initial success of liberal advocacy organizations as well as the conservative response to this challenge. Next, I

From Jeffrey M. Berry, "Citizen Groups and the Changing Nature of Interest Group Politics in America," *The Annals of the American Academy of Political and Social Science,* vol. 528 (July 1993). Copyright © 1993 by The American Academy of Political and Social Science. Reprinted by permission of Sage Publications, Inc. Notes omitted.

will look at the impact of this growth of citizen group politics on the policymaking process. Then I will turn to how Congress and the executive branch have tried to cope with a dense population of citizen groups and the complex policymaking environment that now envelops government.

Finally, I will speculate as to how all of this has affected policymaking in terms of how democratic it is. The popular perception is that the rise of interest groups along with the decline of political parties has had a very negative impact on American politics. Analysis of the decline of parties will be left to others, but a central point here is that the growth in the numbers of citizen groups and of other lobbying organizations has not endangered the political system. There are some unfortunate developments, such as the increasing role of political action committees in campaign financing, but the rise of citizen groups in particular has had a beneficial impact on the way policy is formulated. The overall argument may be stated succinctly: the rise of liberal citizen groups was largely responsible for catalyzing an explosion in the growth of all types of interest groups. Efforts to limit the impact of liberal citizen groups failed, and the policymaking process became more open and more participatory. Expanded access and the growth in the numbers of competing interest groups created the potential for gridlock, if not chaos. The government responded, in turn, with institutional changes that have helped to rationalize policymaking in environments with a large number of independent actors.

The Rise of Citizen Groups

The lobbying organizations that emerged out of the era of protest in the 1960s are tied to the civil rights and antiwar movements in two basic ways. First, activism was stimulated by the same broad ideological dissatisfaction with government and the two-party system. There was the same feeling that government was unresponsive, that it was unconcerned about important issues, and that business was far too dominant a force in policymaking. Second, the rise of liberal citizen groups was facilitated by success of the civil rights and antiwar movements. More specifically, future organizers learned from these social movements. They learned that aggressive behavior could get results, and they saw that government could be influenced by liberal advocacy organizations. Some activists who later led Washington-based citizen lobbies cut their teeth as volunteers in these earlier movements.

For liberal consumer and environmental groups, an important lesson of this era was that they should not follow the protest-oriented behavior of the civil rights and antiwar movements. There was a collective realization that lasting influence would come from more conventional lobbying inside the political system. For consumer and environmental organizers, "power to the people" was rejected in favor of staff-run organizations that placed little emphasis on participatory democracy. This is not to say that these new organizations were simply copies of business lobbies; leaders of these groups like Ralph Nader and John Gardner placed themselves above politics-as-usual with their moralistic rhetoric and their attacks against the established political order.

While there was significant support for these groups from middle-class liberals, a major impetus behind their success was financial backing from large philanthropic foundations. The foundations wanted to support social change during a time of political upheaval, but at the same time they wanted responsible activism. This early support, most notably from the Ford Foundation's program in public interest law, was largely directed at supporting groups relying on litigation and administrative lobbying. The seed money for these organizations enabled them to flourish and provided them with time to establish a track record so that they could appeal to individual donors when the foundation money ran out. Other groups emerged without the help of foundations, drawing on a combination of large donors, dues-paying memberships, and government grants. Citizen lobbies proved remarkably effective at raising money and at shifting funding strategies as the times warranted.

Citizen groups emerged in a variety of areas. In addition to consumer and environmental groups, there were organizations interested in hunger and poverty, governmental reform, corporate responsibility, and many other issues. A number of new women's organizations soon followed in the wake of the success of the first wave of citizen groups, and new civil rights groups arose to defend other groups such as Hispanics and gays. As has been well documented, the rise of citizen groups was the beginning of an era of explosive growth in interest groups in national politics. No precise baseline exists, so exact measurement of this growth is impossible. Yet the mobilization of interests is unmistakable. One analysis of organizations represented in Washington in 1980 found that 40 percent of the groups had been started since 1960, and 25 percent had begun after 1970.

The liberal citizen groups that were established in the 1960s and 1970s were not simply the first ripples of a new wave of interest groups; rather, they played a primary role in catalyzing the formation of many of the groups that followed. New business groups, which were by far the most numerous of all the groups started since 1960, were directly stimulated to organize by the success of consumer and environmental groups. There were other reasons why business mobilized, but much of their hostility toward the expanded regulatory state was directed at agencies strongly supported by liberal citizen groups. These organizations had seemingly seized control of the political agenda, and the new social regulation demanded increased business mobilization. New conservative citizen lobbies, many focusing on family issues such as abortion and the Equal Rights Amendment, were also begun to counter the perceived success of the liberal groups.

The swing of the ideological pendulum that led to a conservative takeover of the White House in 1980 led subsequently to efforts to limit the impact of liberal citizen groups. The Reagan administration believed that the election of 1980 was a mandate to eliminate impediments to economic growth. Environmental and consumer groups were seen as organizations that cared little about the faltering American economy; President Reagan referred to liberal public interest lawyers as "a bunch of ideological ambulance chasers." Wherever possible, liberal citizen groups were to be removed from the governmental process. . . .

The Reagan administration certainly succeeded in reducing the liberal groups' access to the executive branch. On a broader level, however, the conservative counterattack against the liberal groups was a failure. The reasons go far beyond the more accommodating stance of the Bush administration or the attitude of any conservative administrations that may follow. These organizations have proved to be remarkably resilient, and they are a strong and stable force in American politics. Most fundamentally, though, the Reagan attempt failed because the transformation of interest group politics led to large-scale structural changes in the public policymaking process.

Consequences

The rise of citizen groups and the rapid expansion of interest group advocacy in general have had many important long-term consequences for the way policy is formulated by the national government. Most important, policymaking moved away from closed subgovernments, each involving a relatively stable and restricted group of lobbyists and key government officials, to much broader policymaking communities. Policymaking in earlier years is typically described as the product of consensual negotiations between a small number of backscratching participants.

Policymaking is now best described as taking place within issue networks rather than in subgovernments. An issue network is a set of organizations that share expertise in a policy area and interact with each other over time as relevant issues are debated. As sociologist Barry Wellman states, "The world is composed of networks, not groups." This is certainly descriptive of Washington policymaking. Policy formulation cannot be portrayed in terms of what a particular group wanted and how officials responded to those demands. The coalitions within networks, often involving scores of groups, define the divisions over issues and drive the policymaking process forward. Alliances are composed of both old friends and strange bedfellows; relationships are built on immediate need as well as on familiarity and trust. Organizations that do not normally work in a particular issue network can easily move into a policymaking community to work on a single issue. The only thing constant in issue networks is the changing nature of the coalitions.

The result of issue network politics is that policymaking has become more open, more conflictual, and more broadly participatory. What is crucial about the role of citizen groups is that they were instrumental in breaking down the barriers to participation in subgovernments. Building upon their own constituency support and working with allies in Congress, citizen groups made themselves players. They have not been outsiders, left to protest policies and a system that excluded them. Rather, they built opposition right into the policymaking communities that had previously operated with some commonality of interest. Even conservative administrators who would prefer to exclude these liberal advocacy groups have recognized that they have to deal with their opponents in one arena or another. The Nuclear Regulatory Commission, the epitome of an agency hostile to liberal advocacy groups, cannot get away with ignoring groups like the Union of Concerned Scientists. The consensus over nuclear power has long been broken. Critics and advocacy groups like the Union of Concerned Scientists have the technical expertise to involve themselves in agency proceedings, and they have the political know-how to get themselves heard on Capitol Hill and in the news media.

Issue networks are not simply divided between citizen groups on one side and business groups on another. Organizations representing business usually encompass a variety of interests, many of which are opposed to each other. As various business markets have undergone rapid change and become increasingly competitive, issue networks have found themselves divided by efforts of one sector of groups to use the policymaking process to try to gain market share from another sector of the network. Citizen groups, rather than simply being the enemy of business, are potential coalition partners for different business sectors. A characteristic of the culture of interest group politics in Washington is that there are no permanent allies and no permanent enemies.

Citizen groups are especially attractive as coalition partners because they have such a high level of credibility with the public and the news media. All groups claim to represent the public interest because they sincerely believe that the course of action they are advocating would be the most beneficial to the country. Since they do not represent any vocational or business interest, citizen groups may be perceived by some to be less biased—though certainly not unbiased—in their approach to public policy problems. This credibility is also built around the high-quality research that many citizen groups produce and distribute to journalists and policymakers in Washington. Reports from advocacy organizations such as Citizens for Tax Justice or the Center for Budget and Policy Priorities are quickly picked up by the media and disseminated across the country. Most business groups would love to have the respect that these citizen groups command in the press. For all the financial strength at the disposal of oil lobbyists, no representative of the oil industry has as much credibility with the public as a lobbyist for the Natural Resources Defense Council.

Despite the growth and stability of citizen groups in national politics, their reach does not extend into every significant policymaking domain. In the broad area of financial services, for example, citizen groups have played a minor role at best. There are some consumer groups that have been marginally active when specific issues involving banks, insurance companies, and securities firms arise, but they have demonstrated little influence or staying power. There is, however, a vital consumer interest at stake as public policymakers grapple with the crumbling walls that have traditionally divided different segments of the financial services market. Defense policy is another area where citizen groups have been relatively minor actors. But if citizen groups are conspicuous by their absence in some important areas, their overall reach is surprisingly broad. They have become major actors in policy areas where they previously had no presence at all. In negotiations over a free trade agreement with Mexico, for example, environmental groups became central players in the bargaining. These groups were concerned that increased U.S. investment in Mexico would result in increased pollution there from unregulated manufacturing, depleted groundwater supplies, and other forms of environmental degradation. To its dismay, the Bush White House found that the only practical course was to negotiate with the groups.

The increasing prominence of citizen groups and the expanding size of issue networks change our conception of the policymaking process. The basic structural attribute of a subgovernment was that it was relatively bounded with a stable set of participants. Even if there was some conflict in that subgovernment, there were predictable divisions and relatively clear expectations of what kind of conciliation between interest groups was possible. In contrast, issue networks seem like free-for-alls. In the health care field alone, 741 organizations have offices in Washington or employ a representative there. Where subgovernments suggested control over public policy by a limited number of participants, issue networks suggest no control whatsoever. Citizen groups make policymaking all the more difficult because they frequently sharpen the ideological debate; they have different organizational incentive systems from those of the corporations and trade groups with which they are often in conflict; and they place little emphasis on the need for economic growth, an assumption shared by most other actors.

This picture of contemporary interest group politics may make it seem impossible to accomplish anything in Washington. Indeed, it is a popular perception that Congress has become unproductive and that we are subject to some sort of national gridlock. Yet the policymaking system is adaptable, and the relationship between citizen groups and other actors in issue networks suggests that there are a number of productive paths for resolving complicated policy issues.

Complex Policymaking

The growth of issue networks is not, of course, the only reason why the policymaking process has become more complex. The increasingly technical nature of policy problems has obviously put an ever higher premium on expertise. Structural changes are critical, too. The decentralization of the House of Representatives that took place in the mid-1970s dispersed power and reduced the autonomy of leaders. Today, in the House, jurisdictions between committees frequently overlap and multiple referrals of bills are common. When an omnibus trade bill passed by both houses in 1987 was sent to conference, the House and the Senate appointed 200 conferees, who broke up into 17 subconferences. The growth of the executive branch has produced a similar problem of overlapping jurisdictions. In recent deliberations on proposed changes in wetlands policy, executive branch participants included the Soil Conservation Service in the Agriculture Department, the Fish and Wildlife Service in Interior, the Army Corps of Engineers, the Environmental Protection Agency (EPA), the Office of Management and Budget, the Council on Competitiveness, and the President's Domestic Policy Council.

Nevertheless, even though the roots of complex policymaking are multifaceted, the rise of citizen groups has been a critical factor in forcing the

Congress and the executive branch to focus more closely on developing procedures to negotiate settlements of policy disputes. The quiet bargaining of traditional subgovernment politics was not an adequate mechanism for handling negotiations between scores of interest groups, congressional committees, and executive branch agencies.

Citizen groups have been particularly important in prompting more structured negotiations for a number of reasons. First, in many policy areas, citizen groups upset long-standing working arrangements between policymakers and other interest groups. Citizen groups were often the reason subgovernments crumbled; under pressure from congressional allies and public opinion, they were included in the bargaining and negotiating at some stage in the policymaking process.

Second, citizen groups could not be easily accommodated in basic negotiating patterns. It was not a matter of simply placing a few more chairs at the table. These groups' entrance into a policymaking community usually created a new dividing line between participants. The basic ideological cleavage that exists between consumer and environmental interests and business is not easy to bridge, and, consequently, considerable effort has been expended to devise ways of getting mutual antagonists to negotiate over an extended period. As argued above, once accepted at the bargaining table, citizen groups could be attractive coalition partners for business organizations.

Third, . . . citizen groups typically have a great deal of credibility with the press. Thus, in negotiating, they often have had more to gain by going public to gain leverage with other bargainers. This adds increased uncertainty and instability to the structure of negotiations.

Fourth, citizen groups are often more unified than their business adversaries. The business interests in an issue network may consist of large producers, small producers, foreign producers, and companies from other industries trying to expand into new markets. All these business interests may be fiercely divided as each tries to defend or encroach upon established market patterns. The environmentalists in the same network, while each may have its own niche in terms of issue specialization, are likely to present a united front on major policy disputes. In a perverse way, then, the position of citizen groups has been aided by the proliferation of business groups. (Even without the intrusion of citizen lobbies, this sharp rise in the number of business groups would have irretrievably changed the nature of subgovernments.) . . .

Conclusion

Citizen groups have changed the policymaking process in valuable and enduring ways. Most important, they have broadened representation in our political system. Many previously unrepresented or underrepresented constituencies now have a powerful voice in Washington politics. The expanding numbers of liberal citizen groups and their apparent success helped to stimulate a broad mobilization on the part of business. The skyrocketing increase in the numbers of interest groups worked to break down subgovernments and led to the rise of issue networks.

Issue networks are more fragmented, less predictable policymaking environments. Both Congress and the executive branch have taken steps to bring about greater centralized control and coherence to policymaking. Some of these institutional changes seem aimed directly at citizen groups. Negotiated regulations, for example, are seen as a way of getting around the impasse that often develops between liberal citizen groups and business organizations. Centralized regulatory review has been used by Republican administrations as a means of ensuring that business interests are given primacy; regulators are seen as too sympathetic to the citizen groups that are clients of their agencies.

Although government has established these and other institutional mechanisms for coping with complex policymaking environments, the American public does not seem to feel that the government copes very well at all. Congress has been portrayed as unproductive and spineless, unwilling to tackle the tough problems that require discipline or sacrifice. At the core of this criticism is that interest groups are the culprit. Washington lobbies, representing every conceivable interest and showering legislators with the political action committee donations they crave, are said to be responsible for this country's inability to solve its problems.

Although it is counterintuitive, it may be that the increasing number of interest groups coupled with the rise of citizen groups has actually improved the policymaking system in some important ways. More specifically, our policymaking process may be more democratic today because of these developments. Expanded interest group participation has helped to make the policymaking process more open and visible. The closed nature of subgovernment politics meant not only that participation was restricted but that public scrutiny was minimal. The proliferation of interest groups, Washington media that are more aggressive, and the willingness and ability of citizen groups in particular to go public as part of their advocacy strategy have worked to open up policymaking to the public eye.

The end result of expanded citizen group advocacy is policy communities that are highly participatory and more broadly representative of the public. One can argue that this more democratic policymaking process is also one that is less capable of concerted action; yet there is no reliable evidence that American government is any more or less responsive to pressing policy problems than it has ever been. There are, of course, difficult problems that remain unresolved, but that is surely true of every era. Democracy requires adequate representation of interests as well as institutions capable of addressing difficult policy problems. For policymakers who must balance the demand for representation with the need for results, the key is thinking creatively about how to build coalitions and structure negotiations between large groups of actors.

POSTSCRIPT

Is Government Dominated by Big Business?

One of the problems for any pluralist is the danger that many people may not be properly represented. Suppose, for example, that business and environmental groups in Washington compromise their differences by supporting environmental legislation but passing the costs along to consumers. The legislation may be good, even necessary, but have the consumer's interests been taken into account? There are, of course, self-styled consumer groups, but it is hard to determine whether or not they really speak for the average consumer. The challenge for pluralists is to make their system as inclusive as possible.

Social science literature contains a number of works on the issues of pluralism and corporate power. Political scientist Charles E. Lindblom supported pluralism in the 1950s, but he later changed his mind and concluded that big business dominates American policy making. Lindblom takes the pluralist perspective in his early book *Politics, Economics, and Welfare* (Harper, 1953), written with Robert A. Dahl. His repudiation of pluralism was complete by the time he published *Politics and Markets: The World's Political-Economic Systems* (Basic Books, 1977). Ever since the obvious demonstration of corporate influence in the elections of 1980, Lindblom's view has been dominant. More recent works arguing that corporate elites possess inordinate power in American society are G. William Domhoff, *The Power Elite and the State* (Aldine de Gruyter, 1990) and *State Autonomy or Class Dominance?* (Aldine de Gruyter, 1996); Michael Parenti, *America Besieged* (City Lights Books, 1998); Dan Clawson et al., *Money Talks: Corporate PACs and Political Influence* (Basic Books, 1992); and Mark S. Mizruchi, *The Structure of Corporate Political Action: Interfirm Relations and Their Consequences* (Harvard University Press, 1992). For an analysis of the changes taking place in the organization of corporate power, see Michael Useem, *Investor Capitalism: How Money Managers Are Changing the Face of Corporate America* (Basic Books, 1996).

For some pluralist arguments, see Andrew M. Greeley, *Building Coalitions* (Franklin Watts, 1974); David Vogel, *Fluctuating Fortunes: The Political Power of Business in America* (Basic Books, 1989) and *Kindred Strangers: The Uneasy Relationship Between Politics and Business in America* (Princeton University Press, 1996); John P. Heinz, Edward O. Laumann, Robert L. Nelson, and Robert H. Salisbury, *The Hollow Core: Private Interests in National Policy Making* (Harvard University Press, 1993); Lawrence S. Rothenberg, *Linking Citizens to Government: Interest Group Politics at Common Cause* (Cambridge University Press, 1992); and Susan Herbst, *Numbered Voices: How Opinion Polls Shape American Politics* (University of Chicago Press, 1993).

ISSUE 11

Should Government Intervene in a Capitalist Economy?

YES: Ernest Erber, from "Virtues and Vices of the Market: Balanced Correctives to a Current Craze," *Dissent* (Summer 1990)

NO: Milton Friedman and Rose Friedman, from *Free to Choose: A Personal Statement* (Harcourt Brace Jovanovich, 1980)

ISSUE SUMMARY

YES: Author Ernest Erber argues that capitalism creates serious social problems that need to be redressed by an activist government.

NO: Economists Milton Friedman and Rose Friedman maintain that market competition, when permitted to work unimpeded, protects citizens better than government regulations intended to correct for failures of the market.

The expression "That government is best which governs least" sums up a deeply rooted attitude of many Americans. From early presidents Thomas Jefferson and Andrew Jackson to America's most recent leaders, Ronald Reagan, George Bush, and Bill Clinton, American politicians have often echoed the popular view that there are certain areas of life best left to the private actions of citizens.

One such area is the economic sphere, where people make their living by buying, selling, and producing goods and services. The tendency of most Americans is to regard direct government involvement in the economic sphere as both unnecessary and dangerous. The purest expression of this view is the economic theory of *laissez-faire,* a French term meaning "let be" or "let alone." The seminal formulation of *laissez-faire* theory was the work of eighteenth-century Scottish philosopher Adam Smith, whose treatise *The Wealth of Nations* appeared in 1776. Smith's thesis was that each individual, pursuing his or her own selfish interests in a competitive market, will be "led by an invisible hand to promote an end which was no part of his intention." In other words, when people single-mindedly seek profit, they actually serve the community because sellers must keep prices down and quality up if they are to meet the competition of other sellers.

Laissez-faire economics was much honored (in theory, if not always in practice) during the nineteenth and early twentieth centuries. But as the nineteenth century drew to a close, the Populist Party sprang up. The Populists denounced eastern bankers, Wall Street stock manipulators, and rich "moneyed interests," and they called for government ownership of railroads, a progressive income tax, and other forms of state intervention. The Populist Party died out early in the twentieth century, but the Populist message was not forgotten. In fact, it was given new life after 1929, when the stock market collapsed and the United States was plunged into the worst economic depression in its history.

By 1932 a quarter of the nation's workforce was unemployed, and most Americans were finding it hard to believe that the "invisible hand" would set things right. Some Americans totally repudiated the idea of a free market and embraced socialism, the belief that the state (or "the community") should run all major industries. Most stopped short of supporting socialism, but they were now prepared to welcome some forms of state intervention in the economy. President Franklin D. Roosevelt, elected in 1932, spoke to this mood when he pledged a "New Deal" to the American people. "New Deal" has come to stand for a variety of programs that were enacted during the first eight years of Roosevelt's presidency, including business and banking regulations, government pension programs, federal aid to the disabled, unemployment compensation, and government-sponsored work programs. Side by side with the "invisible hand" of the marketplace was now the very visible hand of an activist government.

Government intervention in the economic sphere increased during World War II as the government fixed prices, rationed goods, and put millions to work in government-subsidized war industries. Activist government continued during the 1950s, but the biggest leap forward occurred during the late 1960s and early 1970s, when the federal government launched a variety of new welfare and regulatory programs: the multibillion-dollar War on Poverty, new civil rights and affirmative action mandates, and new laws protecting consumers, workers, disabled people, and the environment. These, in turn, led to a proliferation of new government agencies and bureaus, as well as shelves and shelves of published regulations. Proponents of the new activism conceded that it was expensive, but they insisted that activist government was necessary to protect Americans against pollution, discrimination, dangerous products, and other effects of the modern marketplace. Critics of government involvement called attention not only to its direct costs but also to its effect on business activity and individual freedom.

In the following selections, Ernest Erber argues that although competitive markets are very productive, they bring about a variety of negative consequences, and he concludes that business regulation and other forms of government intervention are necessary to counter some of the harmful effects of the marketplace. Milton Friedman and Rose Friedman argue that the "invisible hand" of the market will work effectively if it is allowed to do so without government interference. Although decades old, this debate may well be one of the major debates of the coming decade.

Ernest Erber

 **YES**

Virtues and Vices of the Market: Balanced Correctives to a Current Craze

Not since they encountered it in nursery rhymes have references to the market so intruded into the consciousness of Americans as in recent months. There is now a virtual consensus that the market is the natural state of economic affairs, and its creation in nations not yet blessed with it is the prescription for every economic ailment. This makes vague good sense to most Americans, for whom the market has pleasant associations. Not surprisingly, for the market has long since come to determine their tastes and values, their very lives....

This worldwide consensus would not exist if it did not reflect a body of evidence that links the market with economic growth, increased productivity, and improved living standards. That this historical progress has been facilitated by the market's competitive and entrepreneurial incentives cannot be contested. Neither can the beliefs that the market's function as a pricing mechanism has historically contributed to economic stability conducive to growth, even if plagued by a persistent tendency toward inflation in recent years, nor that the market's negative, even self-destructive, side effects have been largely diminished by state intervention through regulation, credit-budget-tax policies, price supports, and social welfare programs....

Nature of the Market

... The market as we know it today is the historically specific product of industrial capitalism and can only be understood if perceived as such....

The Market is, essentially, an economic decision-making process that determines the allocation of society's resources by deciding what and how much is produced and how and to whom it is distributed. Those who participate in this process are buyers and sellers who "meet" in the "marketplace," though they are not only individuals, since buyers and sellers also include businesses of all sizes, farmers and professionals as groups, governments at all levels.

As an alternative to the Market, society's resources can also be directly allocated by political decisions of government (that is, by "command"). Government can also act deliberately to influence indirectly how the Market functions indirectly. Those who determine a government's economic role are citizens, governing officials, and administrators (including, sometimes, planners, though every governmental impact upon the economy should not be called "planning" and, in the United States, it almost never is that). Within capitalist economies, the purpose of governmental intervention in the Market is twofold: (1) to facilitate the functioning of the Market by protecting it from its shortcomings, including tendencies toward self-destructiveness; (2) to supplement the Market by providing those goods and services that the Market has no incentive to supply because they do not entail a profit (public schools, social welfare, low-cost housing, infrastructure, and so on).

The extent to which government should influence the economy is an issue that has been fought over for a very long time. Charles E. Lindblom begins his definitive *Politics and Markets* by observing that "the greatest distinction between one government and another is in the degree to which market replaces government or government replaces market. Both Adam Smith and Karl Marx knew this."

⋞◉⋟

The word "degree" is used by Lindblom deliberately, for neither the Market nor government replaces the other completely. Thus all economies are a mix of the Market and political decision making. Even the totally mad Stalinist effort to eliminate the Market in Soviet-type societies fell short of complete success, for these societies had to tolerate market operations in corners of the economy, either by compromise, as in permitted sales from garden plots of collective farmers and *kolkhoz* "surplus" production, or through black market sales of scarce commodities, tolerated because they were considered helpful to the economy.

Another variant of madness, though largely rhetorical, is the Thatcherite and Reaganite pronouncements about getting government out of the economy and "letting the market decide." After a decade of such huffing and puffing, the role of government vis-à-vis the economy, both in Great Britain and in the United States, remains essentially unchanged, some privatizations notwithstanding. . . .

⋞◉⋟

A final aspect of the Market's historical context is the largely forgotten role played by the state in getting market-based economies off the ground in various parts of the world. Japan, Prussia, and Czarist Russia are outstanding examples of the state's role in "jump starting" both capitalist production and market relations through generous credit, subsidies, enactment of special rights, licenses, and so on. Government construction of infrastructure often played a key role.

What we can conclude is that the prevailing view that attributes the material progress of human societies during the last century or two *solely* to the Market is fallacious, because the Market's contribution cannot be sufficiently separated from that of the Industrial Revolution, the capitalist mode of production, or the nourishing role of the state. To the extent that references to the

Market are euphemistic in order to advocate capitalism under another name, there is an implied admission that the Market cannot be separated from capitalism, that is, private property in the means of production, labor as a commodity, unearned income, accumulation, and so forth. But insofar as there now exists an effort to utilize the Market's virtues, while straining out its vices, in order to serve the common welfare, an assessment of its feasibility cannot be made until we have clearer insights into how it would resolve a number of contradictions that seem to make this objective unworkable.

The Market's Side Effects and Political Remedies

The following descriptions of the Market's side effects are valid, on the whole, though in some cases not entirely separable from other causes. The rationale of the Market is competition—for survival and gain. It pits each against all in social Darwinian "survival of the fittest": worker against worker and entrepreneur against entrepreneur, capital against labor and producer against consumer. The weak are eliminated and the strong survive, resulting in the trend toward concentration and monopolies. Businesses live by the "bottom line," with an incentive toward price gouging, adulteration, misrepresentation, environmental degradation. Product or service promotion caters to every human weakness. Advertising seduces consumers to develop endless wants. The central effect is to subvert human solidarity and civic responsibility.

The multitudinous buy/sell decisions that drive the market process are made in total ignorance of their collective impact, as expressed in Adam Smith's now hoary "unseen hand." Its social impact causes society to "fly blind," as when millions of individually bought automobiles collectively spell traffic gridlock and death-dealing air pollution. Government seeks to overcome these destructive results by regulating the manufacture of automobiles and gasoline. If this fails, as is likely, government will have to turn to long-range planning of alternate transportation, replacing private automobile trips with public conveyances. This will be a political decision to allocate resources from the private sector's automobile solution to the public sector's rail and bus solution. This is only one example of the choices between decisions by the Market and by the political process (made with or without planning).

The nineteenth-century laissez-faire market process, almost total economic determination by consumer demand, eventually proved unworkable. This was capitalism as Karl Marx knew it, and unworkable as he had predicted. During the course of the twentieth century, laissez-faire gave way to large-scale political intervention, resulting in state-guided and, increasingly, state-managed capitalism, with the state's control of money flow through central banks (Federal Reserve in the United States), credit control, tariffs and quotas, subsidies, tax policy, industrial and agricultural loans, price supports, wages policy, loan guarantees, savings incentives, marketing assistance, stockpiling, and various regulatory controls. This continuing transformation of market-based economies, which has come to be known as the Keynesian Revolution, is likely to be viewed by historians as of greater significance than the Soviet Revolution.

The proportions of market vs. political decision making in economic affairs does not necessarily reflect the proportions of private vs. state ownership of the economy. State-owned industries in countries such as Austria, Italy, and France, where they form a high proportion of the economy, are largely indistinguishable from the private sector in operating by the rules of the Market to produce in response to consumer demand. On the other hand, despite a relatively small nationalized sector, the state in Sweden is omnipresent in managing economic affairs. *The current widespread tilt toward privatization does not, therefore, diminish the trend toward an increased role of the state in economic affairs.*

The Market process demands that those who wish to participate pay admission. Those who cannot afford to get in—or who drop out—fall through the cracks; if lucky, into a social safety net. As the burden increased beyond private charities' resources, government was forced to assume it and the twentieth century's "welfare state" emerged. Its "transfer" programs of public goods and services exist outside the Market for those who cannot make it within.

The insecurity of various categories of entrepreneurs (such as farmers, oil drillers, ship owners, owners of small businesses, bank depositors), caused by the instability and unpredictability of the market process, led these entrepreneurs to use their political power to seek public assistance through subsidies, loans, insurance, "bailouts," and so forth, eventually becoming entitlements. The latter, together with welfare state transfer payments, proliferated and grew enormously, in part because they reflected the universal transition within affluent societies from satisfying needs to meeting wants. Adding these to the cost of traditional categories of public goods and services (such as national defense, public schools, parks, libraries, streets and roads) resulted in ballooning governmental budgets and the diversion through taxation of increasing proportions of the GNPs of industrial nations to their public sectors.

This had the effect of cutting into the availability of accumulated capital for investment in direct wealth-producing enterprise. Government response differed sharply, depending upon whether it followed a national economic policy or relied upon the Market. Sweden, an example of the former, tapped its Supplementary Pension Program to create the so-called fourth fund for targeted industrial investment, creating and sustaining employment that yielded a flow of payroll deductions back into the fund. The United States, on the other hand, permitted Market forces to drive up interest rates, bringing an inflow of foreign capital and an outflow of dividends and interest.

But, regardless of how the problem is managed, there are political limits to the diversion of funds from the private sector to the public sector via taxation. This can be seen in the "tax revolts" in Europe and the United States in the last two decades, which also had repercussions in the Scandinavian countries, including Sweden. This diversion also triggered the resurgence of laissez-faire ideology and right-wing politics.

Even for those countries in which the Market successfully accumulates the "wealth of nations," there results a lopsided inequality of distribution within the population, resulting in recurring economic instability and social confrontation. (Brazil, a country with the eighth largest Market-based economy in the world, leads all others in polarization between rich and poor.) The Market process generates cyclical and chronic unemployment, bankruptcies, mass layoffs, over- and underproduction, strikes and lockouts, and many other kinds of economic warfare and social tension. There is good reason to believe that the sharp shift in income from earned to unearned during the 1980s will be reflected in rising class conflict in the 1990s.

The Market is not a surefire prescription for the "wealth of nations" because its acclaimed incentives, acting as a spur to economic development, are also historically specific. Just because eighteenth-century England used the Market process to turn itself into a "nation of shopkeepers" and nineteenth-century England used it to lead the way in the Industrial Revolution to become the "world's workshop," is no assurance that, at any other time in history, people of any other culture and level of development can similarly use the Market to the same end—notwithstanding the examples of Western Europe, the United States, Canada, and Japan. (South Korea and Taiwan, judged by their per capita incomes, have not yet made it.)

Internationally, the Market has resulted in hierarchical ranking of nations by wealth, grouping a fortunate few as the rich nations and the rest as relatively or absolutely poor. Market-process relations between the industrially developed nations and the rest take the form of the developed responding to the consumer-driven demands of the underdeveloped for investments, loans, goods, and services, thereby aggravating their dependency, and frustrating their ability to accumulate enough capital to significantly improve their productivity (Argentina, Brazil, Mexico, Egypt, India, to name some).

In summarizing the Market's negative side effects we have noted that it flies blindly; that its growth becomes destructive of communitarian values and institutions and of the natural environment; that its "work ethic" becomes exploitation, even of children (child labor is again on the rise in the United States according to the Department of Labor); that it reduces the cost of production but also triggers inflation; that it produces a cornucopia of goods but also mountains of waste; that its pharmaceutical research lengthens lifespans, but its chemicals (pesticides and herbicides) shorten them; that it makes feverish use of humankind's growing power over nature, born of scientific and technological progress, but puts profits above ecology and market share above the need to conserve natural resources; that it provides conveniences, comforts, and luxuries for an increasing number but shows no ability to close the widening gap between haves and have nots, neither within nor between nations. But, above all, the Market, despite Keynesianism, operates in cycles of boom and bust, victimizing businesses, large and small, farmers, professionals, and wage workers. Left to its own devices, the Market is inherently self-destructive.

Though the Market's negative side effects can be countered through government intervention and largely have been, such countering tends to be ameliorative rather than curative, and often raises new problems requiring additional intervention, thus reinforcing the overall tendency for the state to backstop the Market. But, despite this, Market economies still move blindly, though increasingly within broad channels marked out by government. The Market economy still overheats and runs out of fuel, but government now acts to cool it and then to fuel it (and even attempts to "fine tune" it). Will it prove a viable arrangement in the long term for government to treat the Market as if it were an elemental force of nature?

The people seem to want the benefits of the Market, but look to government to minimize the dreadful side effects that come with it. But one person's "dreadful side effects" are another person's sweet accumulation of capital. Translated into social relations, this conflict of interests expresses itself as interest-group confrontations and social-class struggles. And as decision making in economic affairs continues to shift from the Market to the political process, an ever fiercer political resistance is mounted by the interest groups and classes whose power is far greater and more direct in the Market than in the political arena—for instance, the resurgence of the new right in waging ideological and political warfare on behalf of laissez-faire policies.

The Market's Thrust vs. Societal Guidance

Understanding the direction in which the Market is likely to move in the next few decades is critically important to an assessment of its capacity to accommodate solutions for outstanding problems. In the past, especially since World War II, the Market's contribution to easing the great problems of civilization has been in the form of economic growth. The nature of the problems that now loom, however, makes them less subject to solution through economic growth. The rising tide that once raised all boats now leaves many stuck on muddy bottoms.

Market-based growth has not demonstrated an ability to reduce the glaring inequality in living standards and in educational/cultural levels within and between nations. In the United States during the last decade the gap between the bottom and the top of the income quintiles has widened. And growth solutions now generate new problems: the degradation of the natural environment on earth and in space; the exhaustion of natural resources; the emergence of *social* limits to growth, caused by the level at which acquisition of goods, services, and facilities by enough people spoils the advantages of possessing them; the puzzle of insatiable wants after basic needs have been satisfied (when is enough enough?). There are also the growth of private affluence and public squalor; an individualistic society's reluctance to resort to collective solutions (national health care) before first going through the agony of postponing the inevitable, and other looming problems sensed but seemingly too elusively complex to articulate. These problems join a long list of old problems that go unsolved to become a leaden weight on progress.

Is there reason to believe that the Market's failure to cope with these problems will (or can) be remedied in the future? Is there anything in the nature and function of the Market that is likely to redirect its performance to be able to solve these problems? Are any of its negative side effects going to be eliminated, except insofar as governmentally applied correctives can curb them without altering the overall thrust of the Market? Left to its own devices, the Market's current trends are likely to expand and exacerbate problems. Are any countervailing forces in view? Yes.

One is the sharpening competition in the world market. The latter is being badly misread. True, a coded message on a computer or fax machine can transfer billions of dollars overseas at the end of the business day and retrieve it first thing in the morning—with earnings added. True, multinationals no longer fly a single flag. But national interests are as sharply defined as ever. And waging war with economic weapons has not reduced competitiveness and aggressiveness. The competitors are dividing into several major blocs: North America (the United States plus Canada and Mexico), Japan (plus the Asian rim countries) and a united Europe. The goal: market share. As Japan has shown (and also Europe to a lesser extent), this warfare requires maximum mobilization of economic resources: capital, management, knowledge-industry, and labor. Japan has shown that the way to bring these together is by making them all part of the corporate state. The power of Japan, Inc. is recognized in all American boardrooms, though a much smaller nation, Sweden, has also used the corporate strategy brilliantly. The striking similarity of Japanese and Swedish economic strategies, though for different social ends, is largely overlooked because the former is dominated by corporations and the latter by organized labor acting through the Social Democratic party.

The corporate state strategy has antimarket overtones. Rather than letting the market decide, it operates through strategic planning and a national industrial (investment) policy. If global market share is the goal, the nation's consumers had better not be permitted to decide on the allocation of resources. Laissez-faire America illustrates why not. The consumers opt for second homes, third cars, snowmobiles, Jacuzzis, and Torneau watches, thereby short-changing education at all levels, skill retraining of the labor force, housing, and health care—all essential ingredients in mobilizing resources to fight for market share.

The last thing any nation needs or will ever want after the debacle of the Stalinist model is an administrative-command economy (misnamed "planning"). Let the Market process determine the number, style, size, and color of shoes. And similarly for other basic needs and reasonable wants. But the nation also has collective needs, and the polity should determine the allocation of resources to supply them. Because this cannot be determined by the blind outcomes of the Market, the latter must be subordinated to strategically planned priorities designed to serve an overriding common purpose.

If coping with the major problems facing humankind in both its social and natural environments requires societal guidance, it necessitates setting goals and choosing strategies to achieve them; in short, strategic planning.

This calls for conscious, deliberate, and coordinated measures to mobilize a nation's resources. The American people with its Market-instilled value system is decidedly averse to this (except in time of war, when by political decision a goal-oriented government controlled wages, employment, prices, profits, manufacturing, and construction).

The twenty-first is not likely to be an American Century. Clinging to the Market, the negation of societal guidance, we might not even come in second. More likely we will be third, after a united Europe and an Asian-rim dominant Japan operating with strategic planning. Americans are more likely to be content with nursery reveries of

> *To market, to market, to buy a fat pig,*
> *Home again, home again, to dance a fast jig.*

Free to Choose

The Power of the Market

The Role of Prices

The key insight of Adam Smith's *Wealth of Nations* is misleadingly simple: if an exchange between two parties is voluntary, it will not take place unless both believe they will benefit from it. Most economic fallacies derive from the neglect of this simple insight, from the tendency to assume that there is a fixed pie, that one party can gain only at the expense of another.

This key insight is obvious for a simple exchange between two individuals. It is far more difficult to understand how it can enable people living all over the world to cooperate to promote their separate interests.

The price system is the mechanism that performs this task without central direction, without requiring people to speak to one another or to like one another. When you buy your pencil or your daily bread, you don't know whether the pencil was made or the wheat was grown by a white man or a black man, by a Chinese or an Indian. As a result, the price system enables people to cooperate peacefully in one phase of their life while each one goes about his own business in respect of everything else.

Adam Smith's flash of genius was his recognition that the prices that emerged from voluntary transactions between buyers and sellers—for short, in a free market—could coordinate the activity of millions of people, each seeking his own interest, in such a way as to make everyone better off. It was a startling idea then, and it remains one today, that economic order can emerge as the unintended consequence of the actions of many people, each seeking his own interest.

The price system works so well, so efficiently, that we are not aware of it most of the time. We never realize how well it functions until it is prevented from functioning, and even then we seldom recognize the source of the trouble.

The long gasoline lines that suddenly emerged in 1974 after the OPEC oil embargo, and again in the spring and summer of 1979 after the revolution in Iran, are a striking recent example. On both occasions there was a sharp disturbance in the supply of crude oil from abroad. But that did not lead to gasoline lines in Germany or Japan, which are wholly dependent on imported oil. It led to long gasoline lines in the United States, even though we produce much of our own oil, for one reason and one reason only: because legislation, administered by a government agency, did not permit the price system to function. Prices in some areas were kept by command below the level that would have equated the amount of gasoline available at the gas stations to the amount consumers wanted to buy at that price. Supplies were allocated to different areas of the country by command, rather than in response to the pressures of demand as reflected in price. The result was surpluses in some areas and shortages plus long gasoline lines in others. The smooth operation of the price system—which for many decades had assured every consumer that he could buy gasoline at any of a large number of service stations at his convenience and with a minimal wait —was replaced by bureaucratic improvisation....

The Role of Government

Where does government enter into the picture?...

[W]hat role should be assigned to government?

It is not easy to improve on the answer that Adam Smith gave to this question two hundred years ago:

> ... According to the system of natural liberty, the sovereign has only three duties to attend to; three duties of great importance, indeed, but plain and intelligible to common understandings: first, the duty of protecting the society from the violence and invasion of other independent societies; secondly, the duty of protecting, as far as possible, every member of the society from the injustice or oppression of every other member of it, or the duty of establishing an exact administration of justice; and thirdly, the duty of erecting and maintaining certain public works and certain public institutions, which it can never be for the interest of any individual, or small number of individuals, to erect and maintain; because the profit could never repay the expence to any individual or small number of individuals, though it may frequently do much more than repay it to a great society.

... A fourth duty of government that Adam Smith did not explicitly mention is the duty to protect members of the community who cannot be regarded as "responsible" individuals. Like Adam Smith's third duty, this one, too, is susceptible of great abuse. Yet it cannot be avoided....

Adam Smith's three duties, or our four duties of government, are indeed "of great importance," but they are far less "plain and intelligible to common understandings" than he supposed. Though we cannot decide the desirability or undesirability of any actual or proposed government intervention by mechanical reference to one or another of them, they provide a set of principles that we can use in casting up a balance sheet of pros and cons. Even on the loosest interpretation, they rule out much existing government intervention—all those "systems either of preference or of restraint" that Adam Smith fought against, that were subsequently destroyed, but have since reappeared in the form of today's tariffs, governmentally fixed prices and wages, restrictions on entry into various occupations, and numerous other departures from his "simple system of natural liberty." ...

Cradle to Grave

... At the end of the war [World War II] it looked as if central economic planning was the wave of the future. That outcome was passionately welcomed by some who saw it as the dawn of a world of plenty shared equally. It was just as passionately feared by others, including us, who saw it as a turn to tyranny and misery. So far, neither the hopes of the one nor the fears of the other have been realized.

Government has expanded greatly. However, that expansion has not taken the form of detailed central economic planning accompanied by ever widening nationalization of industry, finance, and commerce, as so many of us feared it would. Experience put an end to detailed economic planning, partly because it was not successful in achieving the announced objectives, but also because it conflicted with freedom....

The failure of planning and nationalization has not eliminated pressure for an ever bigger government. It has simply altered its direction. The expansion of government now takes the form of welfare programs and of regulatory activities. As W. Allen Wallis put it in a somewhat different context, socialism, "intellectually bankrupt after more than a century of seeing one after another of its arguments for socializing the *means* of production demolished—now seeks to socialize the *results* of production."

In the welfare area the change of direction has led to an explosion in recent decades, especially after President Lyndon Johnson declared a "War on Poverty" in 1964. New Deal programs of Social Security, unemployment insurance, and direct relief were all expanded to cover new groups; payments were increased; and Medicare, Medicaid, food stamps, and numerous other programs were added. Public housing and urban renewal programs were enlarged. By now there are literally hundreds of government welfare and income transfer programs. The Department of Health, Education and Welfare, established in 1953 to consolidate the scattered welfare programs, began with a budget of $2 billion, less than 5 percent of expenditures on national defense. Twenty-five years later, in 1978, its budget was $160 billion, one and a half times as much as total spending on the army, the navy, and the air force. It had the third largest budget in the world, exceeded only by the entire budget of the U.S. government and of the Soviet Union....

No one can dispute two superficially contradictory phenomena: widespread dissatisfaction with the results of this explosion in welfare activities; continued pressure for further expansion.

The objectives have all been noble; the results, disappointing. Social Security expenditures have skyrocketed, and the system is in deep financial trouble. Public housing and urban renewal programs have subtracted from rather than added to the housing available to the poor. Public assistance rolls mount despite growing employment. By general agreement, the welfare program is a "mess" saturated with fraud and corruption. As government has paid a larger share of the nation's medical bills, both patients and physicians complain of rocketing costs and of the increasing impersonality of medicine. In education, student performance has dropped as federal intervention has expanded. . . .

The repeated failure of well-intentioned programs is not an accident. It is not simply the result of mistakes of execution. The failure is deeply rooted in the use of bad means to achieve good objectives.

Despite the failure of these programs, the pressure to expand them grows. Failures are attributed to the miserliness of Congress in appropriating funds, and so are met with a cry for still bigger programs. Special interests that benefit from specific programs press for their expansion—foremost among them the massive bureaucracy spawned by the programs. . . .

Created Equal

Capitalism and Equality

Everywhere in the world there are gross inequities of income and wealth. They offend most of us. Few can fail to be moved by the contrast between the luxury enjoyed by some and the grinding poverty suffered by others.

In the past century a myth has grown up that free market capitalism— equality of opportunity as we have interpreted that term—increases such inequalities, that it is a system under which the rich exploit the poor.

Nothing could be further from the truth. Wherever the free market has been permitted to operate, wherever anything approaching equality of opportunity has existed, the ordinary man has been able to attain levels of living never dreamed of before. Nowhere is the gap between rich and poor wider, nowhere are the rich richer and the poor poorer, than in those societies that do not permit the free market to operate. That is true of feudal societies like medieval Europe, India before independence, and much of modern South America, where inherited status determines position. It is equally true of centrally planned societies, like Russia or China or India since independence, where access to government determines position. It is true even where central planning was introduced, as in all three of these countries, in the name of equality. . . .

Who Protects the Consumer?

. . . The pace of intervention quickened greatly after the New Deal—half of the thirty-two agencies in existence in 1966 were created after FDR's election in 1932. Yet intervention remained fairly moderate and continued in the single-industry mold. The *Federal Register*, established in 1936 to record all the regulations, hearings, and other matters connected with the regulatory agencies, grew, at first rather slowly, then more rapidly. Three volumes, containing 2,599 pages and taking six inches of shelf space, sufficed for 1936; twelve volumes, containing 10,528 pages and taking twenty-six inches of shelf space, for 1956; and thirteen volumes, containing 16,850 pages and taking thirty-six inches of shelf space, for 1966.

Then a veritable explosion in government regulatory activity occurred. No fewer than twenty-one new agencies were established in the next decade. Instead of being concerned with specific industries, they covered the waterfront: the environment, the production and distribution of energy, product safety, occupational safety, and so on. In addition to concern with the consumer's pocketbook, with protecting him from exploitation by sellers, recent agencies are primarily concerned with things like the consumer's safety and well-being, with protecting him not only from sellers but also from himself.

Government expenditures on both older and newer agencies skyrocketed— from less than $1 billion in 1970 to roughly $5 billion estimated for 1979. Prices in general roughly doubled, but these expenditures more than quintupled. The number of government bureaucrats employed in regulatory activities tripled, going from 28,000 in 1970 to 81,000 in 1979; the number of pages in the *Federal Register*, from 17,660 in 1970 to 36,487 in 1978, taking 127 inches of shelf space —a veritable ten-foot shelf....

This revolution in the role of government has been accompanied, and largely produced, by an achievement in public persuasion that must have few rivals. Ask yourself what products are currently least satisfactory and have shown the least improvement over time. Postal service, elementary and secondary schooling, railroad passenger transport would surely be high on the list. Ask yourself which products are most satisfactory and have improved the most. Household appliances, television and radio sets, hi-fi equipment, computers, and, we would add, supermarkets and shopping centers would surely come high on that list.

The shoddy products are all produced by government or government-regulated industries. The outstanding products are all produced by private enterprise with little or no government involvement. Yet the public—or a large part of it—has been persuaded that private enterprises produce shoddy products, that we need ever vigilant government employees to keep business from foisting off unsafe, meretricious products at outrageous prices on ignorant, unsuspecting, vulnerable customers. That public relations campaign has succeeded so well that we are in the process of turning over to the kind of people who bring us our postal service the far more critical task of producing and distributing energy....

Government intervention in the marketplace is subject to laws of its own, not legislated laws, but scientific laws. It obeys forces and goes in directions that may have little relationship to the intentions or desires of its initiators or supporters. We have already examined this process in connection with welfare activity. It is present equally when government intervenes in the marketplace, whether to protect consumers against high prices or shoddy goods, to promote their safety, or to preserve the environment. Every act of intervention establishes positions of power. How that power will be used and for what purposes depends far more on the people who are in the best position to get control of that power and what their purposes are than on the aims and objectives of the initial sponsors of the intervention....

Environment

The environmental movement is responsible for one of the most rapidly growing areas of federal intervention. The Environmental Protection Agency, established in 1970 "to protect and enhance the physical environment," has been granted increasing power and authority. Its budget has multiplied sevenfold from 1970 to 1978 and is now more than half a billion dollars. It has a staff of about 7,000. It has imposed costs on industry and local and state governments to meet its standards that total in the tens of billions of dollars a year. Something between a tenth and a quarter of total net investment in new capital equipment by business now goes for antipollution purposes. And this does not count the costs of requirements imposed by other agencies, such as those designed to control emissions of motor vehicles, or the costs of land-use planning or wilderness preservation or a host of other federal, state, and local government activities undertaken in the name of protecting the environment.

The preservation of the environment and the avoidance of undue pollution are real problems and they are problems concerning which the government has an important role to play. When all the costs and benefits of any action, and the people hurt or benefited, are readily identifiable, the market provides an excellent means for assuring that only those actions are undertaken for which the benefits exceed the costs for all participants. But when the costs and benefits or the people affected cannot be identified, there is a market failure....

Government is one means through which we can try to compensate for "market failure," try to use our resources more effectively to produce the amount of clean air, water, and land that we are willing to pay for. Unfortunately, the very factors that produce the market failure also make it difficult for government to achieve a satisfactory solution. Generally, it is no easier for government to identify the specific persons who are hurt and benefited than for market participants, no easier for government to assess the amount of harm or benefit to each. Attempts to use government to correct market failure have often simply substituted government failure for market failure.

Public discussion of the environmental issue is frequently characterized more by emotion than reason. Much of it proceeds as if the issue is pollution versus no pollution, as if it were desirable and possible to have a world without pollution. That is clearly nonsense. No one who contemplates the problem seriously will regard zero pollution as either a desirable or a possible state of affairs. We could have zero pollution from automobiles, for example, by simply abolishing all automobiles. That would also make the kind of agricultural and industrial productivity we now enjoy impossible, and so condemn most of us to a drastically lower standard of living, perhaps many even to death. One source of atmospheric pollution is the carbon dioxide that we all exhale. We could stop that very simply. But the cost would clearly exceed the gain.

It costs something to have clean air, just as it costs something to have other good things we want. Our resources are limited and we must weigh the gains from reducing pollution against the costs. Moreover, "pollution" is not an objective phenomenon. One person's pollution may be another's pleasure. To some of us rock music is noise pollution; to others of us it is pleasure.

The real problem is not "eliminating pollution," but trying to establish arrangements that will yield the "right" amount of pollution: an amount such that the gain from reducing pollution a bit more just balances the sacrifice of the other good things—houses, shoes, coats, and so on—that would have to be given up in order to reduce the pollution. If we go farther than that, we sacrifice more than we gain....

The Market

Perfection is not of this world. There will always be shoddy products, quacks, con artists. But on the whole, market competition, when it is permitted to work, protects the consumer better than do the alternative government mechanisms that have been increasingly superimposed on the market.

As Adam Smith said ..., competition does not protect the consumer because businessmen are more soft-hearted than the bureaucrats or because they are more altruistic or generous, or even because they are more competent, but only because it is in the self-interest of the businessman to serve the consumer.

If one storekeeper offers you goods of lower quality or of higher price than another, you're not going to continue to patronize his store. If he buys goods to sell that don't serve your needs, you're not going to buy them. The merchants therefore search out all over the world the products that might meet your needs and might appeal to you. And they stand back of them because if they don't, they're going to go out of business. When you enter a store, no one forces you to buy. You are free to do so or go elsewhere. That is the basic difference between the market and a political agency. You are free to choose. There is no policeman to take the money out of your pocket to pay for something you do not want or to make you do something you do not want to do.

But, the advocate of government regulation will say, suppose the FDA weren't there, what would prevent business from distributing adulterated or dangerous products? It would be a very expensive thing to do.... It is very poor business practice—not a way to develop a loyal and faithful clientele. Of course, mistakes and accidents occur—but ... government regulation doesn't prevent them. The difference is that a private firm that makes a serious blunder may go out of business. A government agency is likely to get a bigger budget.

Cases will arise where adverse effects develop that could not have been foreseen—but government has no better means of predicting such developments than private enterprise. The only way to prevent all such developments would be to stop progress, which would also eliminate the possibility of unforeseen favorable developments....

What about the danger of monopoly that led to the antitrust laws? That is a real danger. The most effective way to counter it is not through a bigger antitrust division at the Department of Justice or a larger budget for the Federal Trade Commission, but through removing existing barriers to international trade. That would permit competition from all over the world to be even more effective than it is now in undermining monopoly at home. Freddie Laker of Britain needed no help from the Department of Justice to crack the airline cartel. Japanese and German automobile manufacturers forced American manufacturers to introduce smaller cars.

The great danger to the consumer is monopoly—whether private or governmental. His most effective protection is free competition at home and free trade throughout the world. The consumer is protected from being exploited by one seller by the existence of another seller from whom he can buy and who is eager to sell to him. Alternative sources of supply protect the consumer far more effectively than all the Ralph Naders of the world.

Conclusion

... [T]he reaction of the public to the more extreme attempts to control our behavior—to the requirement of an interlock system on automobiles or the proposed ban of saccharin—is ample evidence that we want no part of it. Insofar as the government has information not generally available about the merits or demerits of the items we ingest or the activities we engage in, let it give us the information. But let it leave us free to choose what chances we want to take with our own lives.

POSTSCRIPT

Should Government Intervene in a Capitalist Economy?

Erber concedes that the market should not be abolished. He writes that a "body of evidence . . . links the market with economic growth, increased productivity, and improved living standards," and that this linkage "cannot be contested." Nevertheless, he calls for an activist government to subordinate the market to "planned priorities designed to serve an overriding common purpose." The Friedmans believe that such subordination can only destroy the market. The question, then, is whether or not we can successfully graft the market's "invisible hand" to the arm of the state. Would the graft take? Has the experiment perhaps already proven successful in post–New Deal America? Or is the American government in the process of destroying what gave the nation its growth, prosperity, and living standards?

Erber calls the market a "blind" force. The Friedmans seem to agree that the market in itself is amoral, though they feel that it produces good results. But philosopher Michael Novak goes further, contending that the ethic of capitalism transcends mere moneymaking and is (or can be made) compatible with Judeo-Christian morality. See *The Spirit of Democratic Capitalism* (Madison Books, 1991) and *The Catholic Ethic and the Spirit of Capitalism* (Free Press, 1993). Another broad-based defense of capitalism is Peter L. Berger's *The Capitalist Revolution: Fifty Propositions About Prosperity, Equality and Liberty* (Basic Books, 1988). For an attack on capitalism, see Victor Perlo, *Superprofits and Crisis: Modern U.S. Capitalism* (International Publishers, 1988); Samir Amin, *Spectres of Capitalism* (Monthly Review Press, 1998); Jack Barnes, *Capitalism's World Disorder* (Pathfinders, 1999); and John Gray, *False Dawn: The Delusions of Global Capitalism* (Granta Books, 1998). Two captivating analyses of global capitalism are William Greider's *One World, Ready or Not: The Manic Logic of Global Capitalism* (Simon & Schuster, 1997) and Thomas Friedman's *The Lexus and the Olive Tree* (HarperCollins, 1999). For a feminist critique of capitalism, see J. K. Gibson-Graham, *The End of Capitalism (As We Know It): A Feminist Critique of Political Economy* (Blackwell, 1996). For a mixed view of capitalism, see Charles Wolf, Jr., *Markets or Governments: Choosing Between Imperfect Alternatives* (MIT Press, 1993). A strong attack on government interventions in the market is Jonathan Rauch, *Demosclerosis: The Silent Killer of American Government* (Times Books, 1994).

ISSUE 12

Has Welfare Reform Benefited the Poor?

YES: Ron Haskins, from "Welfare Reform Is Working: For the Poor and Taxpayers Both," *The American Enterprise* (January/February 1999)

NO: Karen Houppert, from "You're Not Entitled! Welfare 'Reform' Is Leading to Government Lawlessness," *The Nation* (October 25, 1999)

ISSUE SUMMARY

YES: Ron Haskins, staff director for the House Human Resources Subcommittee, states that both the poor and the taxpayers are better off due to the recent welfare reform. Haskins uses examples of former welfare recipients to support his assertion.

NO: Author Karen Houppert describes cases of welfare recipients who were denied the assistance to which they were entitled. Houppert also examines the bureaucratic problems that resulted in harmful consequences for the poor, which she asserts are a direct result of welfare reform.

In his 1984 book *Losing Ground: American Social Policy, 1950–1980* (Basic Books), policy analyst Charles Murray recommends abolishing Aid to Families with Dependent Children (AFDC), the program at the heart of the welfare debate. At the time of the book's publication this suggestion struck many as simply a dramatic way for Murray to make some of his points. However, 14 years later this idea became the dominant idea in Congress. In 1996 President Bill Clinton signed into law the Work Opportunity Reconciliation Act and fulfilled his 1992 campaign pledge to "end welfare as we know it." Murray's thesis that welfare hurt the poor had become widely accepted. In "What to Do About Welfare," *Commentary* (December 1994), Murray argues that welfare contributes to dependency, illegitimacy, and the number of absent fathers, which in turn can have terrible effects on the children involved. He states that workfare, enforced child support, and the abolition of welfare would greatly reduce these problems.

One reason why Congress ended AFDC was the emergence of a widespread backlash against welfare recipients. However, such attitudes seem to ignore the fact that most people on welfare are not professional loafers but women with dependent children who have intermittent periods of work, are elderly, or are disabled. Petty fraud may be common since welfare payments are insufficient to live on in many cities, but "welfare queens" who cheat the system for spectacular sums are so rare that they should not be part of any serious debate on welfare issues. The majority of people on welfare are those whose condition would become desperate if payments were cut off. Although many believe that women on welfare commonly bear children in order to increase their benefits, there is no conclusive evidence to support this conclusion. Also, over the last two decades payments to families with dependent children have eroded considerably relative to the cost of living.

Not all objections to AFDC can be easily dismissed, however. There does seem to be evidence that in some cases AFDC reduces work incentives and increases the likelihood of family breakups. But there is also a positive side to AFDC—it helped many needy people get back on their feet. AFDC-type programs will continue for a few years to allow welfare recipients time to be trained for jobs or to complete their schooling. Meanwhile, many have started work or are actively looking for work. This does not end the debate, however, since job retention is a major problem for many recipients.

On July 1, 1997, the Work Opportunity Reconciliation Act went into effect. It is too soon to obtain an accurate assessment of the impacts of the act. Nevertheless, AFDC rolls have declined since the act was passed, so many conclude that it is a success rather than a failure. Of course, the early leavers are the ones with the best prospects of succeeding in the work world; the welfare-to-work transition gets harder as the program works with the more difficult cases. The crucial question is whether or not the reform will benefit those it affects. Already many working former welfare recipients are better off. But what about the average or more vulnerable recipient?

Ron Haskins, in the following selection, finds the effects of welfare reform overwhelmingly positive but admits that the strong economy has greatly helped many programs succeed. What impresses him most is the transformation of welfare offices into job placement centers with the enthusiastic participation of the business community. Karen Houppert, in the second selection, counters that welfare reform is not a success. Houppert asserts that many people have been harmed and that many state and local governments have administered the reform in a cruel manner.

Ron Haskins

 **YES**

Welfare Reform Is Working

As I drove up Interstate 5 from San Diego to Long Beach, I thought back over 20-plus years of visiting welfare offices. Drab operations they were—interviewing moms, filling out 20-page forms, seeking verification of assets and income, calculating benefit amounts, all to spit out the grand product: government checks.

Since the passage of welfare reform in 1996, reports have suggested that a lot is changing in the way states administer welfare. But nothing prepared me for what I was about to witness.

As I pulled into the parking lot of the Regional Work Center in Long Beach, I was greeted by a young man in a blue blazer who ushered me into a large room with 15 people. For the next two hours, I heard a lot about jobs, training, wages, transportation, and child care. But nothing, absolutely nothing, about benefit levels or check writing.

The most striking thing about the meeting was the participants. In addition to the welfare administrators and recipients—standard fare for such meetings—we were joined by the president of Franklin Brass, an assembly and packaging company with about 400 employees; a regional personnel manager for United Airlines; the director of development for Delco Machine and Gear, a small machine company with about 90 employees; and the chief hiring agent for the Volt Company, a temporary employment agency. All were on a first-name basis with the administrator who ran the work program, Frank Mora. Each of the employers told me about their involvement with the program and then introduced one of the former welfare recipients they had hired. The work program administrators jumped in occasionally to explain various details of coordination or to propound their work-first philosophy.

Here's a typical story. Jim was a 19-year-old with two children, a wife, no job, and little education. When he and his wife applied for welfare benefits, Mora gave him an appointment to help him find a job. After Jim missed the appointment, Mora went to his apartment to find out why. Jim lived in a gang-infested neighborhood and had stayed home with a sick child. Mora gave him another appointment, worked with Jim and the local housing authority to find him a better apartment in a better neighborhood, and got him an interview with Delco. After several months on the job, the company was so impressed with Jim they offered to help pay for extensive training as a machine operator. When he finishes the training, Jim will be earning over $15 per hour with benefits.

◦◈◦

Under the old welfare regime, education and training programs for welfare recipients were often used by administrators as diversionary tactics to avoid actual work. By contrast, consider this example of training under the new regime: In his conversations with employers and his reading of want ads, Mora noticed lots of local demand for forklift operators. So he worked with officials at Long Beach City College to design a four-day course in forklift operation. In the first year, about 1,200 adults applying for or receiving welfare completed the course. Mora reports that 90 percent of them are now employed operating forklifts and earning at least $8 per hour with benefits.

My discussion with Bill Allen of United Airlines was equally revealing. He told me that if United places a newspaper ad, about half the people they hire from the ad will be gone within a year. But if they hire welfare participants through the Long Beach office, attrition is cut in half. Given the investment United makes in their employees, cutting attrition saves lots of money. Doubting adults on welfare would be more reliable employees than adults who respond to ads, I asked Allen if he could explain the difference in attrition rates. After considerable discussion it became clear that Mora didn't send just any welfare recipient to United Airlines; he sent only qualified recipients who had good records. In other words, the welfare office was screening people for jobs. The least qualified often started with the temporary employment agency; the best qualified were sent to United and other high-wage employers.

Like the Long Beach office, welfare offices all over Los Angeles County are transforming themselves into job-placement centers. The result is that welfare rolls are dropping precipitously. Over a 10-month period between 1997–98, the rolls in Los Angeles dropped more than 100,000, saving the state $54 million each month. Counties in the rest of California, including those with double-digit unemployment, report similar declines. According to the state's principal economist, it's "the only extended caseload reduction we have ever had."

◦◈◦

Switch coasts. We are now headed to the Anne Arundel County Job Center in Annapolis, Maryland, accompanied by a small delegation of British visitors intent on learning about American welfare reform. The British delegation is headed by Keith Bradley, Undersecretary for Social Welfare in the House of Commons.

We're visiting a program run by Democrats in a state controlled by Democrats, which is nice if you're a member of the British Labour party. Surely here we will find the old entitlement mentality and hostility toward the idea of replacing welfare with work.

On the way to the conference room, however, we pass walls decorated with posters touting the benefits of work and press accounts of former welfare mothers who've left welfare for jobs. As potential welfare dependents talk with job counselors in this converted bank building, a quiet efficiency pervades the place.

In the course of an hour's discussion, we hear more or less the same things the program managers said in Long Beach. Again, no talk about benefits; instead, all the talk is about job placements, child care, transportation, training. The enthusiasm in this office is electric. The attitude of the staff is, We should have been doing this all along.

And what "this" is can be stated simply: helping welfare applicants get a job before they get welfare. The first thing you see on the wall of the Annapolis office are the words "Job Center"—"welfare" is nowhere to be found. And they're not kidding. In a typical month, 1,700 "customers" walk into the Job Center. Fewer than 100 (6 percent) will wind up on cash welfare. The rest are diverted, mostly to employment.

Before the customers can even ask for cash welfare, they are interviewed by a job counselor who believes they can and should work. Then they are helped to prepare a résumé on the Center's public computer, assisted in arranging job interviews (using the phone bank available in the Job Center), provided with on-site child care if necessary, told about available education and training courses (which are not allowed to interfere with getting a job), and signed up for child support. The Job Center even has clothes available so the customers can dress properly for interviews. And if the customer has a transportation problem in this rural county with little public transportation, the job counselor is likely to sign her up for the lease-to-purchase plan for discarded county vehicles.

As in Los Angeles, data on the Annapolis program are clear and consistent. That only 6 percent of the adults who come into the Job Center in a typical month wind up on welfare indicates that this is a completely new kind of "welfare" program. And even among those who actually apply for welfare, only half receive cash benefits before they get a job.

Here are two more striking statistics. In October 1996, when the program started, the county spent $830,000 per month on cash welfare. A year later, the county spent $680,000, a 20 percent reduction. When the county started the Job Center, 9,100 families drew cash welfare. A year later the rolls had plummeted by 40 percent.

⋅❦⋅

Welfare declines like these are completely without historical precedent—but nowadays they are routine. The national rolls have shrunk by an astonishing 40 percent since their peak in March 1994. The highest previous decline in cash welfare rolls over any period of two or more years was 8 percent.

Lest anyone conclude that the current economic boom explains the decline, consider the Reagan expansion that began in 1982. As the economy added 17 million jobs over eight years, the welfare caseload actually increased by 13 percent. Even during the first three years of the current expansion, the welfare caseload expanded even as national employment grew. It was not until 1994, with the states implementing their own partial welfare reforms under Reagan-Bush waivers from federal rules, that the welfare caseload began to decline. Then, after the Republican Congress passed federal reform in 1996, caseloads plummeted. They are now dropping at the rate of nearly 6,000 recipients per day.

Caseload declines are an important indicator of success because they are an indirect measure of welfare families achieving self-reliance. But female employment and earnings are even more important indicators of success, and evidence is accumulating that welfare reform has had major effects on both. The Bureau of Labor Statistics reports that after cruising along at about 136,000 per year, the net increase in single-mothers with jobs rose to 272,000, a figure higher than ever before, in the 12-month period ending in October 1996—just as the states were implementing reforms on a limited basis. Over the next 12 months, after every state had implemented the federal welfare reform law, the figure exploded to 456,000.

As reform began to drive welfare rolls down, the rate of employment among never-married, separated, and divorced mothers with children—precisely the mothers most likely to be on welfare—rose significantly, according to recent studies. John Bishop of Cornell, for example, reports that the percentage of never-married mothers holding jobs jumped an unprecedented 32 percent from 1994–98. By contrast, the rate of work among these mothers had been virtually flat for the previous 15 years. Over this same four-year period (a time of labor shortages in much of the country), fully two-thirds of all increases in U.S. workforce participation were attributable to welfare reform and increases in the federal tax credit for low-income workers.

There is also evidence, from New Jersey and elsewhere, that welfare reforms have helped reduce out-of-wedlock births among welfare mothers. If a better work ethic among unmarried mothers is now combining with reduced illegitimacy, leaving fewer children to grow up without a father in the first place, then some truly profound improvements in American social life will follow. And there are indications this is beginning to happen.

❦

The dramatic decline in welfare rolls has *not* produced the increase in poverty that was widely predicted by opponents of welfare reform. In 1997, the Census Bureau has just reported, children's poverty declined for the fourth year in a row, and the rate for black children declined by the largest single-year amount ever, to the lowest rate on record in the U.S. The poverty rate for black female-headed families with children declined by a remarkable 4.1 percentage points, also by far the greatest decline ever.

Liberal opponents of welfare reform predicted that mothers pushed from public assistance to low-wage jobs would experience substantial declines in their incomes as a result. Now that lots of mothers have made the move, what does the evidence show? An analysis prepared recently by the Clinton administration's Office of Management and Budget finds that single mothers living in the poorest 40 percent of U.S. households received a total of $4 billion less in welfare income in 1997 than in 1993 (after taking inflation into account). But their *earned* income increased by $4.3 billion, and they also received another $2.1 billion increase from the earned income tax credit. Adding up all their sources of income, the nation's poorest mothers had nearly $3.8 billion more in 1997 than 1993. So much for income declines. More importantly, they made their money the old-fashioned way. Next thing you know, they'll be investing.

So while welfare rolls were plummeting, the employment rates of female-headed families soared, their poverty rates dropped, and their income increased. At the same time, the national illegitimacy trends reversed. This happy portrait, based on highly reliable national data, has no precedent in U.S. social history.

Given the modest success or outright failure of most social reforms attempted by government, what accounts for the impressive success of welfare reform? In the next several years, we will be treated to torturous explanations from social scientists. The real answer, though, is quite simple: As long as welfare was an entitlement, with opinion leaders and social workers telling people they had an inalienable right to unlimited benefits, more and more people signed up and stayed for longer and longer spells. By the mid-1980s, the average duration on welfare for families on the rolls at a given moment was an amazing 13 years. In short, millions of young mothers were victims of what psychologists call "learned helplessness."

But then reformers in Congress, joined by the Clinton administration, pushed through a tough set of changes designed to end welfare as a vocation. The essence of their plan was, first, to require persons on welfare to work, beginning the first day they walk through the door seeking benefits. Social workers trying to wrap cocoons of entitlements around able-bodied young Americans had to be converted into social workers who would tell applicants they should, can, and must provide for themselves. Second, firm time limits were placed on benefits, to signal that welfare is an aberration and self-reliance normal. Third, states were given authority to impose sanctions, including the cessation of all cash benefits, on adults not willing to work. Finally, federal entitlements that blindly paid money directly to individuals were converted into block grants to state governments set at a fixed amount. This change gave state and local governments a financial incentive to help people get off welfare. Under the old entitlement system, if states reduced their caseloads, the federal government "rewarded" them by cutting their federal dollars. Now, if states reduce their caseloads, they retain all the savings.

Although liberals in Congress, academia, and the media rarely said so explicitly, they assumed that adults on welfare were incapable of supporting themselves and therefore needed a protective blanket of federal entitlements. Studies will soon provide more detail on why people are leaving welfare at today's unprecedented rates, but we already know enough to conclude that the majority leave because they find work, and most of the rest either were already working or have other means of support. Welfare reformers were correct to predict that most welfare recipients could provide for themselves and their children.

The confidence reformers placed in state and local governments is also paying off. Instead of the slashed benefits and "race to the bottom" predicted by opponents of reform, states are mounting scores of innovative programs. Virtually every state now has offices like those in Long Beach and Annapolis that help low-income families make the transition from welfare to work —or avoid welfare altogether. And states are using the money they save from reduced caseloads to pay for work-promoting services such as child care and transportation, helping former recipients keep their jobs and, in some cases, get the education and training they need for better jobs.

⋘◉⋙

It needs to be remembered that many of the mothers avoiding welfare today receive public subsidies of $5,000 or more even after they leave welfare (providing medical, food, or child care benefits, for instance). Critics may object to these benefits as little more than welfare by a different name. But most Americans believe it is better for adults to be productively employed than idle and dependent, and adults who can command only low wages will not leave welfare until they can actually support themselves and their children.

Starting in the 1980s, Democrats and Republicans began developing a system of non-cash benefits, contingent on work, that makes low-wage jobs economically attractive for mothers with children. Once this system was in place, the 1996 welfare reforms forced welfare-dependent mothers into self-reliance— and the pleasant discovery that they had more money and benefits (not to mention a better feeling about themselves and their place in society) when they were working, even in low-wage jobs.

The nation is now well along in creating a balanced system of public benefits that combines carrots and sticks. This success is producing a social revolution whose beneficial effects on American society are just beginning to emerge. If the nation holds steady on this course—and especially if Congress expands the new requirements to other welfare and unemployment programs— low-skilled parents, their children, and American taxpayers will all be better off.

You're Not Entitled!

According to the 1996 welfare law, Gail Aska was a model recipient. Two years ago, the New York City resident got a job—without health insurance—and promptly informed her caseworker. Because the system took a while to register change in status, she received two welfare checks, which she returned. Meanwhile, her son, who had spinal surgery a year before, needed a follow-up visit with a doctor. To her dismay, Aska discovered that the transitional Medicaid benefits she was supposed to be getting had been cut off. "The caseworker I talked to said my case had been closed because I hadn't picked up my checks," Aska recalls. "But I didn't want to be sanctioned for getting checks when I had a job."

Somehow Aska's case had been miscoded. When she kept insisting that she had a right to transitional Medicaid, she was told she would get a date for a Fair Hearing, where the issue would be arbitrated. She waited for months and months. Finally, she gave up and applied for insurance for her son through a separate government-funded program she had heard about, CHIP, the Children's Health Insurance Program. "My son had some symptoms from the surgery that we needed to get checked out," she said. "You don't play around with that—you don't wait for a Fair Hearing."

Despite all the talk three years ago about "easing the transition from welfare to work," the welfare law has if anything made that transition more difficult. Even for welfare recipients like Aska who are aware of their rights and savvy enough to insist on them, the always lumbering and inefficient system has transformed itself from a bureaucratic behemoth into a whirling dervish, cutting people's benefits in a tangle of confusion that's nearly impossible to correct. In interviews with legal aid attorneys, advocates for the poor, former welfare recipients, local community leaders, nonprofit researchers and charities, *The Nation* discovered that a new lawlessness reigns. Whether out of willful disregard or real misunderstanding, states are failing to fulfill their legal obligations to the poor.

After sixty years of the federal government controlling welfare as an entitlement program—everyone who applied and qualified got aid—the new block grants give states vast discretionary power in distributing cash assistance. But it's not only cash benefits that have been arbitrarily denied. Safeguards written into the law—like making sure a family has health insurance, food stamps and daycare when Mom lands a minimum-wage, no-benefits job at Burger King—have gone largely unenforced. What has evolved instead is a system that pretends to offer such things but in practice withholds them with alarming frequency, vastly expanding the ranks of the working poor.

In 1997 an estimated 675,000 low-income people became uninsured as a result of welfare reform; the majority (62 percent) of those were children who in all likelihood never should have lost their insurance, according to a report by Families U.S.A. A South Carolina study found that 60 percent of former welfare recipients did not know a parent could get transitional Medicaid; nine states had no outreach efforts to inform parents that they could get childcare assistance after welfare. The states of Florida and New York have committed abuses so severe and blatant that former welfare recipients and applicants have filed lawsuits against them for refusing to give Medicaid and food stamp applications to eligible families.

"There used to be some standardization in how welfare recipients were treated and processed at welfare offices," explains Deepak Bhargava, director of public policy for the Center for Community Change. "By eliminating the whole architecture of the old entitlement program, the federal government eliminated a lot of the existing protections for people." Now, with no uniform processes in place, thousands of families never find out that they still qualify for health insurance, childcare or food stamps. Instead, they do without.

Gail Aska, who now works as a program coordinator for the welfare rights organization Community Voices Heard, puts it succinctly. "The real information that people need isn't coming from the system. And why should it? The object of the game is to get as many people off welfare as possible. So why should they share the rules of the game with you?"

Medicaid Emergency

On paper, the rules are pretty straightforward: In August 1996, Congress replaced the New Deal–era Aid to Families with Dependent Children with Temporary Assistance for Needy Families. TANF is not an entitlement program. This means states are under no obligation to provide cash assistance to eligible families. Instead, the federal government gives large block grants to assist poor families, with an emphasis on moving them from welfare to work or deterring them from applying for welfare in the first place. The federal law requires states to impose a five-year limit on welfare but states are free to impose shorter time limits (twenty-two states do) and to set up more rigid work requirements than the federal government's minimum. States are not allowed, however, to divert families from applying for Medicaid or food stamps. If an adult fails to follow any rules a state imposes—for instance, at 10 AM Monday a client must present proof to a welfare worker that she's gone to six job interviews—a state can punish her for these infractions (for being late to the interview or failing to present adequate documentation) by taking away her Medicaid. That is perfectly legal.

States may not, on the other hand, take away a child's Medicaid to punish a parent.

But like a game of telephone, as the welfare reform message has trickled down from Congress to governors to state legislators to counties, cities, welfare administrators and caseworkers, it has grown distorted. The mantra to "end welfare as we know it" has mutated into a message that it's OK to deny all government benefits, regardless of the protective aspects of the law (few and far between as they are). "There is no question that there's tremendous confusion among welfare administrators," says Ron Pollack, executive director of Families U.S.A., which documented the tremendous drop in Medicaid enrollment and the corresponding rise in uninsured children. "And there's no question that beneficiaries are also confused about their rights." Pollack's organization discovered that people across the country are being deprived of Medicaid at various points in the process. "When people apply for welfare, the states have the right to have them do certain things—like do a job search or check with your family to see if they can support you—before they will process an application," explains Pollack. "But when they divert people from filling out a welfare application, they're often diverting them from applying for Medicaid and food stamps, even though it is illegal to do so."

Then, if an applicant temporarily gets welfare but later gets a job, she's often zapped from the computer system in one clean sweep: no more welfare, no more Medicaid, no more food stamps. "In many states, the administrators are unaware of the break in linkage between welfare—no longer an entitlement—and other benefits like Medicaid, which are still entitlements," Pollack says. "Worse, the computers still automatically assume that if you don't qualify for welfare, then you're not eligible for anything else." He believes such problems are caused by carelessness, inadequate training and a poor understanding of the law. "Still," he admits, "there hasn't been overwhelming incentive on the part of the states to correct this because they have to pay part of the Medicaid costs."

After falling by 2.5 million in 1997, last year total Medicaid enrollment dropped by another 1.1 million. Bureaucratic blunders or malfeasance aside, the insurance problem is about to get a whole lot worse. Since Medicaid coverage for those who move from welfare to work is considered a "transitional" benefit, most recipients are eligible for a half-year to one year. "But the people who are moving from welfare to work typically find themselves in low-wage jobs with no health insurance," says Pollack. In most states, unless their earnings are extremely low, they will lose Medicaid. "At the end of the transition period, those folks just become uninsured."

Hungry in New York

When it comes to denying benefits, welfare offices take their cues from the local administration, whose leaders often want impressive numbers—at any cost. In New York City, for example, things got so bad in 1998 that needy residents were forced to take their case to the courts. In April 1998 Mayor Rudolph Giuliani began to make good on his promise to end welfare in New York City by 2000 by converting welfare offices into "job centers" and erecting a series of hurdles designed to discourage applicants from applying for public assistance. The hurdles were effective: During the early weeks of the operation 84 percent of prospective applicants at one job center and 69 percent at another left without filing an application.

But, according to a class action suit filed in December 1998, Giuliani's job centers paid little heed to applicants' rights. The suit, *Reynolds v. Giuliani,* contends that the city is illegally deterring and discouraging thousands of poor people from applying for food stamps, Medicaid and cash assistance, as well as failing to provide written notices of denials and hearing rights. Represented by the Welfare Law Center and the Legal Aid Society, among others, pregnant, disabled and homeless adult and child plaintiffs sought a court order to bar the city from converting more welfare offices into job centers until it stops its illegal practices. Federal District Court Judge William Pauley granted their request, requiring the city to halt its plans until it can prove that the situation has been corrected.

The evidence of illegal activities is credible and considerable. According to court documents, applicants are commonly misinformed. When they first arrive at a job center, receptionists routinely tell them that there is no more welfare, that this office exists solely to see that they get a job, that if they miss any appointments their application will be denied, that emergency food stamps and cash grants don't exist, that there is a time limit on benefits—without explaining that they can apply for Medicaid or food stamps. Receptionists also tell people who arrive after 9:30 AM that they must return another day. If they aren't already deterred, applicants are given a five-page preliminary form to fill out. They must return the next day to get an application. They are fingerprinted, undergo several interviews and are then directed to meet with a financial planner and an employment planner. The financial planner tries to deter people from applying by directing them to churches, charities and food pantries. At various stages, applicants are orally denied benefits or told they are not eligible to apply, but they receive no written notice of denial or their right to appeal the decision.

One plaintiff in the lawsuit was in her fourth month of a high-risk pregnancy, carrying twins, when she repeatedly asked job center employees for emergency assistance (including help buying prenatal vitamins and blood pressure medicine) and expedited food stamps, saying she had no money for food. Instead of being given food stamps, she was referred to two food pantries, places that were closed—except during the daily hours she was required to be present at the job search center. Another plaintiff was referred to three pantries but was turned away and then found another pantry on his own; but when he went there during his lunch break from the job center, all the food, except for some old bananas, was gone. A third plaintiff tried to get food from the American Red Cross and the Salvation Army but was told that both had a three-month waiting period. (As the increasing need for emergency food in New York City strains the existing supply, many people are being turned away. According to a 1998 New York City Coalition Against Hunger report, 58,000 people were turned away from local soup kitchens and food pantries in a single winter month.)

For its part, the city is fairly cavalier about falling short in its responsibility to feed the poor. "There are always lots and lots of problems with any new program," says the city's corporation counsel, Lorna Bade Goodman. Explaining that the sheer size of the city's programs means that they are always complicated to launch, she says a few snafus are common. "We are inevitably sued," she says. "Eventually things get sorted out and begin to run in a more efficient manner."

But Jason Turner, commissioner of the New York City Human Resources Administration (and architect of Wisconsin's aggressive experiment with welfare reform), acknowledged to an audience at the Nelson Rockefeller Institute of Government last year that these policies were not the result of "lengthy planning, followed by implementation." He was direct: "[The city] acted first and worried about the consequences later."

The latest front in Giuliani's lawless war on welfare is drugs: The Mayor has proposed using Medicaid records to uncover any evidence that welfare applicants have sought drug or alcohol treatment in the past, to compel them to undergo further treatment in order to receive benefits. (This, while there are only 200 residential treatment slots in the city for women with children —thanks to Giuliani's slashing of such services.) Although federal law forbids the disclosure of private medical information, Giuliani wants the city's Health and Welfare Department to take advantage of its access to Medicaid records and welfare lists to skirt the law.

Mississippi Burnout

Blatant lawbreaking isn't the only problem. Many states, like Mississippi, are as stingy as possible in their interpretation of the law. Indeed, Mississippi is a good case study of what welfare could look like nationwide when the economy takes a plunge—or how a state's poor can rise or fall at the discretion of local leaders, like notorious antiwelfare Governor Kirk Fordice, whose "internal moral compass" told him to veto 106 of Mississippi's "liberal" legislature's bills during his tenure. ("I just might veto them all, Xerox the durn veto message or whatever," he once threatened, already having gone well beyond the fifty-three bills the two previous governors vetoed during their eight years in office.) With an unemployment rate of more than 13 percent in several counties, jobs are hard to come by. But the welfare rolls are still dropping, in good part because the sanctions for missing appointments or declining work assignments are so harsh: Clients immediately lose their welfare as well as their family's food stamps and the adult's Medicaid.

How are Mississippi families faring? In the eleven-county area of the Delta, the poverty rate hovers at 41 percent, and across the state 32 percent of children live in poverty. A study of eight Mississippi counties showed that only 35 percent of welfare recipients had jobs when they left or were kicked off the welfare rolls. Meanwhile, the state has chosen not to spend millions of federal welfare dollars that could be used for programs assisting the working poor. Mississippi has failed, for instance, to invest available funds in childcare. Although childcare is not an entitlement program like Medicaid and food stamps, it is considered such an integral part of welfare reform's success that Congress included an additional $4.5 billion for childcare—to be spread over five years—in the bill. The welfare law also links cash assistance and childcare by allowing states to move surplus welfare money into childcare programs.

But according to a 1998 report put out by two regional nonprofits, the Mississippi Low-Income Child Care Initiative and Congregations for Children, 90 percent of the Mississippi children eligible for childcare vouchers do not receive them. And with the average cost of childcare for a 4-year-old exceeding that of state college tuition, it's likely that most single parents working full time to bring in $10,712 could use the help. (Otherwise, childcare expenses for two kids consume 61 percent of their total income.) Meanwhile, approximately $25 million in federal childcare money and $17 million in unspent welfare money is sitting in state coffers.

"The state is claiming that the $25 million isn't being spent because it's not needed," says Carol Burnett, director of the Mississippi Low-Income Child Care Initiative and one of the authors of the report. "But they're not really telling people that the money is available." While the state's Department of Human Services contends that it advertises, Burnett is skeptical. "I don't know where it's publicized," she says. "Supposedly there have been ads in newspapers and on TV and the radio, but I've never seen them give a list of media announcements, and I haven't ever seen or heard a single one—and I would notice, because I work in this field."

Furthermore, Burnett argues, even if the state's contention that 90 percent of eligible recipients are forgoing childcare assistance because they don't need it is true, the state could still use the money to improve existing childcare. For example, the state could spend some of the money to reduce the child-teacher ratios; it currently allows one of the highest ratios in the country, with one caregiver allowed to tend fourteen 3-year-olds. It could increase the amount of the childcare voucher that parents turn over to providers (currently $70–$80 a week for a toddler), so that childcare workers—whose average wages are lower than garbage collectors, bus drivers and bartenders—could get a well-deserved raise. It could increase education and training opportunities and requirements in a state where hairdressers have 1,500 hours of mandated training, while childcare teachers have fifteen (in-home providers aren't required to have any training, even in infant CPR).

But Mississippi's Department of Human Services insists it has done plenty, dismissing the report as "a monologue on Ain't It Awful" put out by the "Ain't It Awful Crowd." Ronnie McGinnis, director of the state's Office for Children and Youth, tries to put a positive spin on the report's revelation that 90 percent of eligible families aren't being served. "The truth is . . . the percentage of subsidized parents being served has increased from 5 percent to 10 percent . . . assuming that 100 percent of the eligible population would seek such care." She also points out that the department has introduced a credentialing program that will be a requirement for childcare center directors by the year 2000. "As center directors, you are business operators," she warned a group of daycare center directors. "If you are not carefully managing your center, you may be operating a charity." Although evidence across the country has indicated that it's nearly impossible to run a quality daycare center and make a handsome profit —or any profit at all—McGinnis insists that's what has to happen in Mississippi. "A childcare business is no different from any other," McGinnis says, explaining why the state has moved away from funding daycare centers in favor of vouchers for parents. While childcare advocates contend there is a paucity of centers in poor and rural areas, McGinnis says, "If there is a valid demand for licensed childcare, there will be someone out there who is prepared to open a business."

"Childcare is not an entitlement to parents or providers," McGinnis explains. "Parents seem to understand this."

While it would be easy to dismiss Mississippi as an aberration—after all, the state ranks last or near last among all states in per capita income, percent of children in poverty, infant mortality rate and child deathrate—its response to the welfare law is far from unique. Due to a combination of factors, including a strong economy and the decline in the welfare rolls brought on by the harsh new policies, many states have found themselves with sizable welfare budget surpluses—but according to recent figures, more than half failed to use the full amounts of their federal welfare grants last year, leaving billions of unspent dollars piling up in state treasuries (a total of $6 billion by one estimate). The worst offenders include West Virginia (one of the poorest states in the nation, which left $72 million, 65 percent of its annual grant, unspent), New Jersey ($170 million), New York ($335 million), Colorado ($61 million) and Louisiana ($90 million, more than half the state's total of $168 million). The money can roll over into the next year, but future federal allocations are tied to this spending, as well as to overall state spending levels, which are also dropping.

The states' failure to spend their welfare money isn't illegal, but it vividly shows what's wrong with giving them so much latitude. For years, states argued that they knew best how to spend the money to lift their residents out of poverty. Now that the Feds have given them the autonomy they asked for, they've slashed the welfare rolls but hoarded the money that could actually help the working poor. (Wisconsin went even further, using part of its welfare surplus to fund tax cuts for the middle class.) In early August at an assembly of the nation's governors in St. Louis, Clinton urged states to spend their leftover welfare money on childcare and education for poor children and to invest more in outreach for underused programs like Medicaid, CHIP and food stamps. The President also announced that he would be dispatching federal officials to all fifty states to make sure people aren't being illegally excluded from health programs. But because of the law he endorsed, the most the Administration can do is nudge states to mend their ways. Meanwhile, before Congressional Republicans had the bright idea of fiddling with the earned-income tax credit to balance the budget, they floated the notion of asking states to return their surplus welfare cash to the federal government.

In the past few months, reports on the welfare "leavers" have begun to emerge, painting a bleak portrait of increasing hardship for the country's poor

—and not just in the regional pockets described by Clinton on his recent poverty tour. A study by the Center on Budget and Policy Priorities found that between 1995 and 1997, the poorest fifth of single-parent families suffered nearly a 7 percent loss in income, or $580 per family. Among the poorest of the poor, the loss was even more pronounced. And most of the decline can be attributed to cuts in government benefits—in 1995, for instance, 88 percent of poor children were getting food stamps, but by 1998 food stamps were reaching only 70 percent of poor kids. Moreover, a National Governors' Association survey found that 40–50 percent of those who left the welfare rolls did not have a job, and "most of the jobs [held by former recipients] pay between $5.50 and $7 an hour ... not enough to raise a family out of poverty." Extreme poverty is growing among children, especially those in female-headed households, according to a study released by the Children's Defense Fund and the National Coalition for the Homeless. In a study of the poor in ten states by Network, the National Catholic Social Justice Lobby, 24 percent of those surveyed said they couldn't provide enough food for their children, 46 percent said they were eating less because they couldn't afford food and 36 percent said they had to forgo needed medical care.

According to Jack Tweedie, director of the Children and Families Program at the National Conference of State Legislatures, the welfare rolls dropped faster than states anticipated, and states have not taken advantage of the flexibility they now have to address poverty issues. "States are reluctant to set up new programs if two years down the line they're going to have to shut the programs down—and take the political fallout—or use state money to keep them alive," Tweedie explains.

Activists are challenging such inertia with organizing campaigns focused on investing surplus welfare funds in programs for the working poor. In New York, unions, research nonprofits and welfare advocacy groups formed the Campaign for the Empire State Jobs Program, which called for using $85 million of the welfare surplus to provide subsidized jobs with living wages and childcare benefits to former welfare recipients—with assurances that no permanent workers would be displaced. The state agreed to start a $12 million pilot project based on the proposal, a significant victory that nonetheless leaves the bulk of the surplus unused. Likewise, activists in Pennsylvania and Wisconsin have succeeded in wresting a small amount of the welfare-to-work funds away from states and putting it toward programs for former recipients. In Massachusetts, Parents United for Child Care lobbied successfully for entitlements to childcare assistance on a sliding scale for working-poor families. State-level earned-income tax credits, which subsidize the working poor, have passed in several states, and campaigns are under way to provide transportation assistance and extended job training (in place of the "work first" approach) to those leaving welfare. Perhaps the most important breakthrough has been the expansion of Medicaid to cover working-poor parents in Rhode Island, Connecticut, Wisconsin, California, Ohio and Washington, DC.

Together, these efforts, says Center for Community Change's Bhargava, are "seeds of a national progressive agenda around poverty issues," which may play out in the debate over the reauthorization of the law in 2002. But there is a long way to go. Three years ago the "reformers" declared that welfare was a broken system that needed to be wiped out before it could be improved. Sadly, the same might be said with far greater justice of the replacement they came up with. Unless the federal government unties its own hands, the battle for welfare justice will remain centered in the states, where activists must struggle to bring reason and fairness to a system that has abandoned both.

POSTSCRIPT

Has Welfare Reform Benefited the Poor?

There was considerable national agreement that the old welfare system had to be changed so that it would assist people in finding jobs and achieving self-sufficiency. Much success has been gained regarding this goal so far, but some state that numerous problems still remain. Houppert focuses on the problems with the policies of states and localities and the failure of administrative practices. If these items were fixed so that the truly needy received the assistance that they should have, would we have a welfare system that is ideal?

A related question is: What is the appropriate government structure for the administration of welfare programs? Will decentralizing the control of welfare programs from the federal government to state governments improve the performance of the welfare system?

Michael B. Katz, in *The Undeserving Poor: From the War on Poverty to the War on Welfare* (Pantheon Books, 1989), traces the evolution of welfare policies in the United States from the 1960s through the 1980s. Charles Noble traces the evolution of welfare policies into the late 1990s and argues that the structure of the political economy has greatly limited the welfare state in *Welfare as We Knew It: A Political History of the American Welfare State* (Oxford University Press, 1997). Mary Jo Bane and David T. Ellwood are critical of the organization and administration of welfare. See *Welfare Realities: From Rhetoric to Reform* (Harvard University Press, 1994). Marvin Olasky is critical of big government welfare programs and advocates a return to welfare by faith-based groups or local organizations in *Tough Love: Renewing American Compassion* (Free Press, 1996). Studies of the success of welfare-to-work programs include Daniel Friedlander and Gary Burtless, *Five Years After: The Long-Term Effects of Welfare-to-Work Programs* (Russell Sage Foundation, 1995) and Richard L. Koon, *Welfare Reform: Helping the Least Fortunate Become Less Dependent* (Garland Publishing, 1997). For a review of a range of views on welfare reform see Charles P. Cozic ed., *Welfare Reform* (Greenhaven Press, 1997). Two books that offer explanations as to why welfare provision is so minimal in the United States are Linda Gordon, *Pitied but Not Entitled: Single Mothers and the History of Welfare* (Free Press, 1994) and Joel F. Handler and Yeheskel Hasenfeld, *The Moral Construction of Poverty: Welfare Reform in America* (Sage Publications, 1991).

ISSUE 13

Are Vouchers the Solution to the Ills of Public Education?

YES: Gary Rosen, from "Are School Vouchers Un-American?" *Commentary* (February 2000)

NO: Albert Shanker, from "Privatization: The Wrong Medicine for Public Schools," *Vital Speeches of the Day* (March 15, 1996)

ISSUE SUMMARY

YES: Gary Rosen, an associate editor of *Commentary,* examines the criticisms of public education and argues that vouchers and choice are well suited to correct its deficiencies without damaging education or society.

NO: Albert Shanker, president of the American Federation of Teachers until his death in 1998, argues that there is no evidence that privatizing the public schools works or that the public wants vouchers. He maintains that the public wants discipline and academic standards, which can be provided by public schools modeled after those of countries with better primary and secondary education than the United States.

The quality of American public schooling has been criticized for several decades. Secretary of Education Richard Riley said in 1994 that some American schools are so bad that they "should never be called schools at all." The average school year in the United States is 180 days, while Japanese children attend school 240 days of the year. American schoolchildren score lower than the children of many other Western countries on certain standardized achievement tests. In 1983 the National Commission on Excellence in Education published *A Nation at Risk,* which argued that American education was a failure. Critics of *A Nation at Risk* maintain that the report produced very little evidence to support its thesis, but the public accepted it anyway. Now, almost 20 years and several reforms later, the public still thinks that the American school system is failing and needs to be fixed. The solution most frequently proposed today is school choice, usually involving a voucher system.

The U.S. educational system has a proud record of achievement over the last two centuries. The present system began to take shape in the nineteenth century, when the states set up locally controlled school districts providing free elementary and high school education. Over time the states also passed compulsory schooling laws, which usually were applicable through elementary school and later were raised to age 16. With free and compulsory education, America has always been and still is the world leader in providing mass education. In the twentieth century the expansion of mass education was phenomenal. Today 99 percent of children aged 6 to 13 are in school. In 1900 only about 7 percent of the appropriate age group graduated from high school, but in 1990, 86 percent did. Another success is the extraordinary improvement in the graduation rates for blacks since 1964, when it was 45 percent, to 1987, when it was 83 percent. Now this rate is almost at parity with white graduation rates. And over two-thirds of the present American population have a high school degree. No other nation comes close to these accomplishments.

American education reforms of the past 50 years have focused on quality and on what is taught. In the late 1950s the Soviet Union's launch of the first space satellite convinced the public of the need for more math and science in the curriculum. In the late 1960s and 1970s schools were criticized for rigid authoritarian teaching styles, and schools were made less structured. They became more open, participatory, and individualized in order to stimulate student involvement, creativity, and emotional growth. In the 1980s a crusade for the return to basics was triggered by the announcement that SAT scores had declined since the early 1960s. More recently, the continued problems of public schools have led many to call for their restructuring by means of school choice.

Two questions on the current situation in American schools serve as background for the voucher issue. First, is there really a school performance crisis? David C. Berliner and Bruce J. Biddle, in *The Manufactured Crisis: Myths, Fraud, and the Attack on America's Public Schools* (Addison-Wesley, 1995), argue that school performance has not declined. They point out that the decline in SAT scores since 1960 was due to the changing composition of the sample of students taking the tests, and better indicators of school performance over time show gains, not losses. Second, is the current structure of schools the main reason why schools seem to be failing? Many other trends have also affected school performance. For example, curricula changes away from basics, new unstructured teaching techniques, and the decline of discipline in the classroom have contributed to perceived problems. The relatively poor quality of teachers may be another factor. There is evidence that those who go into teaching score far lower on SATs than the average college student. In addition, societal trends outside the school may significantly impact on school performance. Increasing breakdown of the family, more permissive childrearing, the substantial decline in the amount of time that parents spend with children, and the increased exposure of children to television are trends that are affecting school performance.

In the following selections, Gary Rosen promotes vouchers as a way to improve public education, while Albert Shanker attacks voucher systems as unnecessary, unwanted, and no better than public schools.

 **YES**

Are School Vouchers Un-American?

By any measure, public education in America's cities is in deep trouble, and has been for some time. On any given day in Cleveland, almost one of every six students is likely not to show up. In Washington, D.C., a majority of tenth graders never finish high school. And in Los Angeles, school officials recently retreated from a plan to end the practice of "social promotion," realizing that it would have required holding back for a year more than half of the district's woefully unprepared students. Nor do things look any better in the aggregate. As *Education Week* concluded in a special report two years ago, "Most fourth graders who live in U.S. cities can't read and understand a simple children's book, and most eighth graders can't use arithmetic to solve a practical problem."

The response to this dismal situation has taken many shapes in recent years, but none more radical—or more promising—than the idea of school vouchers. Though little more than a thought-experiment as recently as the late 1980's, vouchers are now being used in one form or another in every major American city, providing low-income families with scholarships or subsidies that allow them to send their children to private schools. Of these programs, the great majority are privately financed, currently sponsoring more than 50,000 students nationwide. Considerably more controversial, despite affecting just some 12,000 students, are the three state-funded programs now in operation. In Milwaukee, in Cleveland, and (as of [the] fall [of 1999]) in the state of Florida, qualifying families are using *public* dollars for *private* education, usually at religious schools.

For the teachers' unions, liberal interest groups, and Democratic politicians who are the most determined foes of vouchers, these programs are objectionable not so much for their scope—after all, the number of students involved is but a tiny fraction of the country's school population—as for the precedent they set and the unmistakable message they send. Whether public or private, today's voucher initiatives are an explicit rebuke to the failing inner-city public-school systems whose students are the chief beneficiaries of the new programs. As activists on all sides of the issue recognize, if these pilot programs succeed, it is far more likely that school choice for the poor will be transformed from a modest, mostly philanthropic experiment into a full-scale public policy.

And it does, in fact, appear that today's voucher programs are succeeding, at least from the perspective of the families taking part in them. Though isolating the deciding factor in improved test scores is a notoriously difficult business, studies by Harvard's Paul E. Peterson and other social scientists have found that students with vouchers perform at least as well—and often much better—than their peers in public schools. Looking at the question from a different angle, John F. Witte of the University of Wisconsin reports that voucher recipients in Milwaukee have resisted the "normal pattern" of declining achievement among inner-city students, maintaining their test scores relative to national averages even as they enter higher grades. Every study has also found that parents who take advantage of vouchers are vastly more satisfied with the quality of their children's education, a sentiment based on everything from more rigorous homework assignments to better classroom discipline.

Unsurprisingly, given these results, interest in school choice has risen greatly over the last few years among inner-city families. One survey found that 85 percent of the urban poor now favor vouchers; another put support for the idea at 59 percent among blacks and 68 percent among Latinos. As if to prove these figures, when the Children's Scholarship Fund, the largest of the private voucher programs, recently announced its first national lottery for 40,000 scholarships, applications poured in from an astonishing 1.25 million children, all from low-income households. Such desperation, in the view of former Mayor Kurt Schmoke of Baltimore—one of a handful of black Democrats who have dissented from their party's line on education—makes the movement for school choice "part of an emerging new civil-rights battle."

This groundswell of grassroots support has created an increasingly uncomfortable situation for those committed to thwarting school choice. When a federal district judge suspended Cleveland's publicly financed voucher program this past August—setting in motion a series of appeals that is still ongoing—local opinion turned sharply against him, with the *Cleveland Plain Dealer* branding him a "voucher vulture" for his "utter disregard for the needs of children across the city." Within days, the judge felt compelled to reverse his order, allowing the program to carry on, as it has continued to do even in the wake of his ruling in December that it is unconstitutional. So, too, the leading groups in the antivoucher movement have been made to see the political awkwardness in taking a stand that so plainly defies the wishes of low-income families eager to improve the lot of their children.

Many of those making the case against school choice are now willing to concede—grudgingly—that the children who participate in these programs may benefit in some way. But, in their view, this is no compensation for the wider harm that vouchers threaten to do. A lucky few may be helped by the government's willingness to underwrite private education, but society as a whole, they insist, will inevitably suffer from a policy so contrary to our most fundamental civic principles and institutions. Indeed, if the most vociferous critics are to be believed, the idea of school vouchers is not just wrongheaded, it is positively un-American.

The most frequently invoked argument on this score is that allowing public dollars to help support sectarian schools is unconstitutional on its face and strikes at the very heart of our tradition of religious freedom. As the American Civil Liberties Union puts it, "vouchers violate the bedrock principle of separation of church and state," forcing "all taxpayers to support religious beliefs and practices with which they may strongly disagree."

In a more strictly legal vein, voucher opponents point to a series of Supreme Court decisions during the 1970's rejecting various forms of government assistance to religious schools. The first and most important of these decisions, in the landmark case of *Lemon* v. *Kurtzman* (1971), set out the criteria the Court has used ever since to determine whether a given state action violates the First Amendment by "establishing" religion. Though the Justices themselves have never ruled on the narrow question of whether vouchers may be used for sectarian schools, several lower courts—including the federal district court in Cleveland—have concluded that such programs are unconstitutional under *Lemon* and its judicial progeny.

A second set of civic-minded objections to school choice has to do with the nation's historic commitment to public education. As a practical matter, opponents charge, government-financed vouchers invariably rob public schools of much-needed resources—not only scarce education dollars but also top students, since private schools exploit voucher programs by "skimming" or "cherrypicking" only the highest achievers. What such a policy amounts to, writes Sandra Feldman, president of the American Federation of Teachers (AFT), is "to hell with all the kids left behind."

Adding to this injustice, antivoucher spokesmen say, is the fact that citizens have virtually no way of knowing whether their tax dollars are being spent well by private schools. People for the American Way, a liberal interest group, warns that the schools receiving vouchers "lack basic standards of public accountability for their funds and management" and have resisted further regulation. Most damning are the problems experienced in Milwaukee, where several scandal-ridden private schools have closed in the middle of the academic year, leaving students and parents to fend for themselves.

Finally, the adversaries of vouchers contend, if private education expands at the expense of the public-school system, the shift will severely weaken America's democratic habits and ideals. Some predict that school choice will place government funds in the hands of extremists—critics warn of "Farrakhan" or "creationist" schools—or that it will serve, in the words of one representative of the NAACP, as a "subterfuge for segregation."

But the broader concern is that the venerable tradition of the "common school"—ingrained in the national imagination by the experience of generations of successfully assimilated immigrants—will be abandoned in the rush to privatize. Reciting the Pledge of Allegiance in a classroom of diverse peers will give way, it is feared, to the (publicly supported) cultivation of narrow religious and ethnic interests, further damaging our already fragile sense of national identity. As the National Education Association (NEA), the country's largest and most powerful teachers' union, has declared, "At a time when America is fractured by race, religion, and income, we can't afford to replace the one remaining unifying institution in the country with a system of private schools pursuing private agendas at taxpayer expense."

_**❦**_

Are the opponents right? Would the spread of school choice, whatever its benefits for a fortunate few, do grave harm to our common culture, and to the republic?

As far as the constitutional question goes, it is useful to start—as these discussions seldom do—with the actual text of the First Amendment, the relevant portion of which reads, "Congress shall make no law respecting an establishment of religion, or prohibiting the free exercise thereof." For most of American history, this language was taken to mean precisely what it says and what its 18th-century authors intended: that the federal government—and the federal government alone—has no authority over religion. The states, by contrast could do as they wished in these matters, limited only by the protections for religious liberty enshrined in their own constitutions.

All this changed in the 1940's, when the Supreme Court decided through a bit of legal legerdemain that *every* level of American government was bound by the religion clauses of the First Amendment. Suddenly, the Court found itself having to rule on the constitutionality of a range of church-state relationships over which it previously had had no say, including the question of whether state and local governments could give aid to religious schools, as many of them had been doing for some time.

In the earliest of these cases, the Court showed some willingness to accommodate the practices that had grown up under the old federalism-based arrangement. Thus, the Justices gave their imprimatur to government assistance whose content was plainly secular, like textbooks and reimbursement for transportation. But by the early 1970's, this attitude had changed dramatically. In *Lemon,* the Court ruled that a secular purpose was not enough. In addition, no program aiding sectarian schools could have the "primary effect" of advancing religion or result in an "excessive entanglement" between church and state—a "test," as it turned out in several cases decided shortly thereafter, that effectively banned almost every form of state aid, including such seemingly innocent items as maps, instructional films, and laboratory equipment.

For the past two decades, the Supreme Court has struggled to make sense of these contradictory precedents. Though accepting the basic standard set by *Lemon,* the Justices have tried to apply it in a way that will not automatically find the "establishment" of religion in any program that somehow benefits a sectarian institution. In the most important of these cases—*Mueller* v. *Allen* (1983), *Witters* v. *Washington Department of Services for the Blind* (1986), *Zobrest* v. *Catalina Foothills School District* (1993), and *Agostini* v. *Felton* (1997)—the Court has upheld several different forms of public aid to students in religious schools. Such assistance is permissible, the Justices have ruled, when it comes about as part of a broader, religiously neutral program and when its benefits accrue to religious schools only indirectly, through the private decisions of individuals.

For school vouchers, the implications could not be clearer. As the highest state courts in both Wisconsin and Ohio have held, the programs currently operating in Milwaukee and Cleveland easily meet the requirements laid down by the Supreme Court: families may opt for a religious *or* a secular school, and the schools themselves receive public funds only as a result of these private choices. Even so strict a church-state separationist as Harvard Law School's Laurence Tribe admits that, "One would have to be awfully clumsy to write voucher legislation that could not pass constitutional scrutiny." . . .

ᴄ⟨◉⟩ᴏ

Of course, the fact that vouchers are constitutional does not make them sound policy. Most Americans are understandably reluctant to see tax dollars spent to support religion, even indirectly. The exceptions to the rule—so commonplace today as to be uncontroversial—are various programs that let sectarian institutions use public funds to meet some obvious secular need: few object when a federal Pell grant allows a low-income college student to attend Notre Dame or Brigham Young, or when New York City subsidizes an Orthodox charity that provides kosher food to housebound elderly Jews.

School vouchers fall into precisely the same category. Yes, they may incidentally promote one or another religious creed, but their primary purpose is to improve the educational prospects of inner-city students trapped in our very worst public schools. Low-income parents who take advantage of vouchers know all this. Asked by researchers why they participate in the programs, they give reasons based overwhelmingly on academic concerns; religious considerations trail far behind. For them, school choice is above all a way to save their children's minds, not their souls.

As for the damage that vouchers would supposedly inflict on public schools, the arguments advanced by the teachers' unions and their allies are deeply disingenuous, if not dishonest. From a financial point of view, it is certainly true that public-school budgets are likely to decline as students leave for private institutions, taking some part of their per-pupil funding with them. But it is unclear why this should create any special hardship, since the schools would be losing money only for students whom they are no longer expected to educate. Moreover, because per-pupil support comes from both state and local funds, and vouchers tend to be financed exclusively with the state's share (and often not even all of that), affected public schools already get to keep much of the money earmarked for students who decide to enroll elsewhere—receiving a bonus, in effect, for driving them away. In the 1996–97 school year, this dividend amounted in both Cleveland and Milwaukee to some $3,000 for each departing voucher student. . . .

⊷◉⊶

The issue of accountability is somewhat more slippery. As one might expect, the private schools that accept vouchers vary in quality, and a few have been truly awful. By all reports, though, the vast majority are reasonably well managed and, more important, employ educators profoundly committed to their disadvantaged students; most work for a fraction of what their unionized public-school counterparts earn.

More to the point, like all private schools, these must comply with state regulations concerning health, safety, attendance, and the basic structure of the curriculum. In order to qualify for vouchers, they often must meet other requirements as well. In Milwaukee, such requirements run the gamut from nondiscrimination laws to accounting practices. Though this sort of regulation hardly ensures that the schools will be problem-free, it does hold them to a meaningful standard of fairness and professional competence. . . .

Needless to say, no one would wish to see public funds wasted on schools that fail to educate or that just function as job services for those who run them. But legitimate as such concerns may be in the case of voucher programs, they apply with still greater force to the massively bureaucratized and patronage-riddled public-school systems of our big cities. After decades of abysmal performance, with no end in sight, how are *they* to be held accountable? For all the talk about the need to impose stricter oversight, private schools are already subject to a form of accountability that inner-city public-school officials almost never have to face: the possibility that dissatisfied families will simply decide to educate their children somewhere else.

In fact, one beneficial consequence of the school-choice programs now in existence is that they have begun to shake this complacency. After the philanthropist Virginia Gilder offered vouchers to every student at the worst elementary school in Albany, New York, local education officials rushed into action, hiring a new principal, sacking 20 percent of the school's teachers, and revamping its reading curriculum. In Florida, the schools whose poor records have made their students eligible for the state's voucher program have begun to "fight back," according to one newspaper report; they have introduced, among other things, after-school and Saturday tutoring, more classroom instruction in the basics, and home visits to parents in order to discourage truancy. Most impressive of all is the case of Milwaukee, where a reformist school board, strongly opposed by the teacher's union whose minions have long dominated school governance in the city, was elected last spring on a platform welcoming the competitive challenge posed by vouchers.

If school choice were implemented on a much grander scale—with full public funding for considerably more low-income families—there is ample reason to think that our inner-city public schools, far from suffering, might just begin to turn themselves around.

As for the alarm sounded by critics about the destructive effect vouchers would have on America's democratic ethos, here too there has been much exaggeration, often of a self-serving nature. The fact is that our public schools, whatever their past glories, are not the engines for Americanization that they once were. On the other hand, private schools turn out to do a much better job these days at citizen education, perhaps because their generally more traditional bent has insulated them to some degree from the antipatriotic dictates of multiculturalism.

On the civics portion of the National Assessment of Educational Progress, the results of which were announced [in] November [1999], 80 percent of private-school seniors demonstrated basic "civic competency," as compared to just 63 percent of their public-school counterparts—roughly the same margin as prevailed in the scores for fourth and eighth graders as well. Significantly, the test measured both knowledge of government and civic disposition in the broadest sense, including the readiness of students to respect "individual worth and human dignity" and to assume "the personal, political, and economic responsibilities of a citizen."

Private schools also do better at approximating the ideal of the American "melting pot," as studies by Jay P. Greene of the Manhattan Institute have shown. Not only are they more racially integrated than public schools, but they are also home to more interracial friendships and less race-related fighting. As far as voucher programs go, rather than serving as a "subterfuge for segregation," they have usually allowed students to enter more racially mixed schools. This is because private schools in our big cities typically enroll students from different parts of the community, while public schools, even after—or perhaps because of—decades of forced busing, tend to reflect the ethnically homogeneous make-up of their neighborhoods.

What, finally, of the extremists who may use vouchers as a vehicle for antidemocratic creeds? It is safe to say that the most extreme of them are unlikely to tolerate the regulations that come along with vouchers, not least the almost universal requirement that schools accept any student interested in attending. But this is not to deny that some of the private schools taking part in voucher programs in inner cities do aim to cultivate narrower identities—identities that make many Americans, particularly of the prosperous, white, secular variety, deeply uneasy . . .

Indeed, for all the civic *angst* displayed by the critics of vouchers, the most urgent threat to the health of our cities is not an excess of religiosity or even of ethnic self-assertion, however worrisome some of its manifestations. Rather, it is that an enormous and growing number of poor, mostly minority teenagers will continue to emerge from our urban public schools utterly lacking in the skills and habits they will need to find a place in the country's social and economic mainstream. Vouchers can help to reverse this cruel process of marginalization, both for the students who receive them and for those who remain in the public schools. What could be more democratic—or more American—than that?

NO

Privatization: The Wrong Medicine
for Public Schools

Delivered to the Joint Economic Committee of the U.S. Senate, Washington, D.C., February 5, 1996

Mr. Chairman and Members of the Committee: I am Albert Shanker, president of the American Federation of Teachers, AFL-CIO, which represents 885,000 teachers and school staff at all levels of the education system, as well as state and local government employees and healthcare professionals. I appreciate the chance to speak to you today about privatization in education.

What's the Real Problem With Schools?

Privatization is not a new idea for fixing public schools. It's been around for a long time. Proponents of privatization see public schools as a monopoly, and, it's always easy to get applause by knocking monopolies. The theory is that monopolies don't produce good results because there's no competition, and without competition, the monopoly has no incentive to strive for quality or efficiency. The obvious conclusion, then, is to inject some good, old-fashioned private-sector competition into the public school system.

There's only one problem with this theory, and that is that there is no evidence that it works. So I think it's important to start by taking a look at why people are dissatisfied with our public schools. Are parents and the public saying get rid of the public school monopoly? No. Are they clamoring for vouchers or private managers? No. In fact, the public—when given a chance to vote on it in California, Oregon, Colorado, and D.C.—has emphatically rejected vouchers.

What do parents and the public say they want? Two things: discipline and academic standards. They've been saying this for at least ten years, but politicians and would-be reformers haven't been listening. They're still not listening.

What parents and the public want are schools that are safe and orderly enough for learning to take place and that set high academic standards for all students. Recent polls, particularly two very interesting studies by the nonpartisan research group Public Agenda, show overwhelming support for greater discipline and higher standards, including among minority parents and those

From Albert Shanker, "Privatization: The Wrong Medicine for Public Schools," *Vital Speeches of the Day* (March 15, 1996). Copyright © 1996 by Albert Shanker. Reprinted by permission of *Vital Speeches of the Day*.

who consider themselves "traditional Christians." Here are a few figures from "First Things First," the first Public Agenda Study:

Sixty-one percent of Americans said that academic standards are too low in their schools, with 70 percent of African-American parents with children in public schools agreeing.

Eighty-two percent supported setting up "very clear guidelines on what students should learn and teachers should teach in every major subject," with 92 percent of African-American parents and 91 percent of traditional Christian parents agreeing.

Seventy percent want to raise standards of promotion from grade school to junior high, letting students move ahead only when they pass a test showing they have met the standards.

Other polls show that these views are also widely supported by teachers and the business community. In a second study, called "Assignment Incomplete," Public Agenda further probed the public's views on school reform, asking a number of questions comparing public and private schools. What they found people liked about private schools was not competition or freedom from monopoly. They believe that private schools are more orderly and disciplined than public schools, and that they have higher academic standards.

When Public Agenda offered a series of proposed solutions for failing public schools, 48 percent of respondents said they wanted to "overhaul the public schools" and "increase the money public schools get," versus 10 percent who favored private management and 28 percent who wanted vouchers. A 1995 Gallup poll on education found that 65 percent of respondents opposed allowing students to attend private schools at public expense.

How should we respond? By giving the public what it doesn't want—vouchers and private management? Or by making the common-sense changes parents and the public are asking for in public schools: order, discipline, and high standards? Public schools can do these things. It's public policies that made them stop, and so it's public policies—not privatization—that can restore discipline and standards.

The Crucial Role of Standards

If I were a businessman and I saw someone else in the same business putting out a better product than mine, I'd sure want to know what the other guy was doing and maybe try to steal some of his ideas. So let's look at the school systems of OECD countries that do a better job with their students. What do we see? Monopolies. And, moreover, the most reviled sort of monopolies—*government* monopolies!

Other countries whose students routinely outperform ours all have education systems that are monopolies, centrally directed or coordinated by their national governments. Not a single one of these countries uses competition or private management or vouchers as an instrument of educational improvement. And not a single one has considered dismantling or selling off their public school systems, which is what some are advocating here.

What all of these countries have in common are a system of clear, common, and rigorous academic standards for all students, at least through their equivalent of our ninth or tenth grades, a set of national or nationally coordinated tests to see if students are meeting the standards, and incentives for students to work hard in school. In these other countries, unlike here, good advanced training or apprenticeships, good jobs, and university admission all depend on doing well in school. Students—and their parents and teachers—know what's expected of them in school, and they know that there will be serious consequences in their lives if they fail to meet the standards. Moreover, since the primary mission of schooling in these countries is academic, students who constantly disrupt classes are suspended or put in alternative placements, so that those who want to learn can do so.

A few of these other countries do subsidize private and religious schools. But the important point is that the state requires private and religious schools to operate according to the same standards as public schools. They must use the same curriculum and the same tests. They get roughly the same level of funding and pay the same teacher salaries as public schools. They are highly regulated within highly centralized education systems. To do that here would breach the wall of separation between church and state, destroy the independence of independent schools; and add to government regulation and costs. It's unthinkable here, given our traditions. Yet without doing these things to ensure accountability, quality and equity, we will further fragment a system that is already dangerously fragmented.

The main exception to these basic operating principles of OECD systems is England, which is actually trying some of the choice and competition experiments proposed here and finding mixed results.

Well, why am I beating the drum for standards again, when your topic is privatization? Because I believe that the effort to privatize schools is completely misguided and destructive. It will erode, not improve, the quality of education and student achievement. I'm arguing that discipline and a system of standards, assessments, and incentives for students are the most essential reforms our schools need right now, and they're standard operating procedure in other successful school systems.

We know that such standards-based systems work in other countries. And standards and discipline are what characterize good schools in this country, public and private. I believe that it is irresponsible and immoral for us to continue ignoring what works while pressing for unproved fads. It's time to stop fooling the public by promising them that privatization panaceas with no evidence of success behind them are the answer to the problems in our public schools. Let's do for all students what we now do only for some students, usually those in more affluent communities, and what other countries do for all their students.

The Promise of Privatization

A leading assumption behind privatization efforts is that competition and private-sector know-how will make public schools more efficient. But there is a large body of literature showing that the assumption is baseless. Here are a few examples.

One recent study found "only weak and inconsistent evidence" for the proposition that competition among schools increased efficiency and concluded that "reforms aimed solely at increasing competition among schools could be ineffectual." Others demonstrate that a voucher system would dramatically increase education costs and shift these costs from the private to the public sector. Yet another argues that "markets are not always more efficient than internal production, especially when the product in question—public benefits in one area or another—is hard to measure and control. The transaction costs involved in regulating private producers may well exceed any of the supposed gains in efficiency from a reduced public sector."

This last point about transaction costs is especially important because it is so often overlooked. Privatization and voucher schemes are more complex transactions than the market analogy suggests. There is a voluminous literature demonstrating that there are huge public costs involved in monitoring and evaluating the performance of private contractors and in running third party payment systems, which is what a voucher system is. And rather than reducing bureaucracy, they increase it. These transaction costs are rarely discussed with the public until a crisis, like healthcare or the Department of Defense contractor scandals, brings them to light.

A Case Study in Private Management: Education Alternatives, Inc.

Let's look briefly at the track record of the only private company that has tried to manage public schools, Education Alternatives, Inc. (EAI). In Baltimore, they promised a dramatic improvement in student achievement in the first year, and they promised to do it for less money. What happened? Test scores went down in EAI schools, while they went up in other Baltimore schools. What did the superintendent and school board do? Nothing, in part because the superintendent was busy running around the country proselytizing for EAI.

What about the second year? EAI schools' test scores were still down. EAI came under investigation for violations of special education laws, and information from the school system showed that EAI increased class size, cut special education services, and took money away from classrooms to pay for corporate overhead. We learned that, not only was EAI failing to cut costs, it was getting about $500 more per student than other schools—money that was drained from other Baltimore schools and is a big part of their current budget shortfall. Meanwhile, the company took home $2.6 million in profits.

In the third year, some test scores in EAI schools started to inch back up, but students are still behind where they were before EAI arrived. An independent evaluation by the University of Maryland/Baltimore County showed that EAI failed to deliver on most of its promises. When they couldn't raise test scores, the company touted its success in cleaning up the schools and supplying computers. But the UMBC evaluation showed that they didn't even do a very good job at that. The evaluation found few differences between EAI schools and other Baltimore schools—and those schools didn't get any extra money.

EAI lied repeatedly about test scores and attendance figures, and when they were caught in their lies, claimed that they were simply "errors." They withheld financial information to the point that the Baltimore city council was forced to subpoena the company for its financial records. In Hartford, they booked the entire Hartford school district budget as revenue, even though they were managing only five schools and did not control the funds. This made the company look more successful on Wall Street than it really was, and city officials criticized the accounting maneuver as misleading and unethical. With no sense of irony, EAI is now claiming that the reason they failed in Hartford was that they didn't control the money they earlier claimed they controlled!

After three-and-a-half years, the Baltimore school board finally pulled the plug on EAI. Who gets to keep the computers is now the subject of a dispute, but there's no disputing the fact that Baltimore got less for more from EAI, not the reverse. The person who benefited most was EAI's executive, John Golle, who made lavish profits by taking public dollars out of Baltimore and trading his EAI stock in timely fashion.

EAI was recently kicked out of Hartford, as well, largely over a financial dispute. EAI is claiming millions of dollars in reimbursement, but the city says EAI agreed that they would only be paid if they could find savings in the school budget. Hartford taxpayers were outraged when EAI billed the city for thousands in first-class travel for EAI staff, public relations fees, and condominium rent. John Golle recently announced that he's now setting his sights on more affluent suburban districts.

The record of EAI demonstrates that private contractors can engineer profit through stock manipulation, inflated claims, and pocketing public funds taken from other schools—all before a single student has shown improvement. The record also shows that EAI knew no more—in fact, a lot less—than public schools about how to improve students achievement.

Behind the zeal to privatize public schools is the assumption that there's a lot of fat to cut out of school budgets. We hear repeatedly that public education costs have gone up, while achievement has remained flat. But as EAI learned, there isn't a lot of fat. Most of the increase in education expenditures over the last twenty years has gone to special education and other hard-to-educate youngsters. In Baltimore, EAI made its profits not from bureaucratic excess—in fact, no central office functions or staff were cut—but by cutting special education and remedial services to disadvantaged students and by increasing class size, that is, by taking money out of classrooms. In Hartford, they didn't get paid because they couldn't identify any savings.

In sum, the case for privatization in education rests only on theory or ideology, not on facts. The facts, with respect to EAI, earlier privatization experiments called "performance contracting," and the Milwaukee voucher program, show that privatization is, at worst, a scandal and a disaster, and, at best, no improvement over the status quo. It has produced no improvement in student achievement, and, in some cases, has depressed it. And student achievement, after all, is our main problem in education. Privatization is a hope and a prayer, when what we need are reliable answers to our problem.

The Role of Public Education in a Democracy

Privatization arguments rest on the argument that education is primarily a private benefit and so best left to parent and private discretion. But in a democracy, education is, first and foremost, a public good. All taxpayers support education, not just the small number of families (somewhere around 27 percent) who actually have children in public schools. Why? Because in a democracy, all citizens have a stake in a well-educated populace and suffer from one that is ill educated. In a diverse and pluralistic country like ours, public schools are the glue that helps hold society together. If we privatize our education system, we would become the only nation on earth to abdicate our responsibility for socializing our young into the common values of our society and the shared duties of citizenship. The Founding Fathers had it right. Only with public education can you have both the unfettered pursuit of individual private interests and a free society.

Despite their dissatisfaction, Americans remain fiercely attached to their public schools. All the polls tell us they want them fixed, not abandoned. In a democracy, when you think the public is wrong, you need to make the case for why they're wrong. If you think they're right, you should give them what they want. The American Federation of Teachers believes that parents and the public are right, and that they should get what they want and what we know works, standards of conduct and achievement, not radical proposals for dismantling our public schools.

POSTSCRIPT

Are Vouchers the Solution to the Ills of Public Education?

With a great deal of public attention focused on school choice, the literature on it has mushroomed. The choice proposal first gained public attention in 1955 when Milton Friedman wrote about vouchers in "The Role of Government in Education," in Robert Solo, ed., *Economics and the Public Interest* (Rutgers University Press). More recent school choice advocates include David Harmer, *School Choice: Why We Need It, How We Get It* (Cato Institute, 1994); Bruce W. Wilkinson, *Educational Choice: Necessary but Not Sufficient* (Renouf, 1994); Terry M. Moe, ed., *Private Vouchers* (Hoover Institution, 1995); and Daniel McGroarty, *Break These Chains: The Battle for School Choice* (Forum, 1996). Some advocates of choice would limit the choices in major ways. Timothy W. Young and Evans Clinchy, in *Choice in Public Education* (Teachers College Press, 1992), contend that there is already considerable choice in public education in that there are alternative and magnet schools, intradistrict choice plans, "second chance" options, postsecondary options, and interdistrict choice plans. Research shows that these options work well, so the authors recommend that they be expanded. They argue against a voucher system, which they feel will divert badly needed financial resources from the public schools to give further support to parents who can already afford private schools. In the end they promote a limited choice plan rather than a fully free market plan. For another proposal of a limited choice plan, see Peter W. Cookson, Jr., *School Choice: The Struggle for the Soul of American Education* (Yale University Press, 1994).

Important critiques of school choice include Jeffrey R. Henig, *Rethinking School Choice: Limits of the Market Metaphor* (Princeton University Press, 1994); Kevin B. Smith and Kenneth J. Meier, *The Case Against School Choice: Politics, Markets, and Fools* (M. E. Sharpe, 1995); and Judith Pearson, *Myths of Educational Choice* (Praeger, 1993). Three works that cover the issue broadly or from several points of view are William L. Boyd and Herbert J. Walberg, eds., *Choice in Education: Potential and Problems* (McCutchan, 1990); Ruth Randall and Keith Geiger, *School Choice: Issues and Answers* (National Educational Service, 1991); and Simon Hakim et al., *Privatizing Education and Educational Choice: Concepts, Plans, and Experiences* (Praeger, 1994). Jerome J. Hanus and Peter W. Cookson, Jr., debate the issue of vouchers in *Choosing Schools: Vouchers and American Education* (American University Press, 1996). On the issue of the impact of choice on the equalization of opportunity, see Stanley C. Trent, "School Choice for African-American Children Who Live in Poverty: A Commitment to Equality or More of the Same?" *Urban Education* (October 1992).

ISSUE 14

Should Doctor-Assisted Suicide Be Legalized for the Terminally Ill?

YES: Marcia Angell, from "The Supreme Court and Physician-Assisted Suicide: The Ultimate Right," *The New England Journal of Medicine* (January 2, 1997)

NO: Paul R. McHugh, from "The Kevorkian Epidemic," *The American Scholar* (Winter 1997)

ISSUE SUMMARY

YES: Marcia Angell, executive editor of *The New England Journal of Medicine*, presents medical and ethical reasons justifying doctor-assisted suicide, including that it honors the autonomy of the patient and is merciful in cases when pain cannot be adequately relieved.

NO: Paul R. McHugh, director of the Department of Psychiatry and Behavioral Sciences at the Johns Hopkins University School of Medicine, argues that sick people who wish to kill themselves suffer from verifiable mental illness and that, since they can be treated for their pain and depressed state, physicians cannot be allowed to kill them.

According to a recent anonymous survey of almost 2,000 doctors who regularly care for dying patients, 6 percent of physicians say they have assisted patient suicides. Only 18 percent had received such requests, and one-third of these had given the requested help. Most physicians who admitted assisting in patients' deaths said they did it only once or twice, so the practice seems to be fairly uncommon. One-third of all doctors surveyed said that they would write prescriptions for deadly doses of drugs in certain cases if the law allowed, and one-quarter would give lethal injections if it were legal. *Officially* the medical community is adamantly opposed to doctor-assisted suicide.

The issue of doctor-assisted suicide is quite complex and confusing. Part of the confusion relates to definitions. Doctor-assisted suicide does not refer to a doctor injecting a patient with a lethal drug nor assisting the suicide of someone who is not terminally ill. The most common method of doctor-assisted suicide is for the doctor to prescribe a drug and then telling the patient how much of it would be lethal. The patient then administers the drug himself or herself. Doctor-assisted suicide lies between letting patients die by removing life-support systems at their request and euthanasia. The first is legal according to the Supreme Court's 1990 decision in *Cruzan v. Director, Missouri Department of Health,* and the latter is considered murder. So the question arises whether doctor-assisted suicide is more like the legal removal of life-support systems or the illegal euthanasia.

The legal, social, and moral issues involved add to the complexity and confusion. First, doctor-assisted suicide is a hotly contested legal issue governed by laws and court decisions. The legal issue was somewhat clarified by the Supreme Court on June 26, 1997, when it unanimously decided that terminally ill people have no constitutional right to die and, therefore, no right to doctor-assisted suicide. Thus, the Supreme Court will not declare invalid state laws that prohibit this practice.

Second, doctor-assisted suicide is a complex social issue with very active groups championing both sides of the debate. Medical technologies have advanced to the point that death can be postponed for a long time after the mind has ceased to function or after the quality of life has declined deeply into the negative. This produces countless situations in which people should not go on living in the judgment of most people. But what should be done for them? The situation for some may suggest that they should be helped to die. How should such a decision be made and how should it be carried out? The patient, of course, should make such decisions, if such decisions are even allowed. Painful ambiguity still remains for those who cannot make intelligent decisions and for those who have chosen to die but may not be competent to make that decision. Furthermore, what are loved ones to do when consulted by the patient or when the patient is no longer capable of making these decisions? The high medical costs for prolonging the lives of some of these very ill people may affect loved ones' decisions regarding the care or life extension of the patient and make the purity of their motives questionable. But costs cannot be totally ignored either.

Third, doctor-assisted suicide is a divisive moral issue. There is no consensus on the norms that should apply to these situations. A strong norm against euthanasia is the belief that stopping someone's life is murder even if that person wants to die. Some people apply the same norm to assisted suicide because they see little difference between injecting a patient with a lethal drug and supplying the patient with the drug to ingest. On the other side, many believe that love and mercy demand assisted suicide or even euthanasia for the terminally ill when great suffering accompanies all other options.

The following selections provide strong arguments for and against doctor-assisted suicide. Marcia Angell contends that the relieving of suffering and honoring the patient's wishes are the overriding concerns, which fully justify the practice in light of the absence of compelling arguments to the contrary. Paul R. McHugh, citing the case of Dr. Jack Kevorkian, maintains that the patients that Kevorkian helped to die were all suffering from depression and that Kevorkian should have advised them to get competent psychological help, which would have restored their desire to live.

Marcia Angell

 **YES**

The Supreme Court and Physician-Assisted Suicide— The Ultimate Right

The U.S. Supreme Court will decide later this year whether to let stand decisions by two appeals courts permitting doctors to help terminally ill patients commit suicide. The Ninth and Second Circuit Courts of Appeals last spring held that state laws in Washington and New York that ban assistance in suicide were unconstitutional as applied to doctors and their dying patients. If the Supreme Court lets the decisions stand, physicians in 12 states, which include about half the population of the United States, would be allowed to provide the means for terminally ill patients to take their own lives, and the remaining states would rapidly follow suit. Not since *Roe* v. *Wade* has a Supreme Court decision been so fateful.

The decision will culminate several years of intense national debate, fueled by a number of highly publicized events. Perhaps most important among them is Dr. Jack Kevorkian's defiant assistance in some 44 suicides since 1990, to the dismay of many in the medical and legal establishments, but with substantial public support, as evidenced by the fact that three juries refused to convict him even in the face of a Michigan statute enacted for that purpose. Also since 1990, voters in three states have considered ballot initiatives that would legalize some form of physician-assisted dying, and in 1994 Oregon became the first state to approve such a measure. (The Oregon law was stayed pending a court challenge.) Several surveys indicate that roughly two thirds of the American public now support physician-assisted suicide, as do more than half the doctors in the United States, despite the fact that influential physicians' organizations are opposed. It seems clear that many Americans are now so concerned about the possibility of a lingering, high-technology death that they are receptive to the idea of doctors' being allowed to help them die.

In this editorial I will explain why I believe the appeals courts were right and why I hope the Supreme Court will uphold their decisions. I am aware that this is a highly contentious issue, with good people and strong arguments on both sides. The American Medical Association (AMA) filed an amicus brief opposing the legalization of physician-assisted suicide, and the Massachusetts

From Marcia Angell, "The Supreme Court and Physician-Assisted Suicide: The Ultimate Right," *The New England Journal of Medicine*, vol. 336, no. 1 (January 2, 1997), pp. 50–53. Copyright © 1997 by The Massachusetts Medical Society. Reprinted by permission. All rights reserved. References omitted.

Medical Society, which owns the *Journal,* was a signatory to it. But here I speak for myself, not the *Journal* or the Massachusetts Medical Society. The legal aspects of the case have been well discussed elsewhere, to me most compellingly in Ronald Dworkin's essay in the *New York Review of Books.* I will focus primarily on the medical and ethical aspects.

I begin with the generally accepted premise that one of the most important ethical principles in medicine is respect for each patient's autonomy, and that when this principle conflicts with others, it should almost always take precedence. This premise is incorporated into our laws governing medical practice and research, including the requirement of informed consent to any treatment. In medicine, patients exercise their self-determination most dramatically when they ask that life-sustaining treatment be withdrawn. Although others may sometimes consider the request ill-founded, we are bound to honor it if the patient is mentally competent—that is, if the patient can understand the nature of the decision and its consequences.

A second starting point is the recognition that death is not fair and is often cruel. Some people die quickly, and others die slowly but peacefully. Some find personal or religious meaning in the process, as well as an opportunity for a final reconciliation with loved ones. But others, especially those with cancer, AIDS, or progressive neurologic disorders, may die by inches and in great anguish, despite every effort of their doctors and nurses. Although nearly all pain can be relieved, some cannot, and other symptoms, such as dyspnea, nausea, and weakness, are even more difficult to control. In addition, dying sometimes holds great indignities and existential suffering. Patients who happen to require some treatment to sustain their lives, such as assisted ventilation or dialysis, can hasten death by having the life-sustaining treatment withdrawn, but those who are not receiving life-sustaining treatment may desperately need help they cannot now get.

If the decisions of the appeals courts are upheld, states will not be able to prohibit doctors from helping such patients to die by prescribing a lethal dose of a drug and advising them on its use for suicide. State laws barring euthanasia (the administration of a lethal drug by a doctor) and assisted suicide for patients who are not terminally ill would not be affected. Furthermore, doctors would not be *required* to assist in suicide; they would simply have that option. Both appeals courts based their decisions on constitutional questions. This is important, because it shifted the focus of the debate from what the majority would approve through the political process, as exemplified by the Oregon initiative, to a matter of fundamental rights, which are largely immune from the political process. Indeed, the Ninth Circuit Court drew an explicit analogy between suicide and abortion, saying that both were personal choices protected by the Constitution and that forbidding doctors to assist would in effect nullify these rights. Although states could regulate assisted suicide, as they do abortion, they would not be permitted to regulate it out of existence.

It is hard to quarrel with the desire of a greatly suffering, dying patient for a quicker, more humane death or to disagree that it may be merciful to help bring that about. In those circumstances, loved ones are often relieved when death finally comes, as are the attending doctors and nurses. As the Second

Circuit Court said, the state has no interest in prolonging such a life. Why, then, do so many people oppose legalizing physician-assisted suicide in these cases? There are a number of arguments against it, some stronger than others, but I believe none of them can offset the overriding duties of doctors to relieve suffering and to respect their patients' autonomy. Below I list several of the more important arguments against physician-assisted suicide and discuss why I believe they are in the last analysis unpersuasive.

Assisted suicide is a form of killing, which is always wrong. In contrast, withdrawing life-sustaining treatment simply allows the disease to take its course. There are three methods of hastening the death of a dying patient: withdrawing life-sustaining treatment, assisting suicide, and euthanasia. The right to stop treatment has been recognized repeatedly since the 1976 case of Karen Ann Quinlan and was affirmed by the U.S. Supreme Court in the 1990 *Cruzan* decision and the U.S. Congress in its 1990 Patient Self-Determination Act. Although the legal underpinning is the right to be free of unwanted bodily invasion, the purpose of hastening death was explicitly acknowledged. In contrast, assisted suicide and euthanasia have not been accepted; euthanasia is illegal in all states, and assisted suicide is illegal in most of them.

Why the distinctions? Most would say they turn on the doctor's role: whether it is passive or active. When life-sustaining treatment is withdrawn, the doctor's role is considered passive and the cause of death is the underlying disease, despite the fact that switching off the ventilator of a patient dependent on it looks anything but passive and would be considered homicide if done without the consent of the patient or a proxy. In contrast, euthanasia by the injection of a lethal drug is active and directly causes the patient's death. Assisting suicide by supplying the necessary drugs is considered somewhere in between, more active than switching off a ventilator but less active than injecting drugs, hence morally and legally more ambiguous.

I believe, however, that these distinctions are too doctor-centered and not sufficiently patient-centered. We should ask ourselves not so much whether the doctor's role is passive or active but whether the *patient's* role is passive or active. From that perspective, the three methods of hastening death line up quite differently. When life-sustaining treatment is withdrawn from an incompetent patient at the request of a proxy or when euthanasia is performed, the patient may be utterly passive. Indeed, either act can be performed even if the patient is unaware of the decision. In sharp contrast, assisted suicide, by definition, cannot occur without the patient's knowledge and participation. Therefore, it must be active—that is to say, voluntary. That is a crucial distinction, because it provides an inherent safeguard against abuse that is not present with the other two methods of hastening death. If the loaded term "kill" is to be used, it is not the doctor who kills, but the patient. Primarily because euthanasia can be performed without the patient's participation, I oppose its legalization in this country.

Assisted suicide is not necessary. All suffering can be relieved if care givers are sufficiently skillful and compassionate, as illustrated by the hospice movement. I have no doubt that if expert palliative care were available to everyone who needed it, there would be few requests for assisted suicide. Even under the best of circumstances, however, there will always be a few patients whose suffering simply cannot be adequately alleviated. And there will be some who would prefer suicide to any other measures available, including the withdrawal of life-sustaining treatment or the use of heavy sedation. Surely, every effort should be made to improve palliative care, as I argued 15 years ago, but when those efforts are unavailing and suffering patients desperately long to end their lives, physician-assisted suicide should be allowed. The argument that permitting it would divert us from redoubling our commitment to comfort care asks these patients to pay the penalty for our failings. It is also illogical. Good comfort care and the availability of physician-assisted suicide are no more mutually exclusive than good cardiologic care and the availability of heart transplantation.

Permitting assisted suicide would put us on a moral "slippery slope." Although in itself assisted suicide might be acceptable, it would lead inexorably to involuntary euthanasia. It is impossible to avoid slippery slopes in medicine (or in any aspect of life). The issue is how and where to find a purchase. For example, we accept the right of proxies to terminate life-sustaining treatment, despite the obvious potential for abuse, because the reasons for doing so outweigh the risks. We hope our procedures will safeguard patients. In the case of assisted suicide, its voluntary nature is the best protection against sliding down a slippery slope, but we also need to ensure that the request is thoughtful and freely made. Although it is possible that we may someday decide to legalize voluntary euthanasia under certain circumstances or assisted suicide for patients who are not terminally ill, legalizing assisted suicide for the dying does not in itself make these other decisions inevitable. Interestingly, recent reports from the Netherlands, where both euthanasia and physician-assisted suicide are permitted, indicate that fears about a slippery slope there have not been borne out.

Assisted suicide would be a threat to the economically and socially vulnerable. The poor disabled, and elderly might be coerced to request it. Admittedly, overburdened families or cost-conscious doctors might pressure vulnerable patients to request suicide, but similar wrongdoing is at least as likely in the case of withdrawing life-sustaining treatment, since that decision can be made by proxy. Yet, there is no evidence of widespread abuse. The Ninth Circuit Court recalled that it was feared *Roe* v. *Wade* would lead to coercion of poor and uneducated women to request abortions, but that did not happen. The concern that coercion is more likely in this era of managed care, although understandable, would hold suffering patients hostage to the deficiencies of our health care system. Unfortunately, no human endeavor is immune to abuses. The question is not whether a perfect system can be devised, but whether abuses are likely to be sufficiently rare to be offset by the benefits to patients who otherwise would be condemned to face the end of their lives in protracted agony.

Depressed patients would seek physician-assisted suicide rather than help for their depression. Even in the terminally ill, a request for assisted suicide might signify treatable depression, not irreversible suffering. Patients suffering greatly at the end of life may also be depressed, but the depression does not necessarily explain their decision to commit suicide or make it irrational. Nor is it simple to diagnose depression in terminally ill patients. Sadness is to be expected, and some of the vegetative symptoms of depression are similar to the symptoms of terminal illness. The success of antidepressant treatment in these circumstances is also not ensured. Although there are anecdotes about patients who changed their minds about suicide after treatment, we do not have good studies of how often that happens or the relation to antidepressant treatment. Dying patients who request assisted suicide and seem depressed should certainly be strongly encouraged to accept psychiatric treatment, but I do not believe that competent patients should be *required* to accept it as a condition of receiving assistance with suicide. On the other hand, doctors would not be required to comply with all requests; they would be expected to use their judgment, just as they do in so many other types of life-and-death decisions in medical practice.

Doctors should never participate in taking life. If there is to be assisted suicide, doctor must not be involved. Although most doctors favor permitting assisted suicide under certain circumstances, many who favor it believe that doctors should not provide the assistance. To them, doctors should be unambiguously committed to life (although most doctors who hold this view would readily honor a patient's decision to have life-sustaining treatment withdrawn). The AMA, too, seems to object to physician-assisted suicide primarily because it violates the profession's mission. Like others, I find that position too abstract. The highest ethical imperative of doctors should be to provide care in whatever way best serves patients' interests, in accord with each patient's wishes, not with a theoretical commitment to preserve life no matter what the cost in suffering. If a patient requests help with suicide and the doctor believes the request is appropriate, requiring someone else to provide the assistance would be a form of abandonment. Doctors who are opposed in principle need not assist, but they should make their patients aware of their position early in the relationship so that a patient who chooses to select another doctor can do so. The greatest harm we can do is to consign a desperate patient to unbearable suffering—or force the patient to seek out a stranger like Dr. Kevorkian. Contrary to the frequent assertion that permitting physician-assisted suicide would lead patients to distrust their doctors, I believe distrust is more likely to arise from uncertainty about whether a doctor will honor a patient's wishes.

Physician-assisted suicide may occasionally be warranted, but it should remain illegal. If doctors risk prosecution, they will think twice before assisting with suicide. This argument wrongly shifts the focus from the patient to the doctor. Instead of reflecting the condition and wishes of patients, assisted suicide would reflect the courage and compassion of their doctors. Thus, patients with doctors like Timothy Quill, who described in a 1991 *Journal* article how he helped a patient take her life, would get the help they need and want, but similar patients with less steadfast doctors would not. That makes no sense.

People do not need assistance to commit suicide. With enough determination, they can do it themselves. This is perhaps the cruelest of the arguments against physician-assisted suicide. Many patients at the end of life are, in fact, physically unable to commit suicide on their own. Others lack the resources to do so. It has sometimes been suggested that they can simply stop eating and drinking and kill themselves that way. Although this method has been described as peaceful under certain conditions, no one should count on that. The fact is that this argument leaves most patients to their suffering. Some, usually men, manage to commit suicide using violent methods. Percy Bridgman, a Nobel laureate in physics who in 1961 shot himself rather than die of metastatic cancer, said in his suicide note, "It is not decent for Society to make a man do this to himself."

My father, who knew nothing of Percy Bridgman, committed suicide under similar circumstances. He was 81 and had metastatic prostate cancer. The night before he was scheduled to be admitted to the hospital, he shot himself. Like Bridgman, he thought it might be his last chance. At the time, he was not in extreme pain, nor was he close to death (his life expectancy was probably longer than six months). But he was suffering nonetheless—from nausea and the side effects of antiemetic agents, weakness, incontinence, and hopelessness. Was he depressed? He would probably have freely admitted that he was, but he would have thought it beside the point. In any case, he was an intensely private man who would have refused psychiatric care. Was he overly concerned with maintaining control of the circumstances of his life and death? Many people would say so, but that was the way he was. It is the job of medicine to deal with patients as they are, not as we would like them to be.

I tell my father's story here because it makes an abstract issue very concrete. If physician-assisted suicide had been available, I have no doubt my father would have chosen it. He was protective of his family, and if he had felt he had the choice, he would have spared my mother the shock of finding his body. He did not tell her what he planned to do, because he knew she would stop him. I also believe my father would have waited if physician-assisted suicide had been available. If patients have access to drugs they can take when they choose, they will not feel they must commit suicide early, while they are still able to do it on their own. They would probably live longer and certainly more peacefully, and they might not even use the drugs.

Long before my father's death, I believed that physician-assisted suicide ought to be permissible under some circumstances, but his death strengthened my conviction that it is simply a part of good medical care—something to be done reluctantly and sadly, as a last resort, but done nonetheless. There should be safeguards to ensure that the decision is well considered and consistent, but they should not be so daunting or violative of privacy that they become obstacles instead of protections. In particular, they should be directed not toward reviewing the reasons for an autonomous decision, but only toward ensuring that the decision is indeed autonomous. If the Supreme Court upholds the decisions of the appeals courts, assisted suicide will not be forced on either patients or doctors, but it will be a choice for those patients who need it and those doctors willing to help. If, on the other hand, the Supreme Court overturns the lower courts' decisions, the issue will continue to be grappled with state by state, through the political process. But sooner or later, given the need and the widespread public support, physician-assisted suicide will be demanded of a compassionate profession.

The Kevorkian Epidemic

D r. Jack Kevorkian of Detroit has been in the papers most days this past summer and autumn [1997] helping sick people kill themselves. He is said to receive hundreds of calls a week. Although his acts are illegal by statute and common law in Michigan, no one stops him. Many citizens, including members of three juries, believe he means well, perhaps thinking: Who knows? Just maybe, we ourselves shall need his services some day.

To me it looks like madness from every quarter. The patients are mad by definition in that they are suicidally depressed and demoralized; Dr. Kevorkian is "certifiable" in that his passions render him, as the state code specifies, "dangerous to others"; and the usually reliable people of Michigan are confused and anxious to the point of incoherence by terrors of choice that are everyday issues for doctors. These three disordered parties have converged as a triad of host-agent-environment to interact synergistically in provoking a local epidemic of premature death.

Let me begin with the injured hosts of this epidemic, the patients mad by definition. At this writing, more than forty, as best we know, have submitted to Dr. Kevorkian's deadly charms. They came to him with a variety of medical conditions: Alzheimer's disease, multiple sclerosis, chronic pain, amyotrophic lateral sclerosis, cancer, drug addiction, and more. These are certainly disorders from which anyone might seek relief. But what kind of relief do patients with these conditions usually seek when they do not have a Dr. Kevorkian to extinguish their pain?

Both clinical experience and research on this question are extensive—and telling. A search for death does not accompany most terminal or progressive diseases. Pain-ridden patients customarily call doctors for remedies, not for termination of life. Physical incapacity, as with advanced arthritis, does not generate suicide. Even amyotrophic lateral sclerosis, or Lou Gehrig's disease, a harrowing condition I shall describe presently, is not associated with increased suicide amongst its sufferers. Most doctors learn these facts as they help patients and their families burdened by these conditions.

But we don't have to rely solely upon the testimonies of experienced physicians. Recently cancer patients in New England were asked about their attitudes toward death. The investigators—apparently surprised to discover a will to live when they expected to find an urge to die—reported in the *Lancet* (vol. 347, pp. 1805–1810, 1996) two striking findings. First, that cancer patients enduring pain were not inclined to want euthanasia or physician-assisted suicide. In fact, "patients actually experiencing pain were more likely to find euthanasia or physician-assisted suicide unacceptable." Second, those patients inclined toward suicide—whether in pain or not—were suffering from depression. As the investigators noted: "These data indicate a conflict between attitudes and possible practices related to euthanasia and physician-assisted suicide. These *interventions* were approved of for terminally ill patients with unremitting pain, but these are not the patients most likely to request such *interventions*.... There is *some* concern that with legislation of euthanasia or physician-assisted suicide non-psychiatric physicians, who generally have a poor ability to detect and treat depression, may allow life-ending *interventions* when treatment of depression may be more appropriate." (Italics added to identify mealymouthed expressions: *interventions* means homicides, and *some* means that we investigators should stay cool in our concerns—after all, it's not we who are dying.)

None of this is news to psychiatrists who have studied suicides associated with medical illnesses. Depression, the driving force in most cases, comes in two varieties: symptomatic depression found as a feature of particular diseases —that is, as one of the several symptoms of that disease; and demoralization, the common state of mind of people in need of guidance for facing discouraging circumstances alone. Both forms of depression render patients vulnerable to feelings of hopelessness that, if not adequately confronted, may lead to suicide.

Let me first concentrate on the symptomatic depressions because an understanding of them illuminates much of the problem. By the term *symptomatic,* psychiatrists mean that with some physical diseases suicidal depression is one of the condition's characteristic features. Careful students of these diseases come to appreciate that this variety of depression is not to be accepted as a natural feeling of discouragement provoked by bad circumstances—that is, similar to the down-hearted state of, say, a bankrupt man or a grief-stricken widow. Instead the depression we are talking about here, with its beclouding of judgment, sense of misery, and suicidal inclinations, is a symptom identical in nature to the fevers, pains, or loss of energy that are signs of the disease itself....

The problematic nature of symptomatic depression goes beyond the painful state of mind of the patient. Other observers—such as family members and physicians—may well take the depressive's disturbed, indeed insane, point of view as a proper assessment of his or her situation. It was this point that Huntington, long before the time of modern anti-depressant treatment, wished to emphasize by identifying it as an insanity. He knew that failure to diagnose this feature will lead to the neglect of efforts to treat the patient properly and to protect him or her from suicide until the symptom remits.

Such neglect is a crucial blunder, because, whether the underlying condition is Huntington's disease, Alzheimer's disease, MS, or something else, modern anti-depressant treatment is usually effective at relieving the mood disorder and restoring the patient's emotional equilibrium. In Michigan and in Holland, where physician-assisted suicide also takes place, these actions to hasten death are the ultimate neglect of patients with symptomatic depression; they are, really, a form of collusion with insanity.

The diagnosis of symptomatic depression is not overly difficult if its existence is remembered and its features systematically sought. But many of its characteristics—such as its capacity to provoke bodily pains—are not known to all physicians. The fact that such depression occurs in dire conditions, such as Huntington's disease, may weigh against its prompt diagnosis and treatment. Again and again, kindly intended physicians presume that a depression "makes sense"—given the patient's situation—and overlook the stereotypic signs of the insanity. They presume justifiable demoralization and forget the pharmacologically treatable depressions.

Over the last decade, at least among psychiatrists, the reality of symptomatic depressions has become familiar and treatment readiness has become the rule. Yet not all sick patients with life-threatening depression have symptomatic depressions. Many physically ill patients are depressed for perfectly understandable reasons, given the grueling circumstances of their progressive and intractable disease. Just as any misfortune can provoke grief and anxiety, so can awareness of loss of health and of a closed future.

Well-titled *demoralization,* this depression, too, has a number of attributes. It waxes and wanes with experiences and events, comes in waves, and is worse at certain times—such as during the night, when contemplating future discomforts and burdens, and when the patient is alone or uninstructed about the benefits that modern treatments can bring him.

In contrast to the symptomatic depressions that run their own course almost independent of events, demoralization is sensitive to circumstances and especially to the conduct of doctors toward the patient. Companionship, especially that which provides understanding and clear explanations of the actions to be taken in opposing disease and disability, can be immensely helpful in overcoming this state and sustaining the patient in a hopeful frame of mind....

This is the point: Depression, both in the form of a symptomatic mental state and in the form of demoralization, is the result of illness and circumstances combined and is treatable just as are other effects of illness. These treatments are the everyday skills of many physicians, but particularly of those physicians who are specialists in these disorders and can advance the treatments most confidently.

Most suicidally depressed patients are not rational individuals who have weighed the balance sheet of their lives and discovered more red than black ink. They are victims of altered attitudes about themselves and their situation, which cause powerful feelings of hopelessness to abound. Doctors can protect them from these attitudes by providing information, guidance, and support all along the way. Dr. Kevorkian, however, trades upon the vulnerabilities and mental disorders of these patients and in so doing makes a mockery of medicine as a discipline of informed concern for patients.

Let us turn to Dr. Kevorkian, the agent of this epidemic in Michigan, and consider why I think that he is "certifiably" insane, by which I mean that he suffers from a mental condition rendering him dangerous to others.

Without question, Dr. Kevorkian has proven himself dangerous, having participated in killing more than forty people already, with no end in sight....

The question is whether his behavior is a product of a mental disorder. Not everyone agrees on an answer. Indeed the *British Medical Journal (BMJ)* described Dr. Kevorkian as a "hero."

His champions see no discernible motive for Dr. Kevorkian other than that he believes his work is fitting. The *BMJ* notes that greed for money or fame or some sadistic urge does not motivate Dr. Kevorkian. They make much of the fact that he does not charge a fee for killing.

Because of the absence of such motives, the editors presume that he is a hero among doctors since it is only a "personal code of honor that admits of no qualification" that leads him into action.

But let us look rather more closely at "personal codes that admit no qualification." We have seen a few of them before and not all were admirable. As Dr. Kevorkian motors around Michigan carrying cylinders of carbon monoxide or bottles of potassium chloride to dispatch the sick, his is the motivation of a person with an "overvalued idea," a diagnostic formulation first spelled out by the psychiatrist Carl Wernicke in 1906. Wernicke differentiated overvalued ideas from obsessions and delusions. Overvalued ideas are often at the motivational heart of "personal codes that admit no qualification" and certainly provide a drive as powerful as that of hunger for money, fame, or sexual gratification.

An individual with an overvalued idea is someone who has taken up an idea shared by others in his milieu or culture and transformed it into a ruling passion or "monomania" for himself. It becomes the goal of all his efforts and he is prepared to sacrifice everything—family, reputation, health, even life itself —for it. He presumes that what he does in its service is right regardless of any losses that he or others suffer for it. He sees all opposition as at best misguided and at worst malevolent.

For Dr. Kevorkian, people may die before their time and the fabric of their families may be torn apart, but it's all for the good if he can presume they were "suffering pain unnecessarily" and he has eliminated it. He scorns all opposition—in particular constitutional democratic opposition—as resting on bad faith or ignorance. Empowered by his idea, he feels free to disregard the law and any of its officers.

An overvalued idea has three characteristics: (1) it is a self-dominating but not idiosyncratic opinion, given great importance by (2) intense emotional feelings over its significance, and evoking (3) persistent behavior in its service. For Dr. Kevorkian, thinking about how to terminate the sick has become his exclusive concern. His belief in the justice of his ideas is intense enough for him to starve himself if thwarted by law.

Dr. Kevorkian thinks that all opposition to him is "bad faith" and thus worthy of contempt—a contempt he expresses with no reservation. He is fond of saying that the judicial system of our country is "corrupt," the religious members of our society are "irrational," the medical profession is "insane," the press is "meretricious."

He considers his own behavior "humanitarian." Dr. Kevorkian holds himself beyond reproach, even after killing one patient he believed had multiple sclerosis but whose autopsy revealed no evidence of that disease and another patient with the vague condition of "chronic fatigue syndrome" in whom no pathological process could be found at autopsy—only Kevorkian's poison. He acts without taking a careful medical history, trying alternative treatments, or reflecting on how his actions affect such people as surviving family members.

Dr. Kevorkian's is a confident business. As the news reports flow out of Michigan, it appears that his threshold for medicide is getting lower. Physician-assisted suicide that had previously demanded an incurable disease such as Alzheimer's is now practiced upon patients with such chronic complaints as pelvic pain and emphysema, whose life expectancy cannot be specified. He can justify the active termination of anyone with an ailment—which is just what might be expected once the boundary against active killing by doctors has been breached. What's to stop him now that juries have found his actions to be de facto legal in Michigan?

A crucial aspect of overvalued ideas is that, in contrast to delusions, they are not idiosyncratic. They are ideas that can be found in a proportion of the public—often an influential proportion. It is from such reservoirs of opinion that the particular individual harnesses and amplifies an idea with the disproportionate zeal characteristic of a ruling passion. That Dr. Kevorkian can find people in the highest places—even within the medical profession—to support his ideas and say that they see heroism in his actions is not surprising, given the passion of the contemporary debate over euthanasia. In this way the person with the overvalued idea may be seen, by those who share his opinion but not his self-sacrificing zeal, as giving expression to their hopes—disregarding the slower processes of democracy, filled with prejudice against all who resist, and pumped up with a sense of a higher purpose and justice.

People such as Dr. Kevorkian have found a place in history. With some, with the passage of time, we come to agree with the idea if not the method by which the idea was first expressed. Such was John Brown, the abolitionist, ready to hack five anonymous farmers to death in the Pottowatomi massacre to advance his cause. With others we may come to tolerate some aspect of the idea but see its expression in actual behavior as ludicrous. Such was Carry Nation, the scourge of Kansas barkeeps and boozers, who went to jail hundreds of times for chopping up saloons with a small hatchet in the cause of temperance. Finally, for some, we come to recognize the potential for horror in an overvalued idea held by a person in high authority. Such was Adolf Hitler.

But how is it that anxieties and confusions about medical practice and death can so afflict the judicious people of Michigan as to paralyze them before the outrageous behavior of Dr. Kevorkian and thus generate an environment for this epidemic? In Michigan these states of mind derive from conflicting concerns over medical decisions. The citizens—like any inexpert group—are relatively uninformed about what doctors can do for patients, even in extreme situations. Conflicting goals and unfamiliar practices—common enough around medical decisions—produce anxiety and confusion every time.

No one thinks happily about dying, especially dying in pain. Death is bad; dying can be worse. Anyone who says he does not fear dying—and all the pain and suffering tied to it—has probably not experienced much in life.

This concern, though, certainly has been exaggerated in our times, even though now much can be done to relieve the heaviest burdens of terminally ill patients. Yet through a variety of sources—such as movies, newspapers, and essays—all the negative aspects of dying have been emphasized, the agonies embellished, and the loss of control represented by disease accentuated. Horror stories feed upon one another, and rumors of medical lack of interest grow into opinions that doctors both neglect the dying and hold back relief. Doctors are regularly accused of surrendering to professional taboos or to legal advice to avoid risk of malpractice or prosecution—and in this way are presumed ready to sacrifice their patients out of selfish fear for themselves.

On the contrary, most doctors try to collaborate with patients and do listen to their wishes, especially when treatments that carry painful burdens are contemplated. As Dr. Kevorkian can demonstrate—with videotapes, no less—the patients he killed asked him repeatedly for help in dying rather than for help in living. Do not they have some right to die at their own hands steadied by Dr. Kevorkian? Is not the matter of assisted suicide simply a matter of rights and wants to which any citizen of Michigan is entitled?

The idea of a right to suicide provokes most psychiatrists. Psychiatry has worked to teach everyone that suicide is not an uncomplicated, voluntary act to which rights attach. It has shown that suicide is an act provoked, indeed compelled, by mental disorder—such as a disorienting depression or a set of misdirected, even delusionary, ideas. In that sense psychiatry taught that suicidal people were not "responsible" for this behavior—no matter what they said or wrote in final letters or testaments—any more than they would be for epileptic seizures.

This idea—generated from the careful study of the clinical circumstances and past histories of suicidal patients—gradually prevailed in civil law and even in the canon law of churches. As a result, laws against suicide were repealed—not to make suicide a "right" but to remove it from the status of a crime.

We psychiatrists thought we had done a worthy thing for our society, for families of patients, and even for patients themselves. We were not saying, not for a moment, that we approved of suicide. Far from it. We knew such deaths to be ugly and misguided—misguided in particular because the disposition to die, the wish for suicide, was, on inspection, often a symptom of the very mental disorders that psychiatry treats. Suicide in almost all cases is as far from a rational choice based on a weighing of the balance books of life as is responding to hallucinated voices or succumbing to the paranoid ideas of a charismatic madman such as Jim Jones, who at Jonestown directed a gruesome exhibition of mass assisted suicide.

Psychiatrists were united in their views about suicide and shook their heads when contemplating past traditions when suicides were considered scandalous. We did not think too deeply into the consequences of our actions. For, after suicide ceased to be a crime, it soon became a right and, conceivably under some circumstances, such as when costs of care grow onerous, an obligation. Psychiatrists, who had worked for decades demonstrating that suicides were insane acts, are now recruited in Holland to assure that requests for suicide made by patients offered "no hope of cure" by their doctors are "rational."

What had begun as an effort at explanation and understanding of the tragic act of suicide has developed into complicity in the seduction of vulnerable people into that very behavior. The patients are seduced just as the victims in Jonestown were—by isolating them, sustaining their despair, revoking alternatives, stressing examples of others choosing to die, and sweetening the deadly poison by speaking of death with dignity. If even psychiatrists succumb to this complicity with death, what can be expected of the lay public in Michigan? . . .

One can think of ways to combat the deadly convergence of madnesses in Michigan and to deter the spread of this local epidemic to other regions of our country. The suicidal patients certainly should be treated for their depressive vulnerabilities by doctors able to assist them with their underlying illnesses. Dr. Kevorkian, the agent of their extinction, should be stopped by whatever means the state has at its disposal to stay dangerous men. And the people of Michigan should be taught about the capacities of modern medicine. With this information, the hope is, they will emerge from their anxious confusions, accept mortality for what it is rather than for what they imagine, and, at last, end their support for this insanity.

POSTSCRIPT

Should Doctor-Assisted Suicide Be Legalized for the Terminally Ill?

Angell tells the story of her father's suicide because he seemed to be a perfect candidate for doctor-assisted suicide. Since it was not available to him, he shot himself before being hospitalized for his cancer. Like any case this one allows for various interpretations, but it points up the problem of a blanket rule for all cases. What if we were to come to the conclusion that doctor-assisted suicide is wrong in most cases when patients request it but right in a minority of cases? Maybe both sides are right at times and wrong at other times. The problem is that it is difficult to make laws that apply only sometimes. Most laws provide too little leeway to be adjusted to the peculiarities of individual cases. For example, if a man goes over the speed limit, he breaks the law, even if he is driving his wife to the hospital to deliver a baby. Fortunately, most policemen would not write this man a ticket but rather turn on their siren and escort him to the hospital. For many laws the discretion of judges and juries, like that of the policeman, provides some badly needed flexibility, but problems will always remain.

The literature on doctor-assisted suicide and the larger issue of euthanasia has mushroomed in the last decade. For arguments against these practices, see Robert Laurence Barry, *Breaking the Thread of Life: On Rational Suicide* (Transaction Publishers, 1994); Tom Beauchamp, *Ethical Issues in Death and Dying* (Prentice Hall, 1996); Herbert Hendin, *Seduced by Death: Doctors, Patients and the Dutch Cure* (W. W. Norton, 1996); and Wesley J. Smith, *Forced Exit: The Slippery Slope from Assisted Suicide to Legalized Murder* (Times Books, 1997).

For works that favor doctor-assisted suicide or euthanasia or that contain various viewpoints, see Ira Byock, *Dying Well: The Prospect for Growth at the End of Life* (Thorndike Press, 1997); Timothy E. Quill, *A Midwife Through the Dying Process* (Johns Hopkins University Press, 1996); and Marylin Webb, *The Good Death: The New American Search to Reshape the End of Life* (Bantam Books, 1997). For works that present or analyze the issues as debates, see Michael M. Uhlman, ed., *Last Rights? Assisted Suicide and Euthanasia Debated* (William B. Eerdmans, 1998); Tamara Roleff, ed., *Suicide: Opposing Viewpoints* (Greenhaven Press, 1998); and Carol Wedesser, ed., *Euthanasia: Opposing Viewpoints* (Greenhaven Press, 1995). For multiple views on doctor-assisted suicide and euthanasia, see Melvin I. Urofsky and Philip E. Urofsky, eds., *The Right to Die: A Two-Volume Anthology of Scholarly Articles* (Garland, 1996) and Robert F. Weir et al., *Physician-Assisted Suicide* (Indiana University Press, 1997).

On the Internet . . .

American Society of Criminology

An excellent starting point for studying all aspects of criminology and criminal justice, this page provides links to sites on criminal justice in general, international criminal justice, juvenile justice, courts, the police, and the government.

http://www.bsos.umd.edu/asc/four.html

Crime-Free America

Crime-Free America is a grassroots, nonprofit group dedicated to ending the crime epidemic that it feels has gripped the United States over the last four decades. This site has links to the Bureau of Justice Statistics, forums, and crime watch profiles.

http://crime-free.org

Crime Times

This site lists research reviews and other information regarding the causes of criminal and violent behavior. It is provided by the nonprofit Wacker Foundation, publishers of Crime Times.

http://www.crime-times.org/titles.htm

Justice Information Center (JIC)

Provided by the National Criminal Justice Reference Service, the JIC site connects to information about corrections, courts, crime prevention, criminal justice, statistics, drugs and crime, law enforcement, and victims, among other topics.

http://www.ncjrs.org

Sociology Library

This site provides a number of indexes of culture and ethnic studies, criminology, population and demographics, and statistical sources.

http://www.library.upenn.edu/resources/subject/
social/sociology/sociology.html

PART 5

Crime and Social Control

*A*ll societies label certain hurtful actions as crimes and punish those who commit them. Other harmful actions, however, are not defined as crimes, and the perpetrators are not punished. Today the definition of crime and the appropriate treatment of criminals is widely debated. Some of the major questions are: Does street crime pose more of a threat to the public's well-being than white-collar crime? Billions of dollars have been spent on the "war on drugs," but who is winning? Would legalizing some drugs free up money that could be directed to other types of social welfare programs, such as the rehabilitation of addicts? What about the death penalty? Do certain crimes justify its use?

- Is Street Crime More Harmful Than White-Collar Crime?

- Should Drug Use Be Decriminalized?

- Is Capital Punishment Justified?

ISSUE 15

Is Street Crime More Harmful Than White-Collar Crime?

YES: John J. DiIulio, Jr., from "The Impact of Inner-City Crime," *The Public Interest* (Summer 1989)

NO: Jeffrey Reiman, from *The Rich Get Richer and the Poor Get Prison: Ideology, Class, and Criminal Justice*, 5th ed. (Allyn & Bacon, 1998)

ISSUE SUMMARY

YES: John J. DiIulio, Jr., a professor of politics and public affairs, analyzes the enormous harm done—especially to the urban poor and, by extension, to all of society—by street criminals and their activities.

NO: Professor of philosophy Jeffrey Reiman argues that the dangers posed by negligent corporations and white-collar criminals are a greater menace to society than are the activities of typical street criminals.

The word *crime* entered the English language (from the Old French) around A.D. 1250, when it was identified with "sinfulness." Later, the meaning of the word was modified: crime became the kind of sinfulness that was rightly punishable by law. Even medieval writers, who did not distinguish very sharply between church and state, recognized that there were some sins for which punishment was best left to God; the laws should punish only those that cause harm to the community. Of course, their concept of harm was a very broad one, embracing such offenses as witchcraft and blasphemy. Modern jurists, even those who deplore such practices, would say that the state has no business punishing the perpetrators of these types of offenses.

What, then, should the laws punish? The answer depends in part on our notion of harm. We usually limit the term to the kind of harm that is tangible and obvious: taking a life, causing bodily injury or psychological trauma, and destroying property. For most Americans today, particularly those who live in cities, the word *crime* is practically synonymous with street crime. Anyone who has ever been robbed or beaten by street criminals will never forget the experience. The harm that these criminals cause is tangible, and the connection between the harm and the perpetrator is very direct.

But suppose the connection is not so direct. Suppose, for example, that A hires B to shoot C. Is that any less a crime? B is the actual shooter, but is A any less guilty? Of course not, we say; he may even be more guilty, since he is the ultimate mover behind the crime. A would be guilty even if the chain of command were much longer, involving A's orders to B, and B's to C, then on to D, E, and F to kill G. Organized crime kingpins go to jail even when they are far removed from the people who carry out their orders. High officials of the Nixon administration, even though they were not directly involved in the burglary attempt at the Democratic National Committee headquarters at the Watergate Hotel complex in 1972, were imprisoned.

This brings us to the topic of white-collar crime. The burglars at the Watergate Hotel were acting on orders that trickled down from the highest reaches of political power in the United States. Other white-collar criminals are as varied as the occupations from which they come. They include stockbrokers who make millions through insider trading, as Ivan Boesky did; members of Congress who take payoffs; and people who cheat on their income taxes, like hotel owner and billionaire Leona Helmsley. Some, like Helmsley, get stiff prison sentences when convicted, though many others (like most of the officials in the Watergate scandal) do little or no time in prison. Do they deserve stiffer punishment, or are their crimes less harmful than the crimes of street criminals?

Although white-collar criminals do not directly cause physical harm or relieve people of their wallets, they can still end up doing considerable harm. The harm done by Nixon's aides threatened the integrity of the U.S. electoral system. Every embezzler, corrupt politician, and tax cheat exacts a toll on our society. Individuals can be hurt in more tangible ways by decisions made in corporate boardrooms: Auto executives, for example, have approved design features that have caused fatalities. Managers of chemical companies have allowed practices that have polluted the environment with cancer-causing agents. And heads of corporations have presided over industries wherein workers have been needlessly killed or maimed.

Whether or not these decisions should be considered crimes is debatable. A crime must always involve "malicious intent," or what the legal system calls *mens rea*. This certainly applies to street crime—the mugger obviously has sinister designs—but does it apply to every decision made in a boardroom that ends up causing harm? And does that harm match or exceed the harm caused by street criminals? In the following selections, John J. DiIulio, Jr., focuses on the enormous harm done—especially to the poor—by street criminals. Not only does street crime cause loss, injury, terror, and death for individuals, he argues, but it also causes neighborhood decline, community disintegration, loss of pride, business decline and failure, hampered schools, and middle-class flight to the suburbs. According to Jeffrey Reiman, white-collar crime also does more harm than is commonly recognized. By his count, white-collar crime causes far more deaths, injuries, illnesses, and financial loss than street crime. In light of this, he argues, we must redefine our ideas about what crime is and who the criminals are.

John J. DiIulio, Jr.    **YES**

The Impact of Inner-City Crime

My grandmother, an Italian immigrant, lived in the same Philadelphia row house from 1921 till her death in 1986. When she moved there, and for the four decades thereafter, most of her neighbors were Irish and Italian. When she died, virtually all of her neighbors were black. Like the whites who fled, the first blacks who moved in were mostly working-class people living just above the poverty level.

Until around 1970, the neighborhood changed little. The houses were well-maintained. The children played in the streets and were polite. The teenagers hung out on the street corners in the evenings, sometimes doing mischief, but rarely—if ever—doing anything worse. The local grocers and other small businesspeople (both blacks and the few remaining whites) stayed open well past dark. Day or night, my grandmother journeyed the streets just as she had during the days of the Great Depression, taking the bus to visit her friends and relatives, going shopping, attending church, and so on.

She was a conspicuous and popular figure in this black community. She was conspicuous for her race, accent, and advanced age; she was popular for the homespun advice (and home-baked goods) she dispensed freely to the teenagers hanging out on the corners, to the youngsters playing ball in the street in front of her house, and to their parents (many of them mothers living without a husband).

Like the generations of ethnics who had lived there before them, these people were near the bottom of the socioeconomic ladder. I often heard my grandmother say that her new neighbors were "just like us," by which she meant that they were honest, decent, law-abiding people working hard to advance themselves and to make a better life for their children.

But in the early 1970s, the neighborhood began to change. Some, though by no means all, of the black families my grandmother had come to know moved out of the neighborhood. The new neighbors kept to themselves. The exteriors of the houses started to look ratty. The streets grew dirty. The grocery and variety stores closed or did business only during daylight hours. The children played in the schoolyard but not in front of their homes. The teenagers on the corners were replaced by adult drug dealers and their "runners." Vandalism

Excerpted from John J. DiIulio, Jr., "The Impact of Inner-City Crime," *The Public Interest,* no. 96 (Summer 1989), pp. 28–46. Copyright © 1989 by National Affairs, Inc. Reprinted by permission of *The Public Interest* and the author.

and graffiti became commonplace. My grandmother was mugged twice, both times by black teenagers; once she was severely beaten in broad daylight.

In the few years before she died at age eighty-four, and after years of pleading by her children and dozens of grandchildren, she stopped going out and kept her doors and windows locked at all times. On drives to visit her, when I got within four blocks of her home, I instinctively checked to make sure that my car doors were locked. Her house, where I myself had been raised, was in a "bad neighborhood," and it did not make sense to take any chances. I have not returned to the area since the day of her funeral.

My old ethnic and ghetto neighborhood had become an underclass neighborhood. Why is it that most readers of this article avoid, and advise their friends and relatives to avoid, walking or driving through such neighborhoods? Obviously we are not worried about being infected somehow by the extremely high levels of poverty, joblessness, illiteracy, welfare dependency, or drug abuse that characterize these places. Instead we shun these places because we suppose them to contain exceedingly high numbers of predatory street criminals, who hit, rape, rob, deal drugs, burglarize, and murder.

This supposition is absolutely correct. The underclass problem, contrary to the leading academic and journalistic understandings, is mainly a crime problem. It is a crime problem, moreover, that can be reduced dramatically (although not eliminated) with the human and financial resources already at hand.

Only two things are required: common sense and compassion. Once we understand the underclass problem as a crime problem, neither of those two qualities should be scarce. Until we understand the underclass problem as a crime problem, policymakers and others will continue to fiddle while the underclass ghettos of Philadelphia, Newark, Chicago, Los Angeles, Miami, Washington, D.C., and other cities burn....

The Truly Deviant

Liberals... have understood the worsening of ghetto conditions mainly as the by-product of a complex process of economic and social change. One of the latest and most influential statements of this view is William Julius Wilson's *The Truly Disadvantaged: The Inner City, the Underclass, and Public Policy* (1987).

Wilson argues that over the last two decades a new and socially destructive class structure has emerged in the ghetto. As he sees it, the main culprit is deindustrialization. As plants have closed, urban areas, especially black urban areas, have lost entry-level jobs. To survive economically, or to enjoy their material success, ghetto residents in a position to do so have moved out, leaving behind them an immobilized "underclass."...

Wilson has focused our attention on the socioeconomic straits of the truly disadvantaged with an elegance and rhetorical force that is truly admirable.[1] But despite its many strengths, his often subtle analysis of the underclass problem wrongly deemphasizes one obvious possibility: "The truly disadvantaged" exist mainly because of the activities of "the truly deviant"—the large numbers of chronic and predatory street criminals—in their midst. One in every nine adult black males in this country is under some form of correctional supervision (prison, jail, probation, or parole).[2] Criminals come disproportionately from underclass neighborhoods. They victimize their neighbors directly through crime, and indirectly by creating or worsening the multiple social and economic ills that define the sad lot of today's ghetto dwellers.

Predatory Ghetto Criminals

I propose [another] way of thinking about the underclass problem. The members of the underclass are, overwhelmingly, decent and law-abiding residents of America's most distressed inner cities. Fundamentally, what makes them different from the rest of us is not only their higher than normal levels of welfare dependency and the like, but their far higher than normal levels of victimization by predatory criminals.

This victimization by criminals takes several forms. There is *direct victimization*—being mugged, raped, or murdered; being threatened and extorted; living in fear about whether you can send your children to school or let them go out and play without their being bothered by dope dealers, pressured by gang members, or even struck by a stray bullet. And there is *indirect victimization*—dampened neighborhood economic development, loss of a sizable fraction of the neighborhood's male population to prison or jail, the undue influence on young people exercised by criminal "role models" like the cash-rich drug lords who rule the streets, and so on.

Baldly stated, my hypothesis is that this victimization causes and perpetuates the other ills of our underclass neighborhoods. Schools in these neighborhoods are unable to function effectively because of their disorderly atmosphere and because of the violent behavior of the criminals (especially gang members) who hang around their classrooms. The truly deviant are responsible for a high percentage of teen pregnancies, rapes, and sexual assaults. Similarly, many of the chronically welfare-dependent, female-headed households in these neighborhoods owe their plights to the fact that the men involved are either unable (because they are under some form of correctional supervision) or unwilling (because it does not jibe well with their criminal lifestyles) to seek and secure gainful employment and live with their families. And much of the poverty and joblessness in these neighborhoods can be laid at the door of criminals whose presence deters local business activity, including the development of residential real estate.

Blacks are victims of violent crimes at much higher rates than whites. Most lone-offender crime against blacks is committed by blacks, while most such crimes against whites are committed by whites; in 1986, for instance, 83.5 percent of violent crimes against blacks were committed by blacks, while 80.3 percent of violent crimes against whites were committed by whites. This monochrome picture of victim-offender relationships also holds for multiple-offender crimes. In 1986, for example, 79.6 percent of multiple-offender violent crimes against blacks were committed by blacks; the "white-on-white" figure was 59.4 percent.

Criminals are most likely to commit crimes against people of their own race. The main reason is presumably their physical proximity to potential victims. If so, then it is not hard to understand why underclass neighborhoods, which have more than their share of would-be criminals, have more than their share of crime.

Prison is the most costly form of correctional supervision, and it is normally reserved for the most dangerous felons—violent or repeat offenders. Most of my readers do not personally know anyone in prison; most ghetto dwellers of a decade or two ago probably would not have known anyone in prison either. But most of today's underclass citizens do; the convicted felons were their relatives and neighbors—and often their victimizers.

For example, in 1980 Newark was the street-crime capital of New Jersey. In the Newark area, there were more than 920 violent crimes (murders, non-negligent manslaughters, forcible rapes, robberies, and aggravated assaults) per 100,000 residents; in the rest of the state the figure was under 500, and in affluent towns like Princeton it was virtually nil. In the same year, New Jersey prisons held 5,866 criminals, 2,697 of them from the Newark area.[3] In virtually all of the most distressed parts of this distressed city, at least one of every two hundred residents was an imprisoned felon.[4] The same basic picture holds for other big cities.[5]

Correlation, however, is not causation, and we could extend and refine this sort of crude, exploratory analysis of the relationship between crime rates, concentrations of correctional supervisees, and the underclass neighborhoods from which they disproportionately come. But except to satisfy curiosity, I see no commanding need for such studies. For much the same picture emerges from the anecdotal accounts of people who have actually spent years wrestling with—as opposed to merely researching—the problem.

For example, in 1988 the nation's capital became its murder capital. Washington, D.C., had 372 killings, 82 percent of them committed on the streets by young black males against other young black males. The city vied with Detroit for the highest juvenile homicide rate in America. Here is part of the eloquent testimony on this development given by Isaac Fulwood, a native Washingtonian and the city's police-chief designate:

> The murder statistics don't capture what these people are doing. We've had in excess of 1,260 drug-related shootings.... People are scared of these kids. Someone can get shot in broad daylight, and nobody saw anything.... Nobody talks. And that's so different from the way it was in my childhood.

The same thing can be said about the underclass neighborhoods of other major cities. In Detroit, for instance, most of the hundreds of ghetto residents murdered over the last six years were killed within blocks of their homes by their truly deviant neighbors.

To devise meaningful law-enforcement and correctional responses to the underclass problem, we need to understand why concentrations of crime and criminals are so high in these neighborhoods, and to change our government's criminal-justice policies and practices accordingly.

Understanding the Problem

We begin with a chicken-and-egg question: Does urban decay cause crime, or does crime cause urban decay?

In conventional criminology, which derives mainly from sociology, ghettos are portrayed as "breeding grounds" for predatory street crime. Poverty, joblessness, broken homes, single-parent families, and similar factors are identified as the "underlying causes" of crime.[6] These conditions cause crime, the argument goes; as they worsen—as the ghetto community becomes the underclass neighborhood—crime worsens. This remains the dominant academic perspective on the subject, one that is shared implicitly by most public officials who are close to the problem.

Beginning in the mid-1970s, however, a number of influential studies appeared that challenged this conventional criminological wisdom.[7] Almost without exception, these studies have cast grave doubts on the classic sociological explanation of crime, suggesting that the actual relationships between such variables as poverty, illiteracy, and unemployment, on the one hand, and criminality, on the other, are far more ambiguous than most analysts freely assumed only a decade or so ago....

Locks, Cops, and Studies

Camden, New Jersey, is directly across the bridge from Philadelphia. Once-decent areas have become just like my grandmother's old neighborhood: isolated, crime-torn urban war zones. In February 1989 a priest doing social work in Camden was ordered off the streets by drug dealers and threatened with death if he did not obey. The police chief of Camden sent some extra men into the area, but the violent drug dealers remained the real rulers of the city's streets.

The month before the incident in Camden, the Rockefeller Foundation announced that it was going to devote some of its annual budget (which exceeds $100 million) to researching the underclass problem. Other foundations, big and small, have already spent (or misspent) much money on the problem. But Rockefeller's president was quoted as follows: "Nobody knows who they are, what they do.... The underclass is not a topic to pursue from the library. You get out and look for them."

His statement was heartening, but it revealed a deep misunderstanding of the problem. Rather than intimating that the underclass was somehow hard to locate, he would have done better to declare that his charity would purchase deadbolt locks for the homes of ghetto dwellers in New York City who lacked them, and subsidize policing and private-security services in the easily identifiable neighborhoods where these poor people are concentrated.

More street-level research would be nice, especially for the networks of policy intellectuals (liberal and conservative) who benefit directly from such endeavors. But more locks, cops, and corrections officers would make a more positive, tangible, and lasting difference in the lives of today's ghetto dwellers.

NOTES

1. In addition, he has canvassed competing academic perspectives on the underclass; see William Julius Wilson, ed., "The Ghetto Underclass: Social Science Perspectives," *Annals of the American Academy of Political and Social Science* (January 1989). It should also be noted that he is directing a $2.7 million research project on poverty in Chicago that promises to be the most comprehensive study of its kind yet undertaken.

2. According to the Bureau of Justice Statistics, in 1986 there were 234,430 adult black males in prison, 101,000 in jail, an estimated 512,000 on probation, and 133,300 on parole. There were 8,985,000 adult black males in the national residential population. I am grateful to Larry Greenfeld for his assistance in compiling these figures.

3. I am grateful to Hank Pierre, Stan Repko, and Commissioner William H. Fauver of the New Jersey Department of Corrections for granting me access to these figures and to related data on density of prisoner residence; to Andy Ripps for his heroic efforts in organizing them; and to my Princeton colleague Mark Alan Hughes for his expert help in analyzing the data.

4. Ten of the thirteen most distressed Newark census tracts were places where the density of prisoner residence was that high. In other words, 76.9 percent of the worst underclass areas of Newark had such extremely high concentrations of hardcore offenders. In most of the rest of Newark, and throughout the rest of the state, such concentrations were virtually nonexistent.

5. In 1980 in the Chicago area, for example, in 182 of the 1,521 census tracts at least one of every two hundred residents was an imprisoned felon. Fully twenty of the thirty-five worst underclass tracts had such extraordinary concentrations of serious criminals; in several of them, more than one of every hundred residents was behind prison bars. I am grateful to Wayne Carroll and Commissioner Michael Lane of the Illinois Department of Corrections for helping me with these data.

6. For example, see the classic statement by Edwin H. Sutherland and Donald R. Cressey, *Principles of Criminology*, 7th rev. ed. (Philadelphia: J. P. Lippincott, 1966).

7. See, for example, James Q. Wilson, *Thinking About Crime* (New York: Basic Books, 1975), especially the third chapter.

 **NO**

A Crime by Any Other Name...

If one individual inflicts a bodily injury upon another which leads to the death of the person attacked we call it manslaughter; on the other hand, if the attacker knows beforehand that the blow will be fatal we call it murder. Murder has also been committed if society places hundreds of workers in such a position that they inevitably come to premature and unnatural ends. Their death is as violent as if they had been stabbed or shot.... Murder has been committed if society knows perfectly well that thousands of workers cannot avoid being sacrificed so long as these conditions are allowed to continue. Murder of this sort is just as culpable as the murder committed by an individual.

— Frederick Engels
The Condition of the Working Class in England

What's in a Name?

If it takes you an hour to read this chapter, by the time you reach the last page, three of your fellow citizens will have been murdered. *During that same time, at least four Americans will die as a result of unhealthy or unsafe conditions in the workplace!* Although these work-related deaths could have been prevented, they are not called murders. Why not? Doesn't a crime by any other name still cause misery and suffering? What's in a name?

The fact is that the label "crime" is not used in America to name all or the worst of the actions that cause misery and suffering to Americans. It is primarily reserved for the dangerous actions of the poor.

In the February 21, 1993, edition of the *New York Times,* an article appears with the headline: "Company in Mine Deaths Set to Pay Big Fine." It describes an agreement by the owners of a Kentucky mine to pay a fine for safety misconduct that may have led to "the worst American mining accident in nearly a decade." Ten workers died in a methane explosion, and the company pleaded guilty to "a pattern of safety misconduct" that included falsifying reports of methane levels and requiring miners to work under unsupported roofs. The company was fined $3.75 million. The acting foreman at the mine was the only individual charged by the federal government, and for his cooperation with the investigation, prosecutors were recommending that he receive the minimum sentence: probation to six months in prison. The company's president expressed regret for the tragedy that occurred. And the U.S. attorney said he hoped the case "sent a clear message that violations of Federal safety and health regulations that endanger the lives of our citizens will not be tolerated."

Compare this with the story of Colin Ferguson, who prompted an editorial in the *New York Times* of December 10, 1993, with the headline: "Mass Murder on the 5:33." A few days earlier, Colin had boarded a commuter train in Garden City, Long Island, and methodically shot passengers with a 9-millimeter pistol, killing 5 and wounding 18. Colin Ferguson was surely a murderer, maybe a mass murderer. My question is, Why wasn't the death of the miners also murder? Why weren't those responsible for subjecting ten miners to deadly conditions also "mass murderers"?

Why do ten dead miners amount to an "accident," a "tragedy," and five dead commuters a "mass murder"? "Murder" suggests a murderer, whereas "accident" and "tragedy" suggest the work of impersonal forces. But the charge against the company that owned the mine said that they "repeatedly exposed the mine's work crews to danger and that such conditions were frequently concealed from Federal inspectors responsible for enforcing the mine safety act." And the acting foreman admitted to falsifying records of methane levels only two months before the fatal blast. Someone was responsible for the conditions that led to the death of ten miners. Is that person not a murderer, perhaps even a *mass murderer?*

These questions are at this point rhetorical. My aim is not to discuss this case but rather to point to the blinders we wear when we look at such an "accident." There was an investigation. One person, the acting foreman, was held responsible for falsifying records. He is to be sentenced to six months in prison (at most). The company was fined. But no one will be tried for *murder.* No one will be thought of as a murderer. *Why not? . . .*

Didn't those miners have a right to protection from the violence that took their lives? *And if not, why not?*

Once we are ready to ask this question seriously, we are in a position to see that the reality of crime—that is, the acts we label crime, the acts we think of as crime, the actors and actions we treat as criminal—is *created:* It is an image shaped by decisions as to *what* will be called crime and *who* will be treated as a criminal.

The Carnival Mirror

. . . The American criminal justice system is a mirror that shows a distorted image of the dangers that threaten us—an image created more by the shape of the mirror than by the reality reflected. What do we see when we look in the criminal justice mirror? . . .

He is, first of all, a *he.* Out of 2,012,906 persons arrested for FBI Index crimes [which are criminal homicide, forcible rape, robbery, aggravated assault, burglary, larceny, and motor vehicle theft] in 1991, 1,572,591, or 78 percent, were males. Second, he is a *youth.* . . . Third, he is predominantly *urban.* . . .

Fourth, he is disproportionately *black*—blacks are arrested for Index crimes at a rate three times that of their percentage in the national population.... Finally, he is *poor:* Among state prisoners in 1991, 33 percent were unemployed prior to being arrested—a rate nearly four times that of males in the general population....

This is the Typical Criminal feared by most law-abiding Americans. Poor, young, urban, (disproportionately) black males make up the core of the enemy forces in the war against crime. They are the heart of a vicious, unorganized guerrilla army, threatening the lives, limbs, and possessions of the law-abiding members of society—necessitating recourse to the ultimate weapons of force and detention in our common defense.

... The acts of the Typical Criminal are not the only acts that endanger us, nor are they the acts that endanger us the most. As I shall show..., we have as great or sometimes even a greater chance of being killed or disabled by an occupational injury or disease, by unnecessary surgery, or by shoddy emergency medical services than by aggravated assault or even homicide! Yet even though these threats to our well-being are graver than those posed by our poor young criminals, they do not show up in the FBI's Index of serious crimes. The individuals responsible for them do not turn up in arrest records or prison statistics. *They never become part of the reality reflected in the criminal justice mirror, although the danger they pose is at least as great and often greater than the danger posed by those who do!*

Similarly, the general public loses more money *by far*... from price-fixing and monopolistic practices and from consumer deception and embezzlement than from all the property crimes in the FBI's Index combined. Yet these far more costly acts are either not criminal, or if technically criminal, not prosecuted, or if prosecuted, not punished, or if punished, only mildly.... *Their faces rarely appear in the criminal justice mirror, although the danger they pose is at least as great and often greater than that of those who do....*

The criminal justice system is like a mirror in which society can see the face of the evil in its midst. Because the system deals with some evil and not with others, because it treats some evils as the gravest and treats some of the gravest evils as minor, the image it throws back is distorted like the image in a carnival mirror. Thus, the image cast back is false not because it is invented out of thin air but because the proportions of the real are distorted....

If criminal justice really gives us a carnival-mirror of "crime," we are doubly deceived. First, we are led to believe that the criminal justice system is protecting us against the gravest threats to our well-being when, in fact, the system is protecting us against only some threats and not necessarily the gravest ones. We are deceived about how much protection we are receiving and thus left vulnerable. The second deception is just the other side of this one. If people believe that the carnival mirror is a true mirror—that is, if they believe the criminal justice system simply *reacts* to the gravest threats to their well-being—they come to believe that whatever is the target of the criminal justice system must be the greatest threat to their well-being....

A Crime by Any Other Name...

Think of a crime, any crime. Picture the first "crime" that comes into your mind. What do you see? The odds are you are not imagining a mining company executive sitting at his desk, calculating the costs of proper safety precautions and deciding not to invest in them. Probably what you do see with your mind's eye is one person physically attacking another or robbing something from another via the threat of physical attack. Look more closely. What does the attacker look like? It's a safe bet he (and it is a *he*, of course) is not wearing a suit and tie. In fact, my hunch is that you—like me, like almost anyone else in America —picture a young, tough lower-class male when the thought of crime first pops into your head. You (we) picture someone like the Typical Criminal described above. The crime itself is one in which the Typical Criminal sets out to attack or rob some specific person....

It is important to identify this model of the Typical Crime because it functions like a set of blinders. It keeps us from calling a mine disaster a mass murder even if ten men are killed, even if someone is responsible for the unsafe conditions in which they worked and died. I contend that this particular piece of mental furniture so blocks our view that it keeps us from using the criminal justice system to protect ourselves from the greatest threats to our persons and possessions.

What keeps a mine disaster from being a mass murder in our eyes is that it is not a one-on-one harm. What is important in one-on-one harm is not the numbers but the *desire of someone (or ones) to harm someone (or ones) else.* An attack by a gang on one or more persons or an attack by one individual on several fits the model of one-on-one harm; that is, for each person harmed there is at least one individual who wanted to harm that person. Once he selects his victim, the rapist, the mugger, the murderer all want this person they have selected to suffer. A mine executive, on the other hand, does not want his employees to be harmed. He would truly prefer that there be no accident, no injured or dead miners. What he does want is something legitimate. It is what he has been hired to get: maximum profits at minimum costs. If he cuts corners to save a buck, he is just doing his job. If ten men die because he cut corners on safety, we may think him crude or callous but not a murderer. He is, at most, responsible for an *indirect harm,* not a one-on-one harm. For this, he may even be criminally indictable for violating safety regulations—but not for murder. The ten men are dead as an unwanted consequence of his (perhaps overzealous or undercautious) pursuit of a legitimate goal. So, unlike the Typical Criminal, he has not committed the Typical Crime—or so we generally believe. As a result, ten men are dead who might be alive now if cutting corners of the kind that leads to loss of life, whether suffering is specifically aimed at or not, were treated as murder.

This is my point. Because we accept the belief... that the model for crime is one person specifically trying to harm another, we accept a legal system that leaves us unprotected against much greater dangers to our lives and well-being than those threatened by the Typical Criminal....

According to the FBI's *Uniform Crime Reports,* in 1991, there were 24,703 murders and nonnegligent manslaughters, and 1,092,739 aggravated assaults.

In 1992, there were 23,760 murders and nonnegligent manslaughters, and 1,126,970 aggravated assaults.... Thus, as a measure of the physical harm done by crime in the beginning of the 1990s, we can say that reported crimes lead to roughly 24,000 deaths and 1,000,000 instances of serious bodily injury short of death a year. As a measure of monetary loss due to property crime, we can use $15.1 billion—the total estimated dollar losses due to property crime in 1992 according to the UCR. Whatever the shortcomings of these reported crime statistics, they are the statistics upon which public policy has traditionally been based. Thus, I will consider any actions that lead to loss of life, physical harm, and property loss comparable to the figures in the UCR as actions that pose grave dangers to the community comparable to the threats posed by crimes....

In testimony before the Senate Committee on Labor and Human Resources, Dr. Philip Landrigan, director of the Division of Environmental and Occupational Medicine at the Mount Sinai School of Medicine in New York City, stated that

> ... [I]t may be calculated that occupational disease is responsible each year in the United States for 50,000 to 70,000 deaths, and for approximately 350,000 new cases of illness.

... The BLS estimate of 330,000 job-related illnesses for 1990 roughly matches Dr. Landrigan's estimates. For 1991, BLS estimates 368,000 job-related illnesses. These illnesses are of varying severity.... Because I want to compare these occupational harms with those resulting from aggravated assault, I shall stay on the conservative side here too, as with deaths from occupational diseases, and say that there are annually in the United States approximately 150,000 job-related serious illnesses. Taken together with 25,000 deaths from occupational diseases, how does this compare with the threat posed by crime?

Before jumping to any conclusions, note that the risk of occupational disease and death falls only on members of the labor force, whereas the risk of crime falls on the whole population, from infants to the elderly. Because the labor force is about half the total population (124,810,000 in 1990, out of a total population of 249,900,000), to get a true picture of the *relative* threat posed by occupational diseases compared with that posed by crimes, we should *halve* the crime statistics when comparing them with the figures for industrial disease and death. Using the crime figures for the first years of the 1990s, ... we note that the *comparable* figures would be

	Occupational Disease	Crime (halved)
Death	25,000	12,000
Other physical harm	150,000	500,000

... Note ... that the estimates in the last chart are *only* for occupational *diseases* and deaths from those diseases. They do not include death and disability from work-related injuries. Here, too, the statistics are gruesome. The National Safety Council reported that in 1991, work-related accidents caused 9,600 deaths and 1.7 million disabling work injuries, a total cost to the economy of $63.3 billion. This brings the number of occupation-related deaths to

34,600 a year and other physical harms to 1,850,000. If, on the basis of these additional figures, we recalculated our chart comparing occupational harms from both disease and accident with criminal harms, it would look like this:

	Occupational Hazard	Crime (halved)
Death	34,600	12,000
Other physical harm	1,850,000	500,000

Can there be any doubt that workers are more likely to stay alive and healthy in the face of the danger from the underworld than in the work-world? . . .

To say that some of these workers died from accidents due to their own carelessness is about as helpful as saying that some of those who died at the hands of murderers asked for it. It overlooks the fact that where workers are careless, it is not because they love to live dangerously. They have production quotas to meet, quotas that they themselves do not set. If quotas were set with an eye to keeping work at a safe pace rather than to keeping the production-to-wages ratio as high as possible, it might be more reasonable to expect workers to take the time to be careful. Beyond this, we should bear in mind that the vast majority of occupational deaths result from disease, not accident, and disease is generally a function of conditions outside a worker's control. Examples of such conditions are the level of coal dust in the air ("260,000 miners receive benefits for [black lung] disease, and perhaps as many as 4,000 retired miners die from the illness or its complications each year"; about 10,000 currently working miners "have X-ray evidence of the beginnings of the crippling and often fatal disease") or textile dust . . . or asbestos fibers . . . or coal tars . . . ; (coke oven workers develop cancer of the scrotum at a rate five times that of the general population). Also, some 800,000 people suffer from occupationally related skin disease each year. . . .

To blame the workers for occupational disease and deaths is to ignore the history of governmental attempts to compel industrial firms to meet safety standards that would keep dangers (such as chemicals or fibers or dust particles in the air) that are outside the worker's control down to a safe level. This has been a continual struggle, with firms using everything from their own "independent" research institutes to more direct and often questionable forms of political pressure to influence government in the direction of loose standards and lax enforcement. So far, industry has been winning because OSHA [Occupational Safety and Health Administration] has been given neither the personnel nor the mandate to fulfill its purpose. It is so understaffed that, in 1973, when 1,500 federal sky marshals guarded the nation's airplanes from hijackers, only 500 OSHA inspectors toured the nation's workplaces. By 1980, OSHA employed 1,581 compliance safety and health officers, but this still enabled inspection of only roughly 2 percent of the 2.5 million establishments covered by OSHA. The *New York Times* reports that in 1987 the number of OSHA inspectors was down to 1,044. As might be expected, the agency performs fewer inspections that it did a dozen years ago. . . .

According to a report issued by the AFL-CIO [American Federation of Labor and Congress of Industrial Organizations] in 1992, "The median penalty paid by an employer during the years 1972–1990 following an incident resulting in death or serious injury of a worker was just $480." The same report claims that the federal government spends $1.1 billion a year to protect fish and wildlife and only $300 million a year to protect workers from health and safety hazards on the job....

Is a person who kills another in a bar brawl a greater threat to society than a business executive who refuses to cut into his profits to make his plant a safe place to work? By any measure of death and suffering the latter is by far a greater danger than the former. Because he wishes his workers no harm, because he is only indirectly responsible for death and disability while pursuing legitimate economic goals, his acts are not called "crimes." Once we free our imagination from the blinders of the one-on-one model of crime, can there be any doubt that the criminal justice system does *not* protect us from the gravest threats to life and limb? It seeks to protect us when danger comes from a young, lower-class male in the inner city. When a threat comes from an upper-class business executive in an office, the criminal justice system looks the other way. This is in the face of growing evidence that for every three American citizens murdered by thugs, at least four American workers are killed by the recklessness of their bosses and the indifference of their government.

Health Care May Be Dangerous to Your Health

... On July 15, 1975, Dr. Sidney Wolfe of Ralph Nader's Public Interest Health Research Group testified before the House Commerce Oversight and Investigations Subcommittee that there "were 3.2 million cases of unnecessary surgery performed each year in the United States." These unneeded operations, Wolfe added, "cost close to $5 billion a year and kill as many as 16,000 Americans."...

In an article on an experimental program by Blue Cross and Blue Shield aimed at curbing unnecessary surgery, *Newsweek* reports that

> a Congressional committee earlier this year [1976] estimated that more than 2 million of the elective operations performed in 1974 were not only unnecessary—but also killed about 12,000 patients and cost nearly $4 billion.

Because the number of surgical operations performed in the United States rose from 16.7 million in 1975 to 22.4 million in 1991, there is reason to believe that at least somewhere between... 12,000 and... 16,000 people a year still die from unnecessary surgery. In 1991, the FBI reported that 3,405 murders were committed by a "cutting or stabbing instrument." Obviously, the FBI does not include the scalpel as a cutting or stabbing instrument. If they did, they would have had to report that between 15,405 and 19,405 persons were killed by "cutting or stabbing" in 1991.... No matter how you slice it, the scalpel may be more dangerous than the switchblade....

Waging Chemical Warfare Against America

One in 4 Americans can expect to contract cancer during their lifetimes. The American Cancer Society estimated that 420,000 Americans would die of cancer in 1981. The National Cancer Institute's estimate for 1993 is 526,000 deaths from cancer. "A 1978 report issued by the President's Council on Environmental Quality (CEQ) unequivocally states that 'most researchers agree that 70 to 90 percent of cancers are caused by environmental influences and are hence theoretically preventable.'" This means that a concerted national effort could result in saving 350,000 or more lives a year and reducing each individual's chances of getting cancer in his or her lifetime from 1 in 4 to 1 in 12 or fewer. If you think this would require a massive effort in terms of money and personnel, you are right. How much of an effort, though, would the nation make to stop a foreign invader who was killing a thousand people and bent on capturing one-quarter of the present population?

In face of this "invasion" that is already under way, the U.S. government has allocated $1.9 billion to the National Cancer Institute (NCI) for fiscal year 1992, and NCI has allocated $219 million to the study of the physical and chemical (i.e., environmental) causes of cancer. Compare this with the (at least) $45 billion spent to fight the Persian Gulf War. The simple truth is that the government that strove so mightily to protect the borders of a small, undemocratic nation 7,000 miles away is doing next to nothing to protect us against the chemical war in our midst. This war is being waged against us on three fronts:

- Pollution
- Cigarette smoking
- Food additives

... The evidence linking *air pollution* and cancer, as well as other serious and often fatal diseases, has been rapidly accumulating in recent years. In 1993, the *Journal of the American Medical Association* reported on research that found "'robust' associations between premature mortality and air pollution levels." They estimate that pollutants cause about 2 percent of all cancer deaths (at least 10,000 a year)....

A... recent study... concluded that air pollution at 1988 levels was responsible for 60,000 deaths a year. The Natural Resources Defense Council sued the EPA [Environmental Protection Agency] for its foot-dragging in implementation of the Clean Air Act, charging that "One hundred million people live in areas of unhealthy air."

This chemical war is not limited to the air. The National Cancer Institute has identified as carcinogens or suspected carcinogens 23 of the chemicals commonly found in our drinking water. Moreover, according to one observer, we are now facing a "new plague—toxic exposure."...

The evidence linking *cigarette smoking* and cancer is overwhelming and need not be repeated here. The Centers for Disease Control estimates that cigarettes cause 87 percent of lung cancers—approximately 146,000 in 1992. Tobacco continues to kill an estimated 400,000 Americans a year. Cigarettes are widely estimated to cause 30 percent of all cancer deaths....

This is enough to expose the hypocrisy of running a full-scale war against heroin (which produces no degenerative disease) while allowing cigarette sales and advertising to flourish. It also should be enough to underscore the point that once again there are threats to our lives much greater than criminal homicide. The legal order does not protect us against them. Indeed, not only does our government fail to protect us against this threat, it promotes it! . . .

Based on the knowledge we have, there can be no doubt that air pollution, tobacco, and food additives amount to a chemical war that makes the crime wave look like a football scrimmage. Even with the most conservative estimates, it is clear that *the death toll in this war is far higher than the number of people killed by criminal homicide!* . . .

Summary

Once again, our investigations lead to the same result. The criminal justice system does not protect us against the gravest threats to life, limb, or possessions. Its definitions of crime are not simply a reflection of the objective dangers that threaten us. The workplace, the medical profession, the air we breathe, and the poverty we refuse to rectify lead to far more human suffering, far more death and disability, and take far more dollars from our pockets than the murders, aggravated assaults, and thefts reported annually by the FBI. What is more, this human suffering is preventable. A government really intent on protecting our well-being could enforce work safety regulations, police the medical profession, require that clean air standards be met, and funnel sufficient money to the poor to alleviate the major disabilities of poverty—but it does not. Instead we hear a lot of cant about law and order and a lot of rant about crime in the streets. It is as if our leaders were not only refusing to protect us from the major threats to our well-being but trying to cover up this refusal by diverting our attention to crime—as if this were the only real threat.

POSTSCRIPT

Is Street Crime More Harmful Than White-Collar Crime?

It is important to consider both the suffering and the wider ramifications caused by crimes. DiIulio captures many of these dimensions and gives a full account of the harms of street crime. Today the public is very concerned about street crime, especially wanton violence. However, it seems relatively unconcerned about white-collar crime. Reiman tries to change that perception. By defining many harmful actions by managers and professionals as crimes, he argues that white-collar crime is worse than street crime. He says that more people are killed and injured by "occupational injury or disease, by unnecessary surgery, and by shoddy emergency medical services than by aggravated assault or even homicide!" But are shoddy medical services a crime? In the end, the questions remain: What is a crime? Who are the criminals?

A set of readings that support Reiman's viewpoint is *Corporate Violence: Injury and Death for Profit* edited by Stuart L. Hills (Rowman & Littlefield, 1987). Further support is provided by Marshall B. Clinard, *Corporate Corruption: The Abuse of Power* (Praeger, 1990). *White-Collar Crime* edited by Gilbert Geis and Robert F. Meier (Free Press, 1977) is a useful compilation of essays on corporate and political crime, as is Gary Green's *Occupational Crime* (Nelson-Hall, 1990). Four other books that focus on crime in high places are J. Douglas and J. M. Johnson, *Official Deviance* (J. B. Lippincott, 1977); J. Anthony Lukas, *Nightmare: The Underside of the Nixon Years* (Viking Press, 1976); Marshall B. Clinard, *Corporate Elites and Crime* (Sage Publications, 1983); and David R. Simon and Stanley Eitzen, *Elite Deviance* (Allyn & Bacon, 1982). A work that deals with the prevalence and fear of street crime is Elliott Currie, *Confronting Crime: An American Challenge* (Pantheon Books, 1985). Two works on gangs, which are often connected with violent street crime, are Martin Sanchez Jankowski, *Islands in the Street: Gangs and American Urban Society* (University of California Press, 1991) and Felix M. Padilla, *The Gang as an American Enterprise* (Rutgers University Press, 1992). William J. Bennett, John J. DiIulio, and John P. Walters, in *Body Count: Moral Poverty—and How to Win America's War Against Crime and Drugs* (Simon & Schuster, 1996), argue that moral poverty is the root cause of crime (meaning street crime). How applicable is this thesis to white-collar crime? One interesting aspect of many corporate, or white-collar, crimes is that they involve crimes of obedience, as discussed in Herman C. Kelman and V. Lee Hamilton, *Crimes of Obedience: Toward a Social Psychology of Authority and Responsibility* (Yale University Press, 1989).

ISSUE 16

Should Drug Use Be Decriminalized?

YES: Ethan A. Nadelmann, from "Commonsense Drug Policy," *Foreign Affairs* (January/February 1998)

NO: James A. Inciardi and Christine A. Saum, from "Legalization Madness," *The Public Interest* (Spring 1996)

ISSUE SUMMARY

YES: Ethan A. Nadelmann, director of the Lindesmith Center, a drug policy research institute, argues that history shows that drug prohibition is costly and futile. Examining the drug policies in other countries, he finds that decriminalization plus sane and humane drug policies and treatment programs can greatly reduce the harms from drugs.

NO: James A. Inciardi, director of the Center for Drug and Alcohol Studies at the University of Delaware, and his associate Christine A. Saum argue that legalizing drugs would not eliminate drug-related criminal activity and would greatly increase drug use. Therefore, the government should continue the war against drugs.

Acentury ago, drugs of every kind were freely available to Americans. Laudanum, a mixture of opium and alcohol, was popularly used as a painkiller. One drug company even claimed that it was a very useful substance for calming hyperactive children, and the company called it Mother's Helper. Morphine came into common use during the Civil War. Heroin, developed as a supposedly less addictive substitute for morphine, began to be marketed at the end of the nineteenth century. By that time, drug paraphernalia could be ordered through Sears and Roebuck catalogues, and Coca-Cola, which contained small quantities of cocaine, had become a popular drink.

Public concerns about addiction and dangerous patent medicines, and an active campaign for drug laws waged by Dr. Harvey Wiley, a chemist in the U.S. Department of Agriculture, led Congress to pass the first national drug regulation act in 1906. The Pure Food and Drug Act required that medicines containing certain drugs, such as opium, must say so on their labels. The Harrison Narcotic Act of 1914 went much further and cut off completely the supply of legal opiates to addicts. Since then, ever stricter drug laws have been passed by Congress and by state legislatures.

Drug abuse in America again came to the forefront of public discourse during the 1960s, when heroin addiction started growing rapidly in inner-city neighborhoods. Also, by the end of the decade, drug experimentation had spread to the middle-class, affluent baby boomers who were then attending college. Indeed, certain types of drugs began to be celebrated by some of the leaders of the counterculture. Heroin was still taboo, but other drugs, notably marijuana and LSD (a psychedelic drug), were regarded as harmless and even spiritually transforming. At music festivals like Woodstock in 1969, marijuana and LSD were used openly and associated with love, peace, and heightened sensitivity. Much of this enthusiasm cooled over the next 20 years as baby boomers entered the workforce full-time and began their careers. But even among the careerists, certain types of drugs enjoyed high status. Cocaine, noted for its highly stimulating effects, became the drug of choice for many hard-driving young lawyers, television writers, and Wall Street bond traders.

The high price of cocaine put it out of reach for many people, but in the early 1980s, cheap substitutes began to appear on the streets and to overtake poor urban communities. Crack cocaine, a potent, highly addictive, smokable form of cocaine, came into widespread use. By the end of the 1980s, the drug known as "ice," or as it is called on the West Coast, "L.A. glass," a smokable form of amphetamine, had hit the streets. These stimulants tend to produce very violent, disorderly behavior. Moreover, the street gangs who sell them are frequently at war with one another and are well armed. Not only gang members but also many innocent people have become victims of contract killings, street battles, and drive-by shootings.

This new drug epidemic prompted President George Bush to declare a "war on drugs," and in 1989 he asked Congress to appropriate $10.6 billion for the fight. Although most Americans support such measures against illegal drugs, some say that in the years since Bush made his declaration, the drug situation has not showed any signs of improvement. Some believe that legalization would be the best way to fight the drug problem.

The drug decriminalization issue is especially interesting to sociologists because it raises basic questions about what should be socially sanctioned or approved, what is illegal or legal, and what is immoral or moral. An aspect of the basic value system of America is under review. The process of value change may be taking place in front of our eyes. As part of this debate, Ethan A. Nadelmann argues that the present policy does not work and that it is counterproductive. Legalization, he contends, would stop much of the disease, violence, and crime associated with illegal drugs. Although Nadelmann concedes that it may increase the use of lower-potency drugs, he believes that legalization would reduce the use of the worst drugs. James A. Inciardi and Christine A. Saum argue that legalization would be madness because "drug prohibition seems to be having some very positive effects and . . . legalizing drugs would not necessarily have a depressant effect on violent crime."

Ethan A. Nadelmann  **YES**

Commonsense Drug Policy

First, Reduce Harm

In 1988 Congress passed a resolution proclaiming its goal of "a drug-free America by 1995." U.S. drug policy has failed persistently over the decades because it has preferred such rhetoric to reality, and moralism to pragmatism. Politicians confess their youthful indiscretions, then call for tougher drug laws. Drug control officials make assertions with no basis in fact or science. Police officers, generals, politicians, and guardians of public morals qualify as drug czars—but not, to date, a single doctor or public health figure. Independent commissions are appointed to evaluate drug policies, only to see their recommendations ignored as politically risky. And drug policies are designed, implemented, and enforced with virtually no input from the millions of Americans they affect most: drug users. Drug abuse is a serious problem, both for individual citizens and society at large, but the "war on drugs" has made matters worse, not better.

Drug warriors often point to the 1980s as a time in which the drug war really worked. Illicit drug use by teenagers peaked around 1980, then fell more than 50 percent over the next 12 years. During the 1996 presidential campaign, Republican challenger Bob Dole made much of the recent rise in teenagers' use of illicit drugs, contrasting it with the sharp drop during the Reagan and Bush administrations. President Clinton's response was tepid, in part because he accepted the notion that teen drug use is the principal measure of drug policy's success or failure; at best, he could point out that the level was still barely half what it had been in 1980.

In 1980, however, no one had ever heard of the cheap, smokable form of cocaine called crack, or drug-related HIV infection or AIDS. By the 1990s, both had reached epidemic proportions in American cities, largely driven by prohibitionist economics and morals indifferent to the human consequences of the drug war. In 1980, the federal budget for drug control was about $1 billion, and state and local budgets were perhaps two or three times that. By 1997, the federal drug control budget had ballooned to $16 billion, two-thirds of it for law enforcement agencies, and state and local funding to at least that. On any day in 1980, approximately 50,000 people were behind bars for violating a drug law. By 1997, the number had increased eightfold, to about 400,000. These are

From Ethan A. Nadelmann, "Commonsense Drug Policy," *Foreign Affairs,* vol. 77, no. 1 (January/February 1998). Copyright © 1998 by The Council on Foreign Relations, Inc. Reprinted by permission of *Foreign Affairs.* Notes omitted.

the results of a drug policy overreliant on criminal justice "solutions," ideologically wedded to abstinence-only treatment, and insulated from cost-benefit analysis.

Imagine instead a policy that starts by acknowledging that drugs are here to stay, and that we have no choice but to learn how to live with them so that they cause the least possible harm. Imagine a policy that focuses on reducing not illicit drug use per se but the crime and misery caused by both drug abuse and prohibitionist policies. And imagine a drug policy based not on the fear, prejudice, and ignorance that drive America's current approach but rather on common sense, science, public health concerns, and human rights. Such a policy is possible in the United States, especially if Americans are willing to learn from the experiences of other countries where such policies are emerging.

Attitudes Abroad

Americans are not averse to looking abroad for solutions to the nation's drug problems. Unfortunately, they have been looking in the wrong places: Asia and Latin America, where much of the world's heroin and cocaine originates. Decades of U.S. efforts to keep drugs from being produced abroad and exported to American markets have failed. Illicit drug production is bigger business than ever before. The opium poppy, source of morphine and heroin, and *cannabis sativa*, from which marijuana and hashish are prepared, grow readily around the world; the coca plant, from whose leaves cocaine is extracted, can be cultivated far from its native environment in the Andes. Crop substitution programs designed to persuade Third World peasants to grow legal crops cannot compete with the profits that drug prohibition makes inevitable. Crop eradication campaigns occasionally reduce production in one country, but new suppliers pop up elsewhere. International law enforcement efforts can disrupt drug trafficking organizations and routes, but they rarely have much impact on U.S. drug markets. . . .

While looking to Latin America and Asia for supply-reduction solutions to America's drug problems is futile, the harm-reduction approaches spreading throughout Europe and Australia and even into corners of North America show promise. These approaches start by acknowledging that supply-reduction initiatives are inherently limited, that criminal justice responses can be costly and counterproductive, and that single-minded pursuit of a "drug-free society" is dangerously quixotic. Demand-reduction efforts to prevent drug abuse among children and adults are important, but so are harm-reduction efforts to lessen the damage to those unable or unwilling to stop using drugs immediately, and to those around them.

Most proponents of harm reduction do not favor legalization. They recognize that prohibition has failed to curtail drug abuse, that it is responsible for much of the crime, corruption, disease, and death associated with drugs, and that its costs mount every year. But they also see legalization as politically unwise and as risking increased drug use. The challenge is thus making drug prohibition work better, but with a focus on reducing the negative consequences of both drug use and prohibitionist policies. . . .

Harm-reduction innovations include efforts to stem the spread of HIV by making sterile syringes readily available and collecting used syringes; allowing doctors to prescribe oral methadone for heroin addiction treatment, as well as heroin and other drugs for addicts who would otherwise buy them on the black market; establishing "safe injection rooms" so addicts do not congregate in public places or dangerous "shooting galleries"; employing drug analysis units at the large dance parties called raves to test the quality and potency of MDMA, known as Ecstasy, and other drugs that patrons buy and consume there; decriminalizing (but not legalizing) possession and retail sale of cannabis and, in some cases, possession of small amounts of "hard" drugs; and integrating harm-reduction policies and principles into community policing strategies. Some of these measures are under way or under consideration in parts of the United States, but rarely to the extent found in growing numbers of foreign countries.

Stopping HIV With Sterile Syringes

The spread of HIV, the virus that causes AIDS, among people who inject drugs illegally was what prompted governments in Europe and Australia to experiment with harm-reduction policies. During the early 1980s public health officials realized that infected users were spreading HIV by sharing needles. Having already experienced a hepatitis epidemic attributed to the same mode of transmission, the Dutch were the first to tell drug users about the risks of needle sharing and to make sterile syringes available and collect dirty needles through pharmacies, needle exchange and methadone programs, and public health services. Governments elsewhere in Europe and in Australia soon followed suit. The few countries in which a prescription was necessary to obtain a syringe dropped the requirement. Local authorities in Germany, Switzerland, and other European countries authorized needle exchange machines to ensure 24-hour access. In some European cities, addicts can exchange used syringes for clean ones at local police stations without fear of prosecution or harassment. Prisons are instituting similar policies to help discourage the spread of HIV among inmates, recognizing that illegal drug injecting cannot be eliminated even behind bars.

These initiatives were not adopted without controversy. Conservative politicians argued that needle exchange programs condoned illicit and immoral behavior and that government policies should focus on punishing drug users or making them drug-free. But by the late 1980s, the consensus in most of Western Europe, Oceania, and Canada was that while drug abuse was a serious problem, AIDS was worse. Slowing the spread of a fatal disease for which no cure exists was the greater moral imperative. There was also a fiscal imperative. Needle exchange programs' costs are minuscule compared with those of treating people who would otherwise become infected with HIV.

Only in the United States has this logic not prevailed, even though AIDS was the leading killer of Americans ages 25 to 44 for most of the 1990s and is now No. 2. The Centers for Disease Control (CDC) estimates that half of new HIV infections in the country stem from injection drug use. Yet both the White House and Congress block allocation of AIDS or drug-abuse prevention

funds for needle exchange, and virtually all state governments retain drug paraphernalia laws, pharmacy regulations, and other restrictions on access to sterile
syringes. During the 1980s, AIDS activists engaging in civil disobedience set up
more syringe exchange programs than state and local governments. There are
now more than 100 such programs in 28 states, Washington, D.C., and Puerto
Rico, but they reach only an estimated 10 percent of injection drug users.

Governments at all levels in the United States refuse to fund needle exchange for political reasons, even though dozens of scientific studies, domestic
and foreign, have found that needle exchange and other distribution programs
reduce needle sharing, bring hard-to-reach drug users into contact with health
care systems, and inform addicts about treatment programs, yet do not increase
illegal drug use. In 1991 the National AIDS Commission appointed by President Bush called the lack of federal support for such programs "bewildering
and tragic." In 1993 a CDC-sponsored review of research on needle exchange
recommended federal funding, but top officials in the Clinton administration
suppressed a favorable evaluation of the report within the Department of Health
and Human Services. In July 1996 President Clinton's Advisory Council on HIV/
AIDS criticized the administration for its failure to heed the National Academy of
Sciences' recommendation that it authorize the use of federal money to support
needle exchange programs. An independent panel convened by the National Institute[s] of Health reached the same conclusion in February 1997. Last summer,
the American Medical Association, the American Bar Association, and even the
politicized U.S. Conference of Mayors endorsed the concept of needle exchange.
In the fall, an endorsement followed from the World Bank.

To date, America's failure in this regard is conservatively estimated to have
resulted in the infection of up to 10,000 people with HIV. Mounting scientific evidence and the stark reality of the continuing AIDS crisis have convinced
the public, if not politicians, that needle exchange saves lives; polls consistently find that a majority of Americans support needle exchange, with approval
highest among those most familiar with the notion. Prejudice and political cow-
ardice are poor excuses for allowing more citizens to suffer from and die of
AIDS, especially when effective interventions are cheap, safe, and easy.

Methadone and Other Alternatives

The United States pioneered the use of the synthetic opiate methadone to treat
heroin addiction in the 1960s and 1970s, but now lags behind much of Europe
and Australia in making methadone accessible and effective. Methadone is the
best available treatment in terms of reducing illicit heroin use and associated
crime, disease, and death. In the early 1990s the National Academy of Sciences'
Institute of Medicine stated that of all forms of drug treatment, "methadone
maintenance has been the most rigorously studied modality and has yielded
the most incontrovertibly positive results.... Consumption of all illicit drugs,
especially heroin, declines. Crime is reduced, fewer individuals become HIV
positive, and individual functioning is improved." However, the institute went
on to declare, "Current policy... puts too much emphasis on protecting society

from methadone, and not enough on protecting society from the epidemics of addiction, violence, and infectious diseases that methadone can help reduce."

Methadone is to street heroin what nicotine skin patches and chewing gum are to cigarettes—with the added benefit of legality. Taken orally, methadone has little of injected heroin's effect on mood or cognition. It can be consumed for decades with few if any negative health consequences, and its purity and concentration, unlike street heroin's, are assured. Like other opiates, it can create physical dependence if taken regularly, but the "addiction" is more like a diabetic's "addiction" to insulin than a heroin addict's to product brought on the street. Methadone patients can and do drive safely, hold good jobs, and care for their children. When prescribed adequate doses, they can be indistinguishable from people who have never used heroin or methadone.

Popular misconceptions and prejudice, however, have all but prevented any expansion of methadone treatment in the United States. The 115,000 Americans receiving methadone today represent only a small increase over the number 20 years ago. For every ten heroin addicts, there are only one or two methadone treatment slots. Methadone is the most tightly controlled drug in the pharmacopoeia, subject to unique federal and state restrictions. Doctors cannot prescribe it for addiction treatment outside designated programs. Regulations dictate not only security, documentation, and staffing requirements but maximum doses, admission criteria, time spent in the program, and a host of other specifics, none of which has much to do with quality of treatment. Moreover, the regulations do not prevent poor treatment; many clinics provide insufficient doses, prematurely detoxify clients, expel clients for offensive behavior, and engage in other practices that would be regarded as unethical in any other field of medicine. Attempts to open new clinics tend to be blocked by residents who don't want addicts in their neighborhood....

The Swiss government began a nationwide trial in 1994 to determine whether prescribing heroin, morphine, or injectable methadone could reduce crime, disease, and other drug-related ills. Some 1,000 volunteers—only heroin addicts with at least two unsuccessful experiences in methadone or other conventional treatment programs were considered—took part in the experiment. The trial quickly determined that virtually all participants preferred heroin, and doctors subsequently prescribed it for them. Last July the government reported the results so far: criminal offenses and the number of criminal offenders dropped 60 percent, the percentage of income from illegal and semilegal activities fell from 69 to 10 percent, illegal heroin *and* cocaine use declined dramatically (although use of alcohol, cannabis, and tranquilizers like Valium remained fairly constant), stable employment increased from 14 to 32 percent, physical health improved enormously, and most participants greatly reduced their contact with the drug scene. There were no deaths from overdoses, and no prescribed drugs were diverted to the black market. More than half those who dropped out of the study switched to another form of drug treatment, including 83 who began abstinence therapy. A cost-benefit analysis of the program found a net economic benefit of $30 per patient per day, mostly because of reduced criminal justice and health care costs.

The Swiss study has undermined several myths about heroin and its habitual users. The results to date demonstrate that, given relatively unlimited availability, heroin users will voluntarily stabilize or reduce their dosage and some will even choose abstinence; that long-addicted users can lead relatively normal, stable lives if provided legal access to their drug of choice; and that ordinary citizens will support such initiatives. In recent referendums in Zurich, Basel, and Zug, substantial majorities voted to continue funding local arms of the experiment. And last September, a nationwide referendum to end the government's heroin maintenance and other harm-reduction initiatives was rejected by 71 percent of Swiss voters, including majorities in all 26 cantons....

Reefer Sanity

Cannabis, in the form of marijuana and hashish, is by far the most popular illicit drug in the United States. More than a quarter of Americans admit to having tried it. Marijuana's popularity peaked in 1980, dropped steadily until the early 1990s, and is now on the rise again. Although it is not entirely safe, especially when consumed by children, smoked heavily, or used when driving, it is clearly among the least dangerous psychoactive drugs in common use. In 1988 the administrative law judge for the Drug Enforcement Administration, Francis Young, reviewed the evidence and concluded that "marihuana, in its natural form, is one of the safest therapeutically active substances known to man."

As with needle exchange and methadone treatment, American politicians have ignored or spurned the findings of government commissions and scientific organizations concerning marijuana policy. In 1972 the National Commission on Marihuana and Drug Abuse—created by President Nixon and chaired by a former Republican governor, Raymond Shafer—recommended that possession of up to one ounce of marijuana be decriminalized. Nixon rejected the recommendation. In 1982 a panel appointed by the National Academy of Sciences reached the same conclusions as the Shafer Commission.

Between 1973 and 1978, with attitudes changing, 11 states approved decriminalization statutes that reclassified marijuana possession as a misdemeanor, petty offense, or civil violation punishable by no more than a $100 fine. Consumption trends in those states and in states that retained stricter sanctions were indistinguishable. A 1988 scholarly evaluation of the Moscone Act, California's 1976 decriminalization law, estimated that the state had saved half a billion dollars in arrest costs since the law's passage. Nonetheless, public opinion began to shift in 1978. No other states decriminalized marijuana, and some eventually recriminalized it.

Between 1973 and 1989, annual arrests on marijuana charges by state and local police ranged between 360,000 and 460,000. The annual total fell to 283,700 in 1991, but has since more than doubled. In 1996, 641,642 people were arrested for marijuana, 85 percent of them for possession, not sale, of the drug. Prompted by concern over rising marijuana use among adolescents and fears of being labeled soft on drugs, the Clinton administration launched its own anti-marijuana campaign in 1995. But the administration's claims to have identified new risks of marijuana consumption—including a purported link between marijuana and violent behavior—have not withstood scrutiny. Neither Congress nor the White House seems likely to put the issue of marijuana policy before a truly independent advisory commission, given the consistency with which such commissions have reached politically unacceptable conclusions. . . .

Will it Work?

Both at home and abroad, the U.S. government has attempted to block resolutions supporting harm reduction, suppress scientific studies that reached politically inconvenient conclusions, and silence critics of official drug policy. In May 1994, the State Department forced the last-minute cancellation of a World Bank conference on drug trafficking to which critics of U.S. drug policy had been invited. That December the U.S. delegation to an international meeting of the U.N. Drug Control Program refused to sign any statement incorporating the phrase "harm reduction." In early 1995 the State Department successfully pressured the World Health Organization to scuttle the release of a report it had commissioned from a panel that included many of the world's leading experts on cocaine because it included the scientifically incontrovertible observations that traditional use of coca leaf in the Andes causes little harm to users and that most consumers of cocaine use the drug in moderation with few detrimental effects. Hundreds of congressional hearings have addressed multitudinous aspects of the drug problem, but few have inquired into the European harm-reduction policies described above. When former Secretary of State George Shultz, then–Surgeon General M. Joycelyn Elders, and Baltimore Mayor Kurt Schmoke pointed to the failure of current policies and called for new approaches, they were mocked, fired, and ignored, respectively—and thereafter mischaracterized as advocating the outright legalization of drugs.

In Europe, in contrast, informed, public debate about drug policy is increasingly common in government, even at the EU level. In June 1995 the European Parliament issued a report acknowledging that "there will always be a demand for drugs in our societies . . . the policies followed so far have not been able to prevent the illegal drug trade from flourishing." The EU called for serious consideration of the Frankfurt Resolution, a statement of harm-reduction principles supported by a transnational coalition of 31 cities and regions. In October 1996 Emma Bonino, the European commissioner for consumer policy, advocated decriminalizing soft drugs and initiating a broad prescription program for hard drugs. Greece's minister for European affairs, George Papandreou, seconded her. Last February the monarch of Liechtenstein, Prince Hans Adam, spoke out in favor of controlled drug legalization. Even Raymond Kendall, secretary general of Interpol, was quoted in the August 20, 1994, *Guardian* as saying, "The prosecution of thousands of otherwise law-abiding citizens every year is both hypocritical and an affront to individual, civil and human rights. . . . Drug use should no longer be a criminal offense. I am totally against legalization, but in favor of decriminalization for the user." . . .

The lessons from Europe and Australia are compelling. Drug control policies should focus on reducing drug-related crime, disease, and death, not the number of casual drug users. Stopping the spread of HIV by and among drug users by making sterile syringes and methadone readily available must be the first priority. American politicians need to explore, not ignore or automatically condemn, promising policy options such as cannabis decriminalization, heroin prescription, and the integration of harm-reduction principles into community policing strategies. Central governments must back, or at least not hinder, the efforts of municipal officials and citizens to devise pragmatic approaches to local drug problems. Like citizens in Europe, the American public has supported such innovations when they are adequately explained and allowed to prove themselves. As the evidence comes in, what works is increasingly apparent. All that remains is mustering the political courage.

James A. Inciardi and
Christine A. Saum

 **NO**

Legalization Madness

Frustrated by the government's apparent inability to reduce the supply of illegal drugs on the streets of America, and disquieted by media accounts of innocents victimized by drug-related violence, some policy makers are convinced that the "war on drugs" has failed. In an attempt to find a better solution to the "drug crisis" or, at the very least, to try an alternative strategy, they have proposed legalizing drugs.

They argue that, if marijuana, cocaine, heroin, and other drugs were legalized, several positive things would probably occur: (1) drug prices would fall; (2) users would obtain their drugs at low, government-regulated prices, and they would no longer be forced to resort to crime in order to support their habits; (3) levels of drug-related crime, and particularly violent crime, would significantly decline, resulting in less crowded courts, jails, and prisons (this would allow law-enforcement personnel to focus their energies on the "real criminals" in society); and (4) drug production, distribution, and sale would no longer be controlled by organized crime, and thus such criminal syndicates as the Colombian cocaine "cartels," the Jamaican "posses," and the various "mafias" around the country and the world would be decapitalized, and the violence associated with drug distribution rivalries would be eliminated.

By contrast, the anti-legalization camp argues that violent crime would not necessarily decline in a legalized drug market. In fact, there are three reasons why it might actually increase. First, removing the criminal sanctions against the possession and distribution of illegal drugs would make them more available and attractive and, hence, would create large numbers of new users. Second, an increase in use would lead to a greater number of dysfunctional addicts who could not support themselves, their habits, or their lifestyles through legitimate means. Hence crime would be their only alternative. Third, more users would mean more of the violence associated with the ingestion of drugs.

These divergent points of view tend to persist because the relationships between drugs and crime are quite complex and because the possible outcomes of a legalized drug market are based primarily on speculation. However, it is possible, from a careful review of the existing empirical literature on drugs and violence, to make some educated inferences.

Considering "Legalization"

Yet much depends upon what we mean by "legalizing drugs." Would all currently illicit drugs be legalized or would the experiment be limited to just certain ones? True legalization would be akin to selling such drugs as heroin and cocaine on the open market, much like alcohol and tobacco, with a few age-related restrictions. In contrast, there are "medicalization" and "decriminalization" alternatives. Medicalization approaches are of many types, but, in essence, they would allow users to obtain prescriptions for some, or all, currently illegal substances. Decriminalization removes the criminal penalties associated with the possession of small amounts of illegal drugs for personal use, while leaving intact the sanctions for trafficking, distribution, and sale.

But what about crack-cocaine? A quick review of the literature reveals that the legalizers, the decriminalizers, and the medicalizers avoid talking about this particular form of cocaine. Perhaps they do not want to legalize crack out of fear of the drug itself, or of public outrage. Arnold S. Trebach, a professor of law at American University and president of the Drug Policy Foundation, is one of the very few who argues for the full legalization of all drugs, including crack. He explains, however, that most are reluctant to discuss the legalization of crack-cocaine because, "it is a very dangerous drug.... I know that for many people the very thought of making crack legal destroys any inclination they might have had for even thinking about drug-law reform."

There is a related concern associated with the legalization of cocaine. Because crack is easily manufactured from powder cocaine (just add water and baking soda and cook on a stove or in a microwave), many drug-policy reformers hold that no form of cocaine should be legalized. But this weakens the argument that legalization will reduce drug-related violence; for much of this violence would appear to be in the cocaine- and crack-distribution markets.

To better understand the complex relationship between drugs and violence, we will discuss the data in the context of three models developed by Paul J. Goldstein of the University of Illinois at Chicago. They are the "psychopharmacological," "economically compulsive," and "systemic" explanations of violence. The first model holds, correctly in our view, that some individuals may become excitable, irrational, and even violent due to the ingestion of specific drugs. In contrast, taking a more economic approach to the behavior of drug users, the second holds that some drug users engage in violent crime mainly for the sake of supporting their drug use. The third model maintains that drug-related violent crime is simply the result of the drug market under a regime of illegality.

Psychopharmacological Violence

The case for legalization rests in part upon the faulty assumption that drugs themselves do not cause violence; rather, so goes the argument, violence is the result of depriving drug addicts of drugs or of the "criminal" trafficking in drugs. But, as researcher Barry Spunt points out, "Users of drugs do get violent when they get high."

Research has documented that chronic users of amphetamines, metham-phetane, and cocaine in particular tend to exhibit hostile and aggressive behaviors. Psychopharmacological violence can also be a product of what is known as "cocaine psychosis." As dose and duration of cocaine use increase, the development of cocaine-related psychopathology is not uncommon. Cocaine psychosis is generally preceded by a transitional period characterized by increased suspiciousness, compulsive behavior, fault finding, and eventually paranoia. When the psychotic state is reached, individuals may experience visual, as well as auditory, hallucinations, with persecutory voices commonly heard. Many believe that they are being followed by police or that family, friends, and others are plotting against them.

Moreover, everyday events are sometimes misinterpreted by cocaine users in ways that support delusional beliefs. When coupled with the irritability and hyperactivity that cocaine tends to generate in almost all of its users, the cocaine-induced paranoia may lead to violent behavior as a means of "self-defense" against imagined persecutors. The violence associated with cocaine psychosis is a common feature in many crack houses across the United States. Violence may also result from the irritability associated with drug-withdrawal syndromes. In addition, some users ingest drugs before committing crimes to both loosen inhibitions and bolster their resolve to break the law....

And Alcohol Abuse

A point that needs emphasizing is that alcohol, because it is legal, accessible, and inexpensive, is linked to violence to a far greater extent than any illegal drug. For example, in the study just cited, it was found that an impressive 64 percent of those women who eventually killed their abusers were alcohol users (44 percent of those who did not kill their abusers were alcohol users). Indeed, the extent to which alcohol is responsible for violent crimes in comparison with other drugs is apparent from the statistics. For example, Carolyn Block and her colleagues at the Criminal Justice Information Authority in Chicago found that, between 1982 and 1989, the use of alcohol by offenders or victims in local homicides ranged from 18 percent to 32 percent.

Alcohol has, in fact, been consistently linked to homicide. Spunt and his colleagues interviewed 268 homicide offenders incarcerated in New York State correctional facilities to determine the role of alcohol in their crimes: Thirty-one percent of the respondents reported being drunk at the time of the crime and 19 percent believed that the homicide was related to their drinking. More generally, Douglass Murdoch of Quebec's McGill University found that in some 9,000 criminal cases drawn from a multinational sample, 62 percent of violent offenders were drinking shortly before, or at the time of, the offense.

It appears that alcohol reduces the inhibitory control of threat, making it more likely that a person will exhibit violent behaviors normally suppressed by fear. In turn, this reduction of inhibition heightens the probability that intoxicated persons will perpetrate, or become victims of, aggressive behavior.

When analyzing the psychopharmacological model of drugs and violence, most of the discussions focus on the offender and the role of drugs in causing or facilitating crime. But what about the victims? Are the victims of drug- and alcohol-related homicides simply casualties of someone else's substance abuse? In addressing these questions, the data demonstrates that victims are likely to be drug users as well. For example, in an analysis of the 4,298 homicides that occurred in New York City during 1990 and 1991, Kenneth Tardiff of Cornell University Medical College found that the victims of these offenses were 10 to 50 times more likely to be cocaine users than were members of the general population. Of the white female victims, 60 percent in the 25- to 34-year age group had cocaine in their systems; for black females, the figure was 72 percent. Tardiff speculated that the classic symptoms of cocaine use—irritability, paranoia, aggressiveness—may have instigated the violence. In another study of cocaine users in New York City, female high-volume users were found to be victims of violence far more frequently than low-volume and nonusers of cocaine. Studies in numerous other cities and countries have yielded the same general findings—that a great many of the victims of homicide and other forms of violence are drinkers and drug users themselves.

Economically Compulsive Violence

Supporters of the economically compulsive model of violence argue that in a legalized market, the prices of "expensive drugs" would decline to more affordable levels, and, hence, predatory crimes would become unnecessary. This argument is based on several specious assumptions. First, it assumes that there is empirical support for what has been referred to as the "enslavement theory of addiction." Second, it assumes that people addicted to drugs commit crimes only for the purpose of supporting their habits. Third, it assumes that, in a legalized market, users could obtain as much of the drugs as they wanted whenever they wanted. Finally, it assumes that, if drugs are inexpensive, they will be affordable, and thus crime would be unnecessary.

With respect to the first premise, there has been for the better part of this century a concerted belief among many in the drug-policy field that addicts commit crimes because they are "enslaved" to drugs, and further that, because of the high price of heroin, cocaine, and other illicit chemicals on the black market, users are forced to commit crimes in order to support their drug habits. However, there is no solid empirical evidence to support this contention. From the 1920s through the end of the 1960s, hundreds of studies of the relationship between crime and addiction were conducted. Invariably, when one analysis would support the posture of "enslavement theory," the next would affirm the view that addicts were criminals first and that their drug use was but one more manifestation of their deviant lifestyles. In retrospect, the difficulty lay in the ways that many of the studies had been conducted: Biases and deficiencies in research designs and sampling had rendered their findings of little value.

Studies since the mid 1970s of active drug users on the streets of New York, Miami, Baltimore, and elsewhere have demonstrated that the "enslavement theory" has little basis in reality. All of these studies of the criminal careers of drug users have convincingly documented that, while drug use tends to intensify and perpetuate criminal behavior, it usually does not initiate criminal careers....

Looking at the second premise, a variety of studies show that addicts commit crimes for reasons other than supporting their drug habit. They do so also for daily living expenses....

With respect to the third premise, that in a legalized market users could obtain as much of the drugs as they wanted whenever they wanted, only speculation is possible. More than likely, however, there would be some sort of regulation, and hence black markets for drugs would persist for those whose addictions were beyond the medicalized or legalized allotments. In a decriminalized market, levels of drug-related violence would likely either remain unchanged or increase (if drug use increased).

As for the last premise, that cheap drugs preclude the need to commit crimes to obtain them, the evidence emphatically suggests that this is not the case. Consider crack-cocaine: Although crack "rocks" are available on the illegal market for as little as two dollars in some locales, users are still involved in crime-driven endeavors to support their addictions. For example, researchers Norman S. Miller and Mark S. Gold surveyed 200 consecutive callers to the 1-800-COCAINE hotline who considered themselves to have a problem with crack. They found that, despite the low cost of crack, 63 percent of daily users and 40 percent of non-daily users spent more than $200 per week on the drug....

Systemic Violence

It is the supposed systemic violence associated with trafficking in cocaine and crack in America's inner cities that has recently received the attention of drug-policy critics interested in legalizing drugs. Certainly it might appear that, if heroin and cocaine were legal substances, systemic drug-related violence would decline. However, there are two very important questions in this regard: First, is drug-related violence more often psychopharmacological or systemic? Second, is the great bulk of systemic violence related to the distribution of crack? If most of the drug-related violence is psychopharmacological in nature, and if systemic violence is typically related to crack—the drug generally excluded from consideration when legalization is recommended—then legalizing drugs would probably *not* reduce violent crime.

Regarding the first question, several recent studies conducted in New York City tend to contradict, or at least not support, the notion that legalizing drugs would reduce violent systemic-related crime. For example, Paul J. Goldstein's ethnographic studies of male and female drug users during the late 1980s found that cocaine-related violence was more often psychopharmacological than systemic. Similarly, Kenneth Tardiff's study of 4,298 New York City homicides found that 31 percent of the victims had used cocaine in the 24-hour period prior to their deaths....

Regarding the second question, the illegal drug most associated with systemic violence is crack-cocaine. Of all illicit drugs, crack is the one now responsible for the most homicides....

Don't Just Say No

The issue of whether or not legalization would create a multitude of new users also needs to be addressed. It has been shown that many people do not use drugs simply because drugs are illegal. As Mark A.R. Kleiman, author of *Against Excess: Drug Policy for Results,* recently put it: "Illegality by itself tends to suppress consumption, independent of its effect on price, both because some consumers are reluctant to disobey the law and because illegal products are harder to find and less reliable as to quality and labeling than legal ones."

Although there is no way of accurately estimating how many new users there would be if drugs were legalized, there would probably be many. To begin with, there is the historical example of Prohibition. During Prohibition, there was a decrease of 20 percent to 50 percent in the number of alcoholics. These estimates were calculated based on a decline in cirrhosis and other alcohol-related deaths; after Prohibition ended, both of these indicators increased.

Currently, relatively few people are steady users of drugs. The University of Michigan's *Monitoring the Future* study reported in 1995 that only two-tenths of 1 percent of high-school seniors are daily users of either hallucinogens, cocaine, heroin, sedatives, or inhalants. It is the addicts who overwhelmingly consume the bulk of the drug supply—80 percent of all alcohol and almost 100 percent of all heroin. In other words, there are significantly large numbers of non-users who have yet to even try drugs, let alone use them regularly. Of those who begin to use drugs "recreationally," researchers estimate that approximately 10 percent go on to serious, heavy, chronic, compulsive use. Herbert Kleber, the former deputy director of the Office of National Drug Control Policy, recently estimated that cocaine legalization might multiply the number of addicts from the current 2 million to between 18 and 50 million (which are the estimated numbers of problem drinkers and nicotine addicts).

This suggests that drug prohibition seems to be having some very positive effects and that legalizing drugs would not necessarily have a depressant effect on violent crime. With legalization, violent crime would likely escalate; or perhaps some types of systemic violence would decline at the expense of greatly increasing the overall rate of violent crime. Moreover, legalizing drugs would likely increase physical illnesses and compound any existing psychiatric problems among users and their family members. And finally, legalizing drugs would not eliminate the effects of unemployment, inadequate housing, deficient job skills, economic worries, and physical abuse that typically contribute to the use of drugs.

POSTSCRIPT

Should Drug Use Be Decriminalized?

The analogy often cited by proponents of drug legalization is the ill-fated attempt to ban the sale of liquor in the United States, which lasted from 1919 to 1933. Prohibition has been called "an experiment noble in purpose," but it was an experiment that greatly contributed to the rise of organized crime. The repeal of Prohibition brought about an increase in liquor consumption and alcoholism, but it also deprived organized crime of an important source of income. Would drug decriminalization similarly strike a blow at the drug dealers? Possibly, and such a prospect is obviously appealing. But would drug decriminalization also exacerbate some of the ills associated with drugs? Would there be more violence, more severe addiction, and more crack babies born to addicted mothers?

There are a variety of publications and theories pertaining to drug use and society. Ronald L. Akers, in *Drugs, Alcohol, and Society* (Wadsworth, 1992), relates drug patterns to social structure. For a comprehensive overview of the history, effects, and prevention of drug use, see Weldon L. Witters, Peter J. Venturelli, and Glen R. Hanson, *Drugs and Society,* 3rd ed. (Jones & Bartlett, 1992) and Mike Gray, *Drug Crazy: How We Got into This Mess and How We Can Get Out* (Random House, 1998). Terry Williams describes the goings-on in a crackhouse in *Crackhouse: Notes from the End of the Zone* (Addison-Wesley, 1992). James A. Inciardi, Ruth Horowitz, and Anne El Pottieger focus on street kids and drugs in *Street Kids, Street Drugs, Street Crime: An Examination of Drug Use and Serious Delinquency in Miami* (Wadsworth, 1993). For an excellent study of how users of the drug ecstasy perceive the experience, see Jerome Beck and Marsha Rosenbaum, *Pursuit of Ecstasy: The MDMA Experience* (SUNY Press, 1994). For studies of female drug-using groups, see Carl S. Taylor, *Girls, Gangs, Women and Drugs* (Michigan State University Press, 1993) and Avril Taylor, *Women Drug Users: An Ethnography of a Female Injecting Community* (Clarendon Press, 1993). For a relatively balanced yet innovative set of drug policies, see Elliott Carrie, *Reckoning: Drugs, the Cities, and the American Future* (Hill & Wang, 1993). William O. Walker III, ed., *Drug Control Policy* (Pennsylvania State University Press, 1992) critically evaluates drug policies from historical and comparative perspectives. On the legalization debate, see Eric Goode, *Between Politics and Reason: The Drug Legalization Debate* (St. Martin's Press, 1997) and Arnold Trebach and James A. Inciardi, *Legalize It? Debating American Drug Policy* (American University Press, 1993). For criticism of the current drug policies, see Dan Baum, *Smoke and Mirrors: The War on Drugs and the Politics of Failure* (Little, Brown, 1996) and Leif Rosenberger, *America's Drug War Debacle* (Avebury, 1996).

ISSUE 17

Is Capital Punishment Justified?

YES: Robert W. Lee, from "Deserving to Die," *The New American* (August 13, 1990)

NO: Eric M. Freedman, from "The Case Against the Death Penalty," *USA Today Magazine* (March 1997)

ISSUE SUMMARY

YES: Editor and author Robert W. Lee argues that capital punishment is needed to deter people from committing murder and other heinous crimes, but more importantly, it is the punishment that is the most appropriate for these crimes.

NO: Legal scholar Eric M. Freedman counters that the death penalty does not deter crime and has unacceptable negative consequences, including the potential of killing innocent people, reducing public safety, and imposing considerable costs on society.

On January 13, 2000 Governor George Ryan of Illinois imposed a moratorium on executions in his state because 13 death row inmates had been released when found to have been wrongly convicted. Ryan was a pro-death-penalty Republican but was deeply concerned about the possibility of executing innocent people. Recent use of DNA evidence had proven that the justice system can be deeply flawed. The Supreme Court supported the constitutionality of the death penalty in 1976 and since then 87 people have been freed from death row on the basis of new evidence.

In 1997 The Death Penalty Information Center issued a report by its director Richard C. Dieter entitled, "The Death Penalty: The Increasing Danger of Executing the Innocent." The executive summary of this report states:

> Twenty-one condemned inmates have been released since 1993 ... Many of these cases were discovered not because of the normal appeals process, but rather as a result of new scientific techniques, investigations by journalists, and the dedicated work of expert attorneys, not available to the typical death row inmate.
>
> This report tells the stories of people like Rolando Cruz, released after 10 years on Illinois's death row, despite the fact that another man had confessed to the crime shortly after his conviction; and Ricardo Aldape Guerra,

who returned to Mexico after 15 years on Texas's death row because of a prosecution that a federal judge called outrageous and designed to simply achieve another notch on the prosecutor's gun. This report particularly looks at the dramatic narrowing of the opportunity to appeal and to raise newly discovered evidence of one's innocence. The federal funding for the death penalty resource centers, which helped discover and vindicate several of the innocent people cited in this report, has been completely withdrawn. Some courts have now taken the position that it is permissible for executions to go forward even in the face of considerable doubt about the defendant's guilt.

How flawed is the criminal justice system? Is there too much potential for error when it comes to capital punishment? Some argue that there is. Too many innocent people die for crimes that they did not commit.

However, some would point out that a murderer, once executed, will never commit murder again. In Utah there have been three executions since 1976. After each execution, the murder rate decreased significantly. It can be argued that the execution acted as a deterrent in those three cases.

Is life imprisonment a suitable alternative to capital punishment? Some state that the rate of escape for "lifers" puts too many innocent people at risk. Does a life sentence provide adequate protection for society? Do the criminals deserve to be killed? Some state that certain crimes warrant the strictest of punishments, thus placing the burden of crime onto the criminal and away from the innocent.

The public currently favors the death penalty according to recent polls. A *Newsweek* poll in 2000 found that 73 percent of Americans support capital punishment, an increase from 42 percent in 1966. Executions have also increased. There were no executions from 1968 to 1976, 117 people were executed in the 1980s, and 478 in the 1990s. Executions have risen rapidly in the 1990s from 14 in 1991 to 98 in 1999, which makes America a world leader behind China with 1,077, Iran with 165, Saudi Arabia with 103, and the Congo with 100. The concern is with victims' rights, while defendants' rights are being cut back because some defendants' rights provisions are perceived as too greatly interfering with effective law enforcement.

Can we evaluate how effective a deterrent capital punishment is? Is there enough information available to make an accurate assessment? Is capital punishment administered in a racially biased manner? Is capital punishment the only way to guarantee adequate protection against people who commit heinous crimes? What burden should society at large assume concerning the few who commit heinous crimes? These are important questions to consider when deciding if capital punishment is justified or not.

In the following selections, Robert W. Lee advocates capital punishment as required justice for certain crimes and the only effective deterrent in some situations. Eric M. Freedman disagrees about the deterrent effect of capital punishment and raises concerns about the execution of innocent people.

Robert W. Lee

 **YES**

Deserving to Die

Akey issue in the debate over capital punishment is whether or not it is an effective deterrent to violent crime. In at least one important respect, it unquestionably is: It simply cannot be contested that a killer, once executed, is forever deterred from killing again. The deterrent effect on others, however, depends largely on how swiftly and surely the penalty is applied. Since capital punishment has not been used with any consistency over the years, it is virtually impossible to evaluate its deterrent effect accurately. Abolitionists claim that a lack of significant difference between the murder rates for states with and without capital punishment proves that the death penalty does not deter. But the states with the death penalty on their books have used it so little over the years as to preclude any meaningful comparison between states. Through July 18, 1990 there had been 134 executions since 1976. Only 14 states (less than 40 percent of those that authorize the death penalty) were involved. Any punishment, including death, will cease to be an effective deterrent if it is recognized as mostly bluff. Due to costly delays and endless appeals, the death penalty has been largely turned into a paper tiger by the same crowd that calls for its abolition on the grounds that it is not an effective deterrent!

To allege that capital punishment, if imposed consistently and without undue delay, would not be a deterrent to crime is, in essence, to say that people are not afraid of dying. If so, as columnist Jenkin Lloyd Jones once observed, then warning signs reading "Slow Down," "Bridge Out," and "Danger—40,000 Volts" are futile relics of an age gone by when men feared death. To be sure, the death penalty could never become a 100-percent deterrent to heinous crime, because the fear of death varies among individuals. Some race automobiles, climb mountains, parachute jump, walk circus high-wires, ride Brahma bulls in rodeos, and otherwise engage in endeavors that are more than normally hazardous. But, as author Bernard Cohen notes in his book *Law and Order,* "there are even more people who refrain from participating in these activities mainly because risking their lives is not to their taste."

Merit System

On occasion, circumstances *have* led to meaningful statistical evaluations of the death penalty's deterrent effect. In Utah, for instance, there have been three executions since the Supreme Court's 1976 ruling:

- Gary Gilmore faced a firing squad at the Utah State Prison on January 17, 1977. There had been 55 murders in the Beehive State during 1976 (4.5 per 100,000 population). During 1977, in the wake of the Gilmore execution, there were 44 murders (3.5 per 100,000), a 20 percent decrease.

- More than a decade later, on August 28, 1987, Pierre Dale Selby (one of the two infamous "hi-fi killers" who in 1974 forced five persons in an Ogden hi-fi shop to drink liquid drain cleaner, kicked a ballpoint pen into the ear of one, then killed three) was executed. During all of 1987, there were 54 murders (3.2 per 100,000). The count for January through August was 38 (a monthly average of 4.75). For September–December (in the aftermath of the Selby execution) there were 16 (4.0 per month, a nearly 16 percent decrease). For July and August there were six and seven murders, respectively. In September (the first month following Selby's demise) there were three.

- Arthur Gary Bishop, who sodomized and killed a number of young boys, was executed on June 10, 1988. For all of 1988 there were 47 murders (2.7 per 100,000, the fewest since 1977). During January–June, there were 26; for July–December (after the Bishop execution) the tally was 21 (a 19 percent difference).

In the wake of all three Utah executions, there have been notable decreases in both the number and the rate of murders within the state. To be sure, there are other variables that could have influenced the results, but the figures are there and abolitionists to date have tended simply to ignore them.

Deterrence should never be considered the *primary* reason for administering the death penalty. It would be both immoral and unjust to punish one man merely as an example to others. The basic consideration should be: Is the punishment deserved? If not, it should not be administered regardless of what its deterrent impact might be. After all, once deterrence supersedes justice as the basis for a criminal sanction, the guilt or innocence of the accused becomes largely irrelevant. Deterrence can be achieved as effectively by executing an innocent person as a guilty one (something that communists and other totalitarians discovered long ago). If a punishment administered to one person deters someone else from committing a crime, fine. But that result should be viewed as a bonus of justice properly applied, not as a reason for the punishment. The decisive consideration should be: Has the accused *earned* the penalty?

The Cost of Execution

The exorbitant financial expense of death penalty cases is regularly cited by abolitionists as a reason for abolishing capital punishment altogether. They prefer to ignore, however, the extent to which they themselves are responsible for the interminable legal maneuvers that run up the costs. . . .

As presently pursued, death-penalty prosecutions *are* outrageously expensive. But, again, the cost is primarily due to redundant appeals, time-consuming delays, bizarre court rulings, and legal histrionics by defense attorneys:

> Willie Darden, who had already survived three death warrants, was scheduled to die in Florida's electric chair on September 4, 1985 for a murder he had committed in 1973. Darden's lawyer made a last-minute emergency appeal to the Supreme Court, which voted against postponing the execution until a formal appeal could be filed. So the attorney (in what he later described as "last-minute ingenuity") then requested that the emergency appeal be technically transformed into a formal appeal. Four Justices agreed (enough to force the full court to review the appeal) and the execution was stayed. After additional years of delay and expense, Darden was eventually put out of our misery on March 15, 1988.

> Ronald Gene Simmons killed 14 members of his family during Christmas week in 1987. He was sentenced to death, said he was willing to die, and refused to appeal. But his scheduled March 16, 1989 execution was delayed when a fellow inmate, also on death row, persuaded the Supreme Court to block it (while Simmons was having what he expected to be his last meal) on the grounds that the execution could have repercussions for other death-row inmates. It took the Court until April 24th of [1990] to reject that challenge. Simmons was executed on June 25th.

> Robert Alton Harris was convicted in California of the 1978 murders of two San Diego teenagers whose car he wanted for a bank robbery. Following a seemingly interminable series of appeals, he was at last sentenced to die on April 3rd of [1990]. Four days earlier, a 9th U.S. Circuit Court of Appeals judge stayed the execution, largely on the claim that Harris was brain-damaged and therefore may possibly have been unable to "premeditate" the murders (as required under California law for the death penalty). On April 10th, the *Washington Times* reported that the series of tests used to evaluate Harris's condition had been described by some experts as inaccurate and "a hoax."

> The psychiatric game is being played for all it is worth. On May 14th, Harris's attorneys argued before the 9th Circuit Court that he should be spared the death penalty because he received

"inadequate" psychiatric advice during his original trial. In 1985, the Supreme Court had ruled that a defendant has a constitutional right to "a competent psychiatrist who will conduct an appropriate examination." Harris had access to a licensed psychiatrist, but now argues that—since the recent (highly questionable) evaluations indicated brain damage and other alleged disorders that the original psychiatrist failed to detect (and which may have influenced the jury not to impose the death sentence)—a new trial (or at least a re-sentencing) is in order. If the courts buy this argument, hundreds (perhaps thousands) of cases could be reopened for psychiatric challenge.

On April 2, 1974 William Neal Moore shot and killed a man in Georgia. Following his arrest, he pleaded guilty to armed robbery and murder and was convicted and sentenced to death. On July 20, 1975 the Georgia Supreme Court denied his petition for review. On July 16, 1976 the U.S. Supreme Court denied his petition for review. On May 13, 1977 the Jefferson County Superior Court turned down a petition for a new sentencing hearing (the state Supreme Court affirmed the denial, and the U.S. Supreme Court again denied a review). On March 30, 1978 a Tattnall County Superior Court judge held a hearing on a petition alleging sundry grounds for a writ of *habeas corpus,* but declined on July 13, 1978 to issue a writ. On October 17, 1978 the state Supreme Court declined to review that ruling. Moore petitioned the U.S. District Court for Southern Georgia. After a delay of more than two years, a U.S. District Court judge granted the writ on April 29, 1981. After another two-year delay, the 11th U.S. Circuit Court of Appeals upheld the writ on June 23, 1983. On September 30, 1983 the Circuit Court reversed itself and ruled that the writ should be denied. On March 5, 1984 the Supreme Court rejected the case for the third time.

Moore's execution was set for May 24, 1984. On May 11, 1984 his attorneys filed a petition in Butts County Superior Court, but a writ was denied. The same petition was filed in the U.S. District Court for Georgia's Southern District on May 18th, but both a writ and a stay of execution were denied. Then, on May 23rd (the day before the scheduled execution) the 11th Circuit Court of Appeals granted a stay. On June 4, 1984 a three-judge panel of the Circuit Court voted to deny a writ. After another delay of more than three years, the Circuit Court voted 7 to 4 to override its three-judge panel and rule in Moore's favor. On April 18, 1988, the Supreme Court accepted the case. On April 17, 1989 it sent the case back to the 11th Circuit Court for review in light of new restrictions that the High Court had placed on *habeas corpus.* On September 28, 1989 the Circuit Court ruled 6 to 5 that Moore had abused the writ process. On December 18, 1989 Moore's attorneys again appealed to the Supreme Court.

Moore's case was described in detail in *Insight* magazine for February 12, 1990. By the end of [1989] his case had gone through 20 separate court reviews, involving some 118 state and federal judges. It had been to the Supreme Court and back four times. There had been a substantial turnover of his attorneys, creating an excuse for one team of lawyers to file a petition claiming that all of the prior attorneys had given ineffective representation. No wonder capital cases cost so much!

Meanwhile, the American Bar Association proposes to make matters even worse by requiring states (as summarized by *Insight*) "to appoint two lawyers for every stage of the proceeding, require them to have past death penalty experience and pay them at 'reasonable' rates to be set by the court."

During an address to the American Law Institute on May 16, 1990, Chief Justice Rehnquist asserted that the "system at present verges on the chaotic" and "cries out for reform." The time expended between sentencing and execution, he declared, "is consumed not by structured review... but in fits of frantic action followed by periods of inaction." He urged that death row inmates be given one chance to challenge their sentences in state courts, and one challenge in federal courts, period.

Lifetime to Escape

Is life imprisonment an adequate substitute for the death penalty? Presently, according to the polls, approximately three-fourths of the American people favor capital punishment. But abolitionists try to discount that figure by claiming that support for the death penalty weakens when life imprisonment without the possibility of parole is offered as an alternative. (At other times, abolitionists argue that parole is imperative to give "lifers" some hope for the future and deter their violent acts in prison.)

Life imprisonment is a flawed alternative to the death penalty, if for no other reason than that so many "lifers" escape. Many innocent persons have died at the hands of men previously convicted and imprisoned for murder, supposedly for "life." The ways in which flaws in our justice system, combined with criminal ingenuity, have worked to allow "lifers" to escape include these recent examples:

- On June 10, 1977, James Earl Ray, who was serving a 99-year term for killing Dr. Martin Luther King Jr., escaped with six other inmates from the Brushy Mountain State Prison in Tennessee (he was captured three days later).
- Brothers Linwood and James Briley were executed in Virginia on October 12, 1984 and April 18, 1985, respectively. Linwood had murdered a disc jockey in 1979 during a crime spree. During the same spree, James raped and killed a woman (who was eight months pregnant) and killed her five-year-old son. On May 31, 1984, the Briley brothers organized and led an escape of five death-row inmates (the largest death-row breakout in U.S. history). They were at large for 19 days.

- On August 1, 1984 convicted murderers Wesley Allen Tuttle and Walter Wood, along with another inmate, escaped from the Utah State Prison. All were eventually apprehended. Wood subsequently sued the state for $2 million for violating his rights by allowing him to escape. In his complaint, he charged that, by allowing him to escape, prison officials had subjected him to several life-threatening situations: "Because of extreme fear of being shot to death, I was forced to swim several irrigation canals, attempt to swim a 'raging' Jordan River and expose myself to innumerable bites by many insects. At one point I heard a volley of shotgun blasts and this completed my anxiety."
- On April 3, 1988 three murderers serving life sentences without the chance of parole escaped from the maximum-security West Virginia Penitentiary. One, Bobby Stacy, had killed a Huntington police officer in 1981. At the time, he had been free on bail after having been arrested for shooting an Ohio patrolman.
- On November 21, 1988 Gonzalo Marrero, who had been convicted of two murders and sentenced to two life terms, escaped from New Jersey's Trenton state prison by burrowing through a three-foot-thick cell wall, then scaling a 20-foot outer wall with a makeshift ladder.
- In August 1989 Arthur Carroll, a self-proclaimed enforcer for an East Oakland street gang, was convicted of murdering a man. On September 28th, he was sentenced to serve 27-years-to-life in prison. On October 10th he was transferred to San Quentin prison. On October 25th he was set free after a paperwork snafu led officials to believe that he had served enough time. An all-points bulletin was promptly issued.
- On February 11, 1990 six convicts, including three murderers, escaped from their segregation cells in the maximum security Joliet Correctional Center in Illinois by cutting through bars on their cells, breaking a window, and crossing a fence. In what may be the understatement of the year, a prison spokesman told reporters: "Obviously, this is a breach of security."

Clearly, life sentences do not adequately protect society, whereas the death penalty properly applied does so with certainty.

Equal Opportunity Execution

Abolitionists often cite statistics indicating that capital punishment has been administered in a discriminatory manner, so that the poor, the black, the friendless, etc., have suffered a disproportionate share of executions. Even if true, such discrimination would not be a valid reason for abandoning the death penalty unless it could be shown that it was responsible for the execution of *innocent* persons (which it has not been, to date). Most attempts to pin the "discrimination" label on capital convictions are similar to one conducted at Stanford University a few years ago, which found that murderers of white people (whether white or black) are more likely to be punished with death than are killers of black people (whether white or black). But the study also concluded that blacks who murdered whites were somewhat *less* likely to receive death sentences than were whites who killed whites.

Using such data, the ACLU attempted to halt the execution of Chester Lee Wicker in Texas on August 26, 1986. Wicker, who was white, had killed a white person. The ACLU contended that Texas unfairly imposes the death penalty because a white is more likely than a black to be sentenced to death for killing a white. The Supreme Court rejected the argument. On the other hand, the execution of Willie Darden in Florida attracted worldwide pleas for amnesty from sundry abolitionists who, ignoring the Stanford study, claimed that Darden had been "railroaded" because he was black and his victim was white.

All criminal laws—in all countries, throughout all human history—have tended to be administered in an imperfect and uneven manner. As a result, some elements in society have been able to evade justice more consistently than others. But why should the imperfect administration of justice persuade us to abandon any attempt to attain it?

The most flagrant example of discrimination in the administration of the death penalty does not involve race, income, or social status, but gender. Women commit around 13 percent of the murders in America, yet, from 1930 to June 30, 1990, only 33 of the 3991 executions (less than 1 percent) involved women. Only one of the 134 persons executed since 1976 (through July 18th [1990]) has been a woman (Velma Barfield in North Carolina on November 2, 1984). One state governor commuted the death sentence of a woman because "humanity does not apply to women the inexorable law that it does to men."

According to L. Kay Gillespie, professor of sociology at Weber State College in Utah, evidence indicates that women who cried during their trials had a better chance of getting away with murder and avoiding the death penalty. Perhaps the National Organization for Women can do something about this glaring example of sexist "inequality" and "injustice." In the meantime, we shall continue to support the death penalty despite the disproportionate number of men who have been required to pay a just penalty for their heinous crimes.

Forgive and Forget?

Another aspect of the death penalty debate is the extent to which justice should be tempered by mercy in the case of killers. After all, abolitionists argue, is it not the duty of Christians to forgive those who trespass against them? In Biblical terms, the most responsible sources to extend mercy and forgiveness are (1) God and (2) the victim of the injustice. In the case of murder, so far as *this* world is concerned, the victim is no longer here to extend mercy and forgiveness. Does the state or any other earthly party have the right or authority to intervene and tender mercy on behalf of a murder victim? In the anthology *Essays on the Death Penalty,* the Reverend E. L. H. Taylor clarifies the answer this way: "Now it is quite natural and proper for a man to forgive something you do to *him.* Thus if somebody cheats me out of $20.00 it is quite possible and reasonable for me to say, 'Well, I forgive him, we will say no more about it.' But what would you say if somebody had done you out of $20.00 and I said, 'That's all right. I forgive him on your behalf'?"

The point is simply that there is no way, in *this* life, for a murderer to be reconciled to his victim, and secure the victim's forgiveness. This leaves the civil authority with no other responsible alternative but to adopt *justice* as the standard for assigning punishment in such cases.

Author Bernard Cohen raises an interesting point: " . . . if it is allowable to deprive a would-be murderer of his life, in order to forestall his attack, why is it wrong to take away his life after he has successfully carried out his dastardly business?" Does anyone question the right of an individual to kill an assailant should it be necessary to preserve his or her life or that of a loved one?

Happily, however, both scripture and our legal system uphold the morality and legality of taking the life of an assailant, if necessary, *before* he kills us. How, then, can it be deemed immoral for civil authority to take his life *after* he kills us?

Intolerant Victims?

Sometimes those who defend the death penalty are portrayed as being "intolerant." But isn't one of our real problems today that Americans are *too tolerant* of evil? Are we not accepting acts of violence, cruelty, lying, and immorality with all too little righteous indignation? Such indignation is not, as some would have us believe, a form of "hatred." In *Reflections on the Psalms,* C. S. Lewis discussed the supposed spirit of "hatred" that some critics claimed to see in parts of the Psalms: "Such hatreds are the kind of thing that cruelty and injustice, by a sort of natural law, produce. . . . Not to perceive it at all—not even to be tempted to resentment—to accept it as the most ordinary thing in the world—argues a terrifying insensibility. Thus the absence of anger, especially that sort of anger which we call indignation, can, in my opinion, be a most alarming symptom."

When mass murderer Ted Bundy was executed in Florida on January 24, 1989, a crowd of some 2000 spectators gathered across from the prison to cheer and celebrate. Many liberal commentators were appalled. Some contended that it was a spectacle on a par with Bundy's own callous disrespect for human life. One headline read: "Exhibition witnessed outside prison was more revolting than execution." What nonsense! As C. S. Lewis observed in his commentary on the Psalms: "If the Jews cursed more bitterly than the Pagans this was, I think, at least in part because they took right and wrong more seriously." It is long past time for us all to being taking right and wrong more seriously. . . .

Seeds of Anarchy

As we have seen, most discussions of the death penalty tend to focus on whether it should exist for murder or be abolished altogether. The issue should be reframed so that the question instead becomes whether or not it should be imposed for certain terrible crimes in addition to murder (such as habitual law-breaking, clearly proven cases of rape, and monstrous child abuse).

In 1953 the renowned British jurist Lord Denning asserted: "Punishment is the way in which society expresses its denunciation of wrongdoing; and in order to maintain respect for law, it is essential that the punishment for grave crimes shall adequately reflect the revulsion felt by a great majority of citizens for them." Nineteen years later, U.S. Supreme Court Justice Potter Stewart noted (while nevertheless concurring in the Court's 1972 opinion that temporarily banned capital punishment) that the "instinct for retribution is part of the nature of man and channeling that instinct in the administration of criminal justice serves an important purpose in promoting the stability of a society governed by law. When people begin to believe that organized society is unwilling or unable to impose upon criminal offenders the punishment they 'deserve,' then there are sown the seeds of anarchy—of self-help, vigilante justice, and lynch law."

To protect the innocent and transfer the fear and burden of crime to the criminal element where it belongs, we must demand that capital punishment be imposed when justified and expanded to cover terrible crimes in addition to murder.

NO

Eric M. Freedman

The Case Against the Death Penalty

On Sept. 1, 1995, New York rejoined the ranks of states imposing capital punishment. Although the first death sentence has yet to be imposed, an overwhelming factual record from around the country makes the consequence of this action easily predictable: New Yorkers will get less crime control than they had before.

Anyone whose public policy goals are to provide a criminal justice system that delivers swift, accurate, and evenhanded results—and to reduce the number of crimes that actually threaten most people in their daily lives—should be a death penalty opponent. The reason is simple: The death penalty not only is useless in itself, but counterproductive to achieving those goals. It wastes enormous resources—fiscal and moral—on a tiny handful of cases, to the detriment of measures that might have a significant impact in improving public safety.

Those who believe the death penalty somehow is an emotionally satisfying response to horrific crimes should ask themselves whether they wish to adhere to that initial reaction in light of the well-documented facts:

Fact: The death penalty does not reduce crime.

Capital punishment proponents sometimes assert that it simply is logical to think that the death penalty is a deterrent. Whether or not the idea is logical, it is not true, an example of the reality that many intuitively obvious propositions—*e.g.*, that a heavy ball will fall faster if dropped from the Leaning Tower of Pisa than a light one—are factually false.

People who commit capital murders generally do not engage in probability analysis concerning the likelihood of getting the death penalty if they are caught. They may be severely mentally disturbed people like Ted Bundy, who chose Florida for his final crimes *because* it had a death penalty.

Whether one chooses to obtain data from scholarly studies, the evidence of long-term experience, or accounts of knowledgeable individuals, he or she

From Eric M. Freedman, "The Case Against the Death Penalty," *USA Today Magazine* (March 1997). Copyright © 1997 by The Society for the Advancement of Education. Reprinted by permission of *USA Today Magazine*.

will search in vain for empirical support for the proposition that imposing the death penalty cuts the crime rate. Instead, that person will find:

- The question of the supposed deterrent effect of capital punishment is perhaps the single most studied issue in the social sciences. The results are as unanimous as scholarly studies can be in finding the death penalty not to be a deterrent.
- Eighteen of the 20 states with the highest murder rates have and use the death penalty. Of the nation's 20 big cities with the highest murder rates, 17 are in death penalty jurisdictions. Between 1975 and 1985, almost twice as many law enforcement officers were killed in death penalty states as in non-death penalty states. Over nearly two decades, the neighboring states of Michigan, with no death penalty, and Indiana, which regularly imposes death sentences and carries out executions, have had virtually indistinguishable homicide rates.
- Myron Love, the presiding judge in Harris County, Tex. (which includes Houston), the county responsible for 10% of all executions in the entire country since 1976, admits that "We are not getting what I think we should be wanting and that is to deter crime.... In fact, the result is the opposite. We're having more violence, more crime."

Fact: The death penalty is extraordinarily expensive.

Contrary to popular intuition, a system with a death penalty is vastly more expensive than one where the maximum penalty is keeping murderers in prison for life. A 1982 New York study estimated the death penalty cost conservatively at three times that of life imprisonment, the ratio that Texas (with a system that is on the brink of collapse due to underfunding) has experienced. In Florida, each execution runs the state $3,200,000—six times the expense of life imprisonment. California has succeeded in executing just two defendants (one a volunteer) since 1976, but could save about $90,000,000 *per year* by abolishing the death penalty and re-sentencing all of its Death Row inmates to life.

In response, it often is proposed to reduce the costs by eliminating "all those endless appeals in death penalty cases." This is not a new idea. In recent years, numerous efforts have been made on the state and Federal levels to do precisely that. Their failure reflects some simple truths:

- Most of the extra costs of the death penalty are incurred prior to and at trial, not in postconviction proceedings. Trials are far more likely under a death penalty system (since there is so little incentive to plea-bargain). They have two separate phases (unlike other trials) and typically are preceded by special motions and extra jury selection questioning—steps that, if not taken before trial, most likely will result in the eventual reversal of the conviction.

- Much more investigation usually is done in capital cases, particularly by the prosecution. In New York, for instance, the office of the State Attorney General (which generally does not participate in local criminal prosecutions) is creating a new multi-lawyer unit to provide support to county district attorneys in capital cases.
- These expenses are incurred even though the outcome of most such trials is a sentence other than death and even though up to 50% of the death verdicts that are returned are reversed on the constitutionally required first appeal. Thus, the taxpayers foot the bill for all the extra costs of capital pretrial and trial proceedings and then must pay either for incarcerating the prisoner for life or the expenses of a retrial, which itself often leads to a life sentence. In short, even if all post-conviction proceedings following the first appeal were abolished, the death penalty system still would be more expensive than the alternative.

In fact, the concept of making such an extreme change in the justice system enjoys virtually no support in any political quarter. The writ of *habeas corpus* to protect against illegal imprisonment is available to every defendant in any criminal case, whether he or she is charged with being a petty thief or looting an S&L. It justly is considered a cornerstone of the American system of civil liberties. To eliminate all those "endless appeals" either would require weakening the system for everyone or differentially with respect to death penalty cases.

Giving less due process in capital cases is the opposite of what common sense and elementary justice call for and eventually could lead to innocent people being executed. Since the rate of constitutional violations is far greater in capital cases than in others—capital defendants seeking Federal *habeas corpus* relief succeed some 40% of the time, compared to a success rate of less than five percent for non-capital defendants—the idea of providing less searching review in death penalty cases is perverse.

Considering that the vast majority of post-conviction death penalty appeals arise from the inadequacies of appointed trial counsel, the most cost-effective and just way of decreasing the number of years devoted to capital proceedings, other than the best way—not enacting the death penalty—would be to provide adequate funding to the defense at the beginning of the process. Such a system, although more expensive than one without capital punishment, at least would result in some predictability. The innocent would be acquitted speedily; the less culpable would be sentenced promptly to lesser punishments; and the results of the trials of those defendants convicted and sentenced to death ordinarily would be final.

Instead, as matters now stand, there is roughly a 70% chance that a defendant sentenced to death eventually will succeed in getting the outcome set aside. The fault for this situation—which is unacceptable to the defense and prosecution bars alike—lies squarely with the states. It is they that have created the endless appeals by attempting to avoid the ineluctable monetary costs of death penalty systems and to run them on the cheap by refusing to provide adequate funding for defense counsel.

Fact: The death penalty actually reduces public safety.

The costs of the death penalty go far beyond the tens of millions of dollars wasted in the pursuit of a chimera. The reality is that, in a time of fixed or declining budgets, those dollars are taken away from a range of programs that would be beneficial. For example:

- New York State, due to financial constraints, can not provide bullet-proof vests for every peace officer—a project that, unlike the death penalty, certainly would save law enforcement lives.
- According to FBI statistics, the rate at which murders are solved has dropped to an all-time low. Yet, empirical studies consistently demonstrate that, as with other crimes, the murder rate decreases as the probability of detection increases. Putting money into investigative resources, rather than wasting it on the death penalty, could have a significant effect on crime.
- Despite the large percentage of ordinary street crimes that are narcotics-related, the states lack the funding to permit drug treatment on demand. The result is that people who are motivated to cure their own addictions are relegated to supporting themselves through crime, while the money that could fund treatment programs is poured down the death penalty drain.

Fact: The death penalty is arbitrary in operation.

Any reasonably conscientious supporter of the death penalty surely would agree with the proposition that, before someone is executed by the state, he or she first should receive the benefits of a judicial process that is as fair as humanly possible.

However, the one thing that is clear about the death penalty system that actually exists—as opposed to the idealized one some capital punishment proponents assume to exist—is that it does not provide a level of fairness which comes even close to equaling the gravity of the irreversible sanction being imposed. This failure of the system to function even reasonably well when it should be performing excellently breeds public cynicism as to how satisfactorily the system runs in ordinary, non-capital cases.

That reaction, although destructive, is understandable, because the factors that are significant in determining whether or not a particular defendant receives a death sentence have nothing at all to do with the seriousness of his or her crime. The key variables, rather, are:

- Racial discrimination in death-sentencing, which has been documented repeatedly. For instance, in the five-year period following their re-institution of the death penalty, the sentencing patterns in Georgia and Florida were as follows: when black kills white—Georgia, 20.1% (32 of 159 cases) and Florida, 13.7% (34 of 249); white kills white—Georgia, 5.7% (35 of 614) and Florida, 5.2% (80 of 1,547); white kills black—

Georgia, 2.9% (one of 34) and Florida, 4.3% (three of 69); black kills black—Georgia, 0.8% (11 of 1,310) and Florida, 0.7% (three of 69).

A fair objection may be that these statistics are too stark because they fail to take into account other neutral variables—*e.g.*, the brutality of the crime and the number and age of the victims. Nevertheless, many subsequent studies, whose validity has been confirmed in a major analysis for Congress by the General Accounting Office, have addressed these issues. They uniformly have found that, even when all other factors are held constant, the races of the victim and defendant are critical variables in determining who is sentenced to death.

Thus, black citizens are the victim of double discrimination. From initial charging decisions to plea bargaining to jury sentencing, they are treated more harshly when they are defendants, but their lives are given less value when they are victims. Moreover, all-white or virtually all-white juries still are commonplace in many places.

One common reaction to this evidence is not to deny it, but to attempt to evade the facts by taking refuge in the assertion that any effective system for guarding against racial discrimination would mean the end of the death penalty. Such a statement is a powerful admission that governments are incapable of running racially neutral capital punishment systems. The response of any fair-minded person should be that, if such is the case, governments should not be running capital punishment systems.

- Income discrimination. Most capital defendants can not afford an attorney, so the court must appoint counsel. Every major study of this issue, including those of the Powell Commission appointed by Chief Justice William Rehnquist, the American Bar Association, the Association of the Bar of the City of New York, and innumerable scholarly journals, has found that the quality of defense representation in capital murder trials generally is far lower than in felony cases.

  The field is a highly specialized one, and since the states have failed to pay the amounts necessary to attract competent counsel, there is an overwhelming record of poor people being subjected to convictions and death sentences that equally or more culpable—but more affluent—defendants would not have suffered.

- Mental disability. Jurors are more likely to sentence to death people who seem different from themselves than individuals who seem similar to themselves. That is the reality underlying the stark fact that those with mental disabilities are sentenced to death at a rate far higher than can be justified by any neutral explanation. This reflects prejudice, pure and simple.

Fact: Capital punishment inevitably will be inflicted on the innocent.

It is ironic that, just as New York was reinstating the death penalty, it was in the midst of a convulsive scandal involving the widespread fabrication of evidence by the New York State Police that had led to scores of people—

including some innocent ones—being convicted and sentenced to prison terms. Miscarriages of justice unquestionably will occur in any human system, but the death penalty presents two special problems in this regard:

- The arbitrary factors discussed above have an enormous negative impact on accuracy. In combination with the emotional atmosphere generally surrounding capital cases, they lead to a situation where the truth-finding process in capital cases is *less* reliable than in others. Indeed, a 1993 House of Representatives subcommittee report found 48 instances over the previous two decades in which innocent people had been sentenced to death.
- The stark reality is that death is final. A mistake can not be corrected if the defendant has been executed.

How often innocent people have been executed is difficult to quantify; once a defendant has been executed, few resources generally are devoted to the continued investigation of the case. Nonetheless, within the past few years, independent investigations by major news organizations have uncovered three cases, two in Florida and one in Mississippi, where people were put to death for crimes they did not commit. Over time, others doubtless will come to light (while still others will remain undiscovered), but it will be too late.

The fact that the system sometimes works—for those who are lucky enough to obtain somehow the legal and investigative resources or media attention necessary to vindicate their claims of innocence—does not mean that most innocent people on Death Row are equally fortunate. Moreover, many Death Row inmates who have been exonerated would have been executed if the legal system had moved more quickly, as would occur if, as those now in power in Congress have proposed, Federal *habeas corpus* is eviscerated.

The death penalty is not just useless—it is positively harmful and diverts resources from genuine crime control measures. Arbitrarily selecting out for execution not the worst criminals, but a racially determined handful of the poorest, most badly represented, least mentally healthy, and unluckiest defendants—some of whom are innocent—breeds cynicism about the entire criminal justice system.

Thus, the Criminal Justice Section of the New York State Bar Association—which includes prosecutors, judges, and defense attorneys—opposed reinstitution of the death penalty because of "the enormous cost associated with such a measure, and the serious negative impact on the delivery of prosecution and defense services throughout the state that will result." Meanwhile, Chief Justice Dixon of the Louisiana Supreme Court put it starkly: "Capital punishment is destroying the system."

POSTSCRIPT

Is Capital Punishment Justified?

The death penalty is currently a hotly debated topic with a rapidly growing literature. The two main arguments in favor of capital punishment consider its deterrence effects and the moral argument that an ultimate punishment is needed for certain heinous crimes. The latter argument is the main thesis of Walter Bern's *For Capital Punishment: Crime and the Morality of the Death Penalty* (University Press of America, 1991). The moral argument against capital punishment is presented in most treatments of the topic but particularly in *Executing Justice: The Moral Meaning of the Death Penalty* by Lloyd Steffen (Pilgrim Press, 1998) and in *Punishment and the Death Penalty: The Current Debate*, Robert M. Baird and Stuart E. Rosenbaum, eds. (Prometheus Books, 1995). Two books that present various religious views are James J. Megivern, *The Death Penalty: An Historical and Theological Survey* (Paulist Press, 1997) and Gardner C. Hanks, *Against the Death Penalty: Christian and Secular Arguments Against the Death Penalty* (Herald Press, 1997). For books that present various viewpoints on this debate see Hugo Adam Bedau, ed., *The Death Penalty in America: Current Controversies* (Oxford University Press, 1997); Mark Costanzo, *Just Revenge: Costs and Consequences of the Death Penalty* (St. Martin's Press, 1997); and Stephen E. Schonebaum, ed., *Does Capital Punishment Deter Crime?* (Greenhaven Press, 1998). The main argument against capital punishment is that innocent people are executed and some recent works that present evidence of this include Barry Scheck, Peter Neufeld, and Jim Dwyer, *Actual Innocence: Five Days to Execution and Other Dispatches from the Wrongly Convicted* (Doubleday, 2000) and Rob Warden and David L. Protess, *A Promise of Justice: The Eighteen-Year Fight to Save Four Innocent Men* (Hyperion Press, 1998). For historical treatments of the death penalty see Laura E. Randa, ed., *Society's Final Solution: A History and Discussion of the Death Penalty* (University Press of America, 1997); James R. Acker, et al., eds., *America's Experiment With Capital Punishment* (Carolina Academic Press, 1998); Bryan Vila and Cynthia Morris, eds., *Capital Punishment in the United States: A Documentary History* (Greenwood Press, 1997); and Herbert H. Haines, *Against Capital Punishment: The Anti-Death Penalty Movement in America 1972–1994* (Oxford University Press, 1996). Two works that explore the racial dimension of this issue are David Cole, *No Equal Justice: Race and Class in the American Criminal Justice System* (New Press, 1999) and Jesse Jackson, *Legal Lynching: Racism, Injustice and the Death Penalty* (Marlowe and Company, 1996).

On the Internet ...

SocioSite: Sociological Subject Areas

This large sociological site from the University of Amsterdam provides many discussions and references of interest to students regarding the environment.

http://www.pscw.uva.nl/sociosite/TOPICS/

United Nations Environment Program (UNEP)

The UNEP offers links to environmental topics of critical concern to sociologists. The site will direct you to useful databases and global resource information.

http://www.unep.ch

William Davidson Institute

The William Davidson Institute at the University of Michigan Business School is dedicated to the understanding and promotion of economic transition. Consult this site for discussions of topics related to the changing global economy and the effects of globalization on society.

http://www.wdi.bus.umich.edu

Worldwatch Institute Home Page

The Worldwatch Institute is dedicated to fostering the evolution of an environmentally sustainable society in which human needs are met without threatening the health of the natural environment. This site provides access to *World Watch Magazine* and *State of the World 2000*.

http://www.worldwatch.org

WWW Virtual Library: Demography and Population Studies

This is a definitive guide to demography and population studies. A multitude of important links to information about global poverty and hunger can be found at this site.

http://coombs.anu.edu.au/ResFacilities/DemographyPage.htm

PART 6

The Future: Population/Environment/ Society

*C**an a world with limited resources support an unlimited population? This question has taken on new dimensions as we start a new century. Technology has increased enormously in the last 100 years, as have worldwide population growth and new forms of pollution that threaten to undermine the world's fragile ecological support system. Will technology itself be the key to controlling or accommodating an increased population along with the resulting increase in waste production? All nations have a stake in the health of the planet and the world economy. Is America in a political and economic position to meet these global challenges? There are also domestic challenges. Is the American economy slipping in its ability to improve the quality of our lives? Are we better off today than two decades ago?*

- Does Population Growth Threaten Humanity?

- Is Life Getting Better in the United States?

ISSUE 18

Does Population Growth Threaten Humanity?

YES: David Pimentel and Marcia Pimentel, from "Population Growth, Environmental Resources, and the Global Availability of Food," *Social Research* (Spring 1999)

NO: D. Gale Johnson, from "Food Security and World Trade Prospects," *American Journal of Agricultural Economics* (December 1998)

ISSUE SUMMARY

YES: Bioscientists David Pimentel and Marcia Pimentel describe the decline and also the limits of the resources used to produce food. They warn that further population growth is likely to increase worldwide malnourishment.

NO: Professor of economics D. Gale Johnson argues that world food security will increase in the next quarter century because incomes are rising. Johnson states that food production increases will exceed increases in demand.

Much of the literature on socioeconomic development in the 1960s was premised on the assumption of inevitable material progress for all. It largely ignored the impacts of development on the environment and presumed that the availability of raw materials would not be a problem. The belief was that all societies would get richer because all societies were investing in new equipment and technologies that would increase productivity and wealth. Theorists recognized that some poor countries were having trouble developing, but they blamed those problems on the deficiencies of the values and attitudes of those countries and on inefficient organizations.

In the late 1960s and early 1970s an intellectual revolution occurred. Environmentalists had criticized the growth paradigm throughout the 1960s, but they were not taken very seriously at first. By the end of the 1960s, however, marine scientist Rachel Carson's book *Silent Spring* (Alfred A. Knopf, 1962) had worked its way into the public's consciousness. Carson's book traced the noticeable loss of birds to the use of pesticides. Her book made the middle and upper classes in the United States realize that pollution affected complex ecological systems in ways that put even the wealthy at risk.

In 1968 Paul Ehrlich, a professor of population studies, published *The Population Bomb* (Ballantine Books), which stated that overpopulation was the major problem facing mankind. Ehrlich explained why he thought the death of the world was imminent:

> Because the human population of the planet is about five times too large, and we're managing to support all these people—at today's level of misery— only by spending our capital, burning our fossil fuels, dispersing our mineral resources and turning our fresh water into salt water. We have not only overpopulated but overstretched our environment. We are poisoning the ecological systems of the earth—systems upon which we are ultimately dependent for all of our food, for all of our oxygen and for all of our waste disposal.

In 1973 *The Limits to Growth* (Universe Publishing) by Donella H. Meadows et al. was published. It presented a dynamic systems computer model for world economic, demographic, and environmental trends. When the computer model projected trends into the future, it predicted that the world would experience ecological collapse and population die-off unless population growth and economic activity were greatly reduced.

Let us examine the population growth rates from the past, present, and future. At about A.D. 0, the world population consisted of approximately one-quarter billion people. It took about 1,650 years to double this number to one-half billion and 200 years to double again to 1 billion. The next doubling took only about 80 years, and the last doubling took about 45 years (from 2 billion in 1930 to about 4 billion in 1975). The world population may double again to 8 billion sometime between 2010 and 2020.

Is population growth jeopardizing the prospects for future generations? Although many argue that population growth does indeed threaten humanity, others counter that the world's supply of food will increase enough to feed the growing population but advances in biological and chemical sciences in recent years can be seen as the answer to potential food shortages. Distributing the food to the entire population is more of a problem than producing enough.

Some important questions to consider include: How much can the human population actually increase? Will it continue to grow at current rates or will it stabilize? Will resources be completely depleted before people figure out ways to replenish them? Can progress compensate for demand? These questions are important to keep in mind as you consider the effects of population growth.

In the following selections, David Pimentel and Marcia Pimentel argue that we need to control population growth and to quickly reverse the deterioration of the environment that is occurring throughout the world. D. Gale Johnson counters that improved technology and increased incomes will increase world food security.

317

David Pimentel and Marcia Pimentel  **YES**

Population Growth, Environmental Resources, and the Global Availability of Food

Agricultural shortages exist because the human population is increasing faster than the food production capability of the agricultural system. Uneven distribution of food, inability to afford food, and political unrest also threaten world food security for human society.

Currently, more than three billion humans worldwide are malnourished; this is the largest number and proportion of hungry people ever recorded in history (WHO, 1996)! Based on current rates of increase, the world population is projected to double to more than 12 billion in less than 50 years (PRB, 1997). As the world population continues to expand at a rate of 1.5%/year—adding more than a quarter million people daily—the task of providing adequate food becomes an increasingly difficult problem. The number of malnourished people could conceivably reach four to five billion in future decades.

Reports from the Food and Agriculture Office (FAO) of the United Nations and the U.S. Department of Agriculture, as well as numerous other international organizations, further confirm the serious nature of the global food supply problem (NAS, 1994). For example, the *per capita* availability of world cereal grains, which make up 80% of the world's food supply, has been declining since 1983 (Figure 1) (Kendall and Pimentel, 1994). These shortages have economic consequences as well, as is reflected in recent major increases in the price of cereal grains (USDA, 1996).

Because the world population continues to expand, more pressure than ever before is being placed on the basic resources that are essential for food production. Unfortunately, the human population is growing exponentially, whereas food production can only increase linearly. Furthermore, degradation of land, water, energy, and biological resources that are vital to a sustainable agriculture continues unabated (Pimentel et al., 1998a).

Figure 1

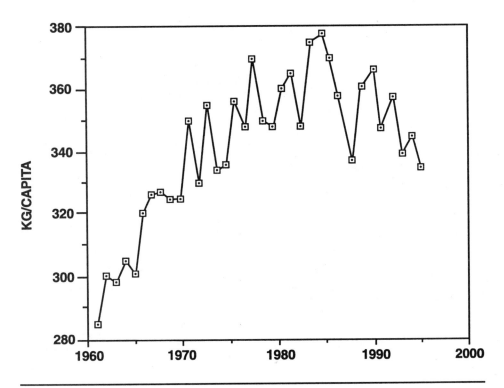

World Cereal Grain Produced Per Capita

Note: Adapted from Harris, 1996; WATI database system compiled by the Economic Research Division, USDA, and FAO Production Yearbooks.

Agricultural Resources

More than 99% of the world's food supply comes from the land; less than 1% is obtained from oceans and other aquatic habitats (FAO, 1991; Pimentel et al., 1998a). As mentioned previously, the continued production of an adequate food supply is directly dependent on the availability of ample quantities of fertile land, fresh water, energy, and natural biodiversity. And obviously, as the human population grows, the requirements for all these resources escalates. Even if these resources are never completely depleted, their supply, on a per capita basis, will decline significantly because they must be divided among more and more people.

Land

Throughout the world, fertile cropland is being lost from production at an alarming rate. This is clearly illustrated by the diminishing amount of land now

Figure 2

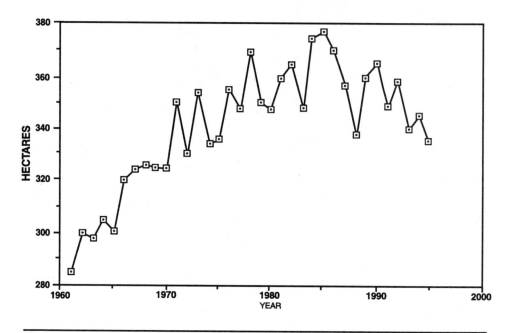

World Cropland in Cereal Grain Production (x 1000 ha).

Note: Adapted from Harris, 1996; WATI database system compiled by the Economic Research Division, USDA, and FAO Production Yearbooks.

devoted to cereal grains (Figure 2). Soil erosion by wind and water, in addition to general overuse of the land, are responsible for the loss of about 30% of the world's cropland during the past 40 years (WRI, 1994; Pimentel et al., 1995). The natural reformation of a mere 25 mm (1 inch) of fertile soil takes 500 years; to sustain adequate crop production, a soil depth of 150 mm is needed.

Most eroded and unproductive agricultural land is now being replaced with cleared forest land and/or marginal land. Indeed, the urgent need for more cropland accounts for more than 60% of the world's deforestation (Myers, 1994). Despite such land replacement strategies, per capita world cropland is declining, currently standing at only 0.27 ha per capita. This is only about 50% of the 0.5 ha per capita that is considered the minimum land area needed for the production of a diverse diet similar to that of the United States and Europe (Lal and Stewart, 1990; Pimentel et al., 1998a). Other countries have even less land; for example, China now has only 0.08 ha available per capita, about 15% of the accepted minimum (Pimentel et al., 1998a).

Water

Rainfall, and its collection in rivers, lakes and vast underground aquifers, provides the water needed by humans for their personal survival and diverse activities.

Fresh water is critical for all vegetation, especially crops. All plants transpire massive amounts of water during the growing season. For example, a hectare of corn, producing about 8,000 kg, transpires more than five million liters of water during just one growing season (Pimentel et al., 1997a). This means that more than eight million liters of water must reach each hectare during the growing season both as rainfall and irrigation, to provide the adequate water supply for crop production. In total, agricultural production consumes more fresh water than any other human activity. About 70% of the world's fresh water supply is consumed, or used up by agriculture, making it unavailable for other uses (Postel, 1996).

Water resources are continually stressed as populous cities, states, and countries increase their withdrawal of water from rivers, lakes, and aquifers every year. For example, by the time the Colorado River reaches Mexico it has dwindled down to a trickle (Sheridan, 1983; Postel, 1996). Also, the great Ogalla aquifer in the central U.S. is suffering an overdraft rate that is about 140% above its natural recharge rate (Gleich, 1993). Water shortages in the U.S. and elsewhere in the world are already reflected in the per capita decline in crop irrigation that has occurred during the past twenty years (Postel, 1996).

To compound the water problem, about 40% of the world population lives in regions that directly compete for shared water resources (Gleick, 1993). In China, for example, more than 300 cities already are short of water, and these shortages are intensifying as Chinese urban areas and industries expand (WRI, 1994). Serious competition for water resources among individuals, industries, and regions both within and between countries is growing throughout the world community (Gleick, 1993).

In addition to the quantity of water available, water purity also is vitally important. Diseases associated with impure and unsanitary water systems rob people of their health, nutrients, and livelihood. These problems are most serious in developing countries, where about 90% of common diseases can be traced to a lack of pure water (WHO, 1992; Pimentel et al., 1998b). Worldwide, about four billion cases of disease and approximately six million deaths are caused by impure water or are water-borne each year (Pimentel et al., 1998b). Furthermore, when a person is stricken with diarrhea, malaria, or other serious disease, from 5% to 20% of an individual's food intake is used by the body to offset the stress of the disease, further diminishing the benefits of his/her food intake (Pimentel et al., 1998b). Disease and malnutrition problems appear to be particularly serious in the third world, where poverty and poor sanitation is endemic (Shetty and Shetty, 1993).

Poverty, disease, and malnutrition are especially serious in cities, particularly third-world cities. The number of people living in urban areas currently doubles every 10 to 20 years, creating environmental problems that include a lack of water and sanitation, increased air pollution, and significant food short-ages. For these reasons, the potential for the spread and increase of disease is especially great in urban areas (Science, 1995).

Energy

Energy from many sources, most importantly fossil energy sources, is a prime resource used in food production. About 75% of the fossil energy used each year throughout the world is consumed by populations living in developed countries. Of this energy, about 17% is expended in the production, processing, and packaging of food products (Pimentel and Pimentel, 1996). In particular, the intensive farming technologies characteristic of developed countries rely on massive amounts of fossil energy for fertilizers, pesticides, irrigation, and machines that substitute for human labor. In contrast, developing countries use fossil energy primarily for fertilizers and irrigation to help maintain yields, rather than to reduce human labor inputs (Giampietro and Pimentel, 1993).

The present world supply of oil is projected to last approximately 50 years at current production rates (Campbell, 1997; Duncan, 1997; Youngquist, 1997; Duncan and Youngquist, 1998; Kerr, 1998). The world's natural gas supply is considered adequate for about 50 years, and the coal supply for about 100 years (Youngquist, 1997). These projections, however, are based on current consump-tion rates and current population numbers; if population and consumption levels continue to increase, these fossil energy stores could be depleted even faster.

Youngquist (1997) reports that current oil and gas exploration drilling data has not borne out some of the earlier optimistic estimates of the amount of these resources projected to be in the United States. Both the production rate and proven reserves have continued to decline. Reliable analyses suggest that by now (1999) the United States has consumed about three-quarters of the re-coverable oil that was ever in the ground, and that we are currently consuming the last 25% of U.S. oil resources (Bartlett, 1998). Projections suggest that U.S. domestic oil and natural gas production will be substantially less in 20 years than it is today. Even now, U.S. oil supplies are not sufficient to meet domestic needs, and oil is imported in increasing yearly amounts (Youngquist, 1997). Im-porting 60% of its oil puts the United States economy at risk, due to fluctuating oil prices and difficult political situations, such as occurred during the 1973 oil crisis and the 1991 Gulf War (U.S. Congressional Record, 1997).

Biodiversity

A productive and sustainable agricultural system, as well as the quality of hu-man life, also depends on maintaining the integrity of the natural biodiversity that exists on earth. Diverse species, though most are small in size, serve as natural enemies to control pests, help degrade wastes, improve soil quality, fix nitrogen for plants, pollinate crops and other vegetation, and provide numerous other vital services for humans and their environment (Pimentel et al., 1997b). Consider that one-third of all crops worldwide require insect pollination. Hu-mans have no technology to substitute for this vital pollination task, or for many of the other contributions provided by the estimated 10 million species that inhabit the earth (Pimentel et al., 1997b).

Biodiversity has an economic value for the world as well. For instance, it is estimated that the benefits of natural species to the U.S. economy is more than $300 billion/year, and approximately $3 trillion/year for the world (Pimentel et al., 1997b).

Food Distribution

Many assumptions have been made as to how market mechanisms and international trade will function to effectively ensure against future food shortages. Unfortunately, the biological and physical limits of resources are typically overlooked in this equation. When these limits of resources are reached, food exports and imports will no longer be a viable options for countries. At that point, food importation for rich countries will only be sustained by starvation of the poor. In the final analysis, the existing biological and physical resource constraints regulate and limit all food production systems.

These concerns about sustainable food sources for the future are supported by two observations. First, most of the 183 nations of the world now are dependent on food imports. Most of these imports are cereal gain *surpluses* produced only in those countries that now have relatively low population densities, where intensive agriculture is practiced and where surpluses are common. For instance, the United States, Canada, Australia, France, and Argentina provide about 80% of the cereal exports of the world market (WRI, 1992). This situation is expected to change, if, the U.S. population doubles in the next 70 years as projected by the current population growth rate (USBC, 1996). Then, instead of exporting cereals and other food resources, these foods will have to be retained domestically to feed 540 million hungry Americans. The United States will no longer be able to serve as a primary food exporter.

In the future, when the four major food exporting countries retain surpluses for home use, Egypt, Jordan, and countless other countries in Africa and Asia will be without the food imports that are essential to their survival. China, which now imports many tons of food, illustrates the severity of this problem. If, as Brown (1995) predicts, China's population increases by 500 million beyond their present 1.2 billion and their soil erosion continues unabated, it will need to import 200–400 million tons of food grains each year starting in 2050. This minimal quantity is equal to more than the current grain exports of *all* the current exporting nations mentioned earlier (USBC, 1996). Based on realistic trends, by 2050, sufficient food supplies probably will not be available for import by China or any other nation on the international market (Brown, 1995).

Technology

Over time, technology has been instrumental in increasing industrial and agricultural production, improving transportation and communications, advancing human health care, and generally improving many aspects of human life. However, much of technology's success is based on the availability of the natural resources of the earth.

In no area is this more evident than in agricultural production. No current or conceivable future technology will be able to double the world's arable land. Granted, technologically produced fertilizers are effective in enhancing the fertility of eroded croplands, but their production relies on the diminishing supply of fossil fuels. In fact, fertilizer use per capita during the past decade has decreased 23% and continues to decline, probably due to increasing economic costs (IFDC, 1998).

The increase in the size and speed of fishing vessels has not resulted in increases in per capita fish catch (Pimentel and Pimentel, 1996). To the contrary, in regions like eastern Canada, over-fishing has become so severe that about 80,000 fisherman have no fish to catch, and the entire industry has been lost (W. Rees, University of British Columbia, personal communication, 1996).

Consider also that the available supplies of fresh water must be shared by more individuals, for the expanding agriculture and industry required to support an increasing population. No currently available technology can double the flow of the Colorado River; the shrinking ground water resources in vast aquifers cannot be refilled by human technology. Rainfall is the only legitimate *supplier* of water.

Certainly improved technology can continue to help increase food production. Technology can result in more effective management and conservation of resources, but technology cannot produce an unlimited flow of those vital natural resources that are the raw material for sustained agricultural production. What technology can be used to stop the decline in per capita cereal grain production, that has been diminishing since 1983 and continues to decline (Figure 1)?

Biotechnology has the potential for some advances in agriculture, provided genetic modifications are cautiously and wisely used. However, the biotechnology developments from more than 20 years ago have not been able to stem the decline in per capita food production during the past 15 years. Currently, about 40% of the research effort in biotechnology is devoted to the development of herbicide resistance in crops (Paoletti and Pimentel, 1996). This technology will not achieve its promise to increase crop yields, but it will increase the use of chemical herbicides and the pollution of the environment.

What of the Future and Ecological Resources?

We can no longer afford to ignore the fact that per capita food production has been declining for more than a decade, that now more than three billion people are malnourished (WHO, 1996). Related to this decline has been a per capita decrease in availability of the following resources: Fertilizers, 23%; cropland, 20%; irrigation, 12%; forest products and fish, 10%.

Strategies for global food security must be based first and foremost on the conservation and ecological management of the land, water, energy, and all biological resources that are essential for a sustainable agricultural system. Our stewardship of world resources must change. The basic needs of all people must be brought into balance with the life sustaining natural resources. The conservation of these resources will require the coordinated efforts of all individuals and all countries. Once these finite resources are exhausted they cannot be replaced by human technology. More efficient and environmentally sound agricultural technologies must be developed and put into practice to support the sustainability of agriculture and life on earth (Pimentel and Pimentel, 1996).

Unfortunately, none of these ecologically sound conservation measures will be sufficient to ensure adequate food supplies for future generations unless the growth in the human population is simultaneously curtailed. Several studies have confirmed that in order to enjoy a relatively high standard of living, the optimum human population should be less than 200 million for the United States and less than two billion for the world (Pimentel et al., 1998a). This seemingly harsh projection assumes, that from now until such an optimum population is achieved, *all* strategies for the conservation of soil, water, energy, and biological resources will be successfully implemented and an ecologically sound, productive environment will be maintained. The lives and livelihood of future generations depend on what the present generation is willing to do now to make agriculture sustainable and conserve the world's ecological resources.

References

"Cities as Disease Vectors," *Science* 270 (1995): 1125.

Bartlett, A. A., "An Analysis of U.S. and World Oil Production Patterns Using Hubbert Curves," *Journal of American Petroleum Geologists,* 1998.

Brown, L. R., *Who Will Feed China?* (New York: W. W. Norton, 1997).

Campbell, C. J., *The Coming Oil Crisis* (New York: Multi-Science Publishing Company & Petroconsultants S. A., 1997).

Duncan, R. C., "The World Petroleum Life-Cycle: Encircling the Production Peak," *Space Studies Institute* (May 9, 1997): 1–8.

Duncan, R. C. and Youngquist, W., *Encircling the Peak of World Oil Production.* Issue # 2 Paper of the World Forecasting Program, 1998, 22 pp.

FAO, *Food Balance Sheets* (Rome: Food and Agriculture Organization of the United Nations, 1991).

Giampietro, M. and Pimentel, D., *The Tightening Conflict: Population, Energy Use, and the Ecology of Agriculture,* Grant, L., ed. (Teaneck, NJ: Negative Population Growth, Inc., 1993).

Gleick, P. H., *Water in Crisis* (New York: Oxford University Press, 1993).

Harris, J. M., "World Agricultural Futures: Regional Sustainability and Ecological Limits," *Ecological Economics* 17:2 (1993): 95.

IFDC, *Global and Regional Data on Fertilizer Production and Consumption 1961/62–1995/96* (Muscle Shoals, AL: International Fertilizer Development Center, 1993).

Kendall, H. W. and Pimentel, D., "Constraints on the Expansion of the Global Food Supply," *Ambio* 23(1994): 198–205.

Kerr, R. A., "The Next Oil Crisis Looms Large—and Perhaps Close," *Science* 281 (21 August, 1998): 1128–1131.

Lal, R. and Stewart, B. A., *Soil Degradation* (New York: Springer-Verlag, 1990).

Myers, N., "Tropical Deforestation: Rates and Patterns," in *The Causes of Tropical Deforestation,* Brown, K. and Pearce, D. W., eds. (Vancouver, British Columbia: UBC Press, 1994).

NAS, *Population Summit of the World's Scientific Academies* (Washington, DC: National Academy of Sciences Press, 1994).

Paoletti, M. G. and Pimentel, D., "Genetic Engineering in Agriculture and the Environment," *BioScience* 46:9 (1996):L 665–673.

Pimentel, D. and Pimentel, M., *Food, Energy and Society* (Niwet, CO: Colorado Press, 1996).

Pimentel, D., Harvey, C., Resosudarmo, P., Sinclair, K., Kurz, D., McNair, M., Crist, S., Sphpritz, L., Fitton, L., Saffouri, R., and Blair, R., "Environmental and Economic Costs of Soil Erosion and Conservation Benefits," *Science* 267(1995): 1117–1123.

Pimentel, D., Houser, J., Preiss, E., White, O., Fng, H., Mesnick, L., Barsky, T., Tariche, S., Schreck, J., and Alpert, S., "Water Resources: Agriculture, the Environment, and Society," *BioScience* 47:2 (1997a): 97–106.

Pimentel, D., Wilson, C., McCullum, C., Huang, R., Dwen, P., Flack, J., Tran, Q., Saltman, T., and Cliff, B., "Economic and Environmental Benefits of Biodiversity," *BioScience* 47:11 (1997b): 747–757.

Pimentel, D., Bailey, O., Kim, P., Mullaney, E., Calabrese, J., Walman, F., Nelson, F., and Yao, X., "Will the Limits of the Earth's Resources Control Human Populations?" *Environment, Development and Sustainability* (1998a).

Pimentel, D., Tort, M., D'Anna, L., Krawic, A., Berger, J., Rossman, J., Mugo, F., Doon, Shriberg, M., Howard, Lee, S., and Talbot, J., "Increasing Disease Incidence: Environmental Degradation and Population Growth," *BioScience* 48:10 (1998b): 817–826.

Postel, S., *Last Oasis: Facing Water Scarcity.* (New York: W. W. Norton and Co., 1996).

PRB, *World Population Data Sheet* (Washington, DC: Population Reference Bureau, 1997).

Sheridan, D., "The Colorado—an Engineering Wonder without Enough Water," *Smithsonian* (February 1983): 45–54.

Shetty, P. S. and Shetty, N., "Parasitic Infection and Chronic Energy Deficiency in Adults," *Supplement to Parasitiology* 107 (1993): S159–S167.

U.S. Congressional Record, "U.S. Foreign Oil Consumption for the Week Ending October 3," *Congressional Record (Senate)* 143 (October 8, 1997): S10625.

USBC, *Statistical Abstract of the United States 1993,* 200th ed. (Washington, DC: U.S. Bureau of the Census, U.S. Government Printing Office, 1996).

USDA, "USDA Weekly Feedstuffs Report," *USDA Weekly Feedstuffs Report* 02 (25) 1996: 1–2.

WHO, *Annual Statistics* (Geneva: World Health Organization, 1992).

WHO, "Micronutrient Malnutrition—Half of the World's Population Affected," 13 November 1996: 1–4.

WRI, World Resources (New York: Oxford University Press, 1997).

WRI, *World Resources 1994–95* (Washington, DC: World Resources Institute, 1994).

Youngquist, W., *Geodestinies: The Inevitable Control of Earth Resources Over Nations and Individuals* (Portland, OR: National Book Company, 1997).

Food Security and World Trade Prospects

F ood security depends on available world supplies of food, the income of the designated population, and the population's access to the available supplies. Consequently, though seldom recognized in national food security policies, there is a direct relationship between food security, world trade in food, and the domestic policies that govern access to international markets for food. On all three scores, I believe we can be optimistic about improvements in world food security over the next quarter century.

Over the next quarter century, the world's supply of food will grow somewhat more rapidly than will the demand for it, leading to lower real prices of food. Thus, the trend of food prices, as measured by grain prices, is likely to continue the trend of the current century, though at a slower rate of decline.[1] The remarkable reduction in the international price of grain that has occurred in [the twentieth] century is given all too little emphasis in discussions of the world food situation, certainly so in the discussions of the food pessimists.

I am confident that the real per capita incomes of the majority of the population in the developing countries will continue to increase, contributing to an improvement in food security. Finally, I believe that, with the changes in agricultural policies in the major industrial countries, world trade in farm products, especially grains, will be further liberalized in the future. In addition, more and more developing countries are reducing barriers to trade, thus increasing access to world food supplies. Thus, all the broad trends point to an improvement in world food security and a reduction in the number of persons adversely affected by both long-term or short-term inadequate access to food.

This does not mean that in every country food security will improve. Some governments may continue to follow national and trade policies related to food that restrict domestic food production, limit the growth of per capita incomes, and restrict access to the available world food supplies. When this happens, food security and adequacy will not be improved or not improved as much as they potentially could be. At this time, there can be little doubt that the poor performance of agriculture and the insecurity of food supplies in sub-Saharan Africa over the past quarter century have been due primarily to inappropriate policies—to policies that discriminated against agriculture and

From D. Gale Johnson, "Food Security and World Trade Prospects," *American Journal of Agricultural Economics*, vol. 80, no. 5 (1998). Copyright © 1998 by The American Agricultural Economics Association. Reprinted by permission of Blackwell Publishers, Ltd. Some notes omitted.

resulted in large-scale governmental interventions in international trade. Misgovernment plus civil and ethnic wars have exacted and continue to exact a heavy toll on the people of Africa.

There are those who argue that Africa's agricultural problems stem from the low and declining real prices of their major exportable products. But even a casual analysis indicates that the prices of agricultural exports from the region declined no more, in real terms, than did the prices of wheat, corn, and rice. Until policies are changed—and they are changing in a number of countries —and peace prevails, there will be little improvement in food security in this region of the world. When policies are inappropriate, farmers find themselves at an enormous disadvantage in making effective use of their natural and human resources.

A Brief Look at the Past

Before looking to the future, let us briefly look at the developments in world food supplies during the last half of the twentieth century. During these years, there has been more improvement in the available supplies of food for the world and in the developing countries than in all of previous human history. Much of the improvement occurred after 1960. Between 1960 and 1990, the per capita caloric supplies in the developing countries increased by 27%, reaching an average of 2,473 in 1988–90 (FAO). The improvement in per capita caloric supplies occurred while population growth was at the highest rate ever recorded and while the real prices of grains in international markets declined by approximately 40% from their levels in the late 1950s. Was it not quite remarkable that per capita food supplies in the developing countries reached their historic peak while grain prices fell to their lowest level in the twentieth century and while population was growing rapidly? This certainly does not support the view that supply lagged behind demand.

What brought about this remarkable development? Basically, it was the application of modern biological and chemical sciences to agriculture, first in the developed countries and, with a lag, in the developing countries. I doubt if there are many who know that, during the last half of the 1930s, the grain yields per hectare were the same in developing and developed countries at 1.15 tons per hectare—world yields are now nearly 2.5 times that amount (FAO). A yield differential soon emerged between the developed and developing countries, reaching 59% in 1961–65 but declining to 29% in 1990–92. I believe that it is reasonable to assume that the differential will narrow even further in the future.

Success Goes Unrecognized

It is perhaps useful to pause at this time to ask why it was that, during a period with such positive developments, there were repeated claims that the growth of demand for food was outpacing the growth of supply. True, since 1960 there have been three price spikes—in 1972–74, 1979–81, and 1995–96. The spikes lasted no more than two or three years and did not interrupt the long-term decline in real grain prices. Yet throughout this period, doom and gloom made the headlines—Lester Brown's repeated and erroneous predictions, Paul Ehrlich's claim that there would be mass starvation in the world in the 1970s, and the Club of Rome's prophecies of doom—to name a few of the doomsayers.

It is quite remarkable that, in 1994, researchers at three international agencies—the Food and Agriculture Organization, the International Food Policy Research Institute (Islam), and the World Bank (Bos et al.)—independently published studies of prospective trends in food demand and supply and came to the same conclusion. This conclusion was that the world food situation would continue to improve over the next two or so decades and that world grain prices would continue to decline (Islam). Yet these three competent studies received hardly any notice in the world's press while claims by Lester Brown that the world faced food shortages were widely reported, and even greater attention was given to his fanciful paper "Will China Starve the World?" What does this prove? A promising view of the future is not news, but a pessimistic view or prediction of a calamity is news. Bad news sells; good news doesn't.

Prospective Growth of Food Supply and Demand

It is difficult to believe that, given the record of the last four or five decades, there should be significant doubt about the world's ability to expand the supply of food more rapidly than the growth of demand over the next quarter century. Some argue that the rate of growth of food supply in the future will be slower than in the recent past—and they will be right. The rate of demand growth over the next three decades will be substantially less than between 1960 and 1990. True, real per capita incomes are anticipated to increase, and this will increase the per capita demand for food, especially through the shift toward livestock products. However, the big shifter of total demand for food is population growth. While you wouldn't believe it from what you read in the press, the rate of growth of population has slowed down, not by a little but by a lot. No country in Europe except Albania is now reproducing its population, and a considerable number of developing countries now have fertility rates below the replacement level as well—South Korea, Taiwan, Singapore, Hong Kong—and Turkey, Sri Lanka, and China have reached or are approaching that level.

The consensus estimate of the three major studies referred to above is that the annual growth in grain use (as a proxy for total food use) for 1990 to 2010 is projected at 1.5%–1.7% (Islam, p. 86). This compares with a growth of 2.46% for 1960–90 and represents a 30%–40% decrease in the rate of growth of world grain use. This is a very large decline.

The projections for 1990 to 2010 of an annual increase in grain production and use can be moved ahead for a further decade. The 1.5%–1.7% projected annual increase in grain production and consumption was based on a projected population growth rate of 1.5% annually. The population projections that Islam used have already been reduced from an annual rate of 1.5% to 1.385%. For 2010 to 2020, the projected annual rate of population growth is now about 1.1%. If the population projections hold true, the growth of per capita consumption in developing countries would be greater than projected in these studies or, more likely, the growth in world demand will be lower than projected.

Nonetheless, let us return to the original studies, accepting their data as then known. Their projections imply no increase in world per capita production and consumption of grain. How can this be? Does this bear out the predictions of the food pessimists? How can world per capita use or production of grain remain constant if the developing countries have income growth and increase their demand for grain both for direct consumption and indirect consumption through livestock products? Hopefully, this is exactly what will occur, and per capita grain use in developing countries will increase over the next quarter century as has been the case over the last half century. Assuming that per capita grain production and use in the developed countries remains constant or increases slightly, why was there not a projected increase in world per capita production or consumption? The reason is that the world per capita figures are almost meaningless in interpreting the changes in production, consumption, or income. The statement that the world's per capita production of grain is declining contains almost no useful information concerning consumption levels in either developing or developed countries.

The world per capita figure holds little meaning because, over time, it is based on shifting weights—the relative importance of the developing countries in world population has increased and is increasing. Since the developing countries have much lower per capita consumption than the developed countries, when they increase their per capita consumption, the world average may be unchanged or actually decline. For example, in the FAO grain production projections for 1990–92 to 2010, world per capita production is constant at 326 kilograms (Islam, p. 27). However, per capita production in both developed and developing countries was projected to increase—by 7% and 4%, respectively. This seeming anomaly resulted from the projected increase in the percentage of the world's population in the developing countries—from 77% in 1990 to 80.7% in 2010. Since per capita grain production in the developing countries in 1990–92 was 214 kilograms versus 692 kilograms in the developed countries, an increase in the relative weight of the developing countries had to have an adverse effect on the world average. The world average, by itself, tells little or nothing about what has occurred in individual regions or income groups when the relative importance of the units is included in the average change.

Much has been made of the decline in the rate of growth of world grain production and yields since 1990. This concern is largely misplaced. Much of the slowdown has been concentrated in Central and Eastern Europe and has occurred without the slightest negative impact on the supply of grain in the rest of the world. In fact, the demand for grain in that region has fallen by more than supply and the import of grain by the countries in the region has declined substantially—by approximately 30 million tons annually since the late 1980s. If the region had maintained grain production at the 1985–89 level, world grain production in 1996 would have been more than 100 million tons greater than it was. It would have increased by 11% compared to 1990 and at a compound annual rate of 1.8%. This is roughly the same as the annual rate of grain output growth during the 1980s, though at a slower rate than for 1960–90, but still faster than the less than 1.5% rate of world population growth for the 1990s (FAO).

Thus, it is not obvious that there has been a significant decline in the rate of growth of world grain production during the 1990s if we account for the drastic adjustments taking place in Central and Eastern Europe resulting from the difficulties of moving from a planned to a market economy. I believe that the territory of the former Soviet Union will emerge as a major grain exporter, though admittedly at a later date than I earlier believed (Johnson 1993). This possibility should be factored into long term projections of the world's supply potential as well as into the trade picture.

Why is it that many believe some reduction in the growth of food output would represent disaster? Given the demand conditions that are likely to prevail, it would be a disaster for the world's farmers if world output grew at the 1960–90 rate. Why is it that the literature on world food supply and demand seldom, if ever, mentions the effects of various outcomes on the welfare of farmers? If I were an agricultural policy maker in a developing country, I would give as much emphasis to the problems associated with low food prices as to food scarcity and high prices over the next quarter century. I believe that grain prices in the early 1990s were at such low levels that they discouraged expansion of grain production during the first half of the decade. Grain inventories declined, but this was a reasonable economic response to low and possibly falling prices. The 1995 and 1996 increases in grain prices were very short lived, with U.S. export prices of wheat and corn returning to the early 1990 prices by the end of 1997.

Price Variability May Increase

Policy developments now underway in the world have both positive and negative effects on price stability in world markets. The governments that have held large stocks of grain have discovered that holding grain stocks is very expensive, and they now have little or no interest in having stocks large enough to play a stabilizing role for world prices. Of course, in the past, the large stocks that had been held did not always restrain the price rises, as was true in 1972–74 because of policy errors made in pricing the grain sold to the USSR by the United States and Canada. On the other hand, there has been the liberalization of international trade in grain that will add a degree of stability to world grain prices. As I argued at the time, the steep increases in world grain prices in 1972–74 did not arise because of any serious shortfall in world grain production but was due to the policies followed by nearly all major exporters to protect their domestic consumers from the large increase in world grain prices (Johnson 1975). The European Community (EC), for example, taxed wheat exports in order to stabilize domestic prices. Both Canada and Australia restricted grain exports and held domestic prices significantly below world prices. Of the major exporters, only the United States permitted its domestic prices to reflect the world market prices and actually sharply increased its grain exports, at the expense of domestic use. This kind of intervention in grain markets is now much less likely than in the 1970s or 1980s, though one may note that, in 1995, the EU once again introduced an export tax on wheat and held domestic prices below world prices. The United States eliminated its export subsidies but at least let its prices equal the world market prices.

If there were (relatively) free trade in grains, world grain prices would be more stable than they are with current policies. Most governmental interventions that affect imports and exports add to price instability in world markets. The exception was when Canada and the United States held very large stocks and were willing to add to or release stocks when world prices moved outside a narrow range. All other policies that result in a difference between domestic and world prices act to destabilize international market prices. In spite of the liberalization of trade that has occurred, there is still some distance to go before the total world supply of a product is available to all at essentially the same price, after adjustment for quality and location.

Prospects for Trade

I find it difficult to say anything about the future of international trade in agricultural products, especially grain. Trade is a residual—for each country, it is the difference between production and consumption. Trade in grain has varied relatively little from an annual average of about 200 to 240 million tons since 1980. Researchers at IFPRI (Pinstrup-Andersen, Pandya-Lorch, and Rosegrant) project an increase in grain imports in the developing countries from approximately 95 million tons in 1993 to about 225 million tons in 2020. This conclusion rests on the expectation that grain imports will increase significantly in developing countries, especially in sub-Saharan Africa, South Asia, Latin America, and China.

Will world grain trade break out of its doldrums and increase by 50% over the next quarter century? I am not so sure. Except for sub-Saharan Africa, there is a significant possibility that the other developing areas will not markedly increase grain imports. Agricultural production growth in much of Latin America has been held back in recent years by overvalued currencies, which have taxed exports and encouraged imports, and high interest rates. The overvalued currencies will not go on forever, and when they are more realistically valued—due in part to a decline in the inflow of foreign capital—then agriculture will face a more encouraging economic environment and output may once again grow at rates that are at least as great as the growth in demand. While there are responsible researchers who believe that China may import 30 to 40 million tons of grain by 2020, I have my doubts. There is considerable potential for further increases in grain yields in China. The current official estimates of grain yields are too high by at least a third. The reason for this is that the grain-sown area is seriously underestimated—the total area of cropland is a third or more greater than is now officially recognized. If the output figure is approximately correct and it is divided by an underestimate of the grain-sown area, yields are significantly overestimated. The Chinese government knows of the underestimate of cropland and presumably will correct its data in the not too distant future, perhaps even in this century!

It needs to be recognized that the growth rate of China's population over the period from 1995 to 2025 is projected to be 23% (Bos et al.), only a little more than a third of the 66% increase in population between 1965 and 1995. It should be remembered that China was a substantial net importer of grain in 1979–84 and a net exporter from 1992–94. While it imported almost 19 million tons of grain in 1995, that year turned out to have a bumper crop and the importation was probably unnecessary and ended up as an addition to stocks and not to consumption. In 1997, China once again became a small net exporter of grain. Consequently, if China met the large increase in demand that occurred between 1979 and 1995, it is highly likely it will be able to meet the much smaller increase in demand over the next thirty years.[2]

I have recently returned from China, where, in May, the government introduced a price support policy designed to increase the real price of grain. The government of China is now concerned about the effects of having too much grain rather than too little. It fears that, if market prices are permitted to go too low, farmers will reduce future grain output, resulting in higher prices at some future date. The plan for grain output for 2000 was 500 million tons; this level was exceeded in 1996. China has huge grain stocks and, if it is successful in increasing the market prices of grain by 20%–30%, it will have even larger stocks. Thus, instead of China being an important importer of grain as the 20th Century ends, it is likely that it will be a net exporter.

During a period of rapid population growth—greater than 2% annually—India has achieved self-sufficiency in grain production over the past three decades. India's population growth rate is projected to decline to 1% annually by 2020. Even with rising incomes due to economic reforms, if realized, for cultural reasons, India is not likely to greatly expand its consumption of meat. The increase in demand for grain will come primarily from direct human consumption. The rate of increase in grain use will only slightly exceed the rate of population growth.

There exists a degree of pessimism about the ability to increase yields, especially of rice, in South Asia. There is evidence that there has been little or no increase in the yields of the high-yielding rice varieties for the past two decades or more. True, the rice yields have increased in South Asia, but this has been due, it is argued, to the replacement of the traditional varieties by the high-yield varieties and not because the yields of the latter have increased very much, if at all. One difficulty with such yield comparisons is that, presumably, the high-yield varieties were first introduced where their yield advantage was the greatest—under relatively favorable growing conditions—and as time went on, replaced the traditional varieties where both the relative advantage was less and the absolute yields were lower. Nonetheless, it probably is true that much of the observed yield increases have been due to the replacement of the traditional varieties and not from significant increases in the yield potential of the existing high-yield varieties.

Is this yield pessimism appropriate? Has IRRI exhausted its capacity to innovate? An announcement, apparently somewhat premature, that IRRI had developed a new high-yield variety that outyielded the current high-yield varieties by at least 20% was made some time ago. If this development is realized, it would go some considerable distance toward meeting the increased demand for rice in South Asia over the next quarter century. Obviously, my crystal ball may be as clouded as that of others. My purpose here is simply to raise questions concerning the prospects for a major increase in world grain trade. It could happen, but if I were a farmer in a country that exports grain, I would not now or in the near future make investments dependent on it actually occurring. I would wait and see.

A major factor of uncertainty with respect to world trade in grain is the prospective development of grain production in the former Soviet Union. The difficulties of the transition process have been much greater than anyone envisaged. Yet I believe that it will be only a matter of time before the combination of human and natural resources are utilized in efficient combinations and the area becomes a net grain exporter once again. . . .

Concluding Comments

I am an optimist about the future trends in food supply and demand. By that, I mean that there will be continued improvements in productivity, the rate of growth of supply will exceed that of demand, and real international prices of food will decline. Farmers will increase their real incomes only as they adjust to the changing conditions. The percentage of the world's resources used to produce food will continue to decline, and farmers must adjust to this fact.

This is not a new conclusion for me. I have been an optimist for the last three decades and I have been right. I have long been confident that farmers could expand food production at least as rapidly as demand. However, I must admit that I did not anticipate the large decline in the real prices of grain that has occurred since 1960. The decline in the real price and cost of grain was little short of a miracle, unprecedented in its magnitude. The gain in welfare for hundreds of millions—no, billions—of people was enormous, and the number that could have benefitted would have been even greater if more governments had followed appropriate policies with respect to agricultural production, prices, and trade.

I do not foresee such a large decline in costs and prices over the next three decades. But I do anticipate, along with some other researchers, that real grain and food prices will continue to decline in the years ahead. Farmers will continue to contribute to the wealth of nations.

Notes

1. Not everyone agrees that real grain or food prices will decline. Two recent studies conclude that real grain or food prices will increase. The studies are the OECD's *The Agricultural Outlook 1998–2003* and Luther Tweeten's recent study of global food supply and demand balance. The OECD study projects international price increases between 1997 and 2003 of 17% for wheat and 7% for corn. Tweeten is quite bullish for food prices, projecting an annual rate of price increase of more than 1.2% for the next two decades.

2. With rising real consumer incomes, there will be a significant increase in the demand for and consumption of livestock products. Will this increase in demand be large enough to offset the decline in growth due to the slowdown in population growth? It is difficult to say. There are currently quite different estimates of the amount of meat consumed in China. The estimates derived from the annual household surveys indicate a per capita consumption of meat and poultry of about 15 kilograms. This presumably refers to consumption in the home and may not count the meat eaten outside the home, which might be another 20%. The data on production of meat and poultry imply per capita availability of 37 kilograms. There may be some difference in what is counted as meat—carcass weight versus retail or home weight. However, the difference is very great and leaves one uncertain about how much meat consumption is likely to increase with increased incomes.

References

Bos, E., M. T. Yu, E. Massiah, and R. A. Bulatao. *World Population Projections: Estimates and Projections with Related Demographic Statistics.* Baltimore MD: The Johns Hopkins Press (for the World Bank), 1994.

Brown, L. R. "Who Will Feed China?" *World Watch* 7 (September/October 1994):10–19.

Ehrlich, P. R. *The Population Bomb,* Revised Ed. New York: Sierra Club/Ballantine Books, year.

Food and Agricultural Organization (FAO). *Production Yearbook.* Rome: FAO. Selected issues.

Islam, N., ed. *Population and Food in the Early Twenty-First Century: Meeting Future Food Demand of an Increasing Population.* Washington DC: International Food Policy Research Institute, 1994.

Johnson, D. G. *World Agriculture in Disarray.* London: Macmillan, 1973.

——. "World Agriculture, Commodity Policy, and Price Variability." *Amer. J. Agr. Econ.* 5 (December 1975):823–28.

——. "Trade Effects of Dismantling the Socialized Agriculture of the Former Soviet Union." *Comparative Econ. Stud.* 35 (Winter 1993):421–34.

Pinstrup-Andersen, P., R. Pandya-Lorch, and M.W. Rosegrant. *The World Food Situation: Recent Developments, Emerging Issues, and Long-Term Prospects.* Washington DC: International Food Policy Research Institute year.

POSTSCRIPT

Does Population Growth Threaten Humanity?

The key issue of this debate is whether or not future technological improvements can feed growing populations. Production increases have slowed down but so has population growth. Is it possible that improvements in the basic grains are reaching their limit? Will future technology continue to have dramatic impacts on world food production? On the other hand, is it unwise to underestimate humankind's inventiveness and its ability to adapt to environmental problems and limits?

Paul R. Ehrlich and Anne H. Ehrlich wrote *Betrayal of Science and Reason: How Anti-Environmental Rhetoric Threatens Our Future* (Island Press, 1996) to refute statements by those who don't agree with the messages of concerned environmentalists. Julian Lincoln Simon counters with *Hoodwinking the Nation* (Transaction, 1999). For a debate on this issue, see Norman Myers and Julian L. Simon, *Scarcity or Abundance? A Debate on the Environment* (W. W. Norton, 1994).

Publications by some that are optimistic about the availability of resources and the health of the environment include Ronald Bailey, ed., *The True State of the Planet* (Free Press, 1995) and Gregg Easterbrook, *A Moment on the Earth: The Coming Age of Environmental Optimism* (Viking Penguin, 1995). Publications by some who state that population growth threatens humanity include Joseph Wayne Smith, Graham Lyons, and Gary Sauer-Thompson, *Healing a Wounded World* (Praeger, 1997); Douglas E. Booth, *The Environmental Consequences of Growth* (Routledge, 1998); and Bill McKibben, *Hope, Human and Wild: True Stories of Living Lightly on the Earth* (Little, Brown, 1995). Works that try to reconcile economic growth with a healthy environment include Paul Ekins, *Economic Growth and Environmental Sustainability: The Prospects for Green Growth* (Routledge, 2000) and Jose I. Dos R. Furtado and Tamara Belt, eds., *Economic Development and Environmental Sustainability: Policies and Principles for a Durable Equilibrium* (World Bank, 2000). For a history of the environmental movement see Laurence P. Pringle, *The Environmental Movement: From Its Roots to the Challenges of a New Century* (HarperCollins, 2000).

Several works relate environmental problems to very severe political, social, and economic problems, including Michael Renner, *Fighting for Survival* (W. W. Norton, 1996) and Michael N. Dobkowski and Isidor Wallimann, eds., *The Coming Age of Scarcity: Preventing Mass Death and Genocide in the Twenty-First Century* (Syracuse University Press, 1998). An important series of publications on environmental problems are by the Worldwatch Institute, including two annuals: *State of the World* and *Vital Signs*.

ISSUE 19

Is Life Getting Better in the United States?

YES: Gregg Easterbrook, from "America the O.K.," *The New Republic* (January 4 & 11, 1999)

NO: Beth A. Rubin, from *Shifts in the Social Contract: Understanding Change in American Society* (Pine Forge Press, 1996)

ISSUE SUMMARY

YES: Author Gregg Easterbrook contends that despite some worrisome trends, "American life is getting better." He maintains that incomes, education levels, and lifespans are increasing, while many negative indicators are declining.

NO: Sociology professor Beth A. Rubin asserts that Americans have not only lost income on average over the past 25 years, but they have also increasingly experienced insecurity and anxiety in their jobs and instability in their family relationships.

After World War II the United States emerged as the most powerful nation in the world. In part, this was because of the cumulative economic costs of two world wars for Germany, Great Britain, Japan, and the Soviet Union. America escaped the physical devastation that these nations suffered, and its economy boomed during and after the wars. With its unequalled prosperity and power, the United States assumed international leadership in armaments, investments, and aid.

Today that prosperity in terms of per capita income is equaled or surpassed by Japan and many European countries, and that leadership is in question. During the 1970s, 1980s, and early 1990s, Japan, Germany, Taiwan, South Korea, China, and other countries in Europe and Asia made enormous economic strides, while America was stuck in first gear. American stores were flooded with foreign-made goods—from shoes and textiles to cars and television sets. America went from winner to loser in many market competitions, resulting in large trade deficits. In the 1990s America's European and Asian competitors have experienced major difficulties and have been trying to climb out of serious recessions. The American economy looks good by comparison.

Because of recent, painful restructuring and downsizing, America now competes more equally with other industrial countries. American business is doing well, but workers are suffering. American workers have been laid off as industries have downsized or moved part of their operations offshore, where they can operate more cheaply than in the United States. Until 1997 the government continued to spend more than it received in revenue, resulting in America's national debt (the total of its accumulated annual budget deficits) growing to more than $5 trillion. Many Americans worry that future generations will be burdened with debts that will drive the nation deeper into economic difficulties.

Despite a long stretch of modest economic growth with relatively low inflation and unemployment, Americans are anxious. Despite an endless array of new technological toys and gadgets, most Americans do not perceive life today as being better than it was a few decades ago, although the majority say that they are better off personally. Visual signs of declining standards of living confront Americans in some of the grim aspects of daily life, particularly in its urban centers: homeless people sprawled on sidewalks, streets lined with boarded-up buildings, crumbling schools with metal detectors at the doors and peeling paint in the classrooms, bridges with chunks of concrete falling off them, and housing projects taken over by drug dealers. Statistical signs of declining standards of living are found in the decline in real wages and in the median income of individuals.

The above factors deal with material standards of living. But it has often been said that money does not buy happiness. In fact, many studies show that once people have enough money to satisfy their basic material needs, additional increments of wealth are not correlated with increasing happiness. Surveys indicate that family, relationships, and meaningful activities are the keys to happiness. What are indicators in these areas telling us? Since 1960 divorce rates have shot upward, fertility rates have plummeted downward, and the time parents devote to children has declined about 10 hours per week. On the other hand, these trends bottomed out in the mid-1980s, and family values are staging a small comeback. Furthermore, Robert Wuthnow, in *Sharing the Journey: Support Groups and America's New Quest for Community* (Free Press, 1994), reveals that more and more Americans participate in small groups and are thereby connecting with God and with other people in the process of dealing with their problems.

So where do we stand? Is the quality of life in America improving? In the following selection, Gregg Easterbrook admits that poverty persists, but he asserts that "the economy is booming" and that most aspects of life are clearly getting better. Beth A. Rubin argues that Americans are victims of the changes taking place in the economy, especially the shrinking commitment of employers to employees. The employers gain flexibility, while the employees, even professionals, lose security. She also sees trouble on the home front and concludes that the quality of life is suffering.

Gregg Easterbrook

 **YES**

America the O.K.

Idon't wish to alarm you, but American life is getting better. Crime has fallen sharply. The economy is booming. Teen pregnancy is declining. The federal budget is in surplus. The air and water are getting cleaner. Health is improving by almost every measure, including the first-ever decline in cancer incidence. Deaths in accidents are decreasing. Standards of living continue to improve. The use of drugs and cigarettes is waning. Levels of education keep rising. Women and minorities are acquiring an ever-larger slice of the national pie. Personal liberty has never been greater, while American culture becomes more and more diverse. Even home runs are at an all-time high! . . .

Of course, there are gloomy trends, worst among them the persistence of poverty. Today, about 13 percent of U.S. households live below the poverty level, which seems ever less tolerable as the nation grows richer. As Michael Novak has noted, when the Bible declared, "You always have the poor with you," the context was a feudal agrarian economy in which some poverty was unavoidable. Today's high-tech, knows-no-obstacle economy could transfer enough goods to everyone, and, until it does, a sword will hang over American abundance.

And, of course, the international scene presents anxieties. Beyond the specters of war and ethnic hostility, the developing world's ecosystems continue to deteriorate. Global population will rise to around nine billion before stabilizing in the twenty-first century. This means the world must eventually feed, educate, employ, and care for the health of a human race half again its present size. There's no way the United States will be able to sit out that great challenge and no sign we are preparing for it.

But, overall, the American scene is progressively more encouraging. Let's review the facts:

Accidents Despite the sirens-and-carnage images projected by local TV news, accidents have been declining pretty much across the board for more than a decade. In 1985, 40 Americans out of every 100,000 died accidental deaths; by 1996, the rate was down to 35 of 100,000, a twelve percent decline. Workplace fatalities dropped spectacularly during this period, from about 11,600 in 1985 to 6,218 in 1997. Traffic fatalities have been declining, too, and in 1997 reached a record low of just 1.6 deaths per 100 million miles driven, the smallest such figure since federal agencies began keeping traffic-death statistics in the 1960s. Highway fatalities are going down in absolute numbers—in 1984, there were 46,200 traffic deaths, for example, versus 41,967 in 1997—even as there are more people driving more cars at faster speeds for more total miles. . . .

Crime   Homicide is down about 20 percent from the level of the early '90s; in 1997, it reached the lowest rate in 30 years. During the '80s, Brooklyn averaged two murders per day; last March, Brooklyn went a full week without a homicide for the first time in a generation. Crime is down in nearly every category, including burglary and robbery. Since 1993, not only has the felony rate dropped, but the total number of violent felonies has fallen 14 percent, even while the population continues to grow. As Gordon Witkin has written, "It's hard to think of a social trend with greater significance."

Many factors are at play here, among them the sheer reduction in perpetrators. Tougher laws and sentences have led to a furious rate of incarceration, with 1.8 million Americans now jailed, more than double the figure of a decade ago. The shift toward "community policing" has helped, though felonies are also falling in cities that have not adopted this system. It's important to note that, while most policing has improved in the past decade, there has been no national initiative on this score, just lots of local experiments.

The adoption of James Q. Wilson's "broken windows" theory of civic propriety has helped, too. Annoying as New York City Mayor Rudy Giuliani's anti-jaywalking campaign might be, there is no doubt that an environment in which people take petty laws seriously creates sociological pressure to respect the sort of laws we really care about. Putting more officers on the street has helped, as has the upgunning of law enforcement. During the '80s, when most police carried revolvers, drug-runners had superior weapons. Now that half of all cops bear the high-rate-of-fire Glock semiautomatic, only a fool would try to shoot his way out of an arrest. . . .

Both a growth economy and social circumstances now work against violent crime. As Jeffrey Fagan, a professor of public health at Columbia University, notes, the kids who became crack-runners in the '80s had been born into a period of upheaval: inner cities were in decline, parents were losing jobs as industry fled urban areas, welfare was pushing fathers out of homes, and, to many whose parents traversed the '60s, rioting—violent contempt for law—had briefly been seen as somehow useful to minority aspirations. Now, Fagan says, "the phase of social reorganization is basically over for the inner city." Downtown areas have stopped declining, and some are improving. People have made their peace with the new service industries, rendering legitimate employment possible again. Stability is returning, and, with it, community contempt for crime. . . .

Drink, drugs, and fooling around   Crack is hardly the only bane in decline. On the key barometer of ingestion by high school seniors, cocaine has declined from something tried by 17 percent of students in 1985 to seven percent in 1996. Twenty-two percent of high school seniors in 1975 had tried stimulant drugs; by 1996, the figure was down to 15 percent. Use of some, though not all, other illegal drugs is also down.

Even legal, socially acceptable forms of indulgence are in remission. In 1965, 42 percent of American adults smoked; today, 25 percent do. Per capita U.S. consumption of spirits has been going down for years. In 1980, 72 percent of high school seniors reported having consumed alcohol recently. This figure has gone down steadily since, falling to 51 percent in 1996. Can it be that half of America's young aren't even sneaking beers anymore?

Another entirely legal (except in Washington) form of earthly pleasure, sex, also seems in decline, at least among the supposedly incorrigible young. The portion of teenage girls reporting to have had intercourse had been climbing steadily since the '60s, a statistic commonly cited—often by middle-age commentators who themselves once devoted countless hours to the pursuit of teenage sex—as a sign of American moral erosion. Now, according to the National Center for Health Statistics, the percentage of sexually active girls ages 15 to 19 has dropped from a peak of 53 percent in 1988 to 50 percent in 1995. Teen pregnancy rates have begun to decline; in 1995, teen pregnancy fell to the same rate as that of 1975, and the downward statistical slope continues. Births to teens have dropped twelve percent since 1991. The number of teen abortions has fallen for seven consecutive years.

Smoking's decline clearly reflects improved awareness of lung cancer. Drug declines probably result from a combination of law-enforcement intensification and rising understanding of the fact that, with the possible exception of marijuana, drugs simply aren't innocuous private choices. Less drinking seems to stem from anti-drunken-driving campaigns and a changing anthropology of the social event, today less viewed as a sanctioned time during which to get schnockered (think *Virginia Woolf*) than as a time at which to sip wine and listen to music.

Less sexual activity among young people may be influenced by concern about sexually transmitted diseases and by religious feeling. A reaction against cultural pressure in favor of sex, especially the repulsively phony Hollywood and rock-video conceptions of sex, might be just as important. Teenage pregnancy decline results directly from higher birth control use—contraceptive use at first intercourse is up from 48 percent among females in the early '80s to 78 percent in 1995. Contraceptives are getting safer (the low-dose Pill) and more convenient (the inject-and-forget Depo-Provera). As important, probably, is a shifting sociology of birth control—which is increasingly seen as smart and responsible.

Less drug use, less drinking, less smoking, and less fooling around hardly synchronize with conventional hand-wringing about the United States as a self-indulgent, libertine realm where anything goes. Rather, these trends suggest that public habits can be moderated through awareness campaigns, rational arguments, and common sense.

The economy   Financial situations can change rapidly, so the milk might curdle; that admonition aside, the American economic outlook is the best it's ever been. Unemployment and inflation are at their lowest points in a quarter-century. Growth is strong, though below record levels. Economic troubles elsewhere in the world seem barely to have dented the system here. Gasoline prices are at a postwar low in real-dollar terms, while mortgage rates are at 30-year lows. Industry isn't disappearing, as is commonly assumed—current U.S. industrial production is 90 percent greater than in 1970, though that figure is achieved with fewer workers. It's common to hear analysts bemoaning the fact that median household income has risen only slightly in the past quarter-century. But the standard concept doesn't take into account that fewer and fewer people live in the median household: factor that in, and household income is up about 15 percent since 1970. The only major negative indicators are the savings rate and the balance-of-trade deficit. As problems go, that's not bad.

The transition from federal deficit to surplus should remind us how often "impossible" problems are solved. Think back to the hollow legislative rituals of the Gramm-Rudman-Hollings law, written to be vacuous on the assumption that real deficit reduction simply could not happen. Now the federal balance sheet has improved so much that lower government borrowing helps drive down interest rates, benefiting everyone. And this has been accomplished without punitive taxation. As Derek Bok pointed out in his 1996 *The State of the Nation,* the American tax burden is 27 percent of GDP, versus 44 percent in France or 50 percent in Sweden.

Having lived the past few years in Europe, I often heard Euros express astonishment at the American economic engine. How could it be, they would ask, that your system has so much litigation, adversarial confrontation, hype, spin, glibness, and overwrought scandal, and yet functions so marvelously? I liked to reply that lawsuits, hype, spin, and scandal must in some way aid American success, forcing our society to accept perpetual change. The sincere answer might be that positive trends in U.S. national wealth have been sparked by ever-greater acceptance of true market economics, with its tumult and endless unanticipated results.

"It's only in the last generation that most people have been converted to the belief that market economics is good for everybody, not just a tool of the wealthy," says John Mueller, a political scientist at the University of Rochester and a rising star in the study of what makes societies run well. Stagflation stopped after Jimmy Carter began deregulation, freeing air travel, energy, and telecommunications. National economic performance shot upward not long thereafter, and, though not all results of deregulation have been favorable, each year brings more evidence that the country is better off with market forces driving most decisions.

Environment Twenty-five years ago, only one-third of America's lakes and rivers were safe for fishing and swimming; today two-thirds are, and the proportion continues to rise. Annual wetlands loss has fallen by 80 percent in the same period, while soil losses to agricultural runoff have been almost cut in half. Total American water consumption has declined nine percent in the past 15 years, even as the population expands, especially in the arid Southwest. Since 1970, smog has declined by about a third, even as the number of cars has increased by half; acid rain has fallen by 40 percent; airborne soot particles are down 69 percent, which is why big cities have blue skies again; carbon monoxide or "winter smog" is down 31 percent; airborne lead, a poison, is down 98 percent. Emissions of CFCs, which deplete stratospheric ozone, have all but ended.

Other environmental measures are almost uniformly positive. Toxic emissions by industry declined 46 percent from 1988 to 1996, even as petrochemical manufacturers enjoyed record U.S. production and copious profits. About one-third of Superfund toxic waste sites are not cleaned up, with the pace of cleanup accelerating. The forested acreage of the United States is expanding, with wildlife numbers up in most areas, led by the comeback of eastern deer, now thought to be at pre-colonial numbers. Since the Endangered Species Act was passed, only a few U.S. species have fallen extinct, not the thousands predicted, while species such as the bald eagle, gray whale, and peregrine falcon have recovered enough to no longer require full legal protection. Only two major U.S. environmental gauges are now negative: continuing inaction against greenhouse gases and continuing loss of wildlife habitats to urban expansion.

An important conceptual lesson is being learned: When pollution stops, natural recovery does not require ponderous geological time. Consider Boston Harbor, whose filth was an issue in George Bush's 1988 campaign against Massachusetts Governor Michael Dukakis. Even as Bush filmed his memorable commercial standing on the sludge-caked Boston shore, a $4 billion water treatment plant was rising in the background. At the time, most experts predicted that it would take 50 years or more to rinse the harbor. Instead, cleanup has been so rapid that Boston Harbor is already safe again for swimming and fishing. Activists, who once had to rail against sludge by the ton, are down to complaining about detection in the harbor of trace parts-per-billion or even parts-per-trillion of compounds. As Paul Levy, who ran the first phase of the cleanup project, has said, the fact that activists now remonstrate about smaller and smaller issues shows that the big issues are under control....

Health   Both incidence and death rates for cancer began to ebb in the early '90s, reversing a 20-year trend of increase. Cancer incidence, or the occurrence of new cases, had risen about 1.2 percent per year from 1973 to 1990; since then, incidence has fallen by almost one percent per year, with the decline manifesting in the big-four cancer forms (lung, prostate, breast, and colon-rectum) for both genders and across all major age and ethnic groups other than black males. Mortality for most cancers is now either level (as it is for breast cancer) or in slight decline. Only melanoma and non-Hodgkin's lymphoma are now rising.

By nearly all other measures, U.S. public health is getting steadily better. Heart disease and stroke are both in decline relative to population growth, with heart disease deaths, the number-one medical killer, falling 3.4 percent from 1996 to 1997. Infant mortality is now down to 0.7 percent of live births, the lowest such figure ever for the United States. (Some European countries do slightly better.) AIDS deaths are declining markedly in the United States. The rate of suicides is declining, falling 4.6 percent in 1997. There are a few worrisome public-health trends, such as the reappearance of TB and the emergence of microbes that resist currently available antibiotics. But, in the main, public health is getting better by leaps and bounds.

Most remarkable is the continued rise in life expectancy, now 76 years at birth for the typical American, up from 54 years when the World War II generation was being born. The rise in life expectancy is global, expressing itself in nearly every country in the world, outside Central Africa. Indeed, the reason there is global population growth is not that the world's women are having more babies—per capita they are having steadily fewer, even in developing nations—but that people the world over are living so much longer.

Most of what's going on in public health appears to be a mix of advancing medical knowledge and public awareness. The biggest factor in the cancer decline, for example, is the drop in smoking. Heart disease decline has been aided by better drugs, better therapy (the coronary-artery bypass operation, touch-and-go 20 years ago, has gotten so much more efficacious that it's now working even for the elderly), and advancing understanding of lifestyle issues such as fat intake. The improving sophistication of medical education and other factors are also at play.

Better public health hasn't come cheaply: medical spending was seven percent of GDP in 1970 and is almost 14 percent now. Yet, much as you may detest your HMO, keep in mind that most trends in health care costs are favorable, too. During the late '80s, costs were rising so rapidly that it was common to predict that 15 to 20 percent of GDP would be spent on health care by the end of the century. If that had happened, American prosperity would have been damaged. Instead, in the past five years, there has been little medical inflation. Managed care creates annoying preapproval hassles and longer waits for some appointments. But on the key points—protecting health at an affordable cost—the system is doing well....

Race   As William Julius Wilson has extensively documented, attention to the problems of inner-city dysfunction causes us to overlook what history will judge as the big racial story of late-twentieth-century America: the emergence of a black middle class.

Through the last generation, the portion of African Americans living in middle-class circumstances has more than doubled. Some kind of watershed was crossed in 1994, when the average income of black families in Queens, long a community treated as symbolic of working-class to middle-class transition, surpassed the average income of white families there. Georgia, Maryland, and other states now contain large, economically independent black middle-class areas where life is suburban, family structures conventional, and values entirely middle-American.

African American income still lags significantly behind that of whites, but, as Steven Holmes has written, in the past few years poverty rates "have dipped below 30 percent of black households for the first time in the country's history." Black male college graduates now make, on average, twelve percent less than their white counterparts, a much smaller gap than a generation ago, while black female college grads now earn slightly more than white female grads. Jencks's 1972 book, *Inequality,* argued that, even if minority education rose, minority income levels would not, owing to barriers of prejudice. Jencks now feels the situation has changed, with minority education "look[ing] far more important than it did in the 1960s," because African American accomplishment in school can now translate into economic success.

Minority educational accomplishment continues to improve. In 1996, black high school graduation rates became about the same as white rates— needless to say, a historical first. The black-white math SAT score gap, which was 140 points in 1976, is 110 points now, owing to black improvements, not white erosion. Bok and William Bowen write in *The Shape of the River* that, although African Americans entering most colleges have lower overall grades and SAT scores than white schoolmates, on the real-world test of what they do when they leave the university, top black students now have about the same career achievement as top whites.

At the turn of the century, many African Americans weren't even literate; today, the college-completion rates of black Americans exceed the comparable figures for much of Europe. If one views African Americans as an immigrant co-hort that "arrived" in the United States with the passage of the civil rights laws, black rates of social progress are similar to those previously displayed by white ethnic immigrant groups, which typically required two to three generations to join the establishment.

Standards of living   Living standards are improving so fast and so consis-tently that to mention them today seems almost banal. Most fundamental is housing. The typical contemporary home is 40 percent larger than a 1970 house, while only three percent of Americans, the lowest percentage ever, live in overcrowded conditions, defined as more than one person per room. That every person should have at least one room to call his or her own is a social innovation of the American present. The majority of today's dwellings have air-conditioning and other improvements. More than half of Americans now live in suburbs, which may be superficial and intellectually insufferable but are physically pleasant: the reason they are popular.

The metric of living standards is rising so rapidly that merely how to track its ascent has become a controversy, centering on whether the Consumer Price Index adequately recognizes such once-rare, now-quotidian indicators as com-puter ownership or eating out. Another way to meter the evolution of living standards, championed by Richard Alm and W. Michael Cox in the forthcom-ing book *Myths of Rich and Poor,* is how long the typical person must work to acquire consumer items. Between rising wages and larger dwellings, for exam-ple, in 1956 the typical worker had to invest 16 weeks at labor to buy 100 square feet of home; now the figure has fallen to less than 14 weeks. The McDonald's brothers' first burgers cost half an hour of work at the time; now 180 seconds buys one. Only health care and university-level education are growing more expensive when measured by work hours required for purchase.

"A seven-day Caribbean cruise," Alm and Cox write, "slipped from 51 hours in 1972 to 45 hours in 1997." Not only are they getting cheaper, excur-sions on 42-deck luxury liners with names like *Insatiable Princess* are another indication of the rising standard of living: such experiences may be stupefy-ing, but what matters is that they are becoming standard middle-class events. Leisure and tourism barely existed as economic sectors a generation ago; today they are a hefty slice of the GDP.

As Robert J. Samuelson has written, overall the U.S. standard of living has continued to rise in the '80s and '90s roughly as rapidly as it did in the '50s and '60s; it's just that we now take out a considerable share of national wealth in forms that don't show up well in price indexes, such as better health, cleaner air, and the ability to fly anywhere, anytime, at an affordable price.

Wedlock   The family-breakup wave may have crested. The divorce rate, which was 2.5 per 1,000 people in 1966, peaked at 5.3 per 1,000 in 1981. The rate leveled off in the early '90s at about 4.7 and now appears to be in a shallow decline. A few years ago, half of all new marriages were expected to fail; now only 40 percent are, with the average length of a marriage starting to creep back up again. And Census Bureau figures suggest that the reduction in conventional two-parent families—which dominated American demographics from 1970 to 1990—is "flattening" and might be about to end.

Whether the decline of divorce is just a blip or suggests some larger social trend can't be determined by only a few years of data. But it's worth noting that sociologists and writers have spent the past decade elaborately documenting the fact, that, whatever it means in terms of adult personal freedom, family breakup harms children. That message may be sinking in.

❧

At first glance, there seems no single thread that runs through the subjects where life is improving. Some seem a case for more Washington: environ-mental protection is arguably the most impressive achievement of progressive government since the establishment of the Social Security system. But "out-side of pollution control, it's hard to see where federal regulations have been the driving factor in recent social improvements," says Gary Becker, a Nobel Prize-winning economist at the University of Chicago. Economic vigor has been aided by deregulation. Crime reduction, welfare reform, and other pos-itive trends have arisen mainly through state and local initiatives. Public health has certainly benefited from federal investments, but advancing knowledge is the primary factor. Betterment of personal behavior, such as the reduction in drunken driving, has been inspired mainly through private efforts.

It's possible that what the surge of national good news tells us is that, as pragmatism supplants ideology, society will get better at fixing things. "We're living in an age with very few romantics and revolutionaries," says Mueller of the University of Rochester. "People with vast, sweeping visions caused most of this century's problems. Most of the time you don't want leaders with visions, you want society run by cautious pragmatists. At the moment, the pragmatists are in control of most nations, and it's making things better." It's possible that the upswing in good news tells us that reform initiatives of the '60s and '70s have finally begun to work. Pollution-control regulations, affirmative action programs, crime crackdowns—all started off clunky and problem-plagued, but, as the snafus were ironed out, results began to flow. And it's possible that what the late-century tidings convey is simply what the United States would have looked like all along if so much of its brainpower and resources had not been diverted to the cold war.

But what the good news unequivocally tells us is that it's never too late to change the world. In that sense, there is a bright thread running through all these examples: intractable or "impossible" dilemmas can be solved. Our efforts matter; when we attempt reform, we can be crowned with success. It is no coincidence that the aspects of life that have gotten better are those that people have dedicated themselves to improving. America can still become whatever it wants to be. We do not have to accept what we see out the window; rather, we can make the view the one of our choosing.

Knowing that reform still works should grant us courage to strive for change in areas where progress now seems "impossible." For instance, the greenhouse effect may seem unstoppable today, but that's only because we have not yet tried to stop it. There is no reason we need accept poverty: it can be bested. Polls show that, far from thinking society spends too much to lift up the poor, 60 percent of Americans think the country should take more action against poverty. So let's—because it will work!

Consider an astonishing figure: The United Nations estimates that it would cost $40 billion per year to provide the basics of life—adequate food, clean water, health care, shelter, and literacy—to every person on the planet. That works out to $151 per American. Every one of us would gladly write that check, if only there were a way to be sure the money were properly used. All that's stopping us from attempting reform of this noble magnitude is the false belief that life is rolling irrevocably downhill.

It's not, and the proof gets stronger each day.

NO

Beth A. Rubin

Shifts in the Social Contract: Understanding Change in American Society

Social Change in the Twentieth Century

Workers who once felt relatively immune from unemployment are discovering that a college degree and a big paycheck are no guarantee against it. Consider the example of IBM, which has long offered many of its workers essentially lifetime employment. In April 1993, in response to declining business conditions, IBM laid off 7,700 workers. Many of these workers were well-paid professionals in their 50s who thought they were at the zenith of their careers. Unlike many blue-collar workers, none of them had ever had to cope with layoffs and employment insecurity. This security was, after all, why they have invested in good educations at colleges and universities. Now, these well-educated, highly skilled, and highly paid workers—who were accustomed to a high standard of living—meet in support/prayer group meetings to discuss their lost careers, provide emotional support for one another, and develop strategies for job hunting and survival. Such support is necessary. In Dutchess County, New York, where three huge IBM plants are located, social service workers report an increase in drinking and family violence, a *New York Times* editorial (The Rise of the Losing Class, Louis Uchitelle, November 20, 1994) claimed that the changing economy was linking the white-collar, skilled, college-educated workers with blue-collar, unskilled, high school educated workers through a shared experience of "uncertainty, insecurity, and anxiety about their jobs and incomes."

Surprisingly, unemployment and layoffs were occurring in a period characterized by economic recovery. But this recovery was an unusual one. Despite economic growth in the early 1990s, economic inequality (the gap between the rich and poor) continued to grow. While inequality has been increasing since the late 1970s, for perhaps the first time in America's history economists were faced with the puzzle of falling *median income* (the income level that half the population is above and half below) at the time of increased economic growth (*New York Times,* October 9, 1994)....

Turmoil is not, of course, confined to the United States. Economic insecurity is so great internationally that the International Labor Organization calls it a "global crisis." One out of three workers in the world's labor force is either unemployed or earning insufficient wages to allow a decent standard of living (*Times-Picayune,* March 7, 1994). Persistent long-term joblessness affects both industrial countries like the United States and developing countries like Mexico.

Global economic hardship has a number of consequences. It can increase competition for resources, engender political conflicts, and foster immigration. Former Secretary of State Lawrence Eagleburger called the current period one of global revolution (*Los Angeles Times,* February 18, 1993). Unchecked, such instability can lead to massive economic depression and even war. In fact, the 1990s provide evidence of such. As the countries that once constituted the Soviet Union struggle to redefine themselves, hatred, ethnic conflict, and bloodshed have often filled the gap left by a once strong centralized government....

Clearly the United States, along with most other countries in the world, is undergoing massive social change. Such change is related to a systematic transformation in the basis of social relations and social institutions (such as the economy, the government, the family).... *[C]ontemporary American society is changing from a social world characterized by long-term, stable relationships to one characterized by short-term, temporary relationships.* This social change alters the *social contract* that underpins society....

This shift results from changes in the economy. Specifically, economic relationships are changing to emphasize flexibility rather than stability in the use of resources. In a larger context the relationships among countries are growing increasingly complex. The result is a kaleidoscope of economic and social changes....

For over 200 years, a central part of American culture has been the belief in the American Dream. When people talk about the American Dream, they are talking about a belief in a society characterized by political and religious freedom in which anyone, regardless of family background, ethnicity, or race, can "make it." By *making it,* we mean that people can—by virtue of education, hard work, luck, and motivation—have a good job, a home, a happy family, and leisure time. Moreover, they can have these in a social climate free from oppression....

This dream continues to motivate people from all over the world. Waves of immigrants continue to come to the United States seeking the same mobility and opportunity that earlier generations sought. Achieving these goals, however, has grown increasingly difficult since the paths to upward mobility have altered.

Accord in the Post–World War II Era

By the beginning of the twentieth century, America was on its way to becoming one of the richest, most successful countries in the world. During the two and half decades following World War II, America was, in many ways, at its zenith. No country appeared richer, more powerful, more sure of itself. The American Dream seemed a reality for unprecedented numbers of Americans. For both blue-collar industrial workers (such as assembly line workers in automobile or electronics plants) and white-collar businessman (such as managers of Dow chemical or Metropolitan Life), upward mobility, comfort, and security appeared to be the norm. Secure workers married, had children, and bought houses. Those who were excluded from this expanding middle class, particularly African-Americans, placed demands on the government for civil rights and equal opportunities. The government responded with a variety of social programs. American culture also reflected the optimism of this period of expansion and growth....

The expansion of the economy provided a certain lifestyle to thousands of American workers. My father-in-law left the army after World War II with a high school degree and got a job with the telephone company. He moved to Santa Barbara, California, and was able to buy a house for $12,000. That house today would cost at least 20 times as much, something a worker with only a high school education is unlikely to have. However, the postwar economy provided him (as it did so many Americans) with a welter of opportunities, such as to marry and raise a family in economic comfort....

Many women who had filled in for absent male workers during World War II returned home, and men filled the jobs in their stead. Those jobs, however, paid well enough to allow a single income to provide for a family. Thus, although later generations of white, middle-class women would fight for the right for equal employment, postwar affluence freed many working-class women from participating in the paid labor force. The breadwinner–homemaker model of families that had dominated the middle class was now a possibility for large portions of the working class as well. In 1940, 70% of families were male breadwinner–female homemaker families. For the next 25 years, more than half of all families conformed to this norm....

End of a Century, End of an Era

While not everyone's experience of life in America during the years 1947–1970 was upbeat, this period was generally one of economic growth, stable work, a liberal and interventionist state, and an increasingly exploratory culture. Once the stability and growth of the economy faltered, however, so too did stability and growth in other institutions. Clearly, the way social life was organized in the period after World War II is extremely different from the way social life is organized at the end of the twentieth century....

For a variety of reasons... the growth of the American economy slowed in the early 1970s. Increased international economic competition and failure to upgrade existing production techniques, among other factors, led to declining business success. As a result, employers experimented with a variety of strategies to maintain their prior economic dominance. All their efforts centered on decreasing the expenses involved in production and finding ways to compete more effectively. The less it costs to produce goods, the more profit businesses can make. Paying workers less, decreasing the number of workers hired, replacing workers with computers, robots, and automated assembly lines, moving to regions of the country and world where production was cheaper—all were ways in which American businesses tried to recoup declining profits.

Moreover, unlike in the decades following World War II, during the 1970s and 1980s other nations were competing successfully with the United States. Whereas American cars, for instance, used to dominate the automobile market, Japanese and German cars now outsold American cars. The increased economic strength of business in other countries also created more economic activity at a *global* level.

The efforts on the part of American business to succeed in the face of newly emerging international economic competitors have changed the national economy and workplace in a number of ways.

• Whereas our economic base previously came from manufacturing (e.g., cars, steel, electronics), it now comes increasingly from services (e.g., education, medical and financial services). This shift in the industrial base of the economy has, like other changes, had enormous consequences for workers and the workplace. Many service-sector jobs (such as restaurant and cleaning services) pay far less than manufacturing jobs. Those that pay well require *at least* a college education. Thus, this change results in fewer opportunities for the non-college-educated.

• Fewer and fewer workers are in jobs in which there is the possibility for continuous movement up a career ladder in a single firm. Like the IBM workers mentioned earlier, more and more workers are finding that jobs they thought they would have for a lifetime, or at least decades, are now part-time and temporary. In their efforts to create greater flexibility in the use of workers, technology, and resources, employers are replacing full-time jobs with temporary or part-time jobs, regardless of the skill or education associated with the occupation. Part-time workers are much cheaper since they receive not only lower wages but also few nonwage benefits such as health and disability insurance, paid vacations, and so forth.

• In manufacturing, roughly 75–80% of the workers used to be unionized (other industry groups such as trucking, mining, and construction had almost as many). Unions provide workers with high wages, benefits, and job security, and they provide employers with a well-disciplined work force. However, unions also create limitations for employers; they do not allow employers to fire workers when business conditions decline, for example. Thus, to increase the flexibility of the work force, employers have sought to rid their workplaces of unions, and so fewer and fewer workers have the economic and job stability that unions provide.

In summary, most of the changes in the economy and the workplace have resulted in far more insecurity and instability for workers. In addition, the paths to upward mobility have changed and have become unclear, and so many workers find themselves unsure of their future....

In addition to economic and political changes, major changes have occurred in another major institution—the family. The nuclear, breadwinner-homemaker family in which husband and wife raise their own biological offspring—once the dominant family form—is now a minority....

The increased divorce rate means that many families are now *blended.* That is, families are increasingly composed of biological parents, stepparents, children from multiple marriages, and so on. Similarly, more and more people in their 20s, instead of forming their own marriages and households, are "returning to the nest" (moving home to live with parents)....

As the question of responsibility has become more important in the context of the family, the same thing has happened in the context of government. Whereas in post–World War II years the government was actively involved in solving problems of poverty, inadequate housing and job and business regulation, in more recent decades it has withdrawn substantially from these commitments. Additionally, with the loss of the Vietnam War and the end of the cold war in the early 1990s, the American government has played an uncertain and vacillating role in international conflicts....

A second factor contributing to the withdrawal of the government from problem solving at home and intervention abroad is the reduction in resources available to the government to finance solutions. A combination of economic and demographic changes (more elderly and more young people, fewer people at high-paying jobs) has decreased the tax base. Moreover, the increasing national debt absorbs any economic surplus that could be used to finance social programs....

From Industrial Economy to Flexible Economy

When I graduated from high school in the Washington, D.C. area in 1972, I went to college, but my old boyfriend Ricky didn't. He looked for a good, unionized factory job. He knew he could make good money and maybe buy a little house in the same neighborhood his parents and sister Sara lived in. His sister didn't go to college, either. She had a job as a typist in a big office building outside the Beltway, in the Maryland suburbs. At the same time, my best friend's father was some sort of researcher. He worked in a big firm located in nearby Bethesda, Maryland, in which he had started out at the bottom and worked his way into one of the nice offices with huge windows. The occupants of those offices had expense accounts, three-martini lunches, and wives at home raising kids like us in well-heeled suburbs.

Now, the factory is gone, and Ricky is trying to figure out how he can keep paying his mortgage on one third of his old salary. The factory moved to Mexico and now employs young Mexican women. The home office is still in Bethesda, Maryland, but it employs only half the number of men it did 20 years ago. Most of the jobs have been taken over by computers or are done on a consulting basis. The only job Ricky could find was as a security guard for one of the new hotels that have opened up in the Washington, D.C. area.

The typewriter Sara used is also gone. When her office switched to computers, Sara had to learn how to use the new system. She thought that when she did, perhaps she could move into a better paying job, but that didn't happen. She still spends all her time typing, but now, instead of getting together with the other "girls in the pool" between typing letters, she sits alone all day in an office with a computer. During her breaks she sometimes logs into a computer bulletin board on the Internet. There, she pretends that she is a famous artist with an international reputation. Nobody knows differently; nobody will ever meet the face behind the computer identity.

My best friend's father doesn't work in Bethesda anymore, either. His office moved to Japan, and he travels back and forth now doing consulting work. He has also learned how to speak Japanese, German, and a little bit of Thai. He travels a lot and misses his family.

Neither Ricky nor his sister votes; they don't see what difference it makes. Sara is divorced and raising two children on her own. She isn't sure how to answer any of the questions her children ask; so they've stopped asking the questions. Ricky drinks too much and worries about losing his house; he blames his problems on welfare cheats and homosexuals. Neither brother nor sister really understands why nothing worked out the way they thought it would, the way it did for their parents.

The difficulty comes in seeing how large-scale social changes are affecting their day-to-day lives; but that's what is happening. From 1972, when they graduated from high school, to 1994 the *economy*—that is, the set of institutions and relationships that produces and distributes goods and services—has changed dramatically....

Bad Jobs: Statically Flexible Workers

Evidence suggest that the majority of workers in the flexible workplace are not in the relatively stable core but are working in an expanded secondary labor market characterized by the *instability* of jobs (Mingione, 1991; Colclough and Tolbert, 1992). This expanded sector is characterized by strategies of static flexibility (or *numerical flexibility*) rather than a dynamically flexible production process. *Static flexibility* refers to the organization of employment around labor demand. Employers attempt to reorganize the labor process so that they have to pay workers only for specific jobs or for short periods of time. Consider the typical secretary, for example. She (about 99% of all clerical workers are female) may be very busy at some times, but under the usual employment contract (8 hours a day, 5 days a week) she may also have long periods when there is very little work to do. Under these conditions, an employer will be paying a worker just to sit around. However, reorganizing the workplace around statically flexible workers might mean that an office does not have a full-time clerical worker but instead uses part-time or temporary clerical workers as needed. This scenario is most feasible where the skills of the statically flexible workers are minimal and interchangeable. In the labor–capital accord era, employers used this strategy only with relatively unskilled workers. In the flexible economy, however, skilled, well-educated workers are used in the same way (Colclough and Tolbert, 1992; Harvey, 1989). In fact, Belous finds that more than half of all temporary workers are employed in technical, sales, and administrative support occupations (1989, p. 28). His research also shows that "at least 17% of the temporary work force is employed in occupations that are managerial, professional, technical or skilled blue collar" (Belous, 1989, p. 29). Those occupations may well include accountants, architects, engineers, financial advisors, lawyers, and doctors, just to name a few....

Displacement   At the extreme, computerization and automation eliminate jobs. More jobs have been lost to subcontracting than to technology; but technology—in combination with industrial shifts, mergers, and general downsizing —has led to a massive displacement of workers. *Displacement* is the loss of jobs for reasons that are completely independent of how well workers have worked. A worker who is habitually late and is subsequently fired leaves an opening that will probably be filled. But a worker who is out of a job because the factory moves to Mexico has been displaced.

Well-paid blue-collar workers who had benefited from the labor–capital accord constituted the majority of displaced workers in the 1970s. In the 1980s, white-collar financial, professional, and managerial workers were also displaced. Using a broad definition of displacement, evidence suggests that "displacement rates have increased by 20% to 40% since the early 1970s" (Doeringer, 1991, p. 49). Displaced workers suffer far more than the pain and economic costs of immediate job loss. Workers who cannot find equivalent jobs right away often experience permanent wage reductions and repeated job instability. Additional problems may include loss of houses, breakup of families, increased rates of alcoholism, illness, and even homelessness.

In the film *Roger and Me,* Michael Moore interviews a woman who has been displaced from her job in the auto industry. Since there were few alternative sources of employment, she resorted to selling rabbits "for pets or meat" (the title of his next movie). In one particularly chilling sequence she calmly skins a rabbit while talking about how General Motors hurt her by closing the plant, leaving her with no option but the one so gruesomely depicted in the film. While all workers do not end up selling bunnies as future stew meat, they do end up strapped for work. In their study of displaced electronics workers in Indiana, Perrucci, Perrucci, Targ, and Targ (1988) found that in addition to lost income, a diminished community tax base, and other economic indicators, the displaced workers evinced "high levels of alienation and distrust of the groups and institutions that comprise the social fabric in the community and at the national level" (p. 123).

The displacement process is one factor that has enabled the creation of a numerically flexible labor force. Workers who have been displaced from a job because of industrial restructuring or downsizing are in very vulnerable positions. When an automobile plant closes, what happens to the 50-year-old who worked in the autobody painting department for the last 30 years? There are no other automobile plants in town for him to get a comparable job. And the sector of the economy that is expanding—services—is unlikely to provide him with a job comparable to the one he's been displaced from. He doesn't have the skills or experience to obtain one of the better paid, more secure jobs in the expanding financial and business sector. The types of jobs to which he will have access (security guard, janitor) are likely to be far less lucrative. Displaced workers may be unable to find any job at all and thus join the ranks of the structurally unemployed.

Workers who are displaced have a variety of strategies for coping. Some of the more skilled and privileged displaced workers are able to start their own businesses. The local paper often has stories of people who have turned their labor market adversity into an opportunity. For example, one woman who had been displaced from an administrative position used the skills and contacts she had gained on the job to develop her own temporary employment agency, a business that has relatively low start-up costs. But not all displaced workers have these opportunities. Some fall back on behaviors that are particularly destructive (like alcoholism and substance abuse).

Contingent Work   One member of my family, Peter, worked in the banking industry for years, developing and using new computer software for the bank's information systems. Over the years Pete's job seemed to develop along the lines of flexibly specialized workers. He continually upgraded and used skills to improve the bank's communications network as part of an ongoing process, and he was rewarded handsomely for this work. When the bank merged with another bank, Pete played a central role in restructuring their communication network. Despite massive layoffs, his skills assured him of his position until his boss—and then he—were fired. For 3 years thereafter, despite an impressive array of skills and an equally impressive resume, he was unable to find another full-time job. Instead he has turned to temporary work. Corporations hire him to do a single job; when he completes the job, he has to look for more work.

Pete is not alone in this experience; he represents part of the new and expanding *contingent labor force*. The contingent labor force includes both part-time and temporary workers—some voluntarily contingent and some involuntarily so. Contingent workers receive lower pay, no fringe benefits, and little occupational protection. Their work is contingent on labor demand, and their security is up for grabs. Most would rather work full-time if they could. Research shows that since 1970, involuntary part-time work has grown 121% (Callaghan and Hartman, 1991, p. 4). It is no wonder that it is involuntary, given these conditions. Part-time workers are six times more likely to work for minimum wage than full-time workers. Additionally, the Internal Revenue Service has estimated that up to 38% of employers deliberately misclassify their workers as independent contractors rather than full-time workers to avoid paying unemployment compensation and social security tax (duRivage, 1992, p. 87). duRivage also finds that only one in six contingent workers is covered by a pension plan.

The involuntary, part-time work force is growing more rapidly than the full-time work force and is becoming a permanent part of the modern workplace (Callaghan and Hartman, 1991). Recent estimates suggest that contingent workers represent 25–30% of the work force and appear most often in the retail trades and in services, which are low-productivity, low-wage jobs (Callaghan and Hartman, 1991). Women make up roughly two thirds of the contingent work force. Black men in temporary, blue-collar manual work constitute the second largest category of contingent workers (duRivage, 1992). One report indicated that "displaced white-collar workers are told up front that any job they get in any company should not be expected to last longer than three to five years—if they are lucky and stay on their toes" (*Times-Picayune,* October 9, 1994).

In contrast to earlier periods, high levels of what economists call *human capital* (e.g., education, training, and skills) no longer ensure status as a primary worker as firms increasingly hire consultants, accountants, marketing researchers, lawyers and technical help on a temporary, as-needed basis. The firm of the future is likely to include very few permanent workers and to subcontract out for the rest of its workers, from the low-skill janitorial and cafeteria staff to the highly skilled workers.

Reliance on a contingent labor force has two major advantages for employers. First, it dramatically decreases labor costs. On average, part-time workers earn 60% of the hourly wages of full-time workers (Belous, 1989; duRivage, 1992, p. 87). Most receive neither pensions, health benefits, fringe benefits, nor unemployment insurance. When banks hire Peter on a contingent basis to do work similar to what he had been doing, they get the same work from him as they used to. Now, however, they do not have to pay for the generous benefits workers at his level usually receive.

Second, reliance on contingent workers also allows employers to use workers only as they need them, rather than maintain a stable work force during, for example, periods of slack demand. Ironically, though, there is evidence that employers are not using contingent workers solely in response to shifting demand conditions (i.e., hiring extra sales workers during the holiday season). Rather, they are using contingent workers on a permanent basis (Belous, 1989; Callaghan and Hartman, 1991; duRivage, 1992)....

Conclusions

Industrial transformation has eliminated many of the good—that is, stable and well-paid—jobs held by workers with only a high school diploma. Now, increasing numbers of jobs require a college education. Moreover, they require complex interpersonal skills and computer literacy, something that schools often fail to provide to all students. These differences pose dilemmas for young entrants into the labor market. Students in wealthy school districts have access to a quality of education, both in content and in resources, that can provide them with the human capital necessary to compete in the future workplace. For many more students, however, particularly those in inner cities or economically depressed rural areas—in fact, all communities that lack sufficient tax monies to maintain and upgrade existing schools—the education is of a quality that leaves them increasingly unprepared for the twenty-first century. Those students who are unable to acquire the necessary skills are likely to fall into the secondary labor market. Unfortunately, given the increasingly rapid pace of knowledge growth, initial deficiencies will be even harder for those students to overcome than they were in earlier periods.

The nature of the flexible economy is such that many workers can no longer anticipate long-term employment relationships with a single employer or a small number of firms over the course of their working lives. Instead of anticipating a relatively predictable career path, more and more workers are becoming contingent workers or homeworkers. The shift to flexible employment threatens the well-being of workers in a number of ways. Workers lose access to stable health care, for instance. Correspondingly, low pay associated with the secondary labor market makes health benefits purchased from private providers harder to afford.

Flexible work arrangements also result in loss of access to retirement and other benefits. This problem is exacerbated by the anticipated increased burden on the social security system as the population ages and fewer labor-market entrants support it. Moreover, lower paid workers contribute less in taxes, reducing government's resources for providing health and retirement benefits.

The flexible workplace is less an actual place than ever before. Workers go to a job, but they are less and less likely to have a "place of work." Likewise, the job ladders they used to climb are broken. Now, they may be confronted with an endless effort to upgrade skills and hustle up jobs, just to pay the rent. Finally, work in modern society has been a major source of identity. Without a stable workplace, what will provide the bond that links people to society? What will replace the social contract that used to be formed within the workplace?

POSTSCRIPT

Is Life Getting Better in the United States?

Easterbrook celebrates the booming American economy and the many benefits associated with it. Although there are social problems and there is still poverty, he asserts that America is "O.K." However, Easterbrook does not discuss the quality of family life and personal relations, which Rubin maintains are highly correlated with happiness, and he omits many other indicators, such as crime rates and measures of anxiety and stress. Rubin focuses on family life and job insecurity and points to ways that America is *not* O.K.

Despite a long period of economic growth in the United States, there are numerous pessimistic analyses on the direction of change in the overall quality of life. America's economic difficulties are analyzed by Jeffrey Madrick in *The End of Affluence: The Causes and Consequences of America's Economic Dilemma* (Random House, 1996). R. J. Douthwaite criticizes growth as illusionary in *The Growth Illusion: How Economic Growth Has Enriched the Few, Impoverished the Many, and Endangered the Planet* (New Society, 1999). Two works are extremely pessimistic about long-term job opportunities: Jeremy Rifkin, in *The End of Work: The Decline of the Global Labor Force and the Dawn of the Post-Market Era* (Putnam, 1995), presents a picture that is more bleak than that of Rubin. Stanley Aronowitz and William DiFazio, in *The Jobless Future: Sci-Tech and the Dogma of Work* (University of Minnesota Press, 1994), focus on the relentless expansion of technology, which displaces workers. For a close-up look at the lives of America's suburban middle class today, see Katherine S. Newman's *Declining Fortunes: The Withering of the American Dream* (Basic Books, 1993). As her title suggests, she portrays the current generation of young adults as worse off than the previous generation. Newman looks closer at downward mobility in *Falling from Grace: Downward Mobility in the Age of Affluence* (University of California Press, 1999). A very different interpretation of the American dream is provided by Robert J. Samuelson in *The Good Life and Its Discontents: The American Dream in the Age of Entitlements* (Times Books, 1996). He argues that the economy is doing quite well and life has improved but that Americans have exaggerated expectations so their dreams have failed and they feel that they are losing ground when they are not. For a more neutral assessment of the state of the nation, see Marc L. Miringoff, *The Social Health of the Nation: How America Is Really Doing* (Oxford University Press, 1999). For the public opinion view of these issues, see Everett C. Ladd and Karlyn H. Bowman, *What's Wrong: A Survey of American Satisfaction and Complaint* (AEI Press, 1998).

Contributors to This Volume

EDITOR

KURT FINSTERBUSCH is a professor of sociology at the University of Maryland at College Park. He received a B.A. in history from Princeton University in 1957, a B.D. from Grace Theological Seminary in 1960, and a Ph.D. in sociology from Columbia University in 1969. He is the author of *Understanding Social Impacts* (Sage Publications, 1980), and he is the coauthor, with Annabelle Bender Motz, of *Social Research for Policy Decisions* (Wadsworth, 1980) and, with Jerald Hage, of *Organizational Change as a Development Strategy* (Lynne Rienner, 1987). He is the editor of *Annual Editions: Sociology* (McGraw-Hill/Dushkin); *Annual Editions: Social Problems* (McGraw-Hill/Dushkin); and *Sources: Notable Selections in Sociology,* 3rd ed. (McGraw-Hill/Dushkin, 1999).

STAFF

Theodore Knight   List Manager
David Brackley   Senior Developmental Editor
Juliana Gribbins   Developmental Editor
Rose Gleich   Administrative Assistant
Brenda S. Filley   Director of Production/Design
Juliana Arbo   Typesetting Supervisor
Diane Barker   Proofreader
Richard Tietjen   Publishing Systems Manager
Larry Killian   Copier Coordinator

AUTHORS

MARCIA ANGELL is a physician, an author, and the executive editor of *The New England Journal of Medicine*. She is the author of *Science on Trial: The Clash of Medical Evidence and the Law in the Breast Implant Case* (W. W. Norton, 1996).

JEFFREY M. BERRY is a professor of political science at Tufts University in Medford, Massachusetts. He is the author of *The Interest Group Society*, 2d ed. (Scott, Foresman, 1989).

PETER BRIMELOW is a senior editor for *Forbes* and *National Review* magazines. He is also the author of *The Patriot Game* (Hoover Institution Press, 1986).

STEPHANIE COONTZ teaches history and family studies at the Evergreen State College in Olympia, Washington. A former Woodrow Wilson fellow, she has also taught at Kobe University in Japan and the University of Hawaii at Hilo. She is coeditor of *American Families: A Multicultural Reader* (Routledge, 1998).

MARY CRAWFORD is a professor of psychology and women's studies at West Chester University of Pennsylvania.

SHELDON DANZIGER is Henry J. Meyer Collegiate Professor of social work and public policy at the University of Michigan at Ann Arbor.

CHRISTOPHER C. DeMUTH is president of the American Enterprise Institute for Public Policy Research.

JOHN J. DiIULIO, JR., is a professor of politics and public affairs at Princeton University in Princeton, New Jersey. His publications include *No Escape: The Future of American Corrections* (Basic Books, 1991).

G. WILLIAM DOMHOFF has been teaching psychology and sociology at the University of California, Santa Cruz, since 1965. His books on political sociology include *Diversity in the Power Elite* (Yale University Press, 1998).

GREGG EASTERBROOK is a senior editor of *The New Republic*. He is also a contributing editor of *The Washington Monthly* and *The Atlantic Monthly*.

ERNEST ERBER is affiliated with the American Planning Association in Washington, D.C., which is involved in urban and rural development.

SUSAN FALUDI is a Pulitzer Prize–winning journalist who writes for magazines such as *The Nation* and the *New Yorker*. She is the author of *Backlash: The Undeclared War Against American Women* (Random House, 1995).

ERIC M. FREEDMAN is a professor of law in the School of Law at Hofstra University. He chairs the Committee on Civil Rights of the Association of the Bar of the City of New York and is a member of the association's Special Committee on Representation in Capital Cases. He earned his M.A. at Victoria University of Wellington in New Zealand and his J.D. at Yale University. He is coauthor, with Monroe H. Freedman, of *Group Defamation and Freedom of Speech: The Relationship Between Language and Violence* (Greenwood, 1995).

MILTON FRIEDMAN is a senior research fellow at the Stanford University Hoover Institution on War, Revolution, and Peace. He was the recipient of the 1976 Nobel Prize in economic science. He and his wife, **ROSE FRIEDMAN,** who also writes on economic topics, have coauthored several publications, including *Tyranny of the Status Quo* (Harcourt Brace Jovanovich, 1984).

JEFF GRABMEIER is managing editor of research news at Ohio State University in Columbus, Ohio.

RON HASKINS is the staff director of the Human Resources Subcommittee of the U.S. House Ways and Means Committee.

GERTRUDE HIMMELFARB is a professor emeritus of history at the Graduate School of the City University of New York. She is the author of *Darwin and the Darwinian Revolution* (I. R. Dee, 1996).

KAREN HOUPPERT is a freelance writer and author of *The Curse: Confronting the Last Unmentionable Taboo: Menstruation* (Farrar, Straus & Giroux, 2000).

JAMES A. INCIARDI is director of the Center for Drug and Alcohol Studies at the University of Delaware, a professor in the Department of Sociology and Criminal Justice at Delaware, an adjunct professor in the Comprehensive Drug Research Center at the University of Miami School of Medicine, and a member of the South Florida AIDS Research Consortium. He has published about three dozen books and more than 180 articles and chapters in the areas of substance abuse, criminology, folklore, social policy, AIDS, medicine, and law.

JOHN ISBISTER is provost of Merrill College at the University of California, Santa Cruz, where he teaches courses on immigration, the economic development of low-income countries, and social change in the Third World. He is the author of *Promises Not Kept: The Betrayal of Social Change in the Third World,* 2d ed. (Kumarian Press, 1991).

WILBERT JENKINS is associate professor of history at Temple University.

D. GALE JOHNSON is the Eliakim Hastings Moore Distinguished Service Professor of Economics Emeritus at the University of Chicago.

ROBERT W. LEE is a contributing editor at *The New American* and the author of *The United Nations Conspiracy* (Western Islands, 1981).

PAUL R. McHUGH is the Henry Phipps Professor and director of the Department of Psychiatry and Behavioral Sciences at Johns Hopkins University School of Medicine.

CHARLES MURRAY is Bradley Fellow at the American Enterprise Institute. He is coauthor, with Richard J. Herrnstein, of *The Bell Curve* (Free Press, 1994).

ETHAN A. NADELMANN is director of the Lindesmith Center, a New York drug policy research institute, and an assistant professor of politics and public affairs in the Woodrow Wilson School of Public and International Affairs at Princeton University in Princeton, New Jersey.

DAVID PIMENTEL is a professor in the College of Agriculture and Life Sciences at Cornell University. He has published extensively and has chaired panels dealing with food, energy, population, and natural resources for the National Academy of Sciences, the American Association for the Advancement of Science, and the U.S. Department of Energy.

MARCIA PIMENTEL is Senior Lecturer (retired), Division of Nutritional Sciences in the College of Human Ecology at Cornell. She has authored a book and several papers dealing with nutrition and human populations.

DAVID POPENOE is a professor of sociology and an associate dean for the social sciences at Rutgers–The State University in New Brunswick, New Jersey. He is the author of *Disturbing the Nest* (Aldine de Gruyter, 1988).

DEBORAH REED is a research fellow at the Public Policy Institute of California.

JEFFREY REIMAN is the William Fraser McDowell Professor of Philosophy at American University in Washington, D.C. He is the author of *Justice and Modern Moral Philosophy* (Yale University Press, 1992).

GARY ROSEN is associate editor of *Commentary* and the author of *American Compact: James Madison and the Problem of Founding* (University Press of Kansas, 1999).

BETH A. RUBIN is an associate professor in the Department of Sociology at Tulane University.

CHRISTINE A. SAUM is a research associate in the Center for Drug and Alcohol Studies at the University of Delaware.

BARRY SCHWARTZ is the Dorwin Cartwright Professor of Social Theory and Social Action and professor of psychology at Swarthmore College. He is the author of *The Costs of Living: How Market Freedom Erodes the Best Things in Life* (W. W. Norton, 1994).

ALBERT SHANKER was president of the American Federation of Teachers in Washington, D.C. until his death in 1998. He is recognized as the first labor leader elected to the National Academy of Education, and he was the author of the Sunday *New York Times* column "Where We Stand."

ANDREW SULLIVAN is a former editor of *The New Republic*. He received a B.A. in modern history and modern language from Oxford University in 1984 and an M.A. in public administration and a Ph.D. in political science from Harvard University in 1986 and 1990, respectively. His articles have been published in the *New York Times*, the *Wall Street Journal*, *Esquire*, *The Public Interest*, and the *Times* of London. He is also the author of *The Distant Intimacy* (Random House, 1999).

DAVID WHITMAN is a senior writer for *U.S. News & World Report*.

WALTER E. WILLIAMS is the John M. Olin Distinguished Professor of Economics at George Mason University.

JAMES Q. WILSON, a criminologist and sociologist, is the James Collins Professor of Management and Public Policy at the University of California at Los Angeles, where he has been teaching since 1985. He has studied and advised on issues in crime and law enforcement for nearly 25 years, serving on a number of national commissions concerned with public policy, and he has authored, coauthored, or edited numerous books on crime, government, and politics, including *Bureaucracy: What Government Agencies Do and Why They Do It* (Basic Books, 1989), *American Government* (Houghton Mifflin, 1996), and *The Moral Sense* (Simon & Schuster, 1997).

PHILIP YANCEY serves as editor-at-large for *Christianity Today* magazine. He has authored numerous books, including *The Jesus I Never Knew* (Zondervan Publishing House, 1995) and *What's so Amazing About Grace?* (Zondervan Publishing House, 1997).

Index